D1356677

OLIVER
TAMBO
REMEMBERED

OLIVER
TAMBO
REMEMBERED

Edited by
Z. Pallo Jordan

MACMILLAN

First published 2007
by Pan Macmillan South Africa
Private Bag x19
Northlands
Johannesburg
2116

www.panmacmillan.co.za

ISBN 978-1-77010-075-6

While every effort has been made to verify and check the facts presented in this book,
the publishers are not able to take responsibility for the accuracy of the information
provided by the various contributors in their recollections of Oliver Reginald Tambo
as well as surrounding people, places and events. Any corrections will be gladly
received and incorporated in the event of a reprint or second edition.

Author royalties from this collection are to be donated to the Oliver Tambo Foundation.

Editing and proofreading by Andrea Nattrass
Design and typesetting by Triple M Design, Johannesburg
Printed and bound in South Africa by CTP Books, Parow, Cape

CONTENTS

ANC AND OTHER COMRADES

ACKNOWLEDGEMENTS

The Publishers would like to thank the Tambo family, and specifically Tembi and Dali Tambo, for their support of the project and their invaluable assistance throughout the editorial process.

Oliver Tambo Remembered was conceptualised by Lindiwe Mabuza, and the book would never have come to fruition without her guidance and assistance. We would also like to thank Z. Pallo Jordan for taking the time to edit the contributions, and for his support of the project.

The Publishers would also like to acknowledge, with thanks, the involvement in this project of Mike Terry, Thami Ntenteni and Andrea Nattrass.

We are grateful to Mats Åsman, Paul Boateng, Nadine Hack and Jerry Dunfey for allowing us to use their photographs. We would also like to thank all other contributors who sent us photographs and documents for consideration.

The publication of this book was only possible because of the generosity of all the contributors who took time out of their schedules to write their contributions, and in doing so have helped us to commemorate and celebrate the life of one of South Africa's most important leaders.

ABBREVIATIONS

AAM Anti-Apartheid Movement
ANC African National Congress
BBC British Broadcasting Corporation
BC Black Consciousness
BCC British Council of Churches
BCM Black Consciousness Movement
BOSS Bureau of State Security
EPG Eminent Persons Group
EU European Union
FCO Foreign and Commonwealth Office
FRELIMO Frente de Libertação de Moçambique
   (Mozambique Liberation Front)
IDAF International Defence and Aid Fund
IRA Irish Republican Army
MK Umkhonto we Sizwe
NEC National Executive Committee
NGO Non-Governmental Organisation
OAU Organisation for African Unity
PAC Pan-Africanist Congress
PLO Palestinian Liberation Organisation
SACC South African Council of Churches
SACP South African Communist Party
SADF South African Defence Force
SAUF South African United Front
SWAPO South West African People's Organisation
UDF United Democratic Front
UK United Kingdom
UN United Nations
US United States
WCC World Council of Churches

OLIVER TAMBO:
'A GREAT GIANT WHO STRODE THE GLOBE LIKE A COLOSSUS'

Thabo Mbeki

The ANC sent Oliver Tambo into exile in 1960, shortly after the Sharpeville massacre. Our leadership expected that the apartheid regime would carry out a campaign of extreme repression to destroy the ANC. It therefore took the decision to locate its Deputy President outside the country to ensure that the ANC would continue to exist and pursue our struggle until victory was won.

I, and others, followed Oliver Tambo into exile in 1962, two-and-half years after he had left. Like him, we were sent out of the country by the ANC, but on a different mission. We were sent out as students charged with the task to study and acquire skills that a liberated South Africa would need.

The fears of the ANC leadership in 1960 had been proved correct. By 1962 our struggle was facing difficult challenges as a result of the apartheid regime's sustained campaign of repression, which was destined to get worse.

As members of the ANC Youth League we were very determined to contribute to the effort to defeat this campaign of repression and intensify the struggle for the victory of the national democratic revolution. Because of this, I was among those of our youth who tried to resist leaving the country to study.

In the end Walter Sisulu directed me to meet two of our leaders, Duma Nokwe and Govan Mbeki, who conveyed the instruction, rather than a proposal of the movement, that I should leave the country. To accommodate my concerns, they undertook that Oliver Tambo would discuss my future with me when I had completed my first year at university in the UK.

On our way out of South Africa, I met the late Joe Modise in the Bechuanaland Protectorate, now Botswana, where he had delivered a new batch of MK recruits. Having returned to Bechuanaland after detention in Southern Rhodesia, present day Zimbabwe, I was convinced that this gave me just cause to return home, arguing that our attempt to leave the country had failed.

Modise, already a member of the then very secretive MK, refused to assist me to return home. Instead he argued in a stern voice that my task was to proceed to the UK as I had been instructed. He made no effort to hide his displeasure at my attempt to persuade him to cooperate in what he considered would be an act of indiscipline.

I first met Oliver Tambo, OR, when we arrived in Dar es Salaam in 1962. As I had been advised, he told me that we would discuss my future when I had completed my first year at university.

One of the passengers on the plane on which I flew out to London to begin my studies was Dr Kenneth Kaunda, KK, later to become President of independent Zambia. At Dar es Salaam airport, in the presence of Mwalimu Julius Nyerere, OR handed me over to KK saying that he would take care of me during the flight to London.

As promised, at the end of my first year at university, in 1963, OR met me in London. Because I insisted that I wanted to join MK, and return home to fight, he agreed that I should terminate my studies. When I informed the university accordingly, it opposed the decision strenuously.

A little more than a week before the university reopened, I received fresh instructions from OR stating that the leadership had reviewed our decision and decided that I should return to university, which I did. In the end this instruction was repeated until I had completed my Master of Arts degree in 1966.

Eight years later, in 1974, the Swedish Liberal Party held an international symposium in Stockholm, which OR had been invited to address. However, he sent an instruction to me to attend in his place. This was during the very week when Zanele and I got married. Despite my protests, which OR rebuffed by insisting on the need to respect the decisions of the ANC, I went to Stockholm as directed.

I returned to Africa in 1971, having stayed in Europe since the early days of my exile in 1962. I came back to the ANC headquarters in Lusaka, Zambia, to serve in the Revolutionary Council as Deputy Secretary to the late Moses Mabhida, with the Council chaired by Oliver Tambo.

Later, appointed to work as Political Secretary to the Acting President of the ANC, Oliver Tambo, I had the responsibility of preparing the drafts of OR's public speeches and the major public documents of our movement.

This work demanded intimate understanding of the strategic and tactical tasks of the movement, the contemporary balance of forces at home and abroad, our objective challenges at all moments, and what the leader of the ANC, Oliver Tambo, would have to say publicly, bearing in mind our domestic and international tasks and audiences, in order to sustain the advance of our struggle.

Many a time I had to live with the embarrassment of OR completely rejecting my draft texts and, on a number of occasions, using his own notes to deliver addresses radically different from the draft speeches I had prepared.

Many a time I had to spend numerous hours with him to discuss specific formulations used in the draft texts, which he thought represented a careless or imprecise use of words, or inaccurate understanding of our movement's policies, history, tradition and values.

Fifteen years after the 1974 Stockholm symposium, in 1989, and having worked with him for many years by then, I visited OR in London as he was recuperating from his stroke. This had occurred soon after we had completed a gruelling trip through a number of countries of southern Africa.

We undertook this trip to consult the Front-line States on a document we had drafted under OR's leadership, which was ultimately called the Harare Declaration. This Declaration served as the basis on which we engaged the apartheid regime in negotiations, starting with the secret discussions in 1989, mainly with the National Intelligence Service.

After the consultations with the Front-line States of southern Africa, the Harare Declaration was adopted by the UDF and the rest of the mass democratic movement in South Africa, the OAU, the Non-Aligned Movement and the General Assembly of the UN.

President Kaunda understood both the importance and urgency of our mission and provided us with a plane to help us undertake our tour of southern Africa. The government of Zambia took care of the costs of the plane while the governments of our region hosted us in all the countries we visited.

Our first meeting in Dar es Salaam was with a government delegation led by the then Prime Minister, Salim Ahmed Salim. When we went to bed that night, our delegation, with the exception of OR, was somewhat depressed. This was because the Tanzanian government delegation had expressed great scepticism at the very idea of engaging the apartheid regime in negotiations.

The following day we met Mwalimu Julius Nyerere. After a presentation by OR, Mwalimu expressed full support for the initiative we had taken. He made a critically important suggestion, which our NEC finally supported, that our document and negotiating stance should recognise the strategic reality that as much as the apartheid regime had not defeated the liberation movement, neither had our movement defeated the white minority regime.

There will be other occasions to make a proper assessment of the impact on our struggle and the evolution of our democracy of the strategic intervention that Mwalimu Julius Nyerere made as we prepared to engage the apartheid regime in a new form of struggle centred on the peaceful transfer of power to the people.

As I have said, I visited OR in London in 1989 as he was recuperating from his stroke. On this occasion we discussed that our movement was faced with conducting our struggle in new and complex circumstances. He then communicated another mission, the most challenging since I first met him in Dar es Salaam 27 years earlier: look after the ANC and make sure we succeed. You will know what needs to be done.

On OR's instruction, in 1989 I began talking to Madiba, Nelson Mandela, by phone, while he was in prison. We continued this telephone contact after he was released in 1990, before I returned home. I must presume that OR authorised this contact to ensure that because of the guidance that his lifelong friend and comrade, Madiba, would provide, I would not make mistakes that would compromise the advance of our struggle and revolution.

An important part of Oliver Tambo's life coincided with critical and defining moments in the evolution of our struggle, each imposing an obligation on our movement, the ANC, to respond in a creative and decisive manner, fully cognisant of our possibilities and constraints.

I am immensely privileged that I had the opportunity to interact with and learn many lifelong lessons from Oliver Tambo during the 31 years from 1962 until he passed away in 1993, which encompassed many of the years when OR led our movement during some of the most critical moments in its history.

It might appear to the casual reader of this contribution to this book of tribute to Oliver Tambo, on what would have been his 90th birthday, that this humble piece is more about myself rather than the immortal hero of our struggle, Oliver Reginald Tambo.

However, the personal stories I have told relate a relationship which positions OR as the subject, and myself as the object of policies and actions that throw light on the character of the subject of this important book, one of the most important founders of democratic South Africa, OR Tambo.

As part of this history, in time I came to understand why he and the rest of our leadership, including Walter Sisulu, Nelson Mandela, Duma Nokwe, Govan Mbeki, Moses Kotane, JB Marks, Mark Shope, Moses Mabhida and others, had been correct in their assessment that I should complete my university education.

This was part of the implementation of a far-sighted programme intended to ensure that our movement took the necessary steps to build a corps of cadres that was both professionally qualified and committed to the national democratic revolution led by the ANC. This remains one of the vital tasks that the national democratic revolution faces, thirteen years after our victory.

I came to understand the significance of the moment at Dar es Salaam airport in 1962, when OR, KK and Mwalimu, comrades in arms, were together, in fact to wish KK success as he travelled to London to negotiate the independence of Zambia, which came in 1964. It is on this basis that the ANC and democratic South Africa have built our contribution to the Renaissance of Africa.

I also came to understand why OR had insisted in 1974 that I should attend the Stockholm symposium. Sweden proved to be one of our most dependable and valued allies as our struggle reached the intensity and global support that produced the historic victory of 1994. The example set by Sweden has enabled democratic South Africa to rally the global support that continues to be a vital factor in our continuing struggle to achieve the fundamental reconstruction and development of our country.

Similarly, I came to understand why OR insisted on maximum precision in the preparation of his public statements. He taught me the obligation to understand the tasks of leadership, including the necessity never to tell lies, never to make false and unrealisable promises, never to say anything you do not mean or believe, and never to say anything that might evoke an enthusiastic populist response, but which would ultimately serve to undermine the credibility of our movement and struggle.

History will make its own judgement about whether or not we have fully honoured the continuing mission that Oliver Tambo gave us in 1989 – to look after the ANC and make sure we succeed.

At least, so far, the historical record will say that our movement handled the process of negotiations successfully, including all fronts of struggle in this regard. It will say that we succeeded in the difficult struggle to establish our democracy and ensure the stability and permanence of the national democratic revolution.

The historical record will also say that we succeeded in reconstructing the ANC that the apartheid regime sought to destroy from 1960, and which Oliver Tambo helped successfully to rebuild from exile.

Building on what was achieved during the years since 1960, under OR's leadership, we have confirmed the ANC as the unchallenged premier representative of the masses of our people, reflected in ever-increasing majorities in all our democratic elections since 1994.

At the same time, we have ensured that our country avoids a destructive racial conflict, and have led the difficult process that has advanced South Africa towards genuine national reconciliation, non-racialism and non-sexism, and a new and shared patriotism.

That record will also say that the ANC has used the years of liberation to ensure that the national democratic revolution makes a measurable and visible impact in terms of materially changing the lives of especially the black poor for the better, without dispossessing the former beneficiaries of colonialism and apartheid.

It will say that in good measure, we owe these positive developments to the leadership provided by Oliver Tambo over many decades.

However, that historical record will also say that we must remain vigilant in the struggle to defeat the abuse of membership of Oliver Tambo's ANC, and the consequent access to state power, as a stepladder to the corrupt acquisition of personal wealth, at the expense of the masses of our people.

The historical record will say that Oliver Tambo's ANC, especially as demonstrated in the run-up to its 2007 52nd National Conference, held during the year of his 90th birthday, faces a continuing challenge to demonstrate to the masses of our people that it remains still a movement of the people, rather than an instrument in the hands of individuals who clothe themselves in ANC garb, while using our colours, black, green and gold, to pursue selfish interests.

When he spoke at Oliver Tambo's funeral on 2 May 1993, Nelson Mandela, OR's closest life comrade, said:

> A great giant who strode the globe like a colossus has fallen. A mind whose thoughts have opened the doors to our liberty has ceased to function. A heart whose dreams gave hope to the despised has for ever lost its beat. The gentle voice whose measured words of reason shook the thrones of tyrants has been silenced ...
>
> We say he has departed. But can we allow him to depart while we live! ...
>
> Dear brother: you set yourself a task which only the brave would dare. Somewhere in the mystery of your essence, you heard the call that you must devote your life to the creation of a new South African nation.

And having heard that call, you did not hesitate to act.

It may be that all of us . . . will never be able to discover what it was in your essence which convinced you that you, and us, could, by our conscious and deliberate actions, so heal our fractured society that out of the terrible heritage, there could be born a nation. All humanity knows what you had to do to create the conditions for all of us to reach this glorious end . . .

Today we stand watching the dawn of a new day. We can see that we have it in our power to remake South Africa into what you wanted it to be – free, just, prosperous, at peace with itself and with the world.

Let all who value peace say together – long live Oliver Tambo!

Let all who love freedom say together – long live Oliver Tambo!

Let all who uphold the dignity of all human beings say together – long live Oliver Tambo!

Let all who stand for friendship among the peoples say together – long live Oliver Tambo!

Let all of us who live say that while we live, the ideals for which Oliver Tambo lived, sacrificed and died will not die!

Today, the official residence of the Deputy President of our Republic in our capital city, Tshwane, carries the official name OR Tambo House. Our principal international and internal airport, formerly Johannesburg International, is OR Tambo International Airport. Our premier National Order, awarded by our democratic state to our international friends who have played a critical role in the struggle to end the apartheid crime and contributed in specific ways to building the new South Africa to which Oliver Tambo dedicated his life, is called the Order of the Companions of OR Tambo. Oliver Tambo's grave in Benoni, in the metropolitan municipality in Ekurhuleni in the Gauteng province is one of our National Heritage sites.

By these means, and other interventions, the new South Africa has tried to pay tribute to, and sustain the memory of, one of its greatest sons. And yet the question continues to trouble the national conscience: have we done everything we should to salute he of whom Nelson Mandela said, 'a mind whose thoughts have opened the doors to our liberty has ceased to function'?

When I first met Oliver Tambo at Dar es Salaam airport and the then headquarters of the ANC in Dar es Salaam, as part of a group of young South African patriots, both of these were humble locations that bear no comparison to OR Tambo International Airport and the Albert Luthuli headquarters of the ANC, located respectively in the South African and Gauteng metropolitan municipalities of Ekurhuleni and Johannesburg.

When I relocated from Europe to Africa and Zambia in 1971, I stayed in a communal farmhouse in Makeni, Lusaka, sharing this residence with OR, the late Chris Hani, the current Director-General of Home Affairs, Mavuso Msimang, former Director-General of the National Intelligence Agency and Soviet University graduate, Sizakele Sigxashe, and other members of the Luthuli Detachment of MK.

Then, together with Oliver Tambo, we slept on padding we would roll out every evening on the cement floor of the house. Then, 35 years ago, the ANC had no money to buy mattresses or beds. And yet nobody left the ranks of our movement to seek comfort elsewhere, even in Lusaka.

The example set by our Acting President, OR Tambo, to whom the ANC had entrusted the historic task of ensuring the survival of our movement, said to all of us that our commitment to the freedom of our people meant that we should be ready to make all necessary sacrifices.

Oliver Tambo faithfully and successfully discharged the mission directly communicated to him by the then President of the ANC, Inkosi Albert Luthuli, that he would have to leave the country to ensure that the ANC would continue to exist and pursue the struggle until victory was won.

For us the challenge remains: have we done, and are we doing everything we must do to discharge successfully the revolutionary mission that OR Tambo handed over to us?

The national monuments and symbols named after him are both necessary and important. However, his most important products are the cadres who learnt to be true representatives of our people because they had the rare fortune to be his students as members of our national liberation movement.

Will these pay tribute to him by defending the tradition he handed down to all of us, aptly identified by Nelson Mandela when he said: 'A mind whose thoughts have opened the doors to our liberty has ceased to function. A heart whose dreams gave hope to the despised has for ever lost its beat'?

Tragically, nobody will ever know what contribution OR Tambo would have made to our continuing revolution as he celebrated his 90th birthday on 27 October 2007. Fortunately, or otherwise, some of us have the possibility to act as his representatives on this historic day.

OLIVER TAMBO: AN APPRECIATION

Z. Pallo Jordan

Oliver Reginald Tambo (often known as OR) was born on 27 October 1917, in the village of Kantolo, in the Mbizana district of eastern Mpondo-land (eQawukeni) in the eastern Cape. After serving the usual rural appren-ticeship as a herdboy he enrolled at an Anglican school before going to St Peter's Secondary School in Rosettenville, Johannesburg. He passed his ma-tric top of his class, including all racial groups, and won a scholarship from the Transkei Bhunga (a dummy parliament used as an instrument of indirect rule) which took him to the University College of Fort Hare. Here OR at-tained a degree in science, qualifying to become a teacher of mathematics and science. From 1943 until 1947 he taught these subjects at his alma mater, St Peter's. He gave up teaching to study law in 1948 and established the first African legal partnership with Nelson Mandela in December 1952.

The National Party's repressive apparatus pre-empted a second career change in December 1956. Two days before the Bishop of Johannesburg was due to prepare him for ordination as a priest, OR was arrested along with 155 others on charges of high treason on 6 December 1956.

OR chose his path when he joined the African National Congress (ANC) after completing his studies at Fort Hare. At the height of the Second World War a small group of young people, members of the ANC, banded together under the leadership of Anton Lembede. Among them were William Nko-mo, Walter Sisulu, Oliver Tambo, Ashby P Mda and Nelson Mandela. In September 1944 they founded the African National Congress Youth League (ANCYL).

Starting out with 60 members concentrated around the city of Johannesburg, they set themselves the formidable task of transforming the ANC into a mass organisation, deriving its strength and motivation from the unlettered millions of ordinary working people of the cities, towns and countryside of South Africa.

This group of zealous young people argued that the 'old guard' leadership of the ANC, reared in the tradition of constitutional struggle and polite petitioning of the white minority government of the day, was proving inadequate to the demands of national emancipation. The old guard's strategy, they asserted, rested on a misconception of the actual power relations in South African society and, consequently, the tactics they had evolved failed to galvanise the disenfranchised black majority. In opposition to the old guard, Lembede and his associates espoused a militant African nationalism grounded in the principle of national self-determination.

At the 1945 annual conference both Lembede and Mda were elected to the National Executive Committee (NEC) of the ANC. Two years later, in 1947, OR became a member of the NEC. At the 1949 annual conference a Programme of Action, inspired by the ANCYL, was adopted as official policy of the ANC.

The adoption of the Programme of Action marked a daring strategic initiative in the politics of black South Africans, which until that decade had been dominated by the educated black elite. The Programme of Action was devised to take politics to the millions of ordinary blacks whom they hoped would, through such mobilisation, become conscious agents of their own emancipation.

The Programme of Action was premised on the notion that the disenfranchised majority would only win their freedom by their own exertions. The violent repression of any protests, it argued, had repeatedly demonstrated that the white minority would not willingly surrender power. It was therefore necessary to devise the means to wrest power from it. The collective might of the disenfranchised – who laboured in the factories, on the mines, on the rich agri-business farms and, invariably, also served the whites as servants in their homes – would be the instrument to attain freedom.

It was this set of young leaders (most at the time in their early thirties) and the thousands of members whose support they won who prepared the ANC for the decade of the 1950s, which witnessed massive non-violent ANC-led campaigns – strikes, civil disobedience, boycotts, mass demonstrations and marches.

To ensure the implementation of the programme, the membership of the ANC elected a number of younger men, among them Oliver Tambo, onto the

NEC. Walter Sisulu, a founding member of the ANCYL was elected as the Secretary-General and the conciliatory Dr AB Xuma was replaced as President by a man with a reputation for greater militancy, Dr JS Moroka. Nelson Mandela also rose into the ranks of the NEC at that same annual conference.

From 1947 until his death in 1993, OR was among the leading figures of the ANC. He has left an indelible mark on South African politics. When Walter Sisulu was forbidden to take an active part in ANC affairs in 1954, OR became Secretary-General of the ANC; by 1957 he had been elected Deputy President to Chief Albert Luthuli. He became Acting President when Chief Luthuli died in 1967 and reluctantly assumed the position of President at the ANC's first consultative conference held in Morogoro in 1969.

Though the campaigns of the 1950s had been militant, they were scrupulously non-violent. The response of the white minority government, however, was not as restrained. In its attempt to cow the movement into quiescence, the government unleashed a wave of repression. Armed police, often assisted by army units, mowed down peaceful demonstrators; police wielding batons, billy clubs and pick-axe handles administered brutal beatings to those not fleet-footed enough to get away; entire villages of people in rural areas were deported to distant areas and the pre-dawn Security Police raid became a regular feature of South African life.

Commencing with the passage of the Suppression of Communism Act of 1950, in small incremental steps the National Party government turned the law into a formidable instrument of repression. That Act gave the Minister power to ban, proscribe and restrict the movements and actions of individuals and entire organisations.

These repressions culminated at Sharpeville in March 1960, when 69 peaceful demonstrators, the majority shot in the back, were massacred by police as they protested against the pass laws. Shortly thereafter, on 30 March, the government instituted a State of Emergency, the first of its kind in peacetime, and declared the ANC an illegal organisation. Before the dawn of 31 March, in well-coordinated raids, the Security Police arrested thousands of political activists, some of whom were detained for up to five months without trial.

A few days prior to 30 March OR was instructed to travel abroad to establish an External Mission for the ANC to mobilise international support and coordinate activities for the anticipated years of underground struggle.

As head of the ANC's organisation in exile, OR travelled widely, appearing before the United Nations (UN) and a host of other international bodies. He spearheaded the setting up of the South African United Front (SAUF) with the Pan-Africanist-Congress (PAC) and the South African Indian Congress (SAIC) in 1960. After the break up of the SAUF, he became the international spokesperson of the South African liberation, enjoying the confidence and respect of the world statesmen he met in every part of the globe.

In March 1961, 1 400 delegates gathered for an All-In Conference at Pietermaritzburg under the ANC's inspiration. Nelson Mandela, emerging from a proscription order that had just expired, was the keynote speaker. In an electrifying address he challenged the white minority government to convene a national convention, representative of all South Africans, to thrash out a new constitution based on democratic principles. Failure to comply, he warned, would compel the disenfranchised to observe the planned inauguration of a republic at the end of May with a mass stay-away from work.

The regime's reaction was predictable. Police reservists and army units were mobilised. Preventative detention of political activists was instituted.

On 29 May, the first of the three days set aside for the celebrations, shops were closed and the streets of Johannesburg were empty as millions of black workers struck.

It was after May 1961 that the ANC leadership set up Umkhonto we Sizwe (MK) – the Spear of the Nation – as the military wing of the ANC. Nelson Mandela was appointed Commander-in-Chief of MK, with Raymond Mhlaba as his deputy. MK went into action on 16 December 1961 by launching simultaneous attacks on targets in three cities: Johannesburg, Port Elizabeth and Durban. From that date the incidence of planned acts of sabotage rose steadily, reaching a peak of 177 acts across the country by 1964.

The National Party regime responded with a more ruthless regime of repression. A new law empowering the Security Police to detain persons for successive periods of 90 days without trial was introduced. Armed with these powers the Security Police commenced a reign of terror against political opponents of apartheid. Harrowing, mind-breaking tortures were routinely employed in all interrogations of political activists; vicious beatings and unexplained deaths occurred in police cells.

It was in this atmosphere that the Security Police swooped on a farm, Liliesl, in Rivonia in July 1963. The upshot was that ten leaders of the ANC, including Nelson Mandela, were put on trial on charges of planning acts of sabotage and conspiring to overthrow the government. Their trial, known as the Rivonia Trial, ended with Nelson Mandela and seven of his colleagues being sentenced to life imprisonment in 1964.

Rivonia and the repression which followed thrust upon the very ample shoulders of OR the responsibility of leading the ANC in exile as well as at home: a task he assumed with a quiet determination and immense dignity.

The dialectics of national liberation

By the time he took over the helm of the ANC, OR was a seasoned political leader with two decades of active engagement behind him. He understood his task as two-fold: to rebuild the ANC as a mass movement inside South Africa, while enhancing its capacity to lead an armed insurgent movement from outside South Africa's borders. He knew that a spontaneous revolution was unlikely if not impossible. Making a revolution, he reasoned, required steady but sure work to bring together a number of factors, chief amongst which was organising the most militant opponents of apartheid to mobilise the people into action to challenge the National Party's regime.

The wave of repression that followed Rivonia had effectively broken up the legal as well as illegal organisational structures of the democratic movement inside South Africa. ANC militants, members and supporters still continued to meet secretly as and when they could, but too many were known to the Security Police and under constant surveillance. The perception that the National Party's secret police were everywhere and had informers, agents and helpers in every nook and cranny of society had frozen thousands into an unnatural silence. Fear, self-doubt and demoralisation seemed to have taken hold of the people.

Nowhere in the world are oppressed people in day to day revolt against their tormentors. But if they are ever to rise, they must continue to resist, fight back and engage in struggles, big and small. OR understood that in order to stimulate the South African people to reclaim their self-confidence it would be necessary to build that self-confidence through small engagements and struggles. Demoralised slaves who are forever on their knees before their masters are unlikely to fight for and win their freedom. But by striving for small immediate gains, low morale could be uplifted and the solidarity so necessary for revolution could also be nurtured.

There is a self-evident paradox in this approach to the politics of national liberation. OR, like his peers in the ANCYL, from the outset of their political careers had always insisted that the oppressed people must be their own liberators. Yet all through those years in exile OR never ceased preaching the need for the ANC to act as the organiser and the external stimulant of mass activity. At the heart of this paradox is a recognition that there is a constant tension between the potential of the oppressed and the state of their day to day morale and preparedness for struggle.

It is a given that struggle does not necessarily end in success. Because there are at least two forces on the field, reverses, partial victories, defeats and even grave setbacks, are inevitable. Any struggle consequently is a cyclical movement with moments of high activity followed by inactivity and quiescence. The responsibility of the national democratic movement, OR maintained, was to sustain the continuity between the previous phases of struggle, the present and future ones by acting as the custodian of the best traditions and the political experience of the people in struggle.

I want to highlight a second paradox to which OR was always alert. Because of the nature of the oppression suffered by the people of South Africa, the ANC was necessarily a broad movement, drawing support from a wide spectrum of social and economic forces. There were people who were drawn to the ANC because freedom from apartheid offered them the opportunity to 'realise their dreams on the Johannesburg Stock Exchange'. Yet others joined and supported it because freedom would open up the chance to rise to the heights to which their talents could take them. Others sought the restoration of the right to the land that had been seized or from which they had been driven by racist laws. Others hoped to restore the dignity and grace of African culture. The movement counted amongst its supporters members of the middle classes, the working class, the rural working poor, aspirant capitalists and entrepreneurs, as well as militant socialists and communists.

There are obvious tensions among these components, yet they had all to be accommodated. OR, perhaps better than many others, understood that it was not possible to suppress and silence the contradictions inherent in such a diverse movement. He mastered the art of giving political leadership to such a movement by the creative management of these contradictions, permitting open and free debate within the movement's ranks, so that every proposed strategy was weighed and tested in the light of reason.

However, he never permitted such debate to impair the movement's capacity for united action in its varied and diverse components. This required that debate, at some point, would have to give way to implementation. To ensure that the energies of the movement were maximised, a minority view would have to submit to a majority view. The practice he encouraged was a continuous search for consensus accompanied by an insistence on disciplined, united action.

It was these qualities which enabled OR to blossom into a truly great leader of the ANC and the South African liberation movement. It was these qualities that endeared him to all the ANC ranks, from its leadership to the youngest cadre.

OR stressed the quality of the movement he led. He insisted on the quality of its leadership as he did on the quality of its actions. But he was also a leader who led from the front. While he was very demanding on those who worked under him, he was himself a tireless worker, very often undertaking far too many tasks and consequently overextending himself. In the end it was the demands he placed on himself that subsequently led to his ill-health and probably hastened his death.

OR's distinguished career in liberation politics began before the National Party came into office in 1948. Despite his best efforts he regrettably did not live long enough to see them turfed out of office. The tragedy is that so many men and women of his calibre were so long denied the opportunity to serve their country and its people as political leaders and as professionals.

Oliver Tambo pursued the goal of liberation and creating a democratic South Africa with an unrelenting energy, a quiet tenacity and stubborn perseverance. By the end of his life, the object of his dreams was within sight. And his contribution to its attainment was second to none.

Cape Town, 2007

FRIENDS AND NEIGHBOURS
IN THE UK

IRRESISTIBLE, INSPIRATIONAL AND DEEPLY BELOVED

Nadine Hack and Jerry Dunfey

When we think of OR what comes to mind is the most gentle soul, with the most tiger-like spirit; the kindest heart, with the fiercest determination; the most compassionate nature, with the strongest moral compass; the warmest, sweetest personality, with an unflinching dedication to honesty; the most loving, peaceful temperament, with the sharpest sense of conscience; the most beautiful smile, with a resolve to accept only absolute integrity; the most noble, patient, calm presence, with the most tenacious fervour for bold, uncompromising action; and the most brilliant intellect, with the most earnest, sincere appreciation for the simplest contribution. What a giant OR was – a steadfast force with such vitality, creativity, courage, clarity, honesty and constancy. How blessed we were to know and work with our dear brother, OR.

The intimate moments we have chosen to share epitomise something about the depth of OR's character. These qualities made him irresistible, inspirational and deeply beloved to us. We sat at his bedside during his final days and, although his physical energy was failing to keep up with his daunting acuity and genius, he grabbed hold of each of our arms. Only when he was completely certain he had our full attention – focusing his penetrating gaze alternately on each of us – he said with extraordinary prescience: 'You must promise me that after our freedom people will understand the importance of creating graduate schools inside South Africa that teach public administration and business management. When we are a free nation, we will have a hand-ful of elite who will be able to assume the highest leadership positions, but we will need thousands of people who can fill positions at every level within government, the private and public sectors if we really want change.'

He was intensely resolute about this insight a full year before the national elections that brought the ANC government to power and a full decade be-fore Black Economic Empowerment became its clarion call. Having had that final directive from him, I was profoundly honoured to be part of the eighteen-strong, official US delegation that President Clinton sent to OR's funeral on 2 May 1993.

In 1988 we joined OR in Lusaka, Zambia, for Johnny Makathini's funeral. Johnny headed International Affairs for the ANC and was the person who introduced many anti-apartheid activists globally to the liberation struggle. OR's story is incomplete without some focus on Johnny's critical role in keeping us all engaged. No matter how serious the situation, Johnny – like OR – maintained an unflappable calm, a fabulous sense of humour and a profound humanity. He was also completely unaware of time zones as he was always working. If you received a call at 3:30 a.m., before you even picked up the phone, you knew it would be Johnny in blessed oblivion, saying, 'Hey, man, I'm in the Cairo airport and I was thinking . . .' So many people were devastated when we lost Johnny. Despite his grief, OR stood steadfast alongside the coffin to greet all those who came to pay tribute. We remem-ber him sharing with Lindiwe Mabuza, Louise Africa and us how his heart was broken knowing that the first time Johnny's mother had seen him in the decades since he'd been in exile was in his coffin.

Even at a time of such grief, OR remained the focused planner. He, Ma/ Sis Adelaide and Pallo Jordan came to the airport when we were leaving Lusaka and explained that, because the ANC was an egalitarian organisa-tion that had lost so many 'unsung' heroes and heroines to the struggle, he could not ask the ANC to take care of Johnny's very young daughter Nandi. But OR was determined that she and children of other fallen ANC leaders would receive a good education. He asked us if we would lead the charge and recruit American friends – Frank Ferrari, Peggy Dulany, Percy Sutton and others – to establish a special education fund for these comrades' chil-dren. We created a fund at the Africa America Institute, which OR and his colleagues on the ANC NEC closely monitored.

We often experienced OR's role as a mentor for younger members of the ANC, many of whom have gone on to become leaders in South Africa's new government and/or in business. In 1985 we were hosting a Global Cit-izens Circle in Boston with OR as the speaker. When we reached the question and answer portion of the programme, OR kept calling on a younger man – Thabo Mbeki – to answer every second question. When we asked Johnny why OR was doing this, he answered, 'The old man is grooming him.' These days when people say 'the old man', they mean Madiba; at that time, this honorific and loving title belonged exclusively to OR.

A few years later we were in Washington, DC, when Mbeki and Lindiwe Mabuza said they'd come to our hotel after meetings. At midnight we assumed we had been trumped by the burdens of their day-long, delicate and strategic interactions with policymakers and we went to bed. At 2:30 a.m., displaying the same indifference to time as all ANC comrades who worked tirelessly around the clock, they called. Since the hour was so late, we invited them to our room where we all sat on the bed – us in pyjamas – regaling each other with stories and much laughter. One of the magnificent qualities that all of OR's protégés shared was an ability to laugh amidst the most trying circumstances. That night ended with, 'We've got to tell the old man about this.'

In 1991 during Nelson Mandela's first visit to New York, a group of us left together after a public event. When we couldn't get a cab near Central Park, we encouraged the driver of a horse-drawn carriage to take us – including Barbara Masekela, Thabo Mbeki and Lindiwe Mabuza – to our destination. When we heard his accent, we knew he was a white South African, so I asked him to take a look at the group, explaining that he had in his carriage the leaders of his nation, including his future President. He looked at us as though we were crazy and again we uttered the famous words, 'We've got to tell the old man about this.'

These anecdotes make clear OR's deep, fatherly connection to Makathini, Mbeki, Masekela and Mabuza, among countless others. In addition, they highlight the critical leadership role OR played while Mandela, Sisulu and others were still in prison. While we've chosen to recount these lighter stories, we trust that readers know there were innumerable painful, heartbreaking situations when OR bravely and unfalteringly led the ANC through unbearably difficult times.

OR and his protégés – Johnny Makathini central among them – guided our support of the struggle. In 1998 when we brought a delegation of sixty-one democracy activists from seven nations on an eight-day tour through post-apartheid South Africa, we established the Oliver Tambo/Johnny Makathini Freedom Award. Recipients include Ma/Sis Adelaide (1998), Leah Tutu (1999), Thabo Mbeki (2000), Donald (posthumously) and Wendy Woods (2001), and Beyers and Ilse Naudé (2003).

Over the several decades before that we organised numerous public forums, primarily with our Global Citizens Circle and/or in association with other organisations. In addition to OR and those described above, these meetings featured Desmond Tutu; Zwelakhe, Max, Lungi, Sheila and Zodwa Sisulu; Aziz and Essop Pahad; Frank Chikane; Albie Sachs; Kader Asmal; Jeff Radebe; Trevor Huddleston; Linda Twala; Richard Goldstone; Themba Vilakazi; Aggrey Mbere; Ken Carstons; Luyanda Kwa Mzuma; George Bizos; and many others.

During these same years we wrote op-ed pieces on South Africa that were published in the *New York Times*, *International Herald Tribune*, *USA Today*, *Boston Globe*, *Miami Herald* and *Crisis Magazine*, among others. And we did fund-raising on behalf of the Oliver Tambo Education Fund, the Walter Sisulu Bursary Fund, the Africa Fund, TransAfrica, Shared Interest, South Africa Partners, the Bishop Tutu Scholarship Fund, the Nelson Mandela Freedom Fund, the IDAF, SAFE and ANSA, among others. We've continued to hold Circles with those who were in jail while OR led the ANC, including with Walter and Albertina Sisulu, Nelson Mandela and Graça Machel, and Ahmed Kathrada.

But, as important, we have remained part of the extended Tambo family through our ongoing relationship with Ma/Sis Adelaide, right until Jerry attended her funeral in February 2007, and with her and OR's children, Dali, Tembi and Tselane, and with their grandchildren Sasha, Oliver, Theodora, Zachary, Anastasia and Oliver. Nandi Makathini is also a member of our extended family. To all of them we are known as Auntie Nadine and Uncle Jerry, and we are forever grateful to OR for the richness and manifold blessings he brought to our lives.

SECRET GATHERINGS

Sally Sampson

I was never as close to the great ANC leader Oliver Tambo as my husband Anthony Sampson was over the years, but I will never forget my meetings with him. I was present at many secret gatherings at our home in Ladborke Grove, organised by Anthony in order to forge links between senior business people in the UK and the ANC. Oliver impressed even the most sceptical business leaders with his quiet authority, his patent honesty and goodness, and his knowledge of the real world. People came away from the meetings with an enormous respect for him, and for his courage in standing up to the forces of evil. Oliver's integrity – and that of Thabo Mbeki, who was present at the same meetings – helped to persuade business people to support the ANC and its aims.

I also met Oliver at his family home in Muswell Hill, North London. The house was always full of activity, with friends and family enjoying meals cooked by Adelaide, and discussing politics in a free and easy way. In spite of all his activities abroad, and the dangers that he lived with, Oliver remained a wonderful family man with an enormous affection for his children. His marriage with Adelaide was a true partnership in every way.

I feel very honoured to have known this great statesman and remarkable human being.

INTERCONNECTED LIVES

Ronald Segal

I cannot recall when it was that Joe Slovo spoke to me so anxiously about Oliver Tambo, though the drift and urgency of his remarks remain vivid. 'I am really worried about OR,' he said. 'He does too much. We tell him, but he won't listen. A little while ago, in the middle of all the pressures on his time, he sat for half an hour talking to someone in the camps whose mother-in-law had sent a letter about the trouble she was having with her teeth and what was she to do about it. He can't go on like this. You must talk to him. And you must promise not to say that I asked you.'

It must have been soon afterwards that Oliver came to London, and I remember driving him from my home in Walton, when I duly reported the concern of his comrades. 'Who spoke to you?' he asked sharply. Since I was driving, I didn't turn to study his reaction, but I supposed that his eyes might be darting from side to side, a habit of his when he was suspicious or disturbed about something. 'I was asked not to tell you,' I replied. 'And anyway, that's not relevant.' He was silent for a few moments and then said, 'It was Joe, I suppose.' I ignored this.

'Aren't you the one', he went on, 'who talks and writes about African leaders so distant from the people they are supposed to lead that they end up talking only to themselves? How am I to know what those in the camps feel or want if I am never there to hear them and talk with them?' He was right, of course, and so, in his own way, was Joe. For the truth is that Oliver did not die by accident or old age. He worked, or more accurately overworked, himself there. It was the only way of leading or serving that he knew.

8

Speak to any of those who served with him on the NEC of the ANC in exile. Of other leaders, before, then or since, they will talk in terms of appreciation, respect and even reverence. Only of Oliver do they use the word 'love' in speaking or writing of him. I too, came to love him, in a close and long friendship that began rather badly.

He would describe this himself in a lengthy letter written to me from Lusaka on 25 March 1970, ten years to the day after a crucial decision in our interconnected lives:

> After all what did I know at that time about Ronald Segal except that he had thrice embarrassed us when –
> • he came out with a Unilateral Declaration of a Boycott of Nationalist products;
> • he waved a £1 note at a crowded ANC conference, and got himself accepted by the cheering delegates as a full ANC member – annual subscriptions paid to the conference (right over the heads of the Leaders – me included!) for the next 8 years!
> • he telephoned me from Cape Town demanding we call a national stay-at-home – a decision the NEC had already taken, but which for tactical reasons we were for the time being keeping secret.
>
> The fact was now beginning to dawn upon me that Ronald Segal was in truth deep 'in it' – the struggle. Hence the repeated 'outbursts'. And hence his split-second decisions that crisis-ridden Friday afternoon.

Oliver had arrived from Johannesburg, and I was telephoned to see someone at the nearby offices of the Food and Canning Workers' Union. Both of us had been banned so that our being caught together amounted to an act of illegality squared. When an official there alerted us to the arrival of police from the Special Branch, we left as quickly as possible and reached the pavement outside to read the headlines of the afternoon paper, announcing the government decision to outlaw the ANC along with various emergency measures. Oliver told me of the NEC decision that in such an event, he was to go abroad and establish the ANC in exile. With no more precise plans made, he wondered how to do this. And I said, 'I'll take you.'

It was 1 600 kilometres by road to Johannesburg, but I had driven that several times before. And the route from there to the border of Bechuanaland (now Botswana) was surely much shorter, though the state of the road or of the border crossing itself was a different matter. I borrowed my mother's car, along with the white coat worn by her driver. Anything more suspect and dangerous at that time than a white man and a black man together alone in a car travelling across country would have been difficult to imagine. But once given a uniform of service, the black man became predictable and safe.

With a futile stop in Kimberley, where Oliver went in search of the ANC leader there, we sped to Johannesburg, which we reached in the early afternoon of the following day. While Oliver went off on his own but with the pledge to return by 9:00 p.m., I deposited myself at the home of a family friend, who displayed particular cool and courage, given that she was, as I recall, head of the Women's Zionist Council at the time, and any political scandal in which I might have involved her would have had considerable reverberations. So many years later, with a seismic shift in the nature of South African society and decades after her death, the historian in me requires that I name her as Inez Gordon.

Oliver arrived at the house two hours late with his wife Adelaide, whose self-control was remarkable given that she must have suspected that she might be saying goodbye to Oliver for the last time. Then the two of us set off for Bechuanaland, to find unexpectedly no more barrier at the border than a single African policeman with a large book in which we were required to inscribe our names. Regrettably, our very success doubtless ensured that security on the South African side would henceforth be tightened.

I drove to Lobatsi, the nearest town, and parked the car outside the single local hotel, dark and locked at 3:30 a.m. We slept until dawn when we went in search of the youthful District Commissioner, who noted Oliver's stated intention to seek political asylum. He then added that there was no accommodation for Oliver available at the hotel, a form of words that exposed the existence of functional segregation in this British High Commission territory, but that he might stay at the Resident Commissioner's hostel for visiting Chiefs a few miles from the town.

There, after an embrace of anxious regret, I parted from Oliver and set off back to Johannesburg. After a night's sleep at her home, Inez woke me early in the morning with news of the announced State of Emergency and police swoops across the country. The events that followed, detailed in my published recollections, *Into Exile*, but scarcely relevant here, convinced me that I might be pressing my luck too far. I drove back across the border and presented myself to a welcoming and unsurprised Oliver. The surprise was all mine as I saw him sitting in the sun with a cross on the beaded necklace round his neck. It had simply never occurred to me that he was a devout Christian.

The rapid discovery of our presence by the press produced a rush of publicity which I gladly fed in the belief that the more of it there was, the more difficult it would be for the South African government to secure or improvise our return and for the British government, if minded, to connive at this. Meanwhile, we had two immediate objectives: travel documents (Oliver might never have been granted a passport, while mine had been confiscated) and a way of using them (preferably a plane to get us over rather than through the risky Central African Federation). The weeks that followed were increasingly frustrating as approaches in both connected directions seemed to lead nowhere.

We drove northwards to Francistown, where soon, judging that the risk of challenging the federal authorities to arrest us was arguably no greater than our being kidnapped, I proposed driving across the border. The history of South Africa might well have been different if a short way from doing so, a cloud of dust had not revealed the car of my elder brother Cyril, a Southern Rhodesian businessman with important political contacts. It had been decided, he informed me, that we would be arrested and returned to South Africa as soon as we crossed the border. Returning to Francistown, we met up with Dr Yusuf Dadoo, former President of the South African Indian Congress, who was on a mission similar to Oliver's.

That night I was visited by two members of the Bechuanaland administration with a report of a plot to kidnap me that they considered credible and required that I move with them at once to their offices. And it was there that I was traced and telephoned by Frene Ginwala, then the East African representative of my magazine *Africa South*, with the news that the Indian government had issued Oliver, Yusuf and me with travel documents and that a plane would be arriving at 6:00 a.m. the next day to collect us.

The airfield turned out to be an unremarkable flat piece of earth with a scattering of stones; the papers brought by the pilot were unconvincing in appearance and language; and the plane itself looked to me scarcely able to lift us let alone carry us to Blantyre, in a Nyasaland soon to become an independent Malawi. But they all served their respective purposes. Two days later we arrived in Dar es Salaam and into the welcoming arms of Julius Nyerere, then Chief Minister of what would soon be an independent Tanganyika.

A few days thereafter, we were on a more reassuring aircraft, travelling first class at the expense of the Ghanaian government, bound for Accra. And it was there that I got a new sense of the complex difficulties with which Oliver was likely to be faced. Geoffrey Bing, the Ghanaian Attorney General, visited us at the hotel and suggested, as though merely in passing, a radical development. The Ghanaian government would be willing to host a South

African government-in-exile, which might then raise a large international loan guaranteed by the Ghanaian government. A specific figure, which struck me as improbably large at the time, was cited as likely encouragement.

Oliver responded, as he was characteristically given to do when so suddenly surprised, by a polite and thoughtful silence. More impulsively I found myself saying, 'Mr Bing, let me put a hypothetical question to you. There is an international meeting at which the Ghanaian government and the South African government-in-exile are both represented, but do not agree on a significant point at issue. Would the government-in-exile be free to vote its own way?' Bing replied at once, 'It would be most unwise.' The subject was immediately changed.

Somewhat more usefully, the Ghanaian government issued three impressive documents, no. 1001 to Oliver, 1002 to Yusuf, and 1003 to me, each inscribed in gold on the green front cover, 'Certificate of Commonwealth Citizenship and Laissez-Passer'. The first part of the inscription was based by Bing on the then operative principle that there was free movement within the Commonwealth and that proof of citizenship in any of the member states was accordingly enough to guarantee this. I was not convinced and relied on the second part, the Ghanaian laissez-passer. It worked well enough, for the various pages in my own document have the visas and corresponding official stamps for Belgium, West Germany, Spain, Italy, Austria, Norway, Sweden and Finland.

These were countries where I went for conferences or lectures in the course of mobilising opposition to apartheid. But my main commitment was to continue the publication of my international quarterly, suitably renamed *Africa South in Exile*, six successive numbers of which eventually appeared. The decision of the South African Reserve Bank to block all my funds in South Africa meant that the sixth was the last. I gladly accepted the invitation from Penguin Books to commission and edit the Penguin African Library, along with occasional other books, and also set out to write my own. This is relevant here because it involved my decision to live in England, formalised in my naturalisation on 25 April 1961, while Oliver's destiny was the infinitely harder and more valuable one of living and leading somewhere in Africa a resurgent ANC.

We continued to keep in touch, and I was all the more delighted when Adelaide and their children came to live in London. I know how much Oliver wanted to be there on 17 July 1962 for my wedding, at which his daughter Tembi was the flower girl and his son Dali the page boy. It seemed to be the closest we could get on that occasion. Nine months later, when our son was born, Susan and I agreed to call him Oliver. At the end of that long letter he would write on the tenth anniversary of our departure, he would sign off, 'Much love to you and the rest of the "Clan", explosive little Oliver not excluded.'

It was impossible not to worry about him, and it was always a relief to get a letter or a message. Through my publishing activities as well as my continuing anti-apartheid campaigning, I came to meet various African leaders. On one occasion I had been taken to meet, in the early hours of the morning, in the VIP lounge at Heathrow, Patrice Lumumba, returning from a visit to the UN on his way back home to what would be his kidnapping and murder. There is no hint of hindsight in this recollection. I simply knew with certainty that I would never see him again. There was out there, in the Cold War, a real Wild West.

I believed then, as I still do, that a popular moral identification across so much of the world with our cause was the essential prerequisite of a successful strategy. And in all this, the wisdom and vision of Oliver were indispensable.

One aspect of such strategy with which I was peculiarly involved was that of the campaign for economic sanctions. I was to be reminded of how this began when in 1994, having been asked by the ANC to help with its election campaign in the Western Cape, I arrived at a house in Cape Town to be greeted by Nelson Mandela with, 'Hello, Ronnie, can you remember when we first met?' Embarrassed to realise that I had no such recollection, I said simply, 'No'. And he responded, 'It was in 1957, to discuss the potato boycott'. My lasting reaction was of wonder, at a memory so prodigious that he could recall not only the year but the subject of a conversation with someone who must have been of marginal interest to him at the time. But it also revived in me the memory of how I first got involved in the economic engagement.

In 1957, courageous black journalists had reported the scandal of effectively forced black labour, hired or otherwise acquired from the prison service, on the potato farms of the Eastern Transvaal in the area of Bethal, from which the ensuing scandal came to be known. The reaction, promoted by the ANC, was a boycott of potatoes – not an easy target, since potatoes were a relatively cheap food that formed a common part of the urban black diet – and the piles of unsold potatoes at railway junctions such as Germiston, pictured in the press, testified to the potential success a consumer boycott might have. It was in consequence of this that I became involved in a consumer boycott of products from companies which supported the apartheid regime; and it was through this involvement that I was invited to speak from the platform at the ANC conference in 1959, when I used the opportunity to apply for membership of the ANC.

By 1963, it was clear to me that a consumer boycott, now expanding abroad, was successful as propaganda, but unlikely to threaten at all seriously the apartheid regime, and that the ultimate economic weapon of international economic sanctions should be our objective. Oliver, whose agreement and association were essential, approved and encouraged me, and with the active engagement of colleagues in the AAM, I convened the International Conference on Economic Sanctions against South Africa, in London, from 14 to 17 April 1964.

Eleven heads of government agreed to be patrons. Mongi Slim, Foreign Minister of Tunisia, acted as Chairman. Official delegates came from thirty countries, and unofficial delegations came from fourteen others. Seventeen papers on various relevant subjects, historical, legal, economic, political, and strategic, were delivered, and five related commissions recorded their findings. Oliver himself had provided the introductory statement on 'Apartheid – the indictment'. And the report was published soon afterwards as a Penguin Special.

The conference did not produce economic sanctions. The view, dominant ever since their ineffectual use by the League of Nations against Italy in its war of 1935–36 on Ethiopia, was still that they were impractical, if not repugnant. Nor, it soon emerged, were those supposedly in support of our campaign all they purported to be. I think it was in July 1964 that the OAU Foreign Ministers met in Cairo, and since the issue of apartheid was on the agenda, Oliver and I, independently, were invited to attend; myself, I assumed, as convenor of the sanctions conference. In the event, we were not expected or even, I inferred, allowed to speak, and the subject of sanctions developed into a series of accusations and counter-accusations of engaging in trade with South Africa while maintaining otherwise. While I fumed in frustration, Oliver presented his impassive face.

Yet the climate did change. Issues of racial conflict rose in importance, not least in the US with the militant civil rights movement; while within South Africa, the increasingly militarised and repressive apartheid regime incited a militant popular reaction, especially in the townships. Young black refugees streamed across the border to join the ANC. At the UN, measures were agreed against the arms and then the oil trade with South Africa. Around the middle of October 1985, I had a phone call from a nephew of mine, then Managing Director of Woolworths in South Africa, asking if I could arrange a meeting with Oliver for Chris Ball, the head of Barclays Bank in South Africa.

On the evening of 29 October, Oliver, along with Thabo Mbeki, arrived at my home for dinner and a discussion with Chris Ball, who informed us that the South African economy was in critical contraction and that if this continued, there would be little left for any revolution to inherit. His own advice was for a short, sharp shock, such as a worldwide rupture in mail and telecommunications with South Africa, so as to bring the government to its senses. It was not a credible proposal. But it was undeniable evidence of the apartheid regime's economic vulnerability.

In August 1986, the US Senate voted a veto-proof 84 to 14 for the imposition of a ban on new investment, loans, airport landing rights and exports of oil to South Africa. This led to increasingly serious financial pressure on a regime many of whose foreign loans, falling due, could now not be easily refinanced. When FW de Klerk came to power, his decision to legalise the ANC and release Mandela was largely due to the scale of the country's economic difficulties. As FW later told his brother Wimpie, 'Internationally we were teetering on the edge of the abyss.'[1]

The issue of economic sanctions was by no means the only one on which my friendship with Oliver had a continuing political dimension. From time to time he would consult me, and the correspondence between us was not always as smooth as we expected it to be. In a typed letter of 14 March 1981, headed 'Office of the President', and in language so unusually official that it must have been meant to be read by others, he made the process formal:

> There are numerous questions which we need to keep under constant study so as to take correct decisions when and as the occasion demands. Your long association with the South African situation enables you to correctly evaluate the relevance and significance, for our struggle, of the developments, events and ideas which are part of the rapidly changing world we live in.
>
> I would like to encourage you, indeed to ask you, to make yourself available to undertake any special study I may require, or on your own initiative, to prepare material, make comments, observations and recommendations in relation to any question or issue which you may feel requires attention or action by the ANC. It will of course be up to me to decide whether and how to use your ideas, but I will certainly give them very careful consideration, and will in any case ensure that your initiatives are put to the best possible use for the advancement of our struggle.
>
> It has happened in the past that documents intended for my attention have not reached my desk. I am taking care of this problem.

Among the few subsequent examples I kept is the telegram dated 1 February 1982: 'HAVE BEEN TRYING FRUITLESSLY TO PHONE YOU YOUR TELEPHONE IS PERMANENTLY ENGAGED PLEASE PHONE BACK URGENTLY OLIVER'. Dated 2/2/82 London, a scrawled hand-written note, headed and underlined confidential, reads:

> Dear Ronald,
>
> I'm enclosing papers from which you'll see I'm due to make a key-note speech here in March. I'd like it to be 'key' in the practical sense of the term and not 'key' in the I-also-ran sense. Do you have any bright ideas? My specialised topic sounds specialised but it must obviously fit into the general framework of the conference theme and, indeed, throw the theme into bold relief. The heading of my topic is broad – perhaps to allow me plenty of elbow room.
>
> Then there is the rally on the 14th. It's not certain if I shall or should speak at the rally. But there may well be things one should say to the British at a rally which would not be appropriate material for a conference – and vice versa.
>
> Again, can you pull out one of your numerous brain waves? This could make the diff [sic] between being or not being at Trafalgar Square on the Sunday in question. I'll be back and around in time to see what use I can make of your 'wild' ideas.

As is evident from this, Oliver prepared carefully and extensively for public speaking engagements. Perhaps, indeed, he did so too much. Certainly he was at his best when he spoke with only a few notes or none at all rather than delivering a written text, but I could never persuade him of this. It was simply that all the preparation came like a screen between his natural eloquence, the projection of his thoughtful, generous, impassioned commitment, and his audience. And this may explain why he was so much more loved the closer that people came to him.

On 17 August 1982, Ruth First, one of the closest and dearest of my friends, was torn apart by a parcel bomb, directed to her and dispatched by the South African security assassins, at the university in Maputo. The tributes paid to her gave rise to the project for a charitable trust that would reflect her work and ideas. I set about raising funds for it and confidently expected a major response from Sweden, where she had been widely admired. When nothing arrived from Sweden, I searched out an explanation. It emerged that the blockage emanated from the ANC office in Stockholm, which objected to this singling out of a white woman for such support when so many black women, no less heroic in their contribution to the struggle, were not being similarly distinguished.

I communicated with Oliver at once and very shortly afterwards, I was informed from Stockholm that there was no longer any resistance to support for the trust. I received a letter from Oliver, dated 8/7/83 in Lusaka.

> My dear Ronald,
> I've written to you officially about the Trust. I make no reference to the race question because anyone who thinks in race terms about Ruth is committing an outrage on a whole lot of us and can only be grossly misrepresenting the ANC.
>
> I'm trying to get a short break and a short rest. But security problems have made me very 'cumbersome' for I have to travel with someone else – and double the cost of going anywhere.
>
> In the meantime, I am getting worried over the Amsterdam University address. I enclose a telex message, from which you'll see there are great expectations. I still haven't thought up a suitable topic and am anxious to know what you have. But I'll contact you. Don't write.
>
> With some luck, I'll be in the UK for the week beginning July 18 (Not to be disclosed) which does not give you too much time.
>
> All of the best & love to the family,
> Oliver

I quote the letter in full because it reveals not only the rage of his response to the attitude of the Stockholm office but also, in all its hurried and varied concerns, the pressures to which he was increasingly subject. There is almost a note of guilt in his choice of the word 'cumbersome', as though he resented any expenditure on himself that even his very protection entailed. And as anyone who knew him well would have inferred, the very admission that he was 'trying to get a short break and a short rest' meant that he must have been feeling close to or at the edge of his capacity to cope.

Just what the subject was of the address at Amsterdam University for which he needed such urgent help, I have kept no record and cannot recall. Indeed, I can remember only two speeches that I wrote for him, one on the issue of violence which may or may not have been delivered, and one on relations between the ANC and the Soviet Union, which certainly was delivered to some high-powered group in the US. In this I argued that the American revolutionaries had experienced no moral or political inhibition in seeking and accepting whatever help they could get from monarchical France in their struggle against monarchical Britain. And the only reason I recall this essence of the argument, which must have been somewhat more extensive, is that Oliver on several occasions mentioned to me how useful the speech had proved to be.

Stress, exhaustion, diet, any number of factors might have contributed to the strokes from which Oliver suffered. The bare truth is that he gave so much of himself that there was little left with which to give even more. The last time we met in London was when he was packing, I seem to remember, with the prospect of his going home. In February 1992, Joe Slovo phoned to say, 'I thought you'd like to know. We've both just been unbanned.' I was so involved in a book I was committed to finishing soon that my own first view of South Africa since leaving it was to be in August, on the tenth anniversary of Ruth's assassination.

The Ruth First Memorial Trust had established an annual award for courageous journalism, and the first presentation of this, with the report of the judges, was to be made at a mass meeting in the great hall at the University of the Western Cape. The platform population, which included Oliver as well as Nelson Mandela, Joe Slovo, Nadine Gordimer (who was due to deliver the decision of the judges) and Pallo Jordan, in the chair, was predictably late, and when we filed onto the stage we were greeted with an explosion of excitement, dancing in the aisles, singing and chanting that might, I suppose, have had some small component of relief at our arrival.

Though my own speech was appropriately concerned mainly with Ruth, there was another aspect to which I began by citing. We had spoken, Oliver and I, during the escape, of when we might be together again in South Africa, and now, 32 years on, this was the occasion. It was not an altogether joyous one, apart from its essential connection with Ruth's murder, as Oliver was still recovering from his stroke. But the trust had specified that he should present the Ruth First award, and having spent some time with him before the meeting began, I knew that he was looking forward to it.

I assumed that he would accompany the presentation with remarks of his own and was somewhat surprised that he did not. And when, after the occasion, I heard that he was upset at not having been allowed to deliver the speech he had prepared, I was furious. Apparently it had been decided, in a mark of misplaced respect, that he should not be subjected in his condition to the stress of such an ordeal. There was not much that I could do afterwards but apologise to him and reassure him, as he must have known, that no slight could ever have been intended.

We had a long breakfast together the following morning at the hotel where we were both staying. That was the last time I saw him, but my son, his namesake, with his wife Lesley, went to visit him in Johannesburg shortly before his death, and I am glad of that.

One recollection is peculiarly precious to me. It involves my late mother, whose long devotion to the ideal of a Jewish homeland left little of her large generosity and imagination for the plight and struggle of black South Africa. A natural opponent of apartheid, which she abhorred not least for its association in her mind with the Afrikaner nationalism that had flirted with anti-Semitism, she did not reach beyond the conventional white liberalism of treating black servants with decent civility. The somewhat different engagement of my own developing politics began to have an effect on her as well.

Oliver himself would occasionally refer to his appreciation at the way she had welcomed him in her home on the day of our escape, and this was strengthened by her subsequent readiness to help with the educational costs of his youngest child. So it might well have been by arrangement that he and Adelaide arrived at my Walton home while my mother, on one of her regular visits from Israel, was staying with me. As Oliver walked through the door and saw her, his face broke into a wonderful smile and he stretched out his arms to embrace her with the cry, 'Mother!' I saw a look of panic flit across her face before she instantly composed herself to be readily embraced.

Perhaps only someone of my own time, country and culture can understand why I found and remember this still as such a beautiful moment.

NOTES
1. In A. Sampson, *Mandela: The Authorized Biography* (New York: Vintage Books, 2000).

FATHER OF A BOISTEROUS FAMILY

Pauline Webb

I first came to know Oliver Tambo, not as a remote, renowned political leader, but as the husband of a good friend of mine, and the father of a boisterous family of young children who had become my near neighbours. In 1960 I had moved to live in the quiet, leafy suburb of Muswell Hill in North London. Not long afterwards I met another new resident in the area, an African lady of most imposing and attractive appearance who, with her three children, including a small baby, had come to live in a large detached house just around the corner from my own flat. When we introduced ourselves to each other I recognised a name that was already becoming well known in the recently formed British branch of the AAM of which I had been a committed member from the days of its foundation in 1956.

At the time when I first met Adelaide Tambo – for that was my new neighbour's name – we were still reeling from the shock of the news of the Sharpeville massacre which signalled to us all how brutal the apartheid regime in South Africa had become. For people living in the country the signs were ominous. The country had now come under martial law. Although the notorious Treason Trial had ended in a shambles, the 156 accused being found not guilty, it was plain that the African political movements, both the ANC and the PAC, would in the very near future almost certainly be banned. Nelson Mandela, who was still in danger of arrest, went underground into hiding. Meanwhile, Oliver Tambo, his colleague, was advised by Chief Albert Luthuli to leave South Africa and go on an External Mission to try to raise international awareness of the dangerously deteriorating situation and to win support for the ANC from around the world.

One of the first heads of government Oliver visited was Kwame Nkrumah of Ghana. With his help and with the aid of the British Defence and Aid Fund, they managed to arrange to fly Oliver's wife Adelaide and their children out to safety and to live in accommodation that had been found for them in London. Adelaide herself was a prominent member of the ANC. Indeed, I was told that she and Oliver first met at a rally of the ANC Youth League in 1955. There, an impressive speech made by Adelaide so inspired Oliver that he wrote to congratulate her. Modestly, she did not reply. Undeterred, Oliver wrote to her again and that was the beginning of their lifelong romance. They were married in December 1956, during the long drawn-out time of the Treason Trial.

I always felt that Oliver's recognition of Adelaide's gifts accounted for his own affirmative attitude to women that I recognised in my rare meetings with him in their home at Muswell Hill. He could visit London only fleetingly between his extensive travel commitments. I remember that at that time I was campaigning for the ordination of women in the Methodist Church. Oliver, who was a devout Anglican, said that he had once wondered whether he had a vocation to the priesthood. But he confessed that there were times when he despaired of the Church which sometimes seemed to lack courage in taking a stand against injustice, though he spoke of his admiration for men such as Father Trevor Huddleston and Canon John Collins, whom we both counted among our close friends.

It was always a great occasion in the Tambo house in Muswell Hill when Oliver did get a chance to come home. He was a devoted father who wanted his children to have every opportunity of education and the chance to develop the talents they all clearly had. Even as small toddlers they were lively and imaginative and would bring out their toys and drawings to show me when I visited. When the children were of school-going age they were all sent to prestigious schools in England.

Although we lost immediate touch with one another when the Tambo family eventually was able to return to South Africa, I have followed the children's careers with interest. Tembi, the eldest, married, with Canon John Collins performing the ceremony. I understand she is now the mother of four children. I was not surprised to learn that both Dali and Tselane have gone into the theatrical profession. I was interested to read the eloquent speech Dali gave at the opening of the Tambo Moot Hall in the Faculty of Law at the University of Cape Town in August 2001, recalling his father's humility and gentleness, and describing him as 'a man of catholic tastes and multiple talents'. Recently I heard that Tselane (who was the baby when I first knew the family) has become the founder of the Tambo Grooming School, a school where students in South Africa are trained in etiquette and fashion along the lines of a European 'finishing' school.

It would seem therefore that the children have inherited their parents' talents: their father's gifts of eloquence and scholarship and their mother's gifts of elegance and hospitality. The Tambo household was never empty of visitors. Adelaide loved entertaining and was a most welcoming hostess as well as an excellent cook. Among the frequent visitors to the house in Muswell Hill were exiled South Africans who had come to Britain to study, including the young Thabo Mbeki. He had come to study economics at Sussex University and then stayed on to run the ANC's London office. On another occasion, in 1962, Nelson Mandela paid a fleeting visit to the Tambo household in London and he and Oliver went on an enthusiastic sight-seeing tour of the metropolis. Among the first overseas visits that Nelson Mandela made immediately after his release from prison, there was another brief, private visit to Adelaide and Oliver's home in London. Little did I realise then how thrilled I would be when in 1991 I was myself able to visit Mandela, newly released from gaol, in his home which was then still in Soweto.

During their stay in London both Oliver and Adelaide devoted their time and their talents to join in all that was being done in support of the anti-apartheid struggle. Adelaide was always a familiar presence at the many women's rallies held by the ANC in London. I was especially grateful to her for agreeing to take part as one of a panel of speakers I had invited for a Church gathering of women held in 1975 to mark International Women's Year. This was a spectacular occasion held in the Royal Albert Hall and attended by some five thousand women from all over the British Isles. It was entitled 'Signs of Hope' and was planned as a positive celebration of the contribution women were making in a variety of spheres of life. Adelaide very much enjoyed the whole programme, which included dance and choral singing as well as displays of fashion and gymnastics.

The panel of speakers was chosen from areas of particular kinds of tension in the world. There was an Indian woman who was a political scientist, a trade unionist who was a leader of the movement known as Women Together in Northern Ireland, a feminist who was campaigning against sex discrimination both in the Church and in society in Britain and, to complete the quartet, Adelaide Tambo represented the struggle of women for freedom in South Africa. As always, Adelaide was exquisitely dressed in African costume, which she often made herself. She spoke with such dignity and authority that, although people had come not expecting this to be a political

gathering, she won the hearts even of some who had criticised me for inviting such controversial speakers to a Church gathering.

I particularly appreciated the effort Adelaide made in coming to this occasion. I knew how hard she was working at the time. She was a nurse in a
major London hospital and was often doing double shifts. I also knew that
she had been injured in an accident that was affecting her mobility a little.
She must also often have been anxious about Oliver who rarely managed to
be home with her more than twice a year, and who was living under tremendous pressure, with an exhausting travel schedule.

Inevitably, there were some social occasions when Adelaide deputised for
Oliver. Diana Collins, in her book *Partners in Protest*, tells how Adelaide represented her husband at the celebration of Canon John Collins's 70th birthday party held at the Stationers' Hall. She even went on to organise a second party for him with all his friends from the AAM. As Diana put it herself,
'Adelaide always does everything with style'. She supplied a splendid birthday cake, a bouquet of flowers for Diana and a wristwatch as a gift for John,
both of whom were among the many personal friends the Tambos made
during their stay in Britain.

There was one important occasion when it was Oliver himself who was
the deputy speaker. It was at a momentous international consultation organised by the WCC to be held in London in May 1969 to inaugurate a
Programme to Combat Racism. The newly appointed Director of the programme, Baldwin Sjollema, went to Dar es Salaam to invite Eduardo Mondlane to be one of the main speakers. Mondlane was President of FRELIMO,
the liberation movement in Mozambique, and was a committed Christian
who was well known in the circles of the WCC. However, three days after
he had accepted the invitation to come to London we heard the tragic news
that Mondlane had been assassinated by a parcel-bomb. Baldwin Sjollema
immediately invited Oliver Tambo, who was also known to be a committed
church man, to come in his place. Despite his already overcrowded schedule, Oliver readily agreed to do this. His presence there was very important,
as we wanted to persuade churches worldwide to give their support to the
liberation movements through grants towards their humanitarian and educational needs, which would be an expression of solidarity and commitment
to their struggle against racial injustice.

The membership of this international consultation was high-powered and
influential. It included several statesmen and Church leaders as well as political activists from those parts of the world where racism was most evident. The
two Chairmen were the Archbishop of Canterbury, the Most Revd Michael
Ramsey, and the Hon. Dr George McGovern, a senator from the US.

Both the consultation and the public meeting that was held in conjunction with it proved to be eventful. In the Methodist hall in Notting Hill where the consultation was held, discussions were on one occasion interrupted by the sudden invasion of black power advocates demanding some form of reparation to be made from the Church for its complicity in racism throughout the centuries. Their anger and the vigour of their protest was matched by a much uglier demonstration in the public meeting that same evening in Church House, Westminster, which was invaded by members of the British National Front, yelling their slogan, 'Keep Britain white!' The police were called and the intruders removed. Oliver Tambo and his fellow speaker, the Rt Revd Trevor Huddleston, both apparently unperturbed by this unexpected interruption, proceeded to deliver two most memorable speeches.

In his address, Oliver Tambo described racism as 'a virulent, aggressive and violent ideology' that threatened to develop into an international conflict far worse than anything the world had yet seen. He responded to this threat in ideological terms, pointing out that all the great faiths adhered to by the vast majority of religious people everywhere upheld the concept of the essential oneness of humanity. He claimed that the once widespread myths of race superiority ought long ago to have been exploded and discarded. He particularly drew attention to the myth of 'white, Western Christian civilisation', which had been totally discredited through the experience of two world wars, in which there had been cold-blooded destruction of masses in the gas chambers, and in which the most advanced scientific discoveries had been applied to the obliteration of cities such as Hiroshima. He suggested that there had always been a disturbing alliance between racism, exploitation and Western Christianity. As an example of this he cited not only the way in which the pious, God-fearing Christians in the Dutch Reformed Churches in South Africa both preached and enacted racism, but also the way in which many others in churches across the world preached against racism but refrained from acting against it. He regarded those who stood up to confront racism in all its overt and covert armoury as 'the vanguard of Christian and other soldiers marching as to war'.

Oliver called on the consultation to urge all the member churches of the WCC, individually and collectively, to throw their moral and material resources behind the struggle for the defeat of racism and 'in support of those who seek to establish a world society of peoples free from hunger, disease and ignorance, rich in its variety of colours, races and creeds'. Recalling the words of a hymn he had learned as a young child, he ended with the challenging question, 'Who is on the Lord's side?'

To that challenge the audience in Church House, still shaken by the blatant racism that had disturbed the meeting and insulted both our distinguished speakers, rose in enthusiastic applause. Their response was further expressed the next day in the strong resolve to call for a programme that would move beyond words into relevant and eloquent action. We felt as though, as the Hebrew prophets used to say, the word of God had not only spoken to us, but had *happened* among us. Oliver Tambo and Trevor Huddleston had been God's messengers to us, both on that day and throughout the time they were among us in London. The two great speeches they made at that consultation were an important contribution to its final positive outcome, the proposing of the Programme to Combat Racism. This has proved over the years to be one of the most controversial and effective consciousness-raising programmes the WCC has ever launched.

AN INSPIRATION
TO THE WHOLE FAMILY

Cora and Peter Weiss

The garden of our home in Riverdale, New York, was filled with family and friends on a brisk, sunny October day in 1963. The back door opened and out came the reason for the celebration – it was our son Danny's first birthday. Danny, who had just started walking, emerged in the loving arms of Oliver Tambo who took responsibility for introducing the young boy to everyone and watched over him, playing and talking all afternoon. That caring side of Oliver was still in evidence some thirty years later when he and Adelaide met us at the airport in Johannesburg to introduce us to the almost free South Africa.

Oliver was in New York in October 1963 to petition the UN General Assembly Special Political Committee. Nelson Mandela, who was already on Robben Island serving a five-year sentence for illegally leaving the country, had just been charged in the Rivonia Trial. Consequently, Diallo Telli, Guinea's Ambassador, who chaired the Special Committee against Apartheid, proposed that his Committee should immediately hear Oliver Tambo. He appeared several times that month before the two UN committees, appealing for the freedom of the South African people.

Oliver stayed with us during that period, bonding with our three children and forming a lifelong friendship that culminated in our trip in 1992 to his and Adelaide's home in Johannesburg. They turned over their pink bedroom to us and Oliver guided us through Soweto, to ANC headquarters, and invited us to join in his early morning speech therapy sessions that were part of his recovery from a stroke.

★ ★ ★

On 21 January 1987 the Riverside Church, one of the two largest in New York City, was packed beyond capacity. The crowd had come to hear Oliver Tambo. It was nearly a year since the assassination of Sweden's Prime Minister Olof Palme, perhaps the most important friend of the ANC and the anti-apartheid movement. The occasion was the Olof Palme Memorial Lecture on Disarmament and Development, which brought Allan Boesak of the UDF together for the first time in public with Oliver Tambo. Also on the programme were Anders Ferm, Sweden's Ambassador to the UN; Jan Martenson, Under-Secretary-General for Disarmament representing Secretary-General Perez de Cuellar; and the Church's Senior Minister, Revd William Sloane Coffin.

Tambo's speech at Riverside was the culmination of over a year's efforts to try to bring him to the church to speak for the Disarmament Programme. At least once a date was actually announced, only to be postponed, as it turned out, to accommodate an appointment with then US Secretary of State George Schultz. Congress had passed sanctions against the apartheid regime over President Reagan's veto, which prompted the Secretary of State to meet with the ANC leadership. That appointment resulted in the transformation of the ANC, in US policy, from a 'terrorist organisation' to a respected political party.

At Riverside, Tambo spoke movingly about Palme's widow, Lisbet, whom he wished had also been there, because 'she would have conveyed something of his vision which she, too, helped to form'. He pointed to Palme's hope of a world 'where each of us would become to all others, friend, comrade, brother and sister'. With his thick, dark-rimmed glasses sliding down his nose, Tambo ridiculed the fact that '... the offspring of the violence of our century remain as yet steeped in the idea that brute force can vanquish reason'.

Citing the assassination of friends and leaders including Palme, Indira Gandhi, Samora Machel, Maurice Bishop, Martin Luther King, Jr., Salvador Allende, as well as Robert and John F. Kennedy, Tambo said they '. . . served to reawaken our sensitivity to the horror of man's violence to man, to the enormity of the crimes of violence that were and are being perpetrated daily against people in many parts of the world'. 'The triumph of world peace,' he continued, would have to be achieved 'against the resistance of those who have a vested interest in the manufacture of weapons.'

In his passionate speech, which wove together Olof Palme's vision with the aspirations of the South African people, Tambo appealed to the West to remember its own struggles for freedom from oppression. 'To reform oppression,' he said, 'is to maintain oppression in an amended form. Liberty is an act of liberation both for the oppressed and the oppressors, a condition for the peaceful coexistence of peoples and individuals.'

Tambo defended the ANC's resort to the use of force, '. . . when we are denied all constitutional possibilities to redress the grievances of the majority'.

The audience that evening was the most racially diverse the church had ever known. Young and not so young were together in a groundswell of admiration and affection for the ANC President.

Revd Jesse Jackson said, 'On this historic evening at Riverside Church, I witnessed the joining of our two great struggles: the demand for peace and the fight for freedom. Let this vision guide us as we pursue what we must – our dignity and our salvation.'

The singer Harry Belafonte and the trade union leader, Cleve Robinson, were among the many dignitaries and well-wishers. Broad press coverage reported a 'rapturous reception', and the *Christian Science Monitor* recorded, 'The huge stone chamber throbbed with organ music as a robed procession – including the Rev. Jesse Jackson and boxing promoter Don King – led Tambo to the high altar and a choir sang "Kum Ba Yah" and "Rock-a-My-Soul".'

Thabo Mbeki, who had replaced the recently deceased Johnny Makathini as head of foreign affairs for the ANC, was part of Tambo's delegation. Don King came with his white stretch limousine to take Tambo and his delegation to his preferred hotel, eschewing the homey arrangements Revd Coffin had made for them to use his quiet, comfortable apartment. The successful evening launched a two-week tour of the US, mobilising support for the ANC.

★ ★ ★

Oliver ended his letter of 20 January 1992, inviting us to South Africa, by saying: 'I hope you are well and sound. I certainly am, and so is Adelaide.' This despite the fact that he was recovering from a stroke.

He was always cheerful, always optimistic, always caring – characteristics that people don't usually associate with a 'rebel leader'.

Adelaide worked as a nurse in England to keep the family fed while Oliver travelled the world mobilising support for the extraordinary dream of bringing freedom to millions of disenfranchised, oppressed people. Oliver could not have achieved his remarkable successes without Adelaide, who provided the warmth of home and love of family. Our whole family is grateful for their friendship and inspiration, and we are proud to have known one of the greatest figures of Africa's liberation struggle.

ANC AND OTHER COMRADES

OUR LODESTAR

Kader Asmal

My first contact with OR was indirect and from a distance. As a school teacher, I was discreetly politically active, living in the small country town of Stanger (now KwaDukuza) on the north coast of Natal. My political hero was Chief Albert Luthuli, then President of the ANC and banished to the magisterial area of Lower Tugela.

'Chief' used to travel to Stanger every now and again from his home in Groutville, an isolated and impoverished location. In 1955, at one of our encounters, he informed me that the ANC had recently elected a Johannesburg lawyer named Oliver Reginald Tambo as its Secretary-General. Albert Luthuli was a large man with a beautiful voice and when he laughed, his whole face was suffused with smiles. He broke into laughter when he told me that Nelson Mandela's law partner was quiet and modest but a man of steel who would galvanise the ANC.

I was to hear little more of OR's life until the early morning arrests of the 156 treason trialists in 1956. All of us involved in the ANC followed the vicissitudes of our heroes and heroines in the charade that passed off as the trial and we celebrated their acquittal. However, what struck me afterwards was the way OR's life resembled the fortunes of the main character in a book that Albert Luthuli had 'lent' to me. I have been re-reading Johan Bunyan's *Pilgrim's Progress* for this tribute. Luthuli's words to me were: read this book as it reflects a life of struggle. We will face similar struggles to those of the hero, Christian, before we win our freedom. At the time, for me as a rationalist, the book was a revelation, and even now provides fresh insights.

Both Luthuli and Tambo were profoundly religious though neither allowed his beliefs to obtrude on personal relations. Both travelled along Christian's allegorical roads – the slough of despond, the hill of difficulty, the valley of humiliation – and neither reached the 'celestial city' of freedom. Both were strong men, and though they must at times have felt despairing we who knew them mostly from a distance were never aware of it.

OR lived his life by the injunctions given to Christian: not to surrender to the forces of evil and not to be deflected from the path of righteousness. Life was not given him, as the editor of the 1921 edition of the book identified, 'merely for ease and pleasure but for the realization of ideals of high endeavour and noble service'.

Indeed, OR sacrificed his life for our freedom as his life reflected 'the ideals of high endeavour and noble service'.

I identify two phases of OR's life which related to my own. The first was the period from 1960 to 1964 when he mobilised people to break the walls of ignorance about apartheid South Africa, and advocated sanctions, culminating in his star performance at the first-ever international conference on sanctions in 1964. It covered too the campaign on behalf of political prisoners, which saved the lives of Nelson Mandela and the Rivonia trialists and then, most important of all, arranged for military and other forms of assistance to the ANC.

I was a law student when OR arrived in London, and deeply involved in the Boycott Movement which began in 1959, a year after Albert Luthuli's famous call to the international community to take action to enable meaningful change in South Africa to take place. A year later, in 1960, the British Anti-Apartheid Movement was established.

Everything at that time was weighed in the calculations of the Cold War, including opposition to or support of apartheid. But OR showed us that it was possible to arouse consciousness about the evils of apartheid by reaching out to ordinary people, by working with civil society in all its manifestations, including political parties, to pressurise governments.

OR was at the centre of our activities. We were all involved with him, either through the anti-apartheid movements or through the ANC or both. The loneliness of exile was largely dissipated for those involved in solidarity work and the comradeship that grew between us all. Of course Oliver was busy with a multitude of concerns, so as young people working at a basic grassroots level we did not meet him often, but we followed his doings eagerly. His stature grew with each appearance at international forums and we revelled in his triumphs. For all of us, including those like myself who only met him after his arrival in London in 1960, he became our lodestar who guided us through the maze of exile politics and relationships with governments and domestic organisations.

He introduced many of us to the burgeoning anti-apartheid and solidarity movements in Europe and elsewhere in the world. He showed us by example the necessity to remove any political or sectarian approach from our solidarity work. His humility drew us to him and strengthened our own understanding as to how we should work towards a non-racial South Africa. He was a truly modest man; for years, he insisted that he was only the Acting President of the ANC and that nothing was to detract from Nelson Mandela's pre-eminent role.

A lesser man might have abandoned what must have seemed a hopeless task, after the incarceration of so many of the experienced leaders in the 1960s, and the suppression of resistance activities. Bunyan's 'hill of difficulty' proved long and steep, but OR's steadfastness helped us to believe that it was not insurmountable.

He also played a part in my personal life, which might have been very different if it were not for his advice and that of Yusuf Dadoo, another stalwart of the struggle whom I had met earlier in my home town in the 1950s. Both of them were based in London in the early 1960s, and both provided leadership to the diverse group of exiles there. From time to time we experienced painful conflicts between our personal lives and our more public struggle lives. Some held the view that there had to be a single-minded devotion to the struggle from which nothing – certainly not private needs and aspirations – must be allowed to deflect us.

The other view was expressed in the advice I received from both these leaders when I visited each of them to inform them that I was considering marriage to an English woman. Apart from wider security considerations, this was of course to preclude my return to South Africa at the end of my studies in 1961.

OR was very clear: an unhappy cadre was not a good activist. Follow your heart, he told me, which I did. Such generosity of spirit from a leader who had at the same time to find cadres to return to South Africa to carry on the underground struggle made an enormous impression on me. Yusuf Dadoo took a similar position.

Nevertheless, generosity of spirit did not preclude toughness. The ANC office in London was a small one, with limited resources, and we were all expected to contribute our time and talents. This meant that we had to find jobs, and I had been offered an appointment lecturing at Trinity College, Dublin, though my heart really lay in Africa. When I mentioned to OR that I was intending to apply for posts in Africa, he unhesitatingly told me that I needed to consider where I would be most effective in the external struggle. The ANC already had offices in a number of African countries, so we were not needed there. Our skills were required in countries which were either collaborating with apartheid or which might be persuaded to support the struggle.

So I duly accepted the Dublin post, and was soon involved in the Irish Anti-Apartheid Movement which was established in 1964, as well as in ANC underground activities. Oliver, however, needed to be in closer contact with the struggle, and was soon based in Lusaka. Our paths did not directly cross again for a period but contact was never lost as we celebrated the ANC's diplomatic and political victories and worked with him in the seminal conferences organised by the UN and solidarity organisations.

Following the 1976 uprising, there was an upsurge of resistance in South Africa. This was followed in the 1980s by the formation of the UDF, in which OR played such an important role. This period, when the situation in southern Africa once again occupied the centre of the world stage, covered the second phase of my relationship with OR.

The ANC's Constitutional Committee

From around the mid-1980s, the ANC came under increasing pressure to put forward concrete proposals for a post-constitutional order. As the situation at home became increasingly repressive and the resistance equally determined, some elements, not necessarily friendly to the ANC, wanted to know what the ANC's vision was for a post-apartheid South Africa. At the same time, the apartheid regime, though it continued to behave in a lawless and criminal fashion, established structures to work out arrangements which would give the appearance of change while retaining white power.

OR recognised that from a strategic perspective it was crucial that we did not appear hesitant or wavering in the face of those proposals and demands. The ANC should not be seen to be responding to others; the ANC had to position itself as the lead agent.

There was another reason why the ANC had to take the initiative. It was a compelling reason but could easily have been overlooked by a lesser man. OR's foresight is attested to by his biographer, Luli Callinicos. She discloses that OR had told Thabo Mbeki that he had a nightmare that when the apartheid regime was ready to talk, the ANC would not be in a position to negotiate or respond. But, uniquely for a liberation movement, the ANC was ready in two ways and we owe this to OR.

Firstly, OR resolved to form a Constitutional Committee to establish what the ANC's idea would be for the constitutional arrangements in a free

South Africa. Secondly, he virtually sacrificed his life to drive the Harare Declaration of 1989, a seminal document which became the foundation for negotiations with the apartheid regime, after its adoption by the OAU and the UN. In order to secure its acceptance, OR criss-crossed Africa in small aircraft to inform our allies who, he always reiterated, had sacrificed so much for our freedom. Intense negotiations took place with the leaders of the Front-line States and OR was the custodian of our interests.

The heart of the Harare Declaration was contained in the pre-conditions for negotiations: the cessation of hostilities, the release of political prisoners and the adoption of a mechanism for drawing up the new constitution. The ANC needed to lay out its ideas as to what the constitution should include, and so the Declaration referred to a number of principles for a democratic society. How these principles emerged has historic significance because of OR's role.

In 1986, OR convened the first meeting of the Constitutional Committee in Lusaka on the 74th anniversary of the foundation of the ANC. For the following four years, chaired by Jack Simons, ANC lawyers worked at meeting the needs of the movement. It was a most exhilarating period of my life as we were involved in an extraordinary exercise – not least because we were working with OR – which few people could have envisaged.

At our first meeting, OR informed us of the efforts of some of the regime's allies, together with the regime, who were attempting to formulate a constitution that in their view would resolve the South African 'conflict'.

However, OR was never seduced by the demands of powerful forces which attempted to prescribe to us. He had met George Schultz, the American Secretary of State, for the first time in 1987 and the latter had enquired about the ANC's intentions. Drawing up a constitution in the middle of a struggle from outside the cockpit of South Africa raised serious questions. Oliver readily agreed with the recommendation of the Constitutional Committee that to draft a constitution externally would be to usurp the right of the people of South Africa to do so. It would be an exercise in gross arrogance, and would deny them their democratic right to choose.

He also agreed that the drafting of the interim constitution would be a matter of negotiations with the apartheid regime and other parties in South Africa. He then fell in line with the recommendation that we should draw up a set of constitutional guidelines, which as it turned out played such a large role in the history of the settlement and subsequent constitution-making process.

Oliver's remit to the Committee demanded a central role for the Freedom Charter. While our efforts were to be guided by the human rights tradition of our movement and the Freedom Charter, our group was expected to look beyond the Freedom Charter and to transform it from a vision of the future into a reality guaranteed by just and concrete constitutional principles.

Under Oliver's stewardship, the ANC produced the first Bill of Rights by a liberation movement. The guidelines of 1988 became the principles reflected in the Harare Declaration and were subsequently adopted by the ANC as the basis for negotiations.

It was the towering presence of OR that enabled the ANC to go into the negotiations in a state of preparedness. We ought to be grateful to him even if this were his only contribution to our freedom.

The Kabwe Conference
I had not attended the first consultative conference called by the ANC at Morogoro in 1969. In exile, the movement could not call a national conference which had constitutional authority. However, the distinction was notional as the Morogoro Conference had earlier adapted the strategy and tactics document which provided the foundation for the ANC activities of the future.

The events in South Africa in the middle of the 1980s required a collective response from the movement. The State of Emergency, the emergence of the UDF and the dramatic success of MK reflected a changing country. So, it was decided that a second consultative conference would be held in Kabwe, near Lusaka in Zambia.

The disinformation from apartheid South Africa was virtually overwhelming. Not only the Afrikaans newspapers but also the 'liberal' white press were full of stories about a *putsch* against Oliver and the rest of the leadership because of alleged dissatisfaction from the rank and file, especially in the ANC camps.

Over 300 delegates from every section of the ANC and from every part of the world where the movement had a presence assembled in Kabwe in June 1985. This conference was the first and only occasion at which I was present when Oliver was the chairperson and leader of the Conference.

OR introduced the political report of the NEC which was wide-ranging and comprehensive. There was overwhelming support for the political position of the NEC but there were some vexed issues to be discussed, such as the increasing impact of the armed struggle and whether membership should be 'open' to all the so-called races prescribed in the apartheid laws.

The ANC constitution did not refer to race at all. However, in the Congress movement, there were structures for the different races and an understanding that the ANC would above all be representative of the most exploited section of our country.

In his political report, the President carefully referred to the membership issue and asked the question as to whether 'we still felt justified to keep the restriction' on membership. Even more carefully, so as not to pre-determine the right of the Conference to decide, he felt that 'it should not be difficult' to reach agreement on a decision that 'will take our movement and struggle further forward'.

The following day, we broke into commissions. I spoke against opening up the membership, partly because of the prejudiced view of some elements hostile to the ANC who argued that the ANC was already dominated by whites and Indians; such a change might confirm them in their prejudices and incite further hostility. Mostly it was because I felt that the ANC should continue to be representative of the vast majority of the most oppressed and nothing should be allowed to dilute this representative capacity.

I was in a small minority of dissenters. Yet, in the middle of the night, I was quietly educated about the nature of the ANC. The group of young combatants from the camps who came to talk to me firmly told me it was wrong that whites and Indians could lay down their lives for our freedom but were not good enough to become full members.

On my way to the plenary where I intended to speak before the vote was taken, the President happened to pass me. He stopped and took me by the arm and without any hint of trying to persuade me, drew my attention to the need to recognise that the ANC represented all oppressed blacks and also those progressive whites who had accepted the policies and programmes of the ANC.

I withdrew my objection at the plenary and the motion to admit all South Africans to membership, including the right to become members of the NEC, was passed overwhelmingly. It was the unobtrusive leadership of the President which enabled all of us to affirm the non-racial character of the ANC and the organisation emerged from the Kabwe Conference more united than ever.

The position of children
By this stage, very few of our comrades who had remained in South Africa had actually met their Acting President. When some of them had the occasion to do so, it was an electrifying moment. Those of us who witnessed it were totally caught by surprise. The event took place in Harare in September 1987 during a breakaway session of an international conference dealing with the appalling treatment of children, thousands of whom had been detained, tortured or imprisoned by the apartheid regime during the so-called State of Emergency.

39

The organisers expected a handful to attend because of the State of Emergency in South Africa. Yet over 300 people came, many of them children. During the first day, we heard the harrowing testimonies of these children. At the opening session, chaired by his great friend, Father Trevor Huddleston, Oliver made one of his best speeches.

He began by reading Ingrid Jonker's moving poem, 'The child is not dead'. His concluding statement about cherishing children is reflected, in my view, in the unique provisions relating to the rights of the child in the present South African constitution.

'We cannot be true liberators unless the liberation we will achieve guarantees all children the rights to life, health, happiness and free development, respecting the individuality, the inclinations and capabilities of each child', he said, drawing attention to the urgent task of a free South Africa to attend to the welfare of the millions of children whose lives had been stunted and 'turned into a terrible misery by the violence of the apartheid system'.

Later that afternoon, a call was made for all the South Africans to gather together, away from the conference.

Oliver Tambo had been out of the country for over 25 years by then. Very few would have seen him as his photograph was banned as were his speeches.

He spoke without notes, welcoming first by name the new members of the NEC of the ANC, who had been elected at the Kabwe Conference of 1985, and drawing attention to the non-racial composition of that body. There was silence when he spoke movingly about violence by the regime and then, about 'necklacing'. There was a hush – exiles did not know what would happen next – but then there was a dramatic full-throated roar of approval when Tambo said, 'This must stop'.

I don't think he had discussed this matter with the NEC of the ANC. His was a cry, drawing on the humanism of our struggle and the need to relate means to ends. He did not need anyone's permission to do this.

Increasing pressure for sanctions
The boycott movement had spread to communities and countries around the globe, and the pressure on governments to impose sanctions against the apartheid regime was meeting with increasing success.

In Ireland, where I had been living since 1964 and working with the Irish Anti-Apartheid Movement, we had seen the Dunnes strike (of ten young women and one young man who spent over three years on the picket line outside the Dunnes supermarket where they worked, because they refused to sell apartheid fruit) result in the Irish government banning the sale of

South African fruit and vegetables. And a visit by the well-known politician and intellectual Dr Conor Cruise O'Brien to South Africa brought down a storm of protest on his head.

These pressures were beginning to have an impact inside South Africa. By the middle of the 1980s, the ANC was engaging with whites who desired some form of progress away from apartheid. Also, under the leadership of the ANC and the UDF, initiatives were being taken to identify new power structures of resistance involving trade unions, education, religion, culture and sport.

What, we asked, should we do when some of these forces wanted to establish links with overseas bodies? Or to make overseas visits? OR's timing was brilliant. We were excited when he spoke at the Canon Collins Memorial Lecture in London in May 1987. Oliver used this occasion to lay down a policy which had enormous implications for our solidarity work. He first traced the effects of the State of Emergency and the way our people were responding. He looked at the serried ranks of the anti-apartheid forces before him and then, quietly and firmly, told us:

> [The] moment is upon us when we shall deal with the structures our people have created and are creating through the struggle and sacrifice as representatives of the masses. Not only should these not be boycotted but more, they should be supported, encouraged and treated as the democratic counterparts within South Africa of similar institutions and organisations internationally. This means that the ANC, the broad democratic movement in all its forms within South African and the international solidarity movement must act together.

It was a dramatic change from the way in which we had operated previously. OR's message reflected the growing broad opposition to apartheid in South Africa. We had to respond, as he had taken us into his confidence. The isolation of apartheid must continue in every area of life; there was to be no let-up. But we had to treat these 'people's movements' in a different way.

The Nkomati Accord

Another insight into OR's remarkable brand of leadership was provided by the events leading to the signing of the Nkomati Accord between Mozambique and the apartheid regime in March 1984. My personal involvement arose from a telephone call from the President of the ANC requesting my presence in Lusaka for an urgent extended meeting of the NEC to discuss the legal and political implications of this agreement for the ANC.

This was a difficult request for me to meet. My students at Trinity College in Dublin were, ironically, due to write an international law paper the following week and there was no guarantee that I could be back in Dublin in time for their examinations. University protocol decreed that the examiner had to be present at the examination.

This was the first time that I had been invited to a meeting of the NEC, and I wanted to take part. I explained my dilemma to OR. His response was understanding, and provided me with an instant solution to my dilemma. Stay in Dublin and do your duty, he advised me, but promise that in the next day or two, you will write an analysis of the Accord from an international law perspective.

This I did in time for the NEC, drawing attention to two features of the agreement that rolled back all the gains there had been made concerning the status of the ANC at the level of international law. Firstly, it assimilated combatants of the ANC to terrorists. Secondly, the agreement compelled both parties not to provide any form of assistance to these 'elements'. Apartheid South Africa had rejected the series of UN General Assembly resolutions which accepted the right of states to provide assistance to liberation movements combating racism, colonialism and foreign occupation; and now it was demanding that allies of the ANC also reject the demands made on them by these resolutions.

The Nkomati Accord stated that all ANC members be removed from Mozambique. This caused a great deal of anger at what we considered to be a betrayal of the legitimacy of our struggle. Yet the NEC statement on the matter was a sober and firm reiteration of the role of the ANC. Oliver Tambo, who had been slighted by Mozambique by not being informed prior to the signing of the treaty, refused to condemn Mozambique. If he felt pushed into the valley of humiliation, he never showed it. He understood the murderous pressures being exercised by PW Botha against Mozambique and he recognised the enormous sacrifices that Mozambique had made in support of the ANC.

In the event, it was South Africa, in the cynical way it treated its neighbours, which violated the agreement. No serious injury was done to the ANC. All of us understood that Oliver's calm and collected approach had been the right one. Rather than driving Mozambique into a corner, he ensured that an unequal and forced treaty would not result in a breach of our relations with a valued partner. Events proved him correct. There is a place for hotheads, but not in this instance. Oliver's sense of history and his innate decency provided the correct response.

OR and reconciliation

In all my contact with OR, the constant refrain I heard from him centred on the need for equality. He insisted that we should reach out to all South Africans, in contrast to apartheid South Africa which violated every canon of equality and thrived on separating our people from each other.

We can see in hindsight that reaching out to all the communities in South Africa in Oliver's case makes him one of the principal architects of reconciliation. Reaching out meant that he took great care to maintain and strengthen the ANC tradition of non-racialism, and that he took a view of our struggle which relied on inclusiveness for its success. It was thus entirely consistent with the character of our movement that it was the ANC which first proposed the setting up of a Truth and Reconciliation Commission (TRC) to investigate and deal with our horrific past.

However, he also applied the principle of inclusiveness to gender issues and was instrumental in placing women's demands before a largely male-dominated ANC. History will judge him as the first leader of a liberation movement who argued passionately for gender equality. On more than one public occasion I heard him express his support for the Women's Charter (adopted by the Federation of South African Women in Johannesburg in 1954) which in many ways was a more revolutionary document in its approach to women's issues than the Freedom Charter adopted a year later.

In the public eye, Nelson Mandela is most closely associated with reconciliation in South Africa through the events following the democratic election in 1994. But long before the establishment of the TRC, Oliver Tambo made the case for reconciliation. I recall this vividly. I had prepared an opening speech for the children's conference in 1987 at Harare. My speech was a legal indictment of apartheid's criminal leaders, based on the Nuremberg Principles, which evolved at the level of international law following the trials of the Nazi leaders after 1945. I had intimated to some ANC leaders that I would call at the conference for the prosecution of apartheid's leaders for crimes against humanity and war crimes following our freedom.

OR took me aside before the opening session and, with quiet persuasiveness, informed me that Nuremberg was 'victors' law'. There was already talk about negotiations with the apartheid regime, and he made it clear that it would be provocative in the extreme to say: we will negotiate with you and, following successful discussions, we will try you for crimes against humanity. The Nuremberg Principles were very important for me. Nearly twenty years later, they formed the basis for the International Criminal Court's jurisdiction. But the facts on the ground in South Africa led all of us to a different conclusion, guided by OR. We were to have talks about talks and then negotiate on the basis of a pre-determined agenda. We could not demand prosecutions and the infliction of condign punishment as a condition for negotiations. If the ANC had done this, there would have been no negotiations. Personally, ten years' work went into the rubbish bin because of OR's intervention and I hurriedly changed my speech. Subsequent events showed the correctness of Oliver's approach.

A war of national liberation

One of Oliver Tambo's abiding qualities was the trust he placed in those who worked with him. This in turn evoked a deep respect, even love, for this highly principled leader who was able to draw on the talents and capacity of so many of the South African men and women in exile in different parts of the world.

I was not 'stationed' in Lusaka, and was thus not in close contact with the ANC leadership. From Dublin, I made an occasional suggestion. Every now and then, Oliver would respond. One such response led to a rather extraordinary series of events on the international scene, which had a substantial effect inside South Africa.

My intervention followed the execution of Solomon Mahlangu, a combatant of MK who had been arrested (and subsequently tortured) following a shoot-out with the regime's police.

We had contended for a number of years that the struggle against apartheid was not simply a civil war, in which case the international community could not have intervened as a civil war was, at that time, a matter of purely domestic concern. Ours was a war for national liberation, which had been legitimated by international law. Consequently, combatants of the ANC should be treated as prisoners of war.

The regime would not budge from its position that 'terrorists' should be given no quarter.

At my suggestion, the ANC agreed that we should focus on the way the Geneva Conventions of 1907, which primarily dealt with inter-state conflicts, had been refined and further developed by recognising that the concept of international armed conflict extended to cover wars of national liberation.

Oliver agreed that we should investigate how the status of the ANC would be enhanced by making a declaration under Protocol I of 1977 which spelled out this development. The Swiss government, the depositary for such declarations, was the authority with which we had to negotiate. But that government refused to accept such a declaration for complex legal reasons. In my view, the Swiss were wrong.

I reported this to OR. We could have made this non-recognition of the right of the ANC to make a declaration with the Swiss government into an international issue, which would have frittered away a great deal of time and energy. Instead, OR accepted my advice that the declaration should be made with the International Committee of the Red Cross (ICRC).

The ICRC is a venerable Swiss organisation with its head office in a beautiful building in Geneva. Such was the importance that the ANC ascribed to the protection of our combatants that the delegation, led by Oliver, included a number of senior members of the NEC.

It was a most impressive ceremony. Having greeted the President of the ICRC, the leader of the ANC rose to the occasion in a sublime fashion. 'We have always defined the enemy in terms of a system of domination and not of a people or a race', he said, 'our values being fundamentally different in contrast to the apartheid regime', which had 'displayed a shameless and ruthless disregard for all the norms of humanity'.

We were all spellbound. Here was our representative, the representative of our liberation movement, who was giving voice to the historic nature of his movement's commitment to humane values in the conduct of war and who in the process moved the staid representatives of the ICRC to loud applause.

The effects of the ANC declaration were felt very quickly in South Africa. Within a short time, lawyers who had defended the SWAPO guerrillas in the apartheid courts and who had invoked the 'new' humanitarian law, felt that earlier inhibitions about claiming a similar status for ANC trialists had now evaporated in the light of the ANC's declaration.

South African lawyers refused to continue with the usual demonisation of the ANC as a result of this declaration. There were also ripples of surprise and support among some Afrikaners. OR, who always respected lawyers (he felt the ANC lawyers were agents of change), had triumphed. The decision to make the declarations was a collective NEC decision, but it was the quality of the presentation by an individual which made the impact. We were not the only ones who admired OR; he evoked this emotion even from unsympathetic sources. He was the liberation movement's most consummate diplomat.

OR's distinguishing qualities
OR possessed something more than the ordinary virtues of leadership. I realised in my contact with him that his distinguishing quality was his accessibility, not simply in the sense that he was available to meet South Africans whether he was in Accra, Lusaka, London or the UN in New York. It was

not his style to be protected by a phalanx of private secretaries or a guard of minders. If you had something to discuss with him, he was there for you.

But by accessibility I mean something more. He had an openness to ideas and a capacity to respond to changing circumstances. I recall a meeting I once attended with traditional leaders from South Africa who had especially come to Lusaka in the 1980s on a mission to see the ANC. He listened to them patiently, took on board some of their suggestions about how to organise in rural areas, and quietly put some challenges before them. Their respect was not given to him simply because he was an older person or because he was President of the ANC, but because of their admiration for the man he was.

But openness to others and their ideas was never an excuse for him to trim the strength of his principles. We all understood the intense pressures brought to bear on him by the conflicting demands of the Cold War externally and by the war in southern Africa internally, which had echoes within the structures of the liberation movement. The unity and integrity of the ANC were his paramount consideration. Uniquely, compared to other liberation movements, he managed to keep us together.

I can attest to his moral courage and pertinacity when he came to Ireland to speak at the first conference on the European Economic Community (EEC) (as it was called then) and apartheid South Africa in 1979.

The Irish government's opposition to apartheid was clear, both at home and at the UN. It opposed the policies of apartheid very strongly and voted in favour of general resolutions against apartheid. Nevertheless, it was reluctant to impose economic sanctions, and it would not support any resolution at the UN which intimated support for the struggle led by the ANC. The inhibition arose because of the IRA campaign which was at its height at that time. How could you support the armed struggle of the ANC when, it was argued in some quarters, the IRA was conducting a similar armed struggle against a similar colonialist master? Such an extrapolation from South Africa to Northern Ireland was obviously invalid but the Irish government was afraid that the argument would result in a loss of support among its voters. Oliver understood the reasons for this approach, though he might not have agreed with it.

Prior to the conference, he met with the Minister for Foreign Affairs, Michael O'Kennedy, for over two hours. O'Kennedy was to open the conference with OR. These meetings usually lasted for an hour. Such was the persuasiveness of OR that the Foreign Minister undertook to provide direct assistance to the ANC, much to the chagrin of his officials whose body-language spoke volumes. Ultimately the Irish Anti-Apartheid Movement was not able to hold the government to this undertaking which was made on the spur of the moment in response to OR's force of argument and quiet passion.

At the conference, OR's speech galvanised the delegates to action. An EEC-wide structure was soon established to coordinate activities of the anti-apartheid movements in the community. There was a striking phrase that OR used, which is not found in his collected speeches. I always thought that when OR diverted from his formal speech, the impact of his contribution was much greater. He did this in Dublin when he described the EEC as the 'life-blood of apartheid' because of the predominant role which the countries of the EEC played in the military, financial, strategic and economic axis of their relations with apartheid South Africa. This was history in the making, as the focus of anti-apartheid activities was no longer limited to national work but took on a collective European perspective through lobbying the Brussels EEC institutions. Oliver provided the impetus for such an innovative development.

One aspect of OR's work as President which has received little acknowledgment is the outstanding role he played in ensuring that internal controls were put in place concerning the treatment of members of the ANC, especially in the camps where our combatants were stationed. This was a sensitive matter as the security department of the ANC had to ensure the welfare and safety of our members and especially of the core leadership, but its behaviour had given rise to criticism.

The Pretoria regime had made no bones about its all-out war against the ANC. Apart from the assassination of our leaders, such as the outstanding Joe Gqabi in Harare, attacks on the Front-line States were part of the destabilising process against the ANC. Even more dangerous was the infiltration of large numbers of agents into the ranks of the ANC with a mission to sow confusion and to attack the leaders.

In this murky world abuses by our security elements did take place. But as was established later in 1993 by a commission of inquiry which was set up by Nelson Mandela to report on the treatment of detainees in some of the ANC camps, there was never a pattern of systematic abuse of rights or a policy of violations.

Although OR always insisted that he was part of a collective and that he acted on the advice of the NEC, there can be little doubt that the initiatives that the ANC took were inspired by him. There was a delicate balance to be maintained between the need for security and the upholding of transparency and the morality of the movement.

Various commissions were set up to investigate irregularities. In one case, the decision of a judicial tribunal to recommend capital punishment was rejected by the NEC and by OR, which reflected our historic opposition to this obscene form of punishment. Capital punishment was of course eventually abolished by the Constitutional Court of a free South Africa. Our liberation movement's hostility to capital punishment was reflected in the early draft of the Bill of Rights produced in 1991, which abolished the death penalty. No international covenant on human rights had renounced the obscenity of capital punishment in such a forthright manner.

Oliver had approved of such an approach when we had discussed an earlier draft. This was real leadership.

Even more significant was the adoption of a code of conduct promulgated after the Kabwe Conference of 1985. This code established a system of justice which was unique among liberation movements in southern Africa.

All this took place in a war context. To insist on proper legal procedures, including the appropriate burden of proof, meant that arbitrary arrests would be reduced and improperly prepared cases thrown out at the hearing. I am not aware of any partisan movement in Europe or a liberation movement anywhere which emphasised the need for restraint and respect for proper procedures during the conduct of hostilities while its very existence was at stake.

Soon after the Kabwe Conference, new allegations of abuse occurred, especially at the Quattro camp in Angola. Against the advice of his security staff, as the situation was fraught with danger, OR visited the camp to investigate matters.

The leadership of the security department was replaced and a restructured directorate of intelligence and security was created to shift responsibility away from the security department.

The response from the combatants at the camp was telling. They had requested OR's presence as they felt that no other leader would be able to deal with their grievances. Tambo the lawyer, with his overpowering sense of justice and his infinite capacity to listen to everyone, even occasional hostile outbursts, was able to reunite the forces in the camp.

OR gave us many gifts: selfless leadership, an extraordinary capacity to listen to others and to be open to new ideas, humility, compassion, and a belief in the capacity of people to be their own saviours. In the hell-holes of apartheid's prisons, in the countless villages and the barren townships, in the loneliness of exile and in the isolated camps of our combatants, his was the voice that spoke for us and provided the hope – no, the certainty – of the freedom which he would sadly not live to see.

It was Seamus Heaney, Ireland's foremost contemporary poet, who wrote that, once in a lifetime, justice can rise up, and hope and history rhyme. He wrote it in response to Nelson Mandela's release in 1990, but there is no doubt that Oliver Tambo's extraordinary determination to uphold the values of inclusiveness, non-racialism, non-sexism and justice, and his capacity to imbue others with the same values, made an incalculable contribution to that rhyme. He was a true hero of our struggle, who helped us all to reach the 'celestial city' of Bunyan's parable – a free and democratic South Africa.

WOMEN AND CHILDREN

Sandi Gladstone Baai

My personal knowledge of Oliver Reginald Tambo goes back to my father's household, and I later met him in some of the countries of the world. Tambo's late father's first wife came from the Njiyela tribe. Her clan name was Manjiyela or Madlabazana, and that is my clan name. My father regarded her as our aunt and Oliver as a member of our extended family. In the early 1950s he was a regular visitor to my father's homestead. As little boys we were pleased to see him sleeping over for a night because we knew that a fat chicken would be slaughtered for him. He was loved and admired by our parents because he was a humble and educated person who had set an example to be followed by schoolgoing children.

In order to know something of Oliver's life story in relation to the freedom of women and children we must define the term 'liberation'. 'Liberation' is a word that best expresses the struggle to construct a just, non-racial, non-sexist democratic society where nations and tribes of different colours can live with dignity and be the agents of their own destinies. The concept implies the creation of a new familyhood in which differences of race, class and gender are transcended.

If what has been said is true, it might be difficult to set the thought of any revolutionary leader, let alone that of a mind as subtle and complex as Oliver Tambo, into a historical perspective with reference to the liberation of women and the welfare of children.

Nevertheless, a close examination of Tambo's social and political thought indicates a holistic liberation which does not exclude the emancipation of women. There is a sense in which we can say that his interpretation of political liberation had been underscored by an interdependent social analysis. We cannot reconstruct his passion for the emancipation of women without looking at the typology of woman; Oliver's Christian ethics; and his political imperatives. Some of these traditions were critiqued with varying degrees as he went around the world articulating the cause for justice of women and children. In conferences, consultations and debates about colonialism and apartheid he lifted out the aspects pertaining to the oppression of women and girls. In this regard he elevated the status of women in the world and in South Africa in particular. This was done to the extent that the convention for a democratic South Africa (CODESA) in 1991 saw the then government joining forces with its political rivals in order to bring about a just and humane society pursuing amidst diversity freedoms, equality and security for women and children.

Black women in South Africa
Tambo knew the different types of work that black women do in South African society. The housewife was a woman who worked at home, taking care of children. There was also the domestic servant who was always away from her own homestead working in a white household, in town, for a meagre wage.

The housewife tended to be entirely on her own as black men were migrant labourers, working away in 'white' South Africa. It suffices at this point to note that women assumed a double role in the running of the home, that is, of both masculine and feminine gender. This entailed a heavy and oppressive responsibility on women, which might have been avoided if they had been allowed to live with their husbands at the workplace.

Of course this constitutes one of the fundamental contradictions underlying the then political structure of South African society. It was a contradiction in the sense that blacks were not citizens of South Africa in the apartheid era. Yet they had to come and work for whites in the cities and had to leave their families in the reserves. Since the Second World War, in particular, this had led to a move towards a matriarchal structure in the traditional African family. This undoubtedly created a chronic dependency on the men who were the sole breadwinners who earned their living by working and remitting their wages to the families back at the homesteads in the reserves.

Moreover, the domestic servant could be defined as primarily a servant who performed domestic labour – from cooking to cleaning and child-minding to gardening – in a white household for a meagre wage. The number of these domestic servants and the roles that they fulfilled varies according to the needs of different households.

Tambo saw that domestic work tended to have a gender bias in the sense that it was most often done by women. This was caused by the fact that there was the division of labour which can be found throughout the world. Particularly in countries where there is a high rate of unemployment, child-rearing, cooking and cleaning are generally assumed to be women's work. The tasks performed in the house underpin the ideology of woman as a wife. It should be remembered that cleaning, cooking and minding children are jobs which are generally regarded as 'socially inferior'; hence they are done by those the political system classifies as black. Indeed, the available evidence shows that from the turn of the twentieth century domestic work in South Africa has been, above all, a black institution compatible with structures of black domination.

The picture I have attempted to paint should not be construed as a comprehensive survey of the oppression of women. Rather, it is meant to support the claims that the oppression of women is based on gender, class and race; it is three-fold. But what precisely is crucial in evaluating these developments? My contention is that although there was a strong ethic of sharing even meals and tobacco in African society, there was division of labour according to gender.

Males did work that was regarded as theirs alone. For example, Tambo was a herd boy and was good at stick fighting. Similarly females did their own work. While the older boys looked after the cattle, sheep, horses and goats, the younger ones had their own responsibilities which involved the tending of calves so that they would be allowed to suckle after their mothers had been milked. Little girls were given simple tasks such as sweeping floors, washing dishes, taking care of younger ones when parents were away and sometimes tending to the kitchen fire.

Correspondingly, the matter of the division of labour also expressed itself in married life as there were divisions between wife and husband in the bedroom. Men would sleep on the bed while their wives would use floor mats for sleeping. Physically they would know each other only when the wife was invited for procreation purposes. Clearly women were generally dependent on males whilst the processes of male domination continued to gather momentum in society. Surprisingly, women diviners and prophetesses enjoyed a fairly large amount of independence.

The Christian tradition
I have said above that South African society is and was generally the representation of male domination. In contrast, the Christian tradition has potentially liberating values. Tambo was deeply religious and knew that New

Testament studies throughout the centuries have always asserted that there is neither male nor female in Christ. In addition, Christianity raised the status of women in that they were not allowed to appear at the place of crucifixion, but when Jesus Christ was crucified women were seen with him at the cross. They were also the first to spread the news that he had been raised from the grave. In brief, women were the eyewitnesses of the resurrection. This tradition challenges male domination in society and seeks to restore the dignity of women.

Christianity is a tradition which instructed Oliver Tambo profoundly. We may identify it by three dominant characteristics including, firstly, the spread of Christian missions. In 1927 Mrs Marjorie Hill went to Holy Cross Anglican Mission in the district of Lusikisiki in response to the world call of the church for more missionaries. She was to take charge of the hostel for girls at the boarding school, but on arrival found that she was wanted for the boys' hostel instead. She decided to ask various friends in Britain to 'adopt' a boy in the school by paying his school fees and by writing to him. As a consequence of Mrs Hill's plea, Oliver Tambo was 'adopted' in 1928. Two sisters, Joyce and Ruth Goddard, undertook to pay his fees and they kept in touch with him until 1940.

The second characteristic was related to the good liberal education that Tambo had received. In those days girls were not encouraged to go to school but the Christian missions fought hard for the education of girls because education empowers and enriches women. Related to the other characteristics was the concept of individual and community development which taught the unlocking of human potential in disadvantaged communities through the process of liberal education which would prepare them for leadership in society. Thirdly, the characteristics noted in Tambo's thought, that of his evangelical background, despite its practical, moral emphasis, was not too great a distance from the women's liberation tradition. He was aware of the limitations that existed in Christianity. For example, some church structures did not seem to wish to move beyond the typology of Christ and the Church as representing the dominant male and submissive female roles. And when addressing a meeting in New York in 1985 Tambo said that if apartheid was Christian then he was not Christian. Nevertheless, the emancipation of women was not incongruous with Tambo's broad religious convictions.

The emancipation of women

As noted earlier, Tambo's interpretation of the struggle involved the emancipation of women. In June 1985 he delivered the political report to the national consultative conference of the party in Zambia. He examined the place of women in the broad liberation movement's strategy and firmly established women's campaigns as a crucial part of the struggle for national and social emancipation.

With the rising crescendo of political oppression in South Africa and the consequent subordination of women in brutal ways he went on to say that the goal of the democratic revolution was to transform this situation. Later he described how many black mothers had to live daily with the agony and trauma of burying their children or searching for their children, who had perhaps been arrested or disappeared without trace. This pain was ironically shared by white mothers who had to see their children 'transformed and perverted' into killers for the apartheid regime, bent on murdering unarmed people. He called on all black and white mothers to reach across the racial divide and create in unity a common struggle.

Tambo's political thought pertaining to the emancipation of women had received its major impetus from many traditions. One of these is the involvement of women in politics, which is closely tied to the formation of the ANC in 1912. Although at that time the ANC had not accorded women voting rights, they transcended their limitations and assisted in the transformation of the South African identity.

This particular tradition comprises Queen Regent Labotsibeni, Charlotte Maxeke, Olive Schreiner, Lilian Ngoyi, Ida Mntwana, Victoria Mxenge, Nomkhosi Mini, Thandi Modise, Theresa Ramashamola and Marion Sparg. Historically the pro-democracy forces would have to take into consideration the disadvantaged position of women in seeking to ensure the substantive transformation of their status.

The other tradition which instructed Tambo is what I shall describe as the march on the Union Buildings on 9 August 1956. For our present discussion this national demonstration in Pretoria is one of the important ones. Over fifty thousand women participated in nationwide demonstrations that culminated in Pretoria where they intended to hand over a petition to JG Strijdom who at the time was Prime Minister of South Africa.

However, Strijdom refused to attend to their grievances which were later handed to their regional leaders. More significantly, before they dispersed the women sang a song they had composed for the day: 'Strijdom, you have tampered with the women; you have struck a rock'.

Much later, in the early 1960s, women challenged the traditional roles of men, attacking the beer halls and spilling over all the beer.

The welfare of children

Tambo also identified children as the most vulnerable of the population.

They suffered terribly under apartheid because the state saw very little difference between children and adults in terms of the application of its oppressive policies.

Moreover, Tambo did not go along with Hendrik Verwoerd's infamous speech in 1953 in which he said that the Native must be taught from childhood to realise that he was not equal with a white person in South Africa. Introducing apartheid into schools he went on to say that the black child must not be misled by showing him the green pastures of European society in which he was not allowed to graze. Earlier on I noted that education was made a tool to keep the white minority group in power. There was no cross-fertilisation of ideas because racial separation was maintained at all levels. Consequently, universities, colleges and schools had become tribalised places of learning.

For three decades Tambo banged the drum about the need for education to be radically altered if race relations were to improve. While he elevated the role of students in the vanguard of liberation, Tambo laid great stress on the importance of integrating the student population within the broad struggle for liberation.

In 1987, during a speech at an international conference on 'Children, Repression and the Law in South Africa' Tambo shared Ingrid Jonker's basic philosophical positions in highlighting the massacre of children in places such as Langa, Nyanga, Orlando, Sharpeville, Soweto, Athlone, Maseru, Gaborone, Galesberry, Maputo and Kassinga. He commented that the apartheid system regarded children as its enemies to be killed and later he said that the apartheid system had failed to take responsibility for the welfare of the children, with regard to their living conditions and medical care.

In Zambia Tambo saw that there was a growing need to bring together all the children who were born while their parents were in exile, including those who came along with their parents. This led to the formation of the Masupatsela cultural group. 'Masupatsela' is a Setswana word which means 'the pioneers'. Its purpose was to express a sense of belonging together in a strange world environment. Together with Rita Mfenyana Tambo taught the children choral music, poetry and African dance. It was there that they learnt to sing 'Nkosi Sikelel' iAfrica'. The UN had declared 1979 the Year of the Child. Consequently, the children were encouraged to broaden their mental and physical horizons by travelling and visiting some of the major cities of the world, including Moscow, Sweden, Luanda and Maputo.

Oliver Tambo ensured that South Africa took its place in the community of nations. He insisted that the right of masculinity was not the right to dominate and ill treat women without concern for children and the disabled.

Oliver would not have spent sleepless nights thinking about who should be the next president of a free and non-sexist South Africa. He would have warmly welcomed a woman as the head of the Republic of South Africa because he believed that women should participate fully in the development of their country.

A LEADING INTERNATIONAL STATESMAN

Ismail Coovadia

From the late 1970s to 1990, my functions at the ANC mission in London brought me in close contact with the ANC President Oliver Reginald Tambo, fondly referred to as 'OR' or 'Chief'.

When I consider our interactions there are innumerable, memorable events that come to mind; choosing some and leaving out others has posed a major dilemma since all are significant in respect of Chief as a statesman and the liberation struggle as a whole, and have value in their own right.

Chief's many outstanding qualities demonstrated world-class leadership. He displayed enduring patience, steadfastness, compassion, calmness, unassuming authority, confidence, moral correctness, extraordinary energy and ability, coupled with a total dedication to the ANC and an unwavering belief in the correctness of the struggle he had been involved in for decades. In addition, he showed an immense trust, confidence and faith in his comrades, which contributed to many individuals' development as they lived up to his expectations.

The ANC was the life and soul of Chief. In pursuing and intensifying the liberation struggle for justice and an end to apartheid, for which he had been sent abroad by his colleagues, he was acutely conscious of his moral, financial and political duties to the organisation's members and the large majority of South Africans, both inside and outside the country.

The management of the ANC's finances was in the hands of the Treasurer-

General, the (late) Thomas Titus Nkobi, but Chief took a deep interest in the movement's finances. He was extremely sensitive to the ANC's short, medium and long-term requirements, and never tired of travelling the world to solicit material and financial aid. Chief exhibited his brilliance in advancing his arguments for financial support. Such was the force of his people-centred humanitarian appeals that he is not known to have returned empty handed.

Much of the needed financial and material assistance came from sympathetic governments, NGOs and individuals (in east and west Europe, Africa, Asia, Latin America and North America). Contributions would be handed to Chief in the form of bank cheques, cash and, in some instances, in promises of support in kind. Because of Chief's confidence and trust in his cadres, he would ask me to make deposits into the ANC's bank account and never asked for proof of deposit!

One of Chief's many attributes was that he would not make a decision without listening to both sides of an argument. His legal mind coupled with his political acumen, authority, tact and thoroughness, protected the ANC from becoming involved in several dubious financial projects. One such project for which a considerable sum of money was required was surrounded by a high degree of controversy.

The ANC mission was offered substantial office premises in Angel, London. The financially lucrative proposition had been recommended to Chief who discussed the matter with the Secretary-General and the Treasurer-General. However, there was opposition to the offer. I was summoned to Lusaka overnight to give my opinion on the proposal. On my arrival, I was driven directly from the airport to the meeting room where I was met by Chief and the Secretary and Treasurer-Generals.

My assessment of support and opposition to the proposition was sought. Most of the ensuing incisive financial and political questions were posed by Chief. The three leaders did not hesitate to discuss the matter further in my presence. The meeting lasted approximately ninety minutes and I took a flight back to London the same evening.

Chief and his colleagues subsequently responded to the offer by declining it, and shortly thereafter it was shown to bear all the hallmarks of another of the apartheid regime's intelligence operations.

Chief's role as the leader of the ANC brought him into contact with world leaders and statespersons in the fields of politics, religion, finance, culture and sports. The international campaign for economic sanctions against apartheid South Africa was furiously debated in the various capitals of the world.

Meanwhile, informal discussions continued between the London-based

ANC representatives and the Secretary to the Board for Social Responsibility of the Church of England over the arguments for and against sanctions and solidarity support for the Solomon Mahlangu Freedom College in Tanzania. Ironically, these discussions led to important developments in favour of the ANC.

In the first of these developments, the ANC in London was asked to address the Board for Social Responsibility, which was chaired by a Bishop. The objective was to solicit support for the school in Tanzania and it was therefore important to familiarise the Board members with the background and requirements of the schoolgoing students and children.

This encounter led, in part, to a subsequent meeting between Chief and twelve of the most prominent and important Bishops in the church hierarchy. Prior to the dinner at which Chief was the guest of honour, Thabo Mbeki and I met with him to go over some of the points that were to be discussed. In particular, Thabo had previously advanced a strong argument for Barclays Bank to disinvest in South Africa. True to form, Chief meticulously covered every conceivable angle to ensure that we were well prepared.

The meeting with the Bishops once again demonstrated Chief's qualities of lucid thinking, infinite tact and astuteness, as well as his incisive and precise political and humanitarian approaches to seemingly intractable politically related issues. The dinner went well and we later learnt that the Bishops had agreed to support the idea that Barclays Bank should disinvest from South Africa. They had also come out in support of the Solomon Mahlangu Freedom College.

Whenever Chief was in London he would conduct secret meetings with leaders, young and old, who were involved in the South and southern African political struggle. Those who met with Chief included the late Joshua Nkomo, leader of the Zimbabwe African People's Union, Archbishop Desmond Tutu, and Gatsha Buthelezi.

Such was the respect and esteem in which Chief was held by Nkomo that he related in confidence a full account of the deliberations at the Lancaster Conference. The briefing to Chief almost seemed like a report back.

On one occasion Chief was invited to the UN in New York to deliver a speech. He was accompanied by his Secretary, Comrade Anthony Mongalo (currently South Africa's High Commissioner to Australia and New Zealand). As a result of a miscommunication, Chief's air ticket to New York had not been purchased. Unbeknown to Chief, at 7:30 a.m. prior to the drive to the airport swift arrangements had been made for the delegation's tickets to be issued at the airport.

The drive to Heathrow could not have been more uncomfortable. The

London traffic had almost come to a standstill and time was passing. The thought of Chief missing the flight began to take a toll on my nerves but he remained calm. With the clock ticking away, we eventually reached the end of the airport tunnel.

It was at this point that Chief asked for the tickets so that they would be readily available for check-in. Only thirty minutes remained to departure time. When he was told of the confusion over the flight tickets, Chief was visibly irritated but he quickly regained his characteristic calmness and composure. With barely twenty minutes to collect the tickets, check-in, clear immigration and board, it was a wonder that they just made it.

On his eventual return to Lusaka, Chief did a pencil sketch of the incident in which he depicted its light-hearted aspect, and he spoke about it with amusement for many years thereafter.

In a world of contradictions, of haves and have nots, and of developed, developing and underdeveloped countries, Chief had the exceptional ability and energy to handle conflicts and pursue international relations. Following in the footsteps of his predecessors, he will always be remembered by South Africans, Africans and citizens of the wider world as a profound national political leader and a leading international statesman.

AN INTERNATIONAL LEGACY

Nkosazana Dlamini Zuma
*(extracts from the inaugural lecture of the Oliver Tambo Lecture Series,
Glasgow, 26 October 2006)*

OR was a unique and extraordinary human being whose personality was moulded by the fusion and mixture of South African life. He came from the rural surroundings of Pondoland where the values of communal sharing in the extended family setting, the ethos of hard work and compassion were instilled in his consciousness from infancy to early adolescence.

The ease with which he settled in the Johannesburg industrial hub of South Africa without losing touch with his rural beginnings armed him with a deep appreciation of all aspects of his people's suffering and tells us of an uncanny start for somebody destined to be a phenomenon.

It is very rare in the annals of human history that this combination of skills can be found all wrapped up in one personality. Science teacher, lawyer, composer, arranger, revolutionary, intellectual and internationalist with an immense spirituality, OR was an unparalleled embodiment of all that is manifestly good in our common humanity despite the bad and negative problems we face.

Nor does his greatness end there. He ensured in his lifetime that he reproduced himself manifold in his students, comrades and in his lieutenants. By example he instilled the culture and values of the community taking precedence over individualism. The organisation, the ANC, was greater than any one individual. He commanded loyalty and commitment by always being the indomitable and principled leader.

Any one of those scores of students, colleagues and comrades who crossed OR's path would talk of him as if this African giant was their father alone, their brother alone, their uncle alone. This was because this leader touched each person profoundly. He had a special gift to listen carefully to each and all. This quality was the converse side of the great communicator that he was, a man who imparted profound lessons that endeared him (and still do) to all. The care and caring boundless enough to enable him to find time and so-lutions to everyone's one problem, however big or small, was the hallmark of his character because his love for his people and humanity was absolutely inexhaustible.

OR remains the immortal true hero of the people. The tragedy is that South Africans were not allowed to know this remarkable leader since the ANC was banned, exiled and in an underground existence. OR could not be seen or quoted in South Africa until the people themselves unbanned him and the ANC by following his command of making 'apartheid unwork-able and the country ungovernable'.

Among friends of our struggle around the world, OR knew and knew too well that he could count on the people of Glasgow to offer us moral, material and political support for the struggle for freedom in our country.

If OR were alive today he would have reminded us of the biggest cam-paign launched in this city by the Glasgow branch of the AAM, led by Brian Filling and others to demand the release of Nelson Mandela and all other political prisoners as well as the unbanning of the ANC.

For this, OR would have directed that during our visit to Glasgow today, we extend our warmest greetings and gratitude to the people of Glasgow for the support and solidarity they offered us during the most difficult times of our struggle – including the cultural, educational and trade union spheres.

OR was a visionary who led our movement, the ANC, with outstand-ing success during the most trying times in our history. The barbarity of the apartheid system as well as the dangers that he faced throughout his life caused him neither to flinch nor lose his determination to lead the libera-tion struggle and belief in the future of South Africa.

In 1955 he was among the pioneers of our movement who were respons-ible for drafting the Freedom Charter, that profound policy declaration on the future of South Africa. Explaining the Freedom Charter to the UN in 1955 he said:

> That statement, which declares South Africa belongs to all who
> live in it, is a drastic concession on the part of the African people,
> but is a demonstration of the willingness of the African people to

> live in South Africa with everybody who wants to live there on
> the basis of absolute equality – no racism, no racial discrimination,
> no superior race, no inferior race. On that basis South Africa be-
> longs to all who live in it.

This was the inspiration that would characterise the work of Oliver Tambo throughout his life and the vision he laid for our movement and indeed for the new democratic South Africa.

South Africa's foreign policy rests on the foundation built by OR. He held the view that 'the struggle for national liberation is by definition, a struggle for peace and that peace is indivisible. For either there is peace every-where or there is no peace anywhere.' A climate of world peace therefore provides a powerful inducement for the speedy resolution of regional con-flicts through the removal by force or by consent, of the cause and source of conflicts. That is why our struggle is an inseparable component of the world-wide struggle for a world free of wars.

It is why even today South Africa feels it has an obligation and a respons-ibility to contribute to peace on the African continent. That view informs us that there can be no peace in the world without peace in the Middle East. The idea that peace is indivisible means that all humanity must strive for world peace.

South Africa believes that the world does not need nuclear weapons. We adhere to the three pillars of the Non-Proliferation Treaty (NPT). There should be no proliferation of nuclear arms. Those who already have them should disarm and those who adhere to the NPT should have access to nuc-lear technology for peaceful use. OR had this to say (in 1987 at the celebra-tion of the 76th anniversary of the great October Socialist Revolution) at the prospect of a treaty to be signed by the USSR and the US: 'This devel-opment has increased the confidence of the rest of humanity in the real pos-sibility of ridding mankind completely of the threat of a nuclear war. It is our view that as long as there are nuclear weapons anywhere there will al-ways be persistent threats of nuclear war or nuclear destruction haunting the whole of mankind.'

In South Africa we are striving according to our own constitution for a non-racial and non-sexist country. The emancipation of women was very dear to OR's heart. At the ANC women's conference held in 1981 in Luanda OR observed: 'If we are to engage our full potential in pursuit of revolutionary goals then, as revolutionaries we should stop pretending that women in our movement have the same opportunities as men.' Very few Presidents are so bluntly honest about the deficiency of their own organisation, but OR was.

In 1985 OR and President Sam Nujoma made a joint pledge to the women of Namibia and South Africa, that they would not consider their objectives achieved, their task completed, or their struggle at an end until the women of South Africa and Namibia are fully liberated.

This is a revolutionary duty that OR has left us with – the full liberation of women, not only in Namibia and South Africa but of women of the world.

OR was a consummate producer and admirer of all forms of the arts. He understood the power of music or a picture and its potential to convey a message with almost immediate impact. Under his leadership the ANC established its Department of Arts and Culture, which produced a quarterly publication, *Rixaka*. Mayibuye, based in London, effectively used music, drama and poetry to win over thousands of ANC supporters around Europe and Scandinavia.

OR's interest in culture reached new heights when in 1979 the Amandla cultural ensemble, based in Angola, was formed. On its first tour of Europe, Amandla performed to packed houses in six countries and in its brief lifespan it produced several records. The ANC art studio in Dakawa, Tanzania, was established with the help of Swedish Artists Against Apartheid with the intention of transporting it to South Africa after liberation. Indeed, today it stands in Grahamstown as one of OR's legacies, still focusing on textile printing, graphics and weaving.

The ANC is the only liberation movement to have produced two publications by women, *Malibongwe, ANC Women Stories* (a poetry collection) and *One Never Knows*, an anthology of short stories. Under OR's leadership all forms of cultural expression became part of the arsenal in highlighting the struggle against apartheid.

OR was an ardent believer in multilateralism. He worked very closely with the OAU, the Non-Aligned Movement (NAM) and the UN. Today South Africa is very involved in building the African Union together with other African countries. The launch of the AU was in South Africa. The NAM has been hosted by South Africa and we have been active in its revitalisation.

In pursuit of South–South Cooperation we co-chair the forum of New Africa Asia Strategic Partnership (NAASP) in an endeavour to deepen understanding and economic, cultural and academic cooperation between African and Asian countries. In addition, the IBSA FORUM which consists of India, Brazil and South Africa is another example of South–South cooperation.

OR bequeathed to South Africa and the world an icon and hero of legendary proportion – Nelson Rolihlahla Mandela. OR led the charge around the globe to free Nelson Mandela and all political prisoners. This ensured that Nelson Mandela did not remain a household name only in South Africa, but became one the world over. The unprecedented outpouring of emotions on Mandela's release and during his first tour around the world is inconceivable without the tireless daunting legwork of OR.

Yet even more remarkable was the manner in which OR was selfless, almost self-effacing, whilst elevating and upholding Mandela's name. But OR could and did do this because he sincerely believed that upon Mandela's release from prison OR would relinquish the presidency of the ANC to Mandela. This remained OR's religiously held principle long before the stroke which eventually ended his illustrious life.

Coming against the background of the 30th anniversary of the 1976 student uprisings in Soweto and elsewhere in our country, Oliver Tambo would have most certainly applauded the role our youth played in the cutting edge of the struggle for freedom, democracy and justice in our country.

The challenges facing the youth of today are fundamentally different from those faced by the youth of yesteryear, including HIV and AIDS, drug misuse and crime. We need to address these challenges squarely as they pose a threat to our democracy built on the sacrifices of millions of our people and solidarity of the peoples of the world.

Recognising that every generation has its historic mission to fulfil, OR would have expressed the confidence that, like their forebears, the youth of today in South Africa will build on the experiences of their forebears in South Africa and their counterparts the world over, and will not abandon their mission.

As millions of people around the world continue to live in conditions of abject poverty and underdevelopment, OR would have asked what the international community is doing to democratise international finance institutions to enable them to respond to the plight of these millions who are knocking at the doors of the rich and powerful with begging bowls.

There is a need to establish, nurture and consolidate democracy and good governance and thus work for the eradication of poverty, the general upliftment of our people and the development of our continent. One of the central pillars of the renaissance of Africa is the need for democratic South Africa to remain part of the African leadership collective to assist the people of these conflict-ridden areas to develop peaceful means of resolving such conflicts for the sake of all our peoples including women and children.

In the global context, we have sought a meaningful role and place for our continent to avoid further marginalisation of Africa and Africans in a globalised world. We extend a hand of friendship and solidarity to Africans in the diaspora who responded to OR's call for solidarity. Now we have to find ways of continuing our solidarity and face the new challenges together.

We are privileged to have shared our lives with this giant of our country, and to have learnt from him the basic teaching that all of us must remain committed to the humble service of the people of our country, our continent and the world.

Today, in Glasgow among friends and colleagues of Oliver Tambo we commit ourselves not to betray his international legacy both in our efforts to rebuild our country into a non-racial, non-sexist and democratic society and also in efforts aimed at the creation of a better Africa in a better world.

It is sad that Oliver Tambo, like Moses, had been to the mountain-top and had seen the promised land, yet never lived to see the freedom of his people. Nonetheless, we shall continue to draw inspiration from his teachings, his commitment and his dedication in the service of the people of our country in building that promised land for which he dedicated his entire life.

GUARD OUR PRECIOUS
MOVEMENT

Frene Ginwala

In late 1959 I returned to South Africa intending to complete the necessary training to practise as an advocate. As a law student in the UK I had worked in organisations involved in the anti-colonial and anti-apartheid campaigns. During holidays spent in South Africa I had associated with the Transvaal Indian Congress (TIC). In Johannesburg we operated out of offices shared with the ANC, and considered ourselves working under one leadership. Many of my former schoolmates were seasoned political activists who had participated in the Defiance Campaign, the Congress of the People and other mass actions. I was inexperienced, and although I was occasionally asked to assist, I felt totally unprepared and ill equipped to undertake the responsibility that was suddenly thrust upon me.

One evening, after a successful street collection for the Treason Trial Defence Fund, a group of us gathered in the Mandela home. As far as I can recall, Nelson Mandela was not there but Comrade Winnie was in.

The conversation focused on recent events in Africa and the gathering demand for independence. Those present spoke about the need for the ANC to have closer links with nationalist movements and the newly independent African countries. Unaware that this was to prove to be a significant discussion, I blithely expanded on the pending emergence of an independent Tanganyika. I suggested that in addition to Ghana we would soon have a strong ally nearer home. Britain had recently agreed in principle that Tanganyika would proceed to independence under an elected government, unlike the white settler colony of Kenya. I expanded on the principled leadership of Julius Nyerere, who had already expressed his support for the boycott of South African goods.

A few days later I was invited to a meeting with Walter Sisulu, the Indian Congress leader Yusuf Cachalia and a few other people including Oliver Tambo, whom I had not previously met. I was informed that the ANC had agreed to establish a presence outside South Africa, and that in view of a series of major campaigns that were about to be launched, the ANC might be banned. The leadership had thought of Ghana as a possible base. Its independence had been an inspiration to the African people and some ANC leaders had attended conferences called by President Nkrumah. London was also considered a possible base. The problem was that it would be difficult for someone without a passport to reach these destinations through white and colonial countries.

Walter Sisulu wanted to know more about what I had said about Tanganyika, and in particular whether anyone entering without a passport would be sent back to South Africa by the British or would be allowed to stay or at least transit safely. In addition, Oliver Tambo asked very detailed questions about why I thought the British would behave differently in Tanganyika.

I expanded on developments in southern Africa and the growing pressures on the British government. The Movement for Colonial Freedom in Britain included a number of members of parliament and other prominent and influential persons. They had campaigned successfully for Seretse Khama to return home with his 'white' wife; were in touch with the African nationalist movements; were currently campaigning for Dr Banda to be released from prison; and supported the demand that Northern Rhodesia and Nyasaland be allowed independence outside the Central African Federation. Christian Action had also mobilised support for the campaigns in central Africa.

This was my first encounter with Oliver Tambo and I was not accustomed to being challenged with such rigour and precision to substantiate the basis of my conclusions. He was not hostile, and gave meticulous attention to every word. His questions were designed to separate events and facts from my personal views and assessments. Again and again he returned to why I thought the British would give in to pressure by Tanganyika, and what was so special about the country and its leader.

I explained that Tanganyika was a UN Trust Territory. Britain had recently announced that in terms of its policy the country was not considered to be a 'colony of white settlement' as were Kenya, the Rhodesias and Nyasaland. There were no pressures from white settlers, and Britain had accepted the principle that the country should proceed to full independence under an elected (majority rule) African government.

Julius Nyerere, the President of the Tanganyika African National Union (TANU), was a strong Christian and respected as a leader of principle. He was a Pan Africanist and had already expressed his commitment to the Boycott South Africa campaign. While I was reasonably confident he would make representations to the British government to allow ANC leaders safe transit, I could not be certain of the British response, except that they would not want additional problems in the area.

Both Comrades Walter and Oliver must have been satisfied with my answers. Comrade Walter asked if I would try to ascertain the likely support from TANU, and consider how the ANC might be able to secure travel documents. I agreed to do so.

During the meeting, I had assumed that the ANC leader who would be leaving was Chief Albert Luthuli. I had interviewed him a few weeks earlier and recorded an appeal from him to the international community calling for support for the international sanctions campaign. During our discussion, he had shown great interest in international developments and likely support, and had indicated he would like to go abroad and explain what was happening in South Africa.

Consequently, I was surprised when I was told that Chief Luthuli's Deputy, Oliver Tambo, would be the person leaving and that I should try to assist him in any way I could. I immediately concluded that this explained Oliver's very penetrating questions, but I was mistaken. While working with Oliver, I came to learn that one of his defining characteristics was to sift facts from assumptions, personal views and opinions. He would consider everything said and then make his own assessment before taking a decision.

There was one further meeting with Comrade Walter and Yusuf Cachalia, at which I was told that events were moving very quickly and I should proceed with haste. I reported that as yet I had had no response from TANU to my rather cryptic message, which had not mentioned the name of the leader involved. However, although Kenya was not independent, an Indian Consul General was based in Nairobi. Through him contact was made with Krishna Menon who would support providing Indian travel documents. Before I left the meeting, Comrade Yusuf gave me a phone number and two addresses to use for communicating further progress, but warned me to use them with caution. That was the last occasion on which I saw Comrade Yusuf. However, I received my final instructions from Comrade Walter on the evening of 21 March 1960.

In Durban, and unaware of the carnage at Sharpeville that morning or its implications, I had arranged to interview the Indian Congress President, Dr Naicker (Monty), that evening. He took a phone call, and told me that Walter Sisulu had been trying to contact me. Comrade Walter said he did not have much time, but had asked Monty to brief me on events that necessitated that we proceed swiftly with arrangements. He asked if I still had a passport, and urged me to visit my parents (who lived in Mozambique). And then, depending on what transpired, I should help my 'big brother' as agreed.

Monty said that he had been asked to impress on me the gravity of the situation for the ANC, and the urgency of acting as my 'big brother' would now be depending on me, since all the leaders might be arrested. I confided what I had been asked to do, and confessed my confusion and sense of a lack of capacity to act on my own. How would I even know where to find Oliver Tambo? From whom could I seek advice? Monty urged me to leave the country as I had been instructed and to use my judgement on how to proceed. He commented that neither Comrades Walter nor Oliver would have told me to act on my own if the ANC did not have confidence in me.

Over the years, it became evident that the confidence of some senior leaders in each other's judgements was the glue that gave coherence and unity to the decisions of the leadership even when they were separated by prison walls and distance. It contributed much to the success and unity of the Congress Movement.

In exile I asked Comrade Oliver the reason why the ANC would have given an untested and ill-equipped person such responsibility. He seemed puzzled by the question and said that Comrade Walter had told him that I would do the job and he had confidence in Walter's judgement. Clearly he expected that I should share that confidence. When I reminded him about the 'grilling' to which he had subjected me at our first meeting, he simply laughed and said he did not doubt Walter, but wanted to satisfy himself that I had thought through my conclusions and had based them on facts. 'You proved then you were someone who could think, so when I was in Bechuanaland I thought we could rely on your judgement . . . You must keep thinking for yourself.'

Thirty years later, when I had the opportunity to seek clarity from Comrade Walter, he appeared surprised that I should ask. He simply said, 'I knew you would do it and so did OR and you did, didn't you?' I continue to wonder, why me, except that I happened to be there at the time, and there was no one else. But why did I not hesitate? What was it about those two leaders, whom I hardly knew, that inspired me to act in a way that changed the direction of my life?

I have no regrets. My mind was opened to new ideas and ways of thinking. I had the privilege to work with and learn from someone of the highest moral integrity. Had Oliver Tambo not provided the leadership he did for thirty years, then certainly the much-acclaimed 'miracle' in South Africa would have been deferred and have had a different character.

I left South Africa for Lourenço Marques on 22 March 1960. The telephone number I had been given was never answered, and the addresses brought no response. In fact, many months later the letters were returned marked 'Addressee Unknown'. Once out of the country I was able to telephone Tanganyika and explain less cryptically what was needed. I also called Rosalynde Ainslee, the Secretary of the Anti-Apartheid Committee, with whom I had worked in London, and sought advice and help. After news reports that Oliver Tambo had escaped to Bechuanaland were confirmed at the UN, I proceeded to Salisbury.

There I found reports of threats on Oliver Tambo's life, and statements by Prime Minister Sir Roy Welensky that if the 'fugitives' tried to enter the Federation they would be promptly returned to South Africa. Comrade OR had worked with Father Trevor Huddleston and had met Canon Collins. Financial support had been sent from Britain to families of those imprisoned for participation in the Defiance Campaign, and later to the Treason Trial Defence Fund. Ros put me in touch with Christian Action contacts in Salisbury and informed me that Canon Collins had already agreed to help with expenses. Professor Terence Ranger and family extended hospitality and friendship and provided a local network for advice and support.

Dr Yusuf Dadoo, the South African Indian Congress and Communist Party leader, had left South Africa and asked to be included in any travel arrangements. His presence brought confidence that the Indian government would provide documents through the local Consulate of India. With funds available from Canon Collins, small planes could be chartered. All that was left was to find a safe route to Dar es Salaam.

In terms of Rhodesian law, a person refused entry would be returned 'from whence he came'. The crucial question was whether that would be to South Africa or Bechuanaland? If it was the latter, Oliver could consider risking even illegal entry. However, local lawyers and legal advice from London was to proceed cautiously, as Salisbury was likely to act quickly and politically. There would be a need to mobilise countervailing pressure on the British government to intervene, at the very least in support of our interpretation of the law.

A charter company that regularly flew into Francistown was prepared to undertake the flight, but we were warned that the small plane would need to refuel on the way to Tanganyika.

By coincidence, Ronald Segal, the Editor of the journal *Africa South*, had volunteered to drive Oliver Tambo from Cape Town to Bechuanaland and had returned there after the widespread arrests in South Africa. I had represented *Africa South*, and Ros worked for it in London. Most people were unaware of the ANC's plans to establish overseas representation, and so it was generally assumed that I had gone to Salisbury to assist Ronald. He was easy to contact and was regularly talking to the press. Warned that all communication with Bechuanaland was via Mafekeng in South Africa, apart from one early call from Tambo, I had discussed possible arrangements with Ronald, including organising a charter flight.

After all plans were finalised, the Indian Consulate and the charter company were suddenly informed that the Francistown airstrip had been closed, that no planes from Salisbury would be allowed to land, and that if Ronald and Comrade OR tried to enter the property they would be arrested and taken to South Africa. I was amazed as the charter company had been chosen precisely because it regularly flew into Francistown and another flight would not attract attention. It subsequently emerged that a request had been made for permission for a charter flight to land in order to fly Ronald and others out.

Local authorities in Bechuanaland and London were now concerned for the safety of the South African group. On Ronald's initiative, they advised me to expedite travel plans. Ronald's statement that denying him entry would cause a constitutional crisis had provoked white settler reaction and Prime Minister Welensky's anger. Of greater concern was a message from South Africa, that my 'big brother' needed to travel urgently as the South African police planned to assassinate or kidnap him. A decision had to be made about the safest and quickest option.

New plans were made and a charter finalised. On 'brother's' instructions communication was limited and only through Dr Dadoo. He was asked to assemble the party in Francistown by a particular day, and to call a number from a public telephone at 10:00 p.m. that night. Later, I issued a statement that the South Africans were proceeding by road and would seek entry into the Federation at a border post the next morning. That night, I received Dr Dadoo's call in a telephone kiosk on the university campus, and immediately started speaking in Gujarati, assuming that even if people were listening in they would not have an interpreter. I explained that they should go to Palapye where someone would meet them with transport and papers. My knowledge of the language was rudimentary, and it was only as we were speaking that I realised I did not know the Gujarati words for airplane or pilot. I improvised, and for years thereafter was teased by both Dr Dadoo and

Oliver Tambo as the word I used, 'chakli', is a tiny Indian bird. Still, I had managed to communicate that they would be flying and not driving.

At daybreak I met the pilot at Salisbury airport and gave him a package of documents that included various legal opinions for OR as well as Indian travel documents for him, Ronald Segal and Dr Dadoo. I instructed the pilot not to land anywhere in southern Rhodesia, but to proceed to Blantyre in Nyasaland where he should refuel.

I then took a commercial flight to Dar es Salaam, via Blantyre. Messages had been sent to Christian Action to meet the flight and have lawyers on standby. I had met and worked with some officials from the Nyasaland Congress Party in London, and managed to send them a message seeking assistance.

The political temperature in the Federation had been rising with increasing pressures from the nationalist movements in Northern Rhodesia and Nyasaland. The British government was in a quandary about whether and when to release Dr Banda from prison. In consultation with London, we assumed that Britain would not want an 'incident' in Nyasaland. If it came to the worst, the courts there were more likely to interpret the law in a way that would allow transit or return to Bechuanaland.

When the plane landed I saw some familiar faces, but was appalled when I was ushered into the transit lounge, a detail that had been overlooked. Desperately I considered ways to go out – an urgent telephone call or an essential medicine I needed to buy? Looking around, I noticed a white-coated waiter standing in a half open doorway beckoning me. I walked across and was quickly whisked through the kitchen into the departure area, where lawyers and others were waiting with tea. They had anticipated the problem and made arrangements with the Congress party members on the airport staff. When I subsequently told Comrade OR how impressed I had been by the cooperation between progressive Christians from Britain and nationalist struggles in southern Africa, he commented that there was a similar situation with some clergy in South Africa, but that one of the areas of international work on which the ANC needed to focus, was to institutionalise the support we had from progressive Christian people.

I explained to the group in Blantyre that the South Africans would be landing there later that day. In case the matter went to the courts, I had brought them the legal opinions and advice we had. I was then led back into the transit lounge and rejoined the flight to Dar es Salaam.

That evening Minister Amir Jamal met Julius Nyerere who was at a TANU Central Committee meeting and informed him that Oliver Tambo and others were arriving the next morning. Nyerere met with British Governor Turnbull that night and secured safe passage for the party through the country. Early the next morning I was informed that a charter flight bound for Dar es Salaam had taken off from Blantyre. (With no CNN there were no instant reports of what had happened in Blantyre.) To our great relief and celebration, Oliver Tambo, Yusuf Dadoo and Ronald Segal arrived safely in Dar es Salaam.

I later learnt that four warrants of arrest were presented in Blantyre, on the assumption that I was also on the chartered flight. However, Salisbury had been taken by surprise, and the Rhodesian warrants were not valid in Nyasaland. The flight took off early the next morning before new valid warrants could be issued.

Oliver Tambo met with Julius Nyerere and spoke to some press, but Dar es Salaam was not yet a centre for political communication. Many Tanganyikans came to the New Africa Hotel to meet us. Two members of the PAC, Nana Mahomo and Peter Raboroko also made contact to inform us that they were on their way to Ghana but had not yet received travel documents.

It was evident that OR had already focused and started to plan the next steps on how he should begin to carry out his responsibilities. After assuring family and colleagues that he had arrived safely, he was anxious to move on as quickly as possible, as already a lot of time had been 'lost', and 'there was a lot of work to be done'.

The next day OR left Dar es Salaam, passing through Nairobi to collect new travel documents. Those that had been sent to me were blank laissez-passer to which the men had attached their pictures on the plane from Bechuanaland.

Notwithstanding OR's work, he made time talk to me. He was the only one to express any appreciation. He commended me for being discreet and said that I had 'kept my head'. He then asked what my plans were and, for the first time, I explained that I had been about to prepare for admission to the Bar in South Africa, and that I would still want to do so. He urged me not to go back to South Africa in a hurry, as even when the State of Emergency was lifted I might be arrested. As yet no one knew what was likely to happen next at home. He had begun to try and anticipate the changes that would be necessary in the new situation, and had to consult and work out what the next steps for him should be. In the meantime, I should try to stay in Dar es Salaam as there would be much to do. He also asked that if I could, I should assist the two PAC officials to reach Ghana.

I was surprised that with so much on his mind OR took time to talk to me and give advice. Later I appreciated that however busy he was, he never failed to concern himself about the most junior of those who worked with him and to attend to their needs.

OR began to travel extensively, explaining what was happening in South Africa and mobilising support for international action against apartheid. As yet there was no organised ANC international presence, no office and no staff. In London he linked up with South African expatriates working there, the Anti-Apartheid Committee (the precursor of the Anti-Apartheid Movement), the Treason Trial Defence Fund, and with Canon and Diana Collins, Father Trevor Huddleston and others. I remained in Dar es Salaam, working as a journalist. President Nkrumah of Ghana sent passports and arrangements were made with TANU to issue them to members of the liberation movements. The assumption was made that I would authenticate at least those who were associated with the ANC.

In South Africa, I had agreed to play what was intended to be a very minor role in facilitating the establishment of the ANC's international presence. Now, however, political developments had overtaken my intentions. Unexpectedly I had acquired a high ANC profile and continuing responsibilities. Yet I had no political or institutional base in South Africa. Those on official missions would contact me to assist with finance and onward transport. Without any formal authority or communication, it appeared I had been designated as the ANC's local travel agent.

In addition to those coming out on behalf of the ANC, groups were being sent out by the Communist Party and by the South African Congress of Trade Unions. Individuals arrived, expecting me (the ANC) to provide them with scholarships or military training. The government of Tanganyika assisted those who qualified as refugees. Generally, there were exaggerated expectations of my authority and capacity, and my anomalous position was becoming difficult.

When I raised my discomfort with Comrade OR, he urged me, much as Comrades Walter and Monty had done in South Africa, to use my own judgement and do whatever I could to help. However, he did explain that he had to make a lot of adjustments as he tried to manage a variety of claims and priorities as the situation in South Africa developed, and that there was no tidy or quick solution.

My discomfort was trivial compared to the immense challenges facing the ANC and requiring the attention of Comrade OR. He was not only the sole authorised spokesperson of the ANC, but had to assume new responsibilities when all other NEC members were either underground or in prison. As the senior and only mandated leader of the ANC, even after a few other NEC members left South Africa, he was anxious to establish decision-making procedures that would be accepted as legitimate.

The ANC had decided on its international representation in a different global scenario. The NEC had not been informed that some members of the SACP, which had been banned in the early 1950s, had decided to set up underground structures as well as an international presence that included a unit in London. How should the alliance function internationally, given the strong anti-communist positions of many potential supporters in Western countries? Yet Britain and the US were the major supporters of the Pretoria regime and Comrade OR's task was to mobilise them instead into the anti-apartheid struggle.

Comrade OR would patiently explain the record of the Communist Party in opposing racist policies in South Africa, and the ongoing determination of the ANC to involve all those prepared to join in bringing an end to apartheid. Notwithstanding Cold War pressures, there was no compromise on the alliance with the Communist Party and later for continued support from the Soviet Union for the armed struggle. Oliver never failed to point out that those who loudly proclaimed democracy did not hesitate to welcome the apartheid regime as part of the 'free world'. Nor were they prepared to support the right of the South African people to take up arms to free themselves.

Later, he courageously engaged those African leaders who might have been seduced by offers of détente and compromise in order to try to win some piecemeal reforms, patiently explaining the impossibility of reformist solutions to eradicate apartheid.

Initially, many African leaders failed to understand the ANC's commitment to non-racism, and had difficulty in dealing with 'non-African' representatives. In the light of Sharpeville and the many reports of brutality and repression, they could not accept the ANC's continued commitment to non-violence. Though the PAC was a member of the newly formed SAUF, its leaders tried to assert political dominance and obtain support by undermining the ANC, alleging that it was not an African organisation but was dominated by communists, Indians and whites. Its political rhetoric, and the violent and brutal response of the regime to the peaceful Sharpeville demonstration on 21 March 1960, which led to the death of over sixty unarmed people, was confused as an example of PAC militancy, rather than irresponsibility.

Though compromise might have brought greater support, Oliver Tambo remained unswerving in his commitment to ANC policies as he addressed the misrepresentations of the PAC. In the 1970s he was careful to distinguish between BC and racism. Calming the fears of some white comrades, the post-1976 youth were drawn into ANC ranks.

Shortly after the youth began leaving South Africa after the uprising of 1976, Oliver had arranged for them to be interviewed not only about their motivation and experiences, but specifically about what they knew about the ANC, and how they had learned about the organisation. In addition, the interviewers were asked to probe the degree and extent of the involvement of parents, family and communities, and the extent of support.

Comrade OR nurtured a deep anger and hurt at the degradation of the African people and was sensitive and conscious of the need to defend the dignity of the African people at all times. Committed to the Freedom Charter declaration that South Africa belonged to all who lived in it, he was determined that every South African who wanted to make a contribution should be allowed to do so. Over the years he worked to balance the need to use the talents available to the ANC, whilst ensuring that it maintained its essential African character. This was not always understood by comrades, who sometimes felt excluded or overlooked without justification.

The main burden of explaining the ANC's shift to armed struggle fell on Comrade OR. While he was a committed Christian, he was not a pacifist. Once convinced that there was no other alternative, he saw no conflict in the decision to take up arms. In large measure it was his sincerity and skilful advocacy that persuaded many countries and people who could not actively support the armed struggle, to support the ANC and recognise it as the leader of the struggle against apartheid, to the extent that they provided much needed non-military material aid.

He advocated a dual strategy: the South African people would take up arms, and the international community should make its contribution through breaking ties with the apartheid regime, isolating it and applying economic sanctions that would serve to weaken it and move it to change its policies.

After the arrest of the leaders of MK, Comrade OR had to function simultaneously as the military leader and the chief diplomat for the ANC. While much of his focus and time had to be on the struggle inside South Africa, he recognised the importance of intensifying international action. He continued to provide strategic guidance to the campaign for sanctions, and often initiated research and action on particular targets, setting up task groups for the purpose. Having identified the potential of a major breakthrough in Sweden, he took personal charge of the presentation to the Swedish parliament, calling on it to support disinvestment in South Africa. He went through the documents and edited them word by word. Our representations were successful and Sweden was the first non-communist European country to stop investment.

On another occasion, I had to report to him that secret South African government documents in the possession of the ANC appeared to indicate that South Africa was building a nuclear weapons capacity. Once again, he interrogated the basis of the conclusion, and asked to be kept informed of the results of further research. In the meantime, the German Anti-Apartheid Movement began a campaign to stop Western nuclear collaboration with South Africa, based on some of the same documents. When the ANC research was completed with the addition of information supplied by some scientists working in South Africa and the US, a very detailed report was presented to Comrade OR. Many questions later, he suggested that while the German Anti-Apartheid Movement and others should continue to focus on the international campaign to stop nuclear and military collaboration, it was incumbent on the ANC to publish whatever information it had in order to alert the world to the potential danger. After publication and the anticipated denials, he asked for a further special report highlighting the evidence that suggested that Mozambique might be a potential target, which he submitted to President Samora Machel.

Similarly, he directed the ANC to focus on preventing oil from reaching South Africa, organising a task group for the purpose.

Comrade OR's concern for the involvement of women in the ANC did not arise simply from recognition that women's involvement in the struggle would strengthen the ANC, but was motivated by a genuine concern for human rights. He believed that ultimately the oppressed should take responsibility for freeing themselves, and so he insisted that women in the ANC be at the forefront of ensuring their participation and securing their rights. At the same time, he accepted the responsibility of the ANC to free all South Africans without distinction, and under his own leadership established an ANC Commission for the Emancipation of Women. In 1985 he addressed a press conference at the 1985 UN Conference on Women, and pledged that the ANC's liberation struggle would not be complete until the women of South Africa were fully emancipated and able to enjoy equally with all others the fruits of democracy. This pledge underpinned the ANC's negotiating positions and its policies in government.

For Oliver Tambo, these were not mere words. They were among the principles that guided his life and his relations with all others, regardless of age or status, and were reflected in the goals and vision he set for the liberation movement. Within the ANC, he never permitted exclusion on the basis of a person's race, religion or ethnicity. In 1979, I demurred at being asked to accompany the Secretary-General on the first ANC visit to post-revolutionary Iran, arguing that a woman might have difficulty being taken seriously in negotiations. I was firmly told that the ANC would never accept the exclusion of a member from participation because she was a woman. Trepidation unabated, I went to Iran.

Over the years, Comrade OR had to cope with personal and political rivalries, the real and imagined grievances of large numbers of members, disillusion as infiltration into the country and military operations became more difficult, real policy differences, personal criticism and challenges.

Most political movements forced to operate from exile or underground succumb to policy and ideological divisions, and challenges to leadership. That the ANC emerged intact and even stronger thirty years after being banned was in no small measure due to the leadership of Oliver Tambo.

His style was inclusive of people and ideas. He was always prepared to listen, to encourage debate and interrogation of all views, proposals and ideas, and to provide guidance towards a collective standpoint. In the mid-1980s, at the same time as the ANC escalated the armed struggle, he encouraged those who postulated that negotiations could come sooner than expected to examine the process and put forward proposals to prepare the ground.

He taught and challenged all those who were privileged to work with him. He was a master of language, expressing himself with precision, requiring others to reflect and often explain their choice of words. On delegations he encouraged all members to participate, to raise issues and seek clarifications. He was a workaholic and drove himself tirelessly, but also worried about whether his assistants and security personnel had managed to eat or attend to family responsibilities.

Justifiably, Oliver Tambo is credited with mobilising the largest and most widespread popular movement in support of a struggle: the international anti-apartheid movement. Yet he remained humble and modest to a fault, never failing to acknowledge his colleagues and especially the internal leadership who were in prison. Rarely articulated, it was evident that he was concerned that while he lived outside the country, his colleagues faced torture, imprisonment and isolation from friends and family. He never failed to acknowledge and seek recognition for them. He refused honours for himself and instead requested that the recipient should be one of the internal leaders. It took a great deal of effort to persuade him eventually to accept an honorary degree.

He believed that Nelson Mandela should succeed Chief Albert Luthuli as President of the ANC, and for a long period insisted on being addressed as 'Acting President', notwithstanding the decision of the NEC.

Nelson Mandela said, 'the struggle is my life'. For his friend and colleague, Oliver Tambo, the ANC and struggle were synonymous, and that was his life.

Many tributes have been paid to him and he has been correctly credited with maintaining the unity of the ANC for over thirty years of exile. But the multifaceted challenges, and the internal, continental and international context in which the ANC had to function under his leadership has yet to be sufficiently or adequately explored.

Notwithstanding the many pressures, Comrade OR survived, and ensured that the ANC survived because he always focused single-mindedly on the responsibility given to him by the NEC. On more than one occasion when someone raised a relatively minor problem caused by a comrade or more seriously on what appeared to be attempts to undermine him, he would raise his head, put down his glasses and patiently respond: 'I have been given a mission by the ANC, and cannot allow myself to be diverted by . . . [whatever]. I suggest you go back and focus on your work.' He would smile to indicate that he understood our concern, and pick up his pen to continue working.

At his welcome home rally in December 1990, he finally acknowledged that his mission had been completed. Addressing the tens of thousands who had assembled, he said: 'I have devotedly watched over the organisation all these years. I now hand it back to you, bigger, stronger – intact. Guard our precious movement.'

THE MOVEMENT'S VOICE
AND HEART

Helen Jackson

Our three children were born in the 1960s. My husband and I were active members of the Labour Party, horrified by events in Africa. We went on marches in Liverpool and London with our small children, who treated these events as days out with Mum or Dad or both. We read of the Rivonia Trial, and later saw the horrific pictures from Soweto. We talked to our children about how remarkable heroes far away were fighting, dying and suffering in prison for standing up for their human rights. They listened to these explanations, though they were not yet old enough to read the newspapers and grasp the reality for themselves.

In those days we believed passionately that international solidarity made a difference, that what we did in our lives in Britain to support the fight against an evil far away was vital. We believed that it was as un-acceptable to eat a juicy 'Cape' orange or apple, as it was to cheat your next door neighbour. We believed that wearing an anti-apartheid badge would really help brave people far away to overcome oppression.

We believed with such conviction partly because we were fortunate enough to have people such as Oliver Tambo as our exiles. It was a privilege to welcome asylum seekers, freedom fighters, to Britain. They inspired us to help the fight for freedom and they gave it a human face, a human heart. They motivated our political activity and added heart and morality to politics. Oliver Tambo was the movement's voice and heart.

We felt a quiet pride one day when we saw that our ten-year-old daughter had put an anti-apartheid picture with Mandela's words from his final Rivonia Trial speech next to her bed, along with her other special possessions. Out of evil comes a stream of hope helped along by those with the energy and determination to fight it. We are grateful to Oliver for his work and life.

THE GLUE THAT BOUND
US TOGETHER

Ronnie Kasrils

Oliver Tambo left an indelible mark on all who were inspired by him. In a poignant eulogy at the final resting place of his comrade in arms, former President, Nelson Mandela, resolutely declared that '… Oliver Tambo has not died because the ideals for which he sacrificed his life can never die …', and accordingly enjoined us '… who became part of his soul … for the victory of his cause …' to remember '… that while we live, Oliver Tambo will not die!'[1]

This statement goes to heart of the rich legacy that is Oliver Reginald Tambo, affectionately known to us as OR. While his passing may have robbed us of his physical presence, his lasting influence remains.

This influence is embedded in the significant advances we have made at home, on the African continent and in the wider world since the dawning of our freedom, which he would have been proud of. It serves as our clarion call to rise to even greater heights in accelerating and deepening these advances, which is what he would expect.

As one of those South Africans who had the distinct privilege of serving with and learning from OR, I count my contemporaries and myself extremely fortunate. We, more than most, carry a very special obligation not only to share but importantly to strive consistently to remain true to and emulate his proud memory.

Tough but fair

OR was a selfless leader of great integrity, who sought neither fame nor glory. He was a tough but fair taskmaster; he set high standards but led by example. This was brought home to me in the very early days of our time in exile, prior to my actually meeting OR, by my wife Eleanor. She was part of a group that was responsible for establishing the ANC office in Dar es Salaam, in preparation for OR, in 1964, while I was on a military training course in Odessa.

In describing him, Eleanor referred to the leisurely pace that had originally prevailed in the office, which was fundamentally altered on OR's arrival. On assuming his post, he immediately called a staff meeting and sternly said that 'from now on everybody will be in at 8 o'clock in the morning'.[2] They could not disobey this modest order as OR himself was in the office by 6:00 a.m., often working relentlessly until well after midnight.

Eleanor's assessment was spot on and when the time came for my first interaction with OR, I was fully briefed and appreciated as well as understood his brisk and no-nonsense manner. This first interaction included the late Chris Hani, who was also summoned to report to OR with me and whose passion for Shakespeare came in a close second to his unstinting dedication to the struggle.

OR's instruction to us was that we should study and comment on a selection of books on guerrilla struggles and counter-revolutionary warfare, which formed part of his commitment to ongoing education so as to ensure informed political debate as well as to broaden our intellectual horizons. I went away completely awestruck and inspired on receiving my first direct and personal tasking from him, with Chris mischievously remarking to me that, as much as he enjoyed revolutionary texts, he had secretly hoped to find time 'to plough through the works of Shakespeare'.[3]

Fatherly concern

OR's austere bearing was, however, matched by his fatherly concern for the well-being of those of us in his charge. When Eleanor and I got married at a registry office in Dar es Salaam, a small reception was arranged for us at a flat close by. It was only years later that we heard from the owner of the flat that OR had come to her and said, 'the children are getting married; we must have a celebration'.[4] He also asked the late JB Marks, another stalwart of the struggle, to make a rousing speech at the function, which he did with characteristic aplomb and humour by invoking sections of the MK Manifesto to illustrate the responsibilities that come with marriage.

Sense of mission

I had initially put down OR's strict demeanour to his background as a teacher at a missionary school, his Christian faith – of which he never spoke – and his career as a lawyer. I slowly came to realise, however, that his demeanour stemmed from his driving sense of mission to fulfil the onerous duties that he shouldered as the person carrying the ANC flag abroad, after the underground inside the country had been smashed and the internal leadership imprisoned following the Rivonia Trial.

Evidence of the full impact of the exacting personal burden that he bore materialised for me near the end of his life. It was only then – once the political prisoners were released and the conditions for negotiations with the apartheid regime were being met, as outlined in the Harare Declaration (which he had worked so hard to mobilise support for) – that he was finally able to relax with us and allow his inner warmth and gentleness to shine through.

It is this sense of mission, coupled with his extraordinary discipline, which enabled OR to rebuild and lead the liberation movement so capably under the most trying of circumstances. He was never one to flinch in the face of the ensuing challenges and always tackled them decisively, no matter how daunting they seemed.

His observations made during his final report to the ANC Congress in 1991, in his capacity as President, are instructive here. He said, '… we did not tear ourselves apart because of a lack of progress at times. We were always ready to accept our mistakes and to correct them … Above all we succeeded to foster and defend [our] unity. Even in bleak moments, we were never in doubt … that our people's cause shall triumph.'[5]

Fostering unity

It is in fostering and defending the unity of the ANC, its Tripartite Alliance and our people that OR played a most instrumental role. Often referred to as the glue that bound us together, out of the diverse ideological strands and experiences of resistance that made up the liberation movement OR was successfully able to forge a common identity and programme against the shared enemy of apartheid.

His ability to do so was heightened by his inclusive and democratic style. As the late Joe Slovo commented: '… [OR] was perhaps one of the greatest listeners that I have come across … who had … the capacity … to summarise the discussion and point the way in the most brilliant fashion … which kept us together, which took into account the differing views'.[6]

As a result, OR was able to discharge his mandate to create a reliable rear base and rally international support with absolute distinction. His efforts enabled the ANC to grow in both stature and effectiveness, which ultimately led to its victory and brought us to where we are today.

There is a particular freedom song, sung in Sesotho and adapted from a religious hymn, which our people creatively composed in honour of our leaders. In many ways it sums up OR's contribution not only to our own liberation, but also to that of oppressed people the world over. It goes as follows: 'Oliver Tambo – *ha ho na ya tshoana le yena*', which when translated means 'Oliver Tambo – there is no one like him'.

OR, with the humility and modesty that was his hallmark, would have been the first to remind us that the ANC is much greater than an individual, that our successes belong to the tireless sacrifices of the collective and our people, and that across the centuries of our struggle South Africa has produced countless leaders and revolutionary icons of note.

While this is true, the fact remains that OR was unique. While many shared his extraordinary talents and qualities, there is 'no one like him'. His life, temperament and role are not only relevant for our work now, but also for that of future generations, as the noble values that he personified are universal and enduring.

The best tribute we could therefore pay him in commemorating the ninetieth anniversary of his birth is to continue our journey on the very same trail that he and so many others blazed. This is what he would want and we dare not fail him; this is precisely what former President Mandela meant when he said that 'while we live, Oliver Tambo will not die'.

NOTES
1. N. Mandela, Address at the funeral of Oliver Tambo, 2 May 1993, Johannesburg.
2. Cited in L. Callinicos, *Oliver Tambo: Beyond the Engeli Mountains* (Cape Town: David Phillip, 2004).
3. Cited in R. Kasrils, *Armed and Dangerous: From Undercover Struggle to Freedom* (Johannesburg: Jonathan Ball Publishers, 2004).
4. In R. Kasrils, *Armed and Dangerous*.
5. O. Tambo, Opening address to the ANC 48th National Conference, 2 July 1991, Durban.
6. Cited in L. Callinicos, 'Oliver Tambo and the Politics of Class, Race and Ethnicity in the African National Congress of South Africa', *African Sociological Review*, 1999.

A FATHER FIGURE

Thandi Lujabe-Rankoe

One thing I will always remember about Oliver Reginald Tambo, besides his great intellect and leadership skills, is the influence and effect he had on the lives of so many people. The mere mention of his name inspired and motivated thousands, including very young children.

My first experience of working with OR was in 1961 when I got to Dar es Salaam. I did a lot of typing for him in the ANC office. It was during this time that I met former President Chissano in the FRELIMO offices as I used to carry messages for OR to the late FRELIMO President Eduardo Mondlane. It was an honour and privilege to serve under OR during that period. Getting to know him on a personal level only further increased my respect and admiration for him.

In 1981 I received a letter from OR requesting me to travel to Nigeria to try to influence the Nigerian government to allow the Amandla group to perform in that country (*see picture section*). It was greatly humbling that he entrusted me with such an important assignment. It showed his belief that women are equal to men and that they can perform any task just as well.

While living in Botswana during the 1980s my daughter, Tshedi, belonged to the ANC children's wing, Masupatsela, which means 'pioneers'. They were taught songs in praise of prominent activists such as Oliver Tambo. Tshedi's favourite song, which I heard her singing many times at home, was:

Uphi u Tambo
U Tambo usehlatini bafana
Wenzani
Ufundisa amajoni
One step!
Two steps!
Bafana!

[Where is Tambo?
Tambo is in the forest.
What is he doing there?
He's training soldiers.]

This song was in praise of Comrade Oliver Tambo and Tshedi was so obsessed with it that she even taught her Norwegian childhood friend to sing it with her. I was amazed and very proud that at such a young age my daughter knew the name and history of one of Africa's greatest sons and that she took immense pride in being able to sing a song about her hero.

I witnessed this same pride and admiration at a later stage. Comrade Tambo suffered a stroke in 1989 and was flown to Sweden for treatment. On his return to London, Lindiwe Mabuza and myself would often visit Comrade Tambo to see that he was being taken care of and if there were anything that we could do for him. I experienced him as someone with immense compassion, humility and patience. It was on these visits that I encountered one of OR's bodyguards, whose name was Mhengu. In my dealings with Mhengu I noticed that he spoke with the same admiration of Tambo as my daughter had done a few years previously. I could see in his eyes and hear in his voice that he had the utmost respect for and loyalty to Tambo. If necessary, he was willing to sacrifice his own life to protect his leader.

I firmly believe that confirmation of a truly humble and great leader will always find expression in the loyalty shown by those closest to him. Oliver Tambo will definitely be remembered as such a man. He treated everyone with the utmost respect and dignity. Not once did I hear anybody saying anything bad about him. As is normal, people will always criticise decisions taken by leaders, but when it came to OR's interactions with other human beings no one could point a finger at him. He treated even his biggest enemies with humility, patience and respect. At conferences and consultations he listened very patiently and carefully to people who defended the apartheid system. He always allowed them to have their say before he replied. This is testimony to the character of a great leader who respected human beings no matter what their convictions.

In 1993 South Africa stood on the doorstep of democracy when two great tragedies befell our nation. These two events could have plunged us into a civil war. On Easter Saturday in 1993 Comrade Chris Hani was assassinated and shortly thereafter, on 23 April 1993, Oliver Tambo passed away. I felt as if democracy was going to slip through our fingers. We were on the brink of losing everything that we had been working so hard for. It felt to me as if there was a dark cloud hanging over the country. I kept asking myself the same questions: 'OR, what are we going to do now? Why don't you wake up and help us?'

Then it dawned on me that OR had not forsaken us. His spirit lived on in our leaders who remained calm in those dark days and led us on to freedom. Through his leadership he had instilled these qualities in our leaders and now they were paying homage to him by acting in a manner that would have made him immensely proud.

I also remember OR as a man who made good on his promises. I recently realised that promises he had made while he was alive, but could not fulfil during his lifetime, are being honoured today, so many years after he has departed.

Moses Mabhida was a senior leader of the ANC, the SACP, MK and the South African Congress of Trade Unions. He was someone in the forefront of the liberation struggle. When he died of natural causes in Maputo, in March 1986, he was given a state funeral. Mozambique's first President, Samora Machel, and the then leader of the ANC, Oliver Tambo, agreed that Mabhida's resting place in Maputo's Lhanguene cemetery would only be temporary. They promised the two nations that after the liberation of South Africa, the body of Comrade Mabhida would be exhumed and taken to South Africa. I am proud to say that OR's promise has now been fulfilled. The remains of Moses Mabhida were exhumed and repatriated to his home town in South Africa on 23 November 2006. Sadly OR died before he could witness the birth of a democratic South Africa, and before he could witness the fulfilment of his promise to the Mabhida family and the people of South Africa.

I will fondly remember OR as a leader, a freedom fighter, a comrade, and a humble and respectful human being. Most of all, I will remember him as a father figure who provided us with guidance and direction and treated all of us with gentleness.

THAT LUCKY HORIZON
WITHOUT END

Lindiwe Mabuza

When I first met ANC President OR Tambo in 1977 in Lusaka, I unthink-ingly called him 'Buti', my brother, stemming from our culture's respect for our seniors. From that day forth any communication from President Tambo to me was signed 'Buti'. And it seemed equally natural that when I first met Mrs Adelaide Tambo in 1978 when she was visiting Lusaka, I called her 'Sisi', my sister.

We adopted one another, but I also knew that I was merely another ad-dition in their lives and in the continuous process of adoptions within the community of South Africans in exile, but especially within the comrades of the ANC. In time, we would discover that some of the relationships estab-lished then would prove themselves to be more enduring than even blood ties.

Buti was the President of all his comrades, his followers. But I once heard a European head of state at a Solidarity Conference say Oliver Tambo was 'the President of Presidents'. The Tambos were family to most of us and our children. Yes, you were formally a comrade to OR, but on another level you were a younger or older sibling or another son or daughter. The Tambos had this abundant capacity to embrace all equally. Away from home this embrace gave substance and a sense of belonging together in the cold world of the intense physical alienation of exile.

One of the earliest impressions I have of Buti is that he was able to listen to people under his care no matter how junior. Comrade Elina Mbeko who had completed her military training in Angola informed one senior leader in Lusaka of her desire to go and study instead of wasting away in Lusaka. Elina, like a few other young women, had come to Lusaka hoping to be deployed in combat. During training some women had distinguished themselves by outmanoeuvring the young men. Nevertheless, there was no support for Elina's wish, which was interpreted as a betrayal of the cause. She became very depressed and even contemplated committing suicide.

Around this time she was selected to be part of OR's delegation to the US. OR always paid close attention to each member of his delegation by opening up conversations with them. When this comrade's turn came she tried to contain herself but the floodgates opened uncontrollably. Eventually she was able to tell him of her problems. By the time they returned to Lusaka things had already been set in motion for Elina to enter the University of Zimbabwe to study Economics. Hers is one life I know OR saved. For many of us, whenever we were confronted with a difficult situation, we thought of OR's wise counsel and quick action.

Culture and the ANC

OR distinguished himself as a supreme patron of the arts. He inspired, nourished and promulgated the development of culture within the ANC. Under his leadership, the very first Chief Representative of the ANC to the UK, Europe and US was the literary giant, Mazisi Kunene. At the time of his death in 2005 Mazisi was both a South African and an African poet laureate.

The inspired decision to appoint an artist to this most important position signalled to all that culture would be integral to the work of liberation. The message not only came through political speeches but also through more dramatic, colourful media whose impact can be more immediate.

At the Africa Centre in London young ANC activists such as Comrades Thabo Mbeki, Essop and Aziz Pahad, Pallo Jordan and Zanele (Dlamini) Mbeki would pluck political and literary wisdom from formidable cultural workers such as President Julius Nyerere of Tanzania, Mazisi Kunene, Cosmo Pieterse and James Phillip.

OR also played a guiding role in the formation of Mayibuye, the ANC performing group based in London. The troupe consisted of Pallo Jordan, Barry Feinberg, Bongi Dlomo, Zareen Maharaj and others. They crisscrossed the UK and Europe mobilising public opinion against apartheid and gathering support for the ANC through freedom songs and struggle poetry.

In turn, Mayibuye inspired the formation of anti-apartheid singing groups in Holland, Sweden, Norway and Germany, which were often workshopped and coordinated by James Phillip, Sobizana Mngqikana and Eddie Fuende. Through our songs, the ANC converted nationals of other countries to being artistic ambassadors of the people of South Africa. Mayibuye and some of the song groups produced records that raised money for the ANC.

I was present in Lusaka when Johnny Makathini, the International Secretary of the ANC before his death in 1988, presented OR with the record *Liberation*, produced by a South African group based in New York. OR's eyes danced as he took off his glasses as if to see better, and put them back on. His smile stretched from ear to ear. This was a special production as the artists included the indomitable maestro, the pianist Abdullah Ibrahim and the brave Thembi Mtshali. Brave because the record was unambiguously an ANC product and Thembi, who was not in exile, still went back to South Africa where association with the organisation could have dire consequences.

Buti took a keen interest in my literary development and in several instances expressed his appreciation, as he must have done with other writers in the ANC. On 8 January 1978, at the 66th anniversary of the founding of the ANC at the Evelyn Holne College in Lusaka, I presented for the first time 'Mangaung', an epic poem I had written on the formation of the ANC.

I was truly overwhelmed at the positive reception the poem received from my comrades. But this pleasure could not match the elation that filled me the next day. A short handwritten note read, 'Cde Lindiwe, thank you for the content and remarkable rendition of your poem "Mangaung" on the birth of our movement. Please continue to write, Buti'.

In 1979, when the apartheid regime decided to hang Solomon Mahlangu, a soldier of MK, I wrote and presented the poem 'Solomon My Brother' at the memorial service in Stockholm. A couple of months later I received a call from Buti – he recounted how whilst flying from Moscow to New Delhi he had discovered 'a gem' in *Sechaba* (the official publication of the ANC). Initially I was puzzled about what he meant, but OR laughed and then he discussed the content, tone, feeling and the imagery of 'Solomon My Brother', and thanked me for articulating the voice of the movement.

OR's involvement with culture included his input into Amandla, the cultural ensemble of the ANC consisting of trained soldiers directed by Jonas Gwangwa. The NEC of the ANC took a decision in late 1978 that there should be a troupe of cultural workers established that could perform around the world as a way of spreading the message of resistance. I had been appointed to head the ANC Cultural Committee based in Lusaka and had the responsibility of developing Amandla.

Then in March 1979 I was asked to go to represent the ANC in the

Nordic countries. When I expressed regrets to Buti that I would not be able to do this important work his answer was simple: 'But we are giving you the authority to implement the idea. As Chief Representative, you can be as creative as you wish without some of us standing in your way'. Indeed, by October 1980, Amandla was on tour in Holland, Germany, Sweden, Finland, Norway and Denmark.

When Amandla arrived in Sweden OR dictated a message to me to share with our comrades: 'Comrades you are on an honourable mission as the cultural ambassadors of our movement. No doubt, you are well rehearsed for your maiden tour. The entire movement is behind you and we all look forward to reports on your success. President Oliver Tambo.'

Denmark was the final country on the tour schedule. About ten minutes before the curtain went up, the most unexpected, unbelievable and overwhelming event occurred for Amandla. Comrade President Tambo appeared before them in person. I had followed OR's instructions to keep his coming a secret.

Later, I wrote an article on the tour which appeared in *Sechaba* (March 1981). Of that particular performance I wrote:

> ... Each and all Amandla was stunned, instantly whirled off their feet and the joke was on them as the President advanced, beaming, holding each hand with both his ...
>
> Many eyes, ignoring make up, floated and danced in tears. After each had greeted him, the person would move back still overcome, still incredulous, making room for other victims of joy. As though rehearsed, the most natural act followed. All around the President, spreading their warmth and happiness, their regained strength plus unspoken gratitude, his comrades and children embraced, hugged and then again embraced ...
>
> If any single performance of the entire tour could be said to have been a rare display of beauty and bounty combined this one must be it. From start to finish without exception, we were to be captives of the most balanced blend of political content and artistic forms ...
>
> Those who know Comrade President Tambo might remember the picture when we say this: countless times the spectacles went off and on. Eyes sparked and darts flew savouring every bit of [the] ANC's own majestic sights and sounds. For honouring them, they played for our President and played as though everything depended on that, in the process elevating all those involved

in the struggle to end the exploitation of man by man. When it was all over, the roses and the standing ovation seemed redundant. Excellence is its own reward. But our Danish friends were entitled to their part.

Many people would not know that the current ANC logo, designed by ANC graphic artists was OR's idea for marking the 75th anniversary of the formation of the ANC in 1912.

In 1986 the ANC set up a 75th Anniversary Preparatory Committee in Zambia coordinated by the late Steve Tshwete. The committee was to organise broad-based celebrations of the movement in 1987 inside and outside the country.

The Arts and Culture Department headed by Barbara Masekela was entrusted with organising a graphic artists' workshop to design a new anniversary logo. There were six graphic artists who participated in the workshop: Ali Mathiba, Jabu Mahlangu, Abel Chabalala (aka Majoro), the late Stobane Nthate (aka Roland Karakash), the late Miles Pelo and the late Joseph Madilo (aka Desmond Sithole). They were briefed to design a logo composed of the following elements of the struggle: the ANC flag, the wheel of unity, the spear of the nation and the shield.

Jabu Mahlangu and Ali Mathiba recall their session:

> The presentation of the designs was at the ANC Headquarters in Lusaka attended by the NEC led by the late OR Tambo. He briefed us about the significance of the 75th Anniversary and the important role of the artists in the struggle. The designs were exhibited and the leadership was given an opportunity to do the critical analysis and raise their personal opinions. He artistically analysed the designs and was keen to hear the views of the artists as well. He created a relaxed atmosphere and the participants were freely expressing their opinions, and the late Joe Modise was more vocal.
>
> They finally agreed on the present ANC logo but OR suggested that the flag should have a wavy shape giving it a feeling of movement (as it is presently) and the hand holding the spear should be firm and strong (comparing it to the other design). The other logos were used for postcards and posters.
>
> The logo was adopted as an ANC national logo after our return from exile in the 1990s with a few changes, for example, the inclusion of eight spokes instead of four to represent all the organisations that participated in the Congress of the People in Cape

Town in 1955.

It was such an honour for the artists to meet with OR and deliberate on our work. It made us feel special and respected in our field.

Around 1986, President OR gave me a letter to deliver personally to Letta Mbulu and Caiphus Semanya. Letta was on a European tour with Harry Belafonte and I travelled from Stockholm to meet her in Vienna.

The letter congratulated the artists for their musical achievements over the years. OR asked them to consider engaging more in the struggle against apartheid. Their response was a proposal presented to OR and the NEC to produce a show.

The idea was to get some of South Africa's best artists including Hugh Masekela, Miriam Makeba, Abdullah Ibrahim, Themba Mkhize and Sipho Gumede to work together.

When the show was ready to tour it started in West Africa – Ghana, Burkina Faso, Nigeria and Senegal. Libya and Zimbabwe were added later. The highlight for the artists was the presence of OR and other members of the NEC at one of the Harare performances. The achievement of touring together with artists who were both internally and externally based was great. Even though not all the major South African artists joined the initiative because of their own commitments, OR had again left his stamp in organising cultural workers to act in unity and to unite in action.

Olof Palme

Over the years I served in Sweden as the ANC's Chief Representative, I came to understand and appreciate the depth of solidarity and affection many Swedes felt toward the oppressed people of South Africa. The ANC leaders who were well known and greatly respected in Sweden were Oliver Tambo, Thabo Mbeki, Johnny Makathini and Thomas Nkobi. When I recall the words with which OR dispatched me to Scandinavia, they still give me goose-pimples: 'Go to Scandinavia, a definite anti-apartheid corner in the world. But Sweden stands as a brilliant landmark on the map of our struggle. You must ensure that through our mission the ANC enters the bloodstream of the entire region.'

While based in Stockholm I came to appreciate the special relationship President Oliver Tambo had with many leaders in Sweden. None meant as much to him as Olof Palme, the leader who started giving support to liberation movements in 1975. Olof and Oliver were brothers in different trenches of the same struggle.

The last time Olof and Oliver were together was 21 February 1986 at the opening of the 'Swedish People's Parliament against Apartheid'. The words spoken by the Prime Minister of Sweden at the conference were powerful in their prophecy: 'If the rest of the world decides that apartheid is abolished, the system will disappear'. A week later, on 28 February, Prime Minister Olof Palme was shot dead on the streets of Stockholm. Advocate George Bizos was in the room when OR received the news of Palme's assassination. OR wept and pain was etched on the faces of OR and Comrade Thabo when they arrived a week later for the memorial service.

Between March and August, I wrote eleven poems dedicated to the memory of Olof Palme. I sent the batch to Buti to preview and he wrote a moving foreword to the collection, which included the words:

> ... There is more to life than the way one dies. It is the way one has lived one's life.
>
> Olof Palme became a friend of the South African people. Sweden gave birth to him and the conscience of Sweden made him the friend he was to us.
>
> Olof Palme was a man of peace. He took his lessons not only from Sweden's past but also from the anti-colonial struggles of peoples around the world to give shape to his quest for peace on the world stage.
>
> How do we thread together his friendship to peoples struggling against colonialism, his abiding repugnance for apartheid and his mission for peace?
>
> Whatever the peculiarities of our peoples, whatever the specifics of our struggles, there is an enduring theme to life: that through our struggles we seek to realise the fullness of humanity that is the property of man.
>
> Olof Palme strode along that path.
>
> Lindiwe Mabuza is a South African who has given her life to the service of the South African struggle. She serves as Chief Representative in Sweden of the African National Congress and over the years has come to know many Swedes, not least, Olof and Lisbet Palme.
>
> She is also a poet of no mean repute – a very South African poet, who often speaks of the agony and the anguish, and of the majesty and fortitude of our South African people in struggle ...
>
> Poetry has a special way of blending passion with truth. I like to think that the poems in this collection are a tribute not only to

Olof Palme and his life – to the Swedish people, but also to the enduring bonds that bind our two peoples in our search for the realisation of man's humanity to man.

The issue of women's emancipation

Not an iota of Buti's bone or blood had a particle of prejudice or discrimination against people on any basis, especially gender. For him the question of women's emancipation was central to the total liberation of the country. The ANC upheld the correct view that the majority of women in our country suffered a triple-fold oppression based on race, class and gender. ANC speeches were full of this. Yet in practice much of our work was devoted to dealing with national or racial and class exploitation. Much of the oppression experienced in terms of gender had this veneer of 'our culture' or 'our traditions' as if these were sacrosanct.

In 1982, following on from the seminal Luanda Conference discussed elsewhere in this book, the ANC Women's Section had a special session to examine obstacles to women in leadership positions within the ANC. The Head of the Women's Section, NEC member, Gertrude Shope, Comrades Florence Maleka (Health), Manko Njobe (Education), Ruth Mompati (NEC member) and myself were present. All the comrades spoke of the difficulties they were constantly confronted with because all decisions in the organisation were essentially the right and privilege of men. We took a decision that we should request a special NEC meeting exclusively for this matter. NEC members present included OR, Comrades Alfred Nzo (Secretary-General), Thomas Nkobi (Treasurer), Josiah Jele (International Secretary), John Nkadimeng and Thabo Mbeki. The comrades had asked me to paint the broad picture of the discrepancy within the ANC of professed ideals and actual practices. As I made my introduction I was quite intimidated when a senior NEC member interrupted my presentation, 'Do you mean that this august movement of ours with its history of opposing discrimination in all forms is discriminating against our own women comrades?' A strong chorus of 'Yes!' came from the women comrades. As arranged, the comrades presented obstacles department by department.

One by one, OR asked his NEC colleagues for a response. Comrade Thabo had to leave, asked by the President to attend to some other urgent business, but we already knew that he was on our side as he had helped to ensure the meeting took place. Generally the comrades were in denial except for Comrade John Nkadimeng and the President. The former applauded the fact that we had 'come home' to expose to the leadership a problem with a huge potential danger.

Only Comrade Thabo had been at the Luanda Women's Section meeting where OR had identified the problem as well as our joint responsibilities as comrades in arms to work for the total emancipation of women. So OR, very much conscious that this was about moving forward the agenda we had written ourselves after his riveting challenge came back to some of the points he had made in Luanda. He not only voiced his appreciation of the challenge for the organisation but also expressed confidence that the ANC was up to the challenge and he would do everything in his power to ensure that the malady was corrected.

But it was what OR had said at the Luanda Conference which set us free as women – intellectually, mentally and politically – and revolutionised our own thinking as to our own place in the organisation and country. The Luanda Conference represents a milestone for the women of South Africa and served as a significant precursor to our meeting with the NEC. One of the sons of Oliver Tambo, President Thabo Mbeki, now forges ahead with OR's revolutionary agenda for the total emancipation of women.

Chris Hani

On the day Comrade Chris Hani was assassinated the news came to me at 4.00 a.m. local time in the US. The pain in Sis Adelaide's voice was palpable. She and OR had been among the first to arrive at Chris's home with his body still lying in a pool of blood, she said, and their anguish over such savagery visited on their son, Chris, was incalculable. 'You have to ask one of our friends to give you a ticket to come home as soon as you can,' she said.

The phone at the ANC office in Washington was ringing off the hook. A few weeks previously Chris had done a speaking tour of the US and had made an impressive political, ideological, intellectual and emotional impact. 'When will the memorial service be held?' most callers from coast to coast wanted to know. I phoned Sis Adelaide to inform her that I couldn't come to Chris's funeral because I had to work on his memorial service in the US. A few hours later she called back with the instruction: 'Lindiwe, Papa says you must come home for Chris's funeral or you will be sorry for the rest of your life!'

When I arrived at the Johannesburg airport, a car Sisi had sent drove me straight to the Tambo residence. 'You had to be home Lindiwe and I'm pleased you will be with all of us during these difficult hours,' OR commented.

Under ordinary circumstances in our African society, these days before the funeral amount to individual and communal therapy sessions. The death of Chris Hani was no ordinary event. Chris's wife, Dimpho, the children,

Lindiwe, Lineo, the extended family including the ANC, and the entire nation was bleeding.

The venue for the vigil and the funeral service was the FNB Stadium. Appropriately, the ANC had foreseen the numbers and accurately gauged our people's sentiments around Chris's death. The only venue large enough to contain the outpouring from trains, buses, taxis and all manner of transport from around the entire country was indeed this people's soccer stadium.

Although not officially declared as such, this was the first state funeral the ANC had arranged. The apartheid regime was still in power, but the scale, content and logistical detail clearly demonstrated that the ANC was de facto in power. An explosion was averted and calm settled over the whole nation because the President of the ANC, Nelson Mandela, and all the leaders sent out the same message, 'Let us bury Comrade Chris with dignity'. And that's exactly what happened.

I spent the days following Comrade Chris's funeral with the Tambos. I had ample time with Buti and Sisi to discuss the ANC's work in the US. The ANC had been in the forefront in advocating and campaigning for sanctions. Now it was in the forefront again in calling for re-engagement with and investment in South Africa. In particular, OR wanted to know how much was being done to get assistance for the education and development of skills of the youth.

On one of the occasions when the three of us were together, I asked Buti what he thought I might do in the future as the ANC moved into government. After some reflection he told us that indeed there would be many new challenges and opportunities. He said: 'You could be a Director-General or Deputy Minister or even Minister if the organisation so decides and you agree. You could manage any of these many new possibilities in parastatals. But I believe you should remain in diplomacy. You have a flair and a talent for it and we shall need an army of skilled diplomats.'

I was filled with trepidation. 'Exile again Buti?' He burst out laughing. 'No, Lindiwe, we will all be with you out there, without leaving our posts!' As always, OR had a way with words, a turn of phrase that could completely disarm. Now that Sis Adelaide has gone to join him, I feel their presence even more strongly in my diplomatic assignment from the ANC and my government.

Just a few days later, before I embarked on a weekend trip to visit my brother in Pietermaritzburg, Sis Adelaide sent for me. I found her busy massaging OR's back to release some phlegm. The moment she saw me Sis Adelaide shouted 'Look, look Papa, she's wearing my dress!' OR puzzled, looked at me, then looked at Adelaide, and then I said, 'You know what

99

Buti, I've had this dress for three years. Over the years people kept on gossiping about Sis Adelaide's habits of giving you something and then the next day claiming that it was hers and I've been wearing it for three years, but it's still hers!' Buti looked at Sis Adelaide and looked back at me and almost as if speaking to himself asked, 'But, is it true?' I protested at the solidarity and bonding against me and we all laughed together. The next day, OR passed on and from then on all my conversations with Sis Adelaide would end with '. . . But, is it true?'

As shock gripped every person in our country and the world, I remembered with a particular poignancy Sis Adelaide's words on the telephone in Washington DC: 'Lindiwe, Papa says you must come home for Chris's funeral or you will be sorry for the rest of your life!' Had I not obeyed that instruction, I don't know how I could have lived with myself thereafter:

> Then you fell into the wakeless sleep
> Where we cannot reach to touch
> With all our cravings
> And yet you did return
> You found the hand of Thabo
> Pouring out his orphaned heart
> Trembling
> It flowed over flowed
> Letting streams of grief
> Drench all those pages
> Then you moved
> Moved over to your son numbed by the gash
> Your absence left
> Moving him
> You moved
> Looked over his shoulder
> When suddenly
> The poet in you stopped stark
> Thought
> Looking over the same shoulder again
> Stopped
> Slowly pulled off your glasses
> To see better.

There you stood perplexed
In childlike awe
Your eyes flashed back and forth
From side to side
With the swiftness of any mamba
You were again a child in awe
For verily
Your very own son
Scripted
As none else ever could
That oration
Sealed
Insured
From heart to heart
As your Chief
Pensive
Slowly walked off
To that lucky horizon without end

WE NEED OUR HISTORY

Winnie Madikizela-Mandela
(extracts from an interview with Lindiwe Mabuza)

Lindiwe Mabuza (LM): I want to start right away by asking you about the Mbizana district. That's where Oliver Tambo was born and that's your birthplace as well.

Winnie Madikizela-Mandela (WM): You want to know about our background, our roots, what it was like growing up there in Mbizana?

LM: Yes. The landscape, the pictures, the things that influenced the personalities you both became.

WM: I think it has to do not only with the beautiful geography of that part of the Eastern Cape. But also a great deal to do with our cultural upbringing. We had so much in common. We came from exactly the same village [Kantolo].

WM: So when I ultimately met OR in Johannesburg, we always revisited our home spiritually and we had so much in common. He adopted me as his own daughter because of our cultural upbringing. We came from Bizana, the proud Pondo warriors, of the day. We were born into traditional Pondoland where a child was born not to parents, but into the community. Some people could not understand why we meant so much to the masses, but it's because a child is born into the community, into the tribe. There was no such thing as an individual child and our upbringing was a communal thing. Although the family was extremely important in the sense that it was the nucleus of the tribe, and then the nucleus of the nation. There was such unity in the family that all the mothers had the responsibility of grooming the children as members of society.

LM: For me, the importance of understanding that philosophical world, that cultural environment, is in relation to Oliver Tambo becoming the father of the organisation [the ANC]. Every member of the organisation became a member of his family. You know, because of that I couldn't say President, I would say Buti.

WM: Exactly. Nowadays people would not understand why. You see, during his leadership, there could never ever be cliques. There could never be camps because of that common background we came from. He could never entertain any type of criticism of others. OR had this ability to keep us together, those of us who were underground, and those of us who were operating internally, during extremely difficult times. At the mere mention of OR's name, you stood at attention. You automatically waited for an order.

LM: He was the Commander-in-Chief.

WM: His name you knew. No matter how dangerous an order they had given you, if it was for OR, you never questioned it. Because you knew it was genuine, it was honest, it was sincere. He was so unbelievably selfless. To the extent that it would have actually been a danger to himself, being so selfless. He would never think of himself in any regard.

LM: Can I just go back a little bit. The whole of South Africa heard when OR got his First Class pass, surpassing white students sitting for the same exams. What was your reaction to that? How did it inspire you? You probably were one of the few women out of Mbizana to have gone as high as you did with your education. Was OR an inspiration?

WM: He was this amazing inspiration to us all. I grew up knowing of Oliver Tambo at home because my father knew him. And my mother was the school principal, so in her teaching, she would tell us about this brilliant student, this child called Oliver. When we heard he'd made it, all of us walked tall because of him. I had never identified with any human being as I do with him to this day. You just claim him and the mere mention of his name brings such pride within you.

LM: Tell me about arriving in Johannesburg.

WM: When I came to Johannesburg as a young girl I'd never been on a train in my life. My father entrusted me to one of the miners who was going to the gold mines. This miner, Gikiza, had been working on his fields, my father's fields, before, and then he decided that, you know, he wanted to go and try his luck in Johannesburg, in the gold mines. My father gave me ten shillings for my pocket money. I had never owned ten shillings in my life. And I went to do my social work studies.

LM: When did you first meet Sis Adelaide?

WM: In 1953 I stayed in a girl's hostel, run by a Mrs Bruce. It was for black girls – the Helping Hand Hostel. So I met Matlala [Adelaide] there. She just liked me and there I was, a student in social work while she was a beauty queen nursing sister. You know, Sis Adelaide, you would end up even washing her feet. Without realising it. She would talk so sweetly to you, and you literally ran her errands. She would be sitting down and you would do everything.

LM: Like a matron.

WM: She's always been that duchess. She has always been that matron. And she did that at the Helping Hand. And she didn't do that with me alone. She used to command all of us young girls. It was nothing for her. That one must go and polish her shoes, that one must go and get her something. And we used to.

LM: But you did it with delight.

WM: We loved her. And she got to a point where she would make me change. She said my appearance wasn't appropriate. And because it was Adelaide, I would.

LM: You had to be well groomed.

WM: You had to be well groomed before Matlala. On one occasion she made me wash my face because I had applied the wrong make-up to my eyebrows. And she said: "Go and wash that thing off your face. You look terrible." She was like that. And, of course, when Sis Adelaide was with Oliver, she would groom herself, my dear. She was a picture of perfection. She was so immaculate. The stockings she wore, the type of shoes, must match the outfit. She has always been like that.

LM: But she has always had this love for others.

WM: She has this amazing love. She doesn't even know you but she assumes responsibility for you.

LM: It is the same quality that you talked about Oliver having.

WM: Yes. That is why that union was blessed in heaven.

LM: How fortunate to have found people like that. Tell me, when did you actually meet Oliver?

WM: The first time I heard the combination of the name Mandela and Tambo was from our schoolteachers in 1949 when there was a train disaster. And then later on we heard again that the OR we knew from home was now working with a Mandela in Johannesburg. I was a high school student. And we actually had held a strike at school, where we demonstrated against the conditions in the school. That is when the name of OR really started in my mind. Because, as the children were screaming against the school administration, the older teachers from Fort Hare explained to us that we have leaders in our country – Mandela and Tambo. And they're in Johannesburg. You must understand that our people are fighting for their rights. So that's when we learnt of this Mandela and Tambo. So when Sis Adelaide spoke about them one day, I already knew of them.

LM: So she brought up the name.

WM: Yes, she brought up the name. She told me of this Tambo. So I said, I know him. Because we're from the same place. One day I was in Park Station with Sis Adelaide. She was meeting Oliver Tambo. From there, we went to Oliver Tambo's office in Fox Street and met Mandela.

LM: His partner.

WM: His partner. But that is not what we are talking about. When we were in the offices, OR would monitor me. And he was the one who coined my name Nomzamo. Oliver knew my father.

LM: Really?

WM: Nomzamo comes from my real name Zanyiwe, from which OR coined Nomzamo. That's how I become Nomzamo. It is not in my ID.

LM: Nomzamo was not given to you by your parents.

WM: No. It was OR who coined it for easy pronunciation..

LM: 'Mother of struggle'...

WM: Yes. I am Zanyiwe. Nomzamo is mother of struggle. But what OR coined is the name that stuck.

LM: Nomzamo.

WM: Because it was easier for him. Instead of saying Zanyiwe he said Zami, and then we ended up with Nomzamo

LM: You must hold it very close. That's your identity now.

WM: He is so dear to me. Not even my biological father evokes the same love in me as OR. Because here I was, a young girl, in the heart of the Transvaal [now Gauteng], and he just took over as a parent just as Adelaide had already started. It was an umbilical cord type of relationship. And it reminded me of that very traditional background we came from.

LM: It's a relationship that is stronger than blood ties. And then you add the struggle dimension to this . . .

WM: Yes, the struggle dimension comes to it. Only if you had had that kind of background, would you be so loved. So, I battle to put it into words. I get so emotional about the struggle, it's not mine as an individual . . .

LM: It is ours.

WM: It is that background I came from. That community that made me. It was never mine alone. It could never be an individual. And OR never led as an individual.

LM: Go back to the law firm. You saw OR in operation. What is your assessment of him and his role in that firm?

WM: OR was a great thinker. And when a client walked into OR's office, you know, you could see the heavy load on the client's shoulders literally melting when he spoke to OR. Because he was that sort of person. He made you feel so safe.

LM: He would take care of you.

WM: And he didn't have to tell you. It was in his eyes, his expressions, his humbleness. You just felt: I'm protected here; I'm safe.

LM: We all had that experience.

WM: But what hurts, is that we never told him. We, who were in that crossfire, ducking and diving bullets, we wanted to say so much to him. You know, had it not been for him we wouldn't have had that courage to go on; the more difficult the going was, the more he propelled us to go on and on. You just had to think of OR and you knew you could undertake any task. He exuded an amazing amount of strength that was all embracing and, above all, you felt it was so honest. You felt you could never be in danger under OR.

LM: I could never let him down.

WM: And I could never do an about turn. I could never betray him. I could never do anything he would be ashamed of. That's what happened when clients walked in there. They felt their problems were solved and he would spend so much time, so much time on people. And as a lawyer, there are really few who will measure up to what OR meant to the people of this country. His genius, in law, and his intellectual ability was beyond description.

LM: You know, you were saying that it was a pity that we never told him. Maybe those of us who were with him outside could have told him. He would never give you the opportunity to do that. Because it was not about himself.

WM: He always said that. He said that to Zeni so many times, 'It's not about me. Your father and all those who are on Robben Island, should have been here to receive this. Remember, always, that I'm not here receiving it all on my behalf, it is for your father.' My goodness. How many people are humble enough to say: I don't want this recognition. He told Zeni, our eldest daughter, that she was 'Acting President' of the ANC for as long as her father was on Robben Island. He would add that he was President by default! That was the most amazing OR, if you contrast that to today's vicious succession debate. The unassuming OR did not care for power, for power's sake. The Freedom Charter's 'The People Shall Govern' was sacrosanct to him. Even to me, he would say he was Acting President because the people of South Africa did not elect him but the leadership in exile did.

LM: He would say: 'Not for me, but for Nelson Mandela and all the political prisoners.' Would you say, Winnie, that he actually created Nelson Mandela?

WM: Of course.

LM: Nelson Mandela was an icon when he went to jail inside the country. And it is through the international campaign that he got to be known internationally.

WM: Yes. You see this is the mistake that is very often made. It is not actually the men and women who sat in prison as such, who made our country what it is today. It was the sustained campaigns and a decision to say that Mandela would then be used, a deliberate decision was made. Mandela would be used as a symbol of resistance, a symbol of the ANC internationally so that people could focus on the ANC through this particular name. The ANC has always been all about the collectivity and centrality of the leadership of the people's popular movement. As such, there ought not be individualism which leads to autocracy. The masses will always remove such a leader in whatever manner necessary, no matter how long it takes them – OR knew that and preached that.

LM: Could it have been another man?

WM: It could have been Sisulu, it could have been Duma Nokwe, who is hardly remembered today. It was all those people on Robben Island. It was the campaigns of those women and the children of 1976 who said: 'This far and no further.' But had it not been for the sustained campaigns led by Oliver Tambo then those campaigns I've mentioned within the country, would have remained in the country itself, because apartheid was too harsh. Had it not been for OR, and other great men and women, the ANC would not have been where it is today. If he had not been there, if he had not led us from outside, very few of us would have survived.

LM: You were a leader yourself. You inspired us all the time within and out of jail. You were banished to Brandfort. What did it mean to get messages from OR over these difficult days?

WM: He was a mentor to me and he monitored me even in Brandfort. He telephoned me monthly at a public phone. It was at the time 051 999 Brandfort. He sought me out wherever I was. The very first contact I had from the outside world was from him. I broke down. I said, 'Buti, what do I do now? I am here, I cannot speak the language, they have banished me to this area. I don't know if you know where Zenani is? I'm with Zindzi. What do I do?' Then OR said, 'Zami history provides. Do not do anything. History will provide a situation for you to react. Do not say anything. Remember that always in life. Sit when times are difficult, and just wait there. History will come to rescue you. You will get guidance from within, from yourself.' And I adopted that attitude from that day. I don't react to any crisis. I just wait for history to take its course. And I know I will be guided.

LM: I know that during this same period there were lots of visitors. Some visitors came to you with messages. Did you get any messages from the Tambos, from maybe members of church organisations, or journalists who were passing by?

WM: I didn't get just a few. Amazingly enough, dangerous as that situation was, I got hundreds and hundreds of messages. Matlala was one extremely vociferous link. She would write letters via a law firm and the letters reached me. I had a lot of visitors from the Christian fraternity, from the international community and, of course, from democratic formations that were banned at the time. People also came as individuals. I remember Trevor Manuel. He was a boy from Cape Town and he used to come and visit. And there was one politician who visited me under those very difficult circumstances. That was Helen, Helen Suzman. She braved it, and she came to see me in Brandfort quite a few times.

LM: Our questions have ranged over quite a large landscape. To get back to the present, recently Johannesburg International Airport was renamed after OR, the man who has been our gateway to the world. React to that. What do you think?

WM: Frankly I thought it was long overdue. I was so overjoyed and at the same time so disappointed that we were doing that only now. I think that, as far as I'm concerned, OR deserves so much more. OR deserves to be re-membered. As far as I'm concerned, in his own village, Kantolo, we should have a monument of OR. And I think we could have done something more in Mbizana to remember OR's name. Because he is the father of the strug-gle, the father of democracy in this country. He is the man we should hon-our and venerate as being responsible for the fact that the leaders from Rob-ben Island, from all the prisons, were able to come out and still lead the country to freedom. It was because of OR. No one could have kept the ANC together the way OR did. No one could have led us to freedom the way OR did – unassumingly and without any recognition. He didn't want it. But I think we owe it to his legacy to at least honour him more than we are doing so that future generations do not forget OR and so that it never happens again, that, post-revolution, history consumes its heroes.

LM: With that, I think we have come to the end of our conversation. And what a conversation. What revelations. Thank you so much.

WM: I am so glad to have had this opportunity. I and so many people of my generation haven't had opportunities like this. This history is something you can capture for future generations. Because I think our children often don't even know who I'm talking about. We need our history to be recorded.

OR TAMBO
INTERNATIONAL AIRPORT

Nelson Mandela
(remarks made on the renaming of the airport
in Johannesburg, 27 October 2006)

'In December 1990 Oliver returned to South Africa, having been in exile from his native land for three decades. It was wonderful to have him near.'

That is a quote. I wrote those words in *Long Walk to Freedom*.

The words are coming back to me strongly tonight. The day was a Thursday, the 13th of December, 1990, a summer's day in South Africa. I was of course among those there to meet OR, along with our comrades.

We sat and spoke in the back of a motor car for a while before Oliver, who was very frail by then, got out to acknowledge the thunderous welcome of the crowds that had gathered. I had the honour to tell those crowds: 'Our President wishes to say he is happy to be home.'

I remember the widest grin on Oliver's face as the crowd erupted. I remember also that Oliver had said, while I was still in prison: 'The moment of our freedom will come in the lifetime of Nelson and myself.' He was not to savour that moment of freedom in the way he deserved.

What I have not said so far is where we were; where the homecoming of Oliver Reginald Tambo occurred.

It was here, at an airport then called Jan Smuts, in a country not yet liberated, but certain it would be. Commentators at the time noted that this was the largest welcoming crowd ever to gather at Johannesburg's airport –

much larger than that which greeted Hendrik Verwoerd on his return from the Commonwealth Conference of 1961. And so it should have been, and so it was.

At Oliver's funeral, in Johannesburg on the 2nd of May 1993, just a year before the elections that marked the victory of the struggle for democracy in our land, I delivered a eulogy in which I said, 'Oliver has not died – because the struggle for freedom and justice lives.' I also said: 'We will not fail you.'

And so here we are tonight to celebrate the renaming of this airport in honour of a South African hero, an African hero, a world hero.

I close by saying this. In 1990 Oliver returned to South Africa. It was wonderful to have him near. In 2006 we bring him near again. And that is wonderful.

I thank you.

AN UNSURPASSED CONTRIBUTION

Joe Matthews

Oliver Tambo arrived in London during April 1960 and immediately set about laying the foundation for what would eventually develop into a formidable international solidarity movement against apartheid. He always believed that the efforts of the people of South Africa and their liberation movement had to be completed by an international movement that would take steps to isolate the apartheid regime.

The choice of London as the base of the international effort was deliberate. London was the metropolis for a worldwide group of nations that were formerly and were still parts of an empire. Communications of all kinds were unrivalled. In addition, there was a huge constituency of South Africans and British sympathisers who were only too willing to assist in any anti-apartheid effort.

At the outset Oliver Tambo, together with Dr Yusuf Dadoo of the South African Indian Congress set up the SAUF. This operated from offices in the Strand that were previously occupied by Krishna Menon when he was campaigning for the independence of India.

The campaigns of the SAUF at the UN and in Europe occurred during the State of Emergency in South Africa that saw almost the entire leadership of the ANC imprisoned. The State of Emergency was lifted at the end of August 1960. The SAUF scored a major success in 1961, during the Commonwealth Heads of Government meeting in London. Persistent lobbying had produced a groundswell of opposition to South Africa's continued membership among Asian and African member states. They succeeded in winning the support of Canada. At the conference Hendrik Verwoerd announced that South Africa was withdrawing from the Commonwealth. The first significant act of international isolation. The SAUF disbanded later that year and the External Mission of the ANC was established to organise the international solidarity movement against apartheid.

The ANC moved to Africa Unity House, which had been provided by Nkrumah's Ghana to house African and Caribbean liberation movements. Oliver Tambo appointed Raymond Kunene as the ANC Chief Representative in London.

Oliver also supervised the change of the committee for the boycott of South African goods into the AAM with the active help of Vella Pillay and Abdul Minty and many others too numerous to mention.

In 1961 the Treason Trial, which had begun in 1956 with the arrest of 156 accused, had sputtered to an inglorious end with the acquittal of all the remaining accused. The Treason Trial Fund organised by Canon John Collins of St Paul's Cathedral worked with Oliver Tambo to transform into the IDAF. This fund developed into a huge arm of the international solidarity movement against apartheid with funds and humanitarian aid, which came largely from the Scandinavian countries, Sweden in particular. The Oliver Tambo network extended to the UN Committee on Apartheid with Mr Enuga Reddy as its tireless executive.

Even with his prodigious energy Oliver sometimes had to rest. His favourite hideaway was the Community of the Resurrection at Mirfield. There he would be surrounded by familiar Fathers who had established the famous secondary school at St Peter's in Rosettenville, Johannesburg, where he had received his secondary education and also taught mathematics and science to scholars for many years.

The Fathers, who included such famous names as Bishop Trevor Huddleston, were well known symbols of the Church Militant in their unstinting opposition to the racist policies of the apartheid regime. A weekend at Mirfield was sufficient to galvanise Oliver into a further burst of political activity.

One of the happiest moments for Oliver in London in 1962 was an unexpected visit from Nelson Mandela who had illegally left South Africa to travel to Britain and to Africa. The meeting in London and their subsequent joint visit to Nigeria and Ethiopia were memorable events. The fact that Mandela was arrested on his return to South Africa and incarcerated for almost three decades lent special poignancy to these meetings.

Adelaide Tambo had joined Oliver in London and they set up their home, but the arrests of the entire leadership at Rivonia in 1963 and the life sentences imposed at the Rivonia Trial meant that henceforth Oliver became a commuter between London and the various headquarters of the ANC in Tanzania and Zambia. As the struggle developed his visits to London became more and more infrequent as he now assumed leadership of the entire struggle for liberation.

But the networks established by Oliver Tambo and his colleagues in London took root and grew to become formidable instruments in the international solidarity movement against apartheid. The complementary structures that he built in Africa from 1964 onwards were to be the decisive factor that brought the evil system of apartheid to an end. In both cases the contribution of the indefatigable Oliver Tambo was unsurpassed.

AN ORDINARY HUMAN BEING

Zanele Mbeki

In this contribution, Zanele Mbeki, through an interview with Lindiwe Mabuza, reflects on Oliver Tambo, the man, the leader, and the meaning of his life. Of necessity, Mabuza asks Ms Mbeki about how she became politicised and what the name Oliver Tambo and other leaders meant to her youth. By focusing on OR in the domestic sphere and moments of silence in his peripatetic life enforced on him by his role as a leader of the ANC and a Commander of MK, an apparently low-key conversation offers us glimpses of OR's life as a political and private man.

Interestingly, Ms Mbeki also links domestic situations with political situations in ways that activists of the women's movements from the 1960s onwards have sought to do. Looking at OR's self-representation, humility, meticulous approach to his work and his concern for the well-being of the larger ANC family as well as his own family unit, provides a rare glimpse into aspects of his life which have not been fully recorded.

Lindiwe Mabuza (LM): Zanele, thank you so much for having this conversation around Oliver Tambo, one of the greatest icons of South Africa. Let me start by asking you about your reaction to the renaming of Johannesburg International Airport to OR Tambo International. How do you feel about this?

Zanele Mbeki (ZM): You know when I heard the news of the renaming of Johannesburg airport after OR Tambo, I followed the radio discussions intellectually; I felt that it was the right thing to do, but I had no emotional reaction towards an outcome. Because of other commitments I did not attend the actual renaming ceremony. However, soon after the event, I went to Cape Town. Driving to the airport I saw the OR Tambo International Airport motorway billboards and I suddenly got goose pimples everywhere. The depth of feeling came a few days later. As he was preparing the passengers for landing back in Johannesburg an air steward matter-of-factly announced that we were landing at OR Tambo International Airport. My eyes just filled with tears. It was very, very emotional for me. The emotion grew stronger on the ground when I saw this huge poster of OR watching me walk in. Even though I'd only been to

Cape Town, I felt as though I was returning to South Africa for the first time from exile; that this was my true home coming. I came to understand the feelings of people who kiss the ground upon landing. The moment was at once political, private and personal. It also made me understand the shrill protests of those opposing apartheid name changes. Historical apartheid figures that are being replaced are part of their souls as OR is part of mine.

LM: I think it is also so emotional because it brings to mind the greatness of OR, which has not fully been recognised. Because first of all, during the struggle, he couldn't be quoted. People could hear him on the ANC's Radio Freedom, but nothing written by him was available to people except through the underground structures. And suddenly, now, he is a public figure. Our Minister of Foreign Affairs says that OR was South Africa's gateway to the world. And somehow the airport picks up on that.

ZM: Yes, you are so right. The intensity of emotion rises surreptitiously because in everyday life OR was never larger than life. His greatness did not overwhelm. He remained a very ordinary human being.

LM: When did you first know, hear or read about Oliver Tambo?

ZM: When I was growing up Oliver Tambo was not a big name in Alexandra township politics. I mean, as a schoolgirl in Alexandra the big names were Dr Dadoo, Kotane, Madzunya and Chief Luthuli. Tambo was himself still a young man, working in a law firm in Johannesburg with Mandela. In my circles Tambo and Mandela were known as people's defenders. As a university student I actually visited his law firm at Macosa House where I met with Mandela. Tambo was not there. I first met Tambo in London. By this time his reputation as the ANC international envoy was very well known.

LM: Not in Zambia when you were still working there?

ZM: I first went to Zambia in 1964, then left for London in 1966 and returned to Zambia again in 1974. In the early years (1964–66) I did not meet OR in Zambia because his visits were confined to Lusaka and Kitwe; I was stationed at the Nchanga mines in Chingola. His base at the time lay between Tanzania and London. It was in London that I met OR, through Mazisi Kunene.

LM: Mazisi was the Chief Representative of the ANC in the UK at the time, not so?

ZM: Yes. I was introduced to Mazisi very early upon arrival in 1966. I later came to know that Mazisi welcomed all South African newcomers to London. Through him I joined the Youth Section of the ANC and got to participate in its programmes. Hey, why am I talking about myself and not about OR?

LM: It's fine. You are talking about the youth, about your interactions with him.

ZM: Okay. Many of us became part of the ANC Youth Section. Doing what youth does. This would bring us closer to the leadership. The Youth Section included Thabo Mbeki, Pallo Jordan, Essop and Aziz Pahad, Sobizana Mngqikana, Thami Mhlambiso, Teresa Maimane and so on. One joined a group that had a much longer ANC political history than some of us who were informed mainly by student politics. One of the key people I met at this time was Mrs Adelaide Tambo through her open house for the ANC youth. I came to admire Sis Adelaide very much for her selfless struggle of bringing up her children virtually on her own while also doing both political and diplomatic work. She had very high hopes for the children. She placed them in expensive private schools. Asked why she should do this when there were less expensive state schools, she said, 'When I am in England where I can get the best education available for my children, why should I settle for less? In South Africa I could not do this.' In between her jobs and family responsibilities, Sis Adelaide constantly received international envoys and British anti-apartheid missions while also participating in the ANC programmes.

LM: Sometimes she was doing two jobs.

ZM: Yes. At one time she worked around eighteen hours a day because she had a day and a night job. It was then that I took a personal decision to be an aide to Sis Adelaide because I deeply appreciated that she had set OR free to lead our struggle. Thus my involvement with the Tambo family in London consisted of assisting Sis Tambo periodically by taking over some of her responsibilities around the children or the house. After my work day at Slough, in Buckinghamshire, I would travel to their house in London to be of assistance: babysit Tselane, clean the house, accompany Dali to Chichester, do some shopping, and so on.

LM: But it was a revolutionary contribution for you to help. You became like a sister to the children, you were a helpmate to Adelaide.

ZM: Yes, I reckoned that Sis Adelaide had set OR free to do national work that he could not avoid; an act which came at a cost on his time with the family. They all missed him. In some ways, the role that women such as Sis Adelaide played in the domestic sphere must be re-examined, especially when we look at the relationship between the personal and the political. By not affirming women's contribution at this level we fall into the trap of accepting the binary approach that says this is a political contribution and this is the private sphere and is therefore not taken into consideration.

Sis Adelaide was an activist in her own right and she played this role effectively. But by choosing to raise the children and look after the family, her children and other ANC members, she was making it possible for OR to be the leader he was.

There are many women in our struggle whose contribution has not been accorded its rightful place. These are women, mothers, who opened their homes and made it possible for young ANC exiles and leaders to have an address to fill in on their landing forms when they arrived in Zambia, Swaziland, Botswana and the UK.

In addition, their contribution remains difficult to quantify because in many ways they held the lives of young people together when they were far from home. The ANC could not have survived without these sacrifices and deep commitment to provide, guide and look after so many young people, and even leaders.

Here I am thinking of Mrs Tiny Nokwe, Mrs Winnie Nkobi, Mrs Pulane Ngcakane, Mrs Regina Nzo, Mrs Gertrude Shope, Mrs Ray Simons, Mrs Ntombi Mavuso, Mrs Sophie de Bruyn, Mrs Ruth Makiwane, Mrs Nomvuyo Masondo, Mrs Thandi Rankoe and Mrs Tikilili Mabizela.

If we view history from a narrow political perspective, we marginalise and erase many women's roles whose lives were not only tied to the ANC but who made tremendous contributions in keeping some kind of social fabric and safety net out there in exile. If our account of what is political and revolutionary does not address this, the historical narrative we are likely to produce will be based on gross misrepresentation.

And this is one of OR's qualities, his ability to bring people together, to make all people's contributions be seen for what they really were. In reflecting on OR, I would like to pay tribute to his inclusive sensitivity to different roles and different locations. No contribution was insignificant.

LM: Didn't Thabo live with the family when he was in London?

ZM: He did, but that was before I came to London. Thabo arrived four years before me. He was like a big brother to the children and an additional responsibility for Adelaide because he too depended on her as the children did. I remember once when we visited Muswell Hill, Tembi was very angry that her father was not there when she needed him (in fact she wanted a new pair of winter boots!). Thabo told her some story in an effort to placate her. This did not wash with Tembi because she reckoned his explanations could not deliver a pair of boots that she wanted before going back to school. Thabo was obliged to deliver as big brother!

LM: Although there were times when OR was around.

ZM: Of course; as often as he could be. On one occasion when OR was in London and Sis Adelaide could not accompany him to Tembi's school on Founder's Day, I went along with him. Upon arrival we joined all parents at the opening devotions at the school chapel. I was amazed at how familiar OR was with the English High Church service rituals and hymns. Knowing that he had just arrived from revolutionary Lusaka or Morogoro, I had expected the chapel environment to be alien to him; and here was this person who suddenly just blended in. He followed the prayers and music with ease and enjoyment. He even joined in with the English anthem 'God save our gracious queen'. And right there was, you know, Tambo the 'priest'.

LM: You had to have known then that he had actually wanted to be an Anglican priest.

ZM: Yes, but you get to hear many things and the reality still does not sink in. It is like the airport renaming story. To me OR the revolutionary leader of the ANC, the leader of MK, did not translate into a priest. It did not bring to mind a spiritual being. Hence the surprise when, suddenly, you find that the leader of all these firebrand revolutionaries is such a humble, pious, priestly man.

LM: How did you get your political education? In your student activities, in your interactions?

ZM: In retrospect, I was politicised by the living conditions of Alexandra township. Living in Alexandra and commuting daily to Wits University was itself a very big political education. Your sense of difference is heightened daily. You study by candlelight, wake up every day to make a fire in a coal stove to wash and emerge to dusty, smoke-filled streets where you join a long bus queue to get to Johannesburg's bright lights and flatland. At Wits your classmates are white, drive to school in brand new MGs, take overseas holidays, have parents who own factories. You interact with them, compete in studies and then hitch rides from them on fieldwork trips. At the end of the day you go to the Alexandra bus queue to go home to study by candle-light. That is political education at a personal level. This contrast stays in your mind daily. Alexandra has, however, always been a very political place. One grew up with the Bethal potato boycott, the prolonged Alexandra bus boy-cott, the ANC mobilisation marches every Sunday, and the emergence of the Madzunya and the PAC rallies at No. 1 square. I attended a primary school that was created by the ANC and led by teachers like the Messrs Tsele, Mosia and Pelie, families who anchored the ANC in Alexandra. At universi-ty one began to ground one's childhood thinking to theoretical foundations through vibrant debates with the PAC, NEUM, SOYA, UPDUSA, Congress of Democrats, ASA and ASUSA. It was a big ideological marketplace!

LM: Did you see OR often in Lusaka?

ZM: Almost every time he visited Zambia in the 1970s. For a long time OR did not have a permanent residence in Lusaka. This came later in the strug-gle. He very often shared collective accommodation with specific comrades at Makeni, a fair distance from Lusaka. Because our flat was on the way from the Lusaka airport to Makeni and the comrades who collected him from the airport may not have known his final destination they would drop him at our place. In the 1970s the ANC had very limited residential accommoda-tion and had access to very few cars. Therefore employed spouses with rent-ed homes provided transit accommodation for all comrades. This applied es-pecially to the homes of Mrs Nkobi, Mrs Nokwe and Mrs Ngcakane. Our flat just added to this pool. At that time Tambo's official space was a collec-tive ANC residence out of town in Makeni. The stopover at our flat was so that someone from Makeni would eventually collect him after completing their daily tasks or occasionally I would drive him there after work. At times I would come home from work and find OR in the spare room, usually reading. I can't think what conversations we had. I really can't – because we did not engage on anything political. In my absence Mr Mwanza, my house-keeper, would always be there to let OR in and attend to his needs. What would happen was that if Makeni colleagues were not able to pick him up I would do the driving. This was not encouraged because access to Mak-eni was restricted. One day, I arrived home and found OR sleeping in the spare room. When he woke up in the evening he wanted to go to Makeni.

It was raining quite heavily. We waited for Comrade Nxumalo to come and pick him up but Nxumalo did not arrive and so eventually OR asked me to take him. The flat/townhouse had huge sliding doors leading to the garden where my car was parked next to a big pine tree. The rain had stopped. As we approached the car we saw a small snake slithering across our path towards the car. I got a fright and stepped back; when I looked around for OR he was not there. I looked back into the house and saw him peeping [laughter] . . . from a half open door of the bedroom. He wanted me to deal with the snake. He would not come out. Also afraid to step out, I started looking for a stick around the house to sort the snake out. No luck. Eventually I took courage and got out into the driver's seat and hooted for him to come out. As we drove along I thought to myself how ironic it was that this great revolutionary of the South African struggle, a leader who was taking on the whole of apartheid South Africa, was afraid of a little snake. It is the ordinariness of the people leading our struggle that I find so amazing and reassuring. He was an ordinary human being, retaining childhood phobias – a small snake being one of them. We laughed a lot about it.

LM: Tell me about the relationship between Thabo and OR.

ZM: Thabo worked with OR a lot, especially in terms of intellectual production. Thabo gets things down on paper very easily. He gets started and moves on. OR by contrast struggled, probably because of his self-criticism and drive for perfection. He would fill a wastepaper basket with discarded formulations. Thabo and OR would sit talking for hours on end – before speech writing began. Thabo would mostly be absorbing the gist of OR's message. (During that time we had no computers in the ANC. We depended on manual typewriters.) OR was very careful with his language. He did not like jargon in his speeches and therefore would not hesitate to return a draft four or five times for the correction of words and formulations. If inappropriate formulations appeared, the speech would be typed all over again. The 'delete' and 'insert' technology of the computer age did not exist. The to and fro of draft rewrites required a dedicated team of drivers, typists and proofreaders.

LM: He was such a perfectionist. Do you remember any of his speeches in particular?

ZM: His speech to the ANC Women's Section in Angola (1987) during the National Union of Mineworkers' strike was memorable. I remember also his press conference in Nairobi in 1985 at the UN Women's Conference. He was there with SWAPO President Sam Nujoma. OR defined to the world's media the struggle for women's emancipation as the struggle not of women alone, but that of men and women in society. Society as a whole had to be challenged. This was an important intervention where even women radical feminists attempted to appropriate the women's struggle. I often draw strength from his positions and his example.

LM: Yes, he used to take the emotion out of a situation.

ZM: There was a meeting of the ANC Youth Section in 1979 in London. We were discussing the visit of Dr Mangosuthu Buthelezi and the issue of the Bantustans. The Youth Section wanted to organise a demonstration against Buthelezi's visit. OR called us in for a meeting to discuss our concerns. He listened and listened and listened. At the end, he said: 'You know, you occupy a particular position as young people of the struggle. I am impressed with your concerns and you are correct to take issue with the Bantustans and their leaders. It is your right as young people to do so. We are not stopping you from demonstrating and expressing your views on the Bantustans. But I am not a young person. I am a leader of the ANC. The ANC wants to achieve unity for the South African people. Buthelezi represents a large section of the South African people and we have to work with him and others to see how we can get to a position that is correct and that is for all our people.' I mean, he used words to that effect. He was talking about the responsibilities of leadership in a national movement; making us understand how he as the leader of the ANC had to hold discussions with Dr Buthelezi; to try to sort out problems between various opposing organisations for the sake of all the people in our country. It was a salutary lesson for many of the Young Turks.

LM: He was so good at calming the waters.

ZM: On another occasion there was much contestation of views within the ANC when those who came to be called the Group of Eight questioned ANC decisions on membership. Before their expulsion from the organisation there were continuous discussions revolving around the impending inclusion of different national groups – Indians, coloureds and whites – into full ANC membership. This approach was resisted by some and supported by many. OR and Mzwai Piliso came to London from Tanzania to calm the waters. Many platforms were provided to discuss these issues. There was so much debate and people were taking different and very strong positions. A person would seem at one time to be on both sides of the debate; saying one thing at one meeting and the opposite at another. As a group of young people we detected what we thought was dishonesty from one such leader. So a group of us thought that it was important for us to inform OR what was happening; what was dishonestly said and by whom.

LM: Where did you see him?

ZM: I think it was at his home in Muswell Hill. We went to see OR. He listened carefully and quietly. Then, finally, he said to us: 'And what did you say to him? Did you confront him for his duplicity?' Nobody said a word. He asked again: 'What did you say when people were saying all of these things?' Again there was silence. Then he commented: 'I think it is your responsibility, all of you, to defend the organisation when it is under attack from anybody. Do not come and report to me what others are saying. Rather you must tackle any wrongdoing where you see it and whenever you come across it.' He was forthright. He discouraged storytelling by self-styled informers even when it was to his support.

LM: He was such a principled man. And that was part of the way he educated us, by correcting our mistakes all the time.

ZM: Yes.

LM: Can you comment on the relationship of OR and Thabo and Johnny [Makathini]? They were such a close-knit threesome in terms of international mobilisation.

ZM: You know, it is strange that you should ask that. I was with Shukti Naidoo, Phyllis Naidoo's daughter, a few weeks ago. She was talking about how she never realised the greatness of so many people of the struggle that she interacted with at her home until long after they were gone. She lived with all those people simply as uncles and brothers who came and went; now she wishes that she had listened more and absorbed a whole lot more from them. I feel the same about OR and Johnny, in particular, as well as others. I probably took OR and Johnny for granted because I lived with them in a sort of domestic fashion. It is easier for me to talk about their food tastes, music preferences and clothing styles, even their social likes and dislikes. Many comrades were embarrassed when OR sent them back home for a change of clothes if he was not impressed with their outfits when they constituted part of his delegation. He was a stickler for neatness and formality. OR preferred a very simple diet and drank weak, black tea. He loved music and poetry. He listened especially to South African music and, as you know, got involved in the rearrangement and new lyrics for ANC songs and Amandla music. I have snippets of poetic correspondence between OR and Mazisi Kunene from the early 1970s. Johnny started talking as he walked into the house. He was loquacious. They held very late night discussions on all sorts of issues internal and external to the ANC. They were interdependent in crafting ANC positions on internal, national and international matters. I think that Thabo was a great beneficiary of their thoughts and insights which they shared and hoped he would capture in his writings.

LM: Was OR at your wedding?

ZM: No, he wasn't. The evening reception was at his house and his whole family was there, but he had to be somewhere else. When I think of OR as a leader, I do not have an image of a towering giant. Not like a Kaunda or a Nyerere who stand out because I saw them only as public figures who made speeches and changed societies. With OR I was not there for most his public political speeches and even organisational meetings. I always saw him afterwards in a more domestic setting at review time. Yet there is no question of his impact; a steadfastly amazing man who was at the helm of the ANC. I remember how hard he worked. I was on part of his journey when he, Tshwete, Maduna, Modise, Thabo and others travelled through nine countries in ten days canvassing for the Harare Declaration. He participated fully in the detailed drafting process the night before the trip. The drafting took place in our flat with Maduna on the computer. When we got to Zimbabwe the next day he was preoccupied with the diplomatic and logistical details, seeking and confirming flights and landing permission for the borrowed plane; personally reconfirming appointments with regional heads of state. At 4:00 a.m. when all were fast asleep, he called me to reconfirm various logistical arrangements for the next stop in Angola. I don't think that he slept that night. I remember his patience, his humanity, the way he agonised both about substantive political issues as well as about mundane concerns of the ordinary membership in the Lusaka ANC community. He would respond to their general but frustrated welfare needs and help to solve non-political problems including purchasing a supply of baby nappies.

LM: Yes, all the people were his children. Thank you so much, Zanele, for sharing your rich recollections with us.

THANK YOU TATA

Baleka Mbete

This tribute to Oliver Tambo was commissioned by the ANC Women's League. It was written and presented on 31 October 1998.

Here we are
in the company
of your presence
made so palpable
by your absence.
Since your Departure
we have tried in
our individual corners
of pain to grapple with
memory which sticks
to us like our very skins.

We have missed you in this strange place
called freedom to which
you personally delivered us
We wish to dance
to your life
to say Thank You
for letting the hippos

and the crocodiles of
the Zambezi know the
touch of the skin
of an MK cadre
know our song and
the smell of our fear

Our tears have dried
into silver stripes
into lines of seasons
which point to our past
which in turn must point
to the future
Uncle Mark in bidding
us farewell said we must
remember where we have come from

Tata you tricked us
that morning lying
on that bed a
Mona Lisa smile lingering
around your gentle face
as if still about to
caress our eager hungry souls
only to find things had changed
It was not to be like
the other morning
when we all rushed to
your bedside
which turned out to be
the rendezvous with
the last smile from
Comrade Chris Hani.
That morning we were
greeted by your easy smile
which carried our relief
that we could still hold
your warm guiding hand

As I've said Tata
this place called freedom
is strange a
strangeness made stranger
by your absence
when through decades
of desert times
our eyes were glued
to your head in the air
your erect back marching
leading us through thunderstorms
kneading us into a dough.
We will never know why
your eye never touched the cake.

You taught us to be upright
to work hard,
to be proud in humility
you told us
we had to look good
not to take nonsense from
anyone even when some
of us meandered through
years of statelessness
as if we had no country,
You led the way as we
wandered, waded and swam
over mountains, mud and
across rivers to reach
tonight to listen
to the echo from Mulungushi
and Morogoro, Dakawa,
Iringa, Uganda, Angola,
How can I ever
mention them all
'Koba njani sesihleli no Tambo'
Little did we know
that tonight you would
look at us from across
in the land of our ancestors

Tata tonight I wish
I were a poet
I would summon a giant
river of words to match
the monument you are.
Here I stand
I tremble at the feet
of my wish to find
the words to resurrect
your gentle eloquence
through your eye
through your voice
so many times we need it
here to tell the world
where we have come from
Uncle Mark said we must
never forget that
so we always know
where we are going

Tata, I wish I could
be a painter
I would pluck all
the colour from everywhere
I would scoop up gallons
nay barrels of seawater
suck colours from
the trees and flowers
I'd even reach out for
the blue of the sky
so I could fill up
dams with different
colours to paint a
mural across the land
so the women of this
nation can ululate
their salute to your
distinct voice which
rose to be counted and
heard as the debates

rolled and raged
through the forties
Let the women be
mobilised and organised!
Let equal membership
be theirs as much as
humanity is theirs!
the ANC Women's League was born!

I would carefully select
colours fitting in texture
and brilliance to paint
symphonies of music
whose notes would leap
swing and sway with
the volume tempo and rhythm
suited to our celebration
of the hope you hammered
out of years of people's
struggle for liberation.

From Angola you reminded
the woman's place is in
the struggle as indeed
the lives of many heroines
had told us
from Maxeke to Ngoyi and
countless others whose
brave and determined deeds
remain an articulate statement

The rolling drums of memories
summoned by your presence
here tonight will bolster
our longing and resolve
THANK YOU
for bringing us here
to this place called freedom
THANK YOU
for your presence here tonight.

AS I REMEMBER HIM

Rita Mfenyana

Execution of Solomon Mahlangu, 6 April 1979

The ANC community in Lusaka gathered before sunrise in Lilanda, the ANC residence. We were quiet and tense. Somehow there was hope that at the last moment Solomon Mahlangu would not be hanged. We were seated on the benches under the dark sky, partially covered by flimsy corrugated iron sheets.

Only Comrade OR (as we generally called him) was at the front table, facing us. As dawn broke, a telephone rang somewhere inside the house. Somebody came out and whispered into OR's ear. He raised his head towards us and said: 'They have done it; they have killed him!' There was pain and dejection in his face; the burden was too heavy. We all gasped. Oh! Many cried. Then the singing of hymns and freedom songs started.

Nkomati Accord, February 1984

A meeting was called at the Makeni residence where the Department of Information and Publicity was, formerly Dr Randeree's house. It was mostly the Mgwenya, the older generation MK cadres. I cannot remember what the agenda was, but there were strong rumours that OR would be there. The mood in Lusaka amongst the ranks was quietly tense. Some enemy agents had been discovered. Lusaka was in a state of continuous alert. We had been advised not to sleep at our places; to go to our Zambian friends; to leave the town; to sleep outside of the house, maybe in the car, within a short distance, or even go for a night drive.

Comrade Mzwai Piliso was chairing. He talked about generalities and people hardly listened. Then OR came from inside the house to join Mzwai. He told us that there was some important information.

He said that the pressure of the apartheid regime was too strong. Our friends were suffering; their countries were collapsing. Samora Machel, on behalf of the government of Mozambique, had signed a peace agreement with South Africa in a place called Nkomati. We could no longer operate in Mozambique or even be there. Our presence was to be reduced to ten people at the ANC office. Our people would be moved from Mozambique to other places, some to Lusaka.

A cry of disbelief and anger followed. 'Sell-outs! They have betrayed us! We will fix them, we will teach FRELIMO a lesson.' Without raising his voice, OR calmed us. He spoke about the sacrifices of the Front-line States, of Africa, in support of our struggle. He said that we could not expect, we did not want, the demise of these young independent states. We would continue the struggle, and we would win. We would not turn against our friends and allies. That was what the enemy wanted. Then he said: 'Sometimes I think that our situation will be resolved differently, not through the destruction . . .' We were depressed and puzzled. The meeting soon dispersed, without the usual barrage of complaints about supplies and the Regional Political Committee inefficiency.

Then people started arriving from Mozambique. Some were sent to East Africa (Morogoro in Tanzania). The trained cadres went to Angola.

The man himself
OR had a unique ability to find something useful and constructive in his discussions with anyone. At times it would be a character known for unruly behaviour, for continuous complaints, real riff-raff and social misfits, waylaying him in the yard of the ANC headquarters in Lusaka. OR would stop and listen attentively, and would always find some potential gems of information in whatever the person had to say. He was a truly inspirational leader.

A MAN OF MANY TALENTS

Sindiso Mfenyana

Whatever strengths and influence the ANC had in 1956–57 to myself as an ANC Youth League matric student in a rural college, faced with taunts from a rival youth organisation about us selling the country by declaring that South Africa belongs to 'black and white', my abiding faith stemmed from the fact that the ANC leadership included the top black lawyers in the country Oliver Tambo, Nelson Mandela and Advocate Duma Nokwe.

I worked under Mandela and Nokwe for the entire year of 1961, and I was to meet Comrade Oliver Tambo in early 1962 in exile.

The experienced teacher
The scores of young people who participated in the 1976 student uprising (generally referred to as the Soweto uprising) were assembled at Mazimbu in the Tanzanian town of Morogoro in 1979 in order to get remedial and ba- sic schooling at the ANC school named the Solomon Mahlangu Freedom College (SOMAFCO).

The young people had survived a hostile environment in the bush as they sought to escape from the South African police to join the liberation move- ments in exile. For days they had walked, eaten and slept together as com- rades and now the school authorities insisted on separate quarters for boys and girls. Some of the students understood freedom to mean that they did not have to do any manual labour, including the cleaning of their sleep- ing quarters. Some insisted on smoking in class, and boys refused to take off their headgear. The situation was developing into a confrontation between students and teachers.

As the then acting ANC Secretary for Education, I consulted the experienced teacher Oliver Tambo. I had learnt that in the 1950s, when practically all black colleges were experiencing continuous waves of strikes, there had been no strikes at St Peter's Secondary School, in Rosettenville, where he had been teaching.

Acting on Comrade OR's advice, the students were assembled and told to discuss among themselves what kind of school they wanted and what kind of behaviour was expected of each and every one of them.

The document that the students produced surprised everybody. It set high standards of behaviour, emphasised that knowledge was the instrument that would help defeat apartheid, and stressed that self-reliance meant cleaning the rooms and premises, and producing food in the school garden.

The students identified themselves as soldiers in the struggle for knowledge and gave military titles to their supervisors and team leaders. In no time it became policy that those who completed their studies would undergo military training, and soldiers with field experience would be eligible for production, skills training and the pursuit of academic studies.

The choirmaster

During one of his visits to SOMAFCO, Comrade OR found the school choir rehearsing. The teacher who was conducting, Phumzile Zulu, was herself a passionate music teacher and composer, held in high esteem. The choir was enthusiastically singing one of the songs about self-liberation. Comrade OR quietly asked to conduct the choir. Within a minute, the choir that had been signing rather indifferently was giving a rendition that would have rivalled the best choirs in a Choir Competition Festival. The students obviously wanted to impress their President but there was no doubt that under his baton, he made them dig deep into their untested capabilities. The students testified that they had never encountered such a conductor.

The perfectionist

Comrade OR would enter an office and notice a framed picture that was skew, water served in a stained glass or any object that seemed out of place. His perfectionism also displayed itself in written speeches. During the year that I served as his secretary, drafting his responses to received mail, I quickly learnt that I could never produce the perfect draft. He did, however, restore my self-esteem by pointing out that nobody could draft the perfect reply for him. All he needed from the draft were ideas, but the final wording would be his.

Those of us who had participated in preparing his draft speeches learnt to tell from a slight pause during his delivery, that a correction had been made.

The consummate diplomat

In the early 1980s together with Johnny Makathini we accompanied Comrade OR to Ghana where he also addressed the students at the University of the Cape Coast. We sat there highly embarrassed as the Rector, in his opening remarks, recounted how black South African teachers had come to the help of Ghana in the late 1950s (after 1957 Independence). And now, the Rector announced proudly, we are returning the favour by sending our teachers to help the newly independent African states (referring to the so-called Bantustans) in South Africa.

In response, Comrade OR chose not to comment on this, but simply elaborated on the strength of the enemy we were facing as well as its powerful allies who controlled the media. Our well-meaning friends had been co-opted into rendering apartheid acceptable and workable, but fortunately the apartheid regime was digging its own grave by increasing the numbers of first-hand witnesses to the horrors of apartheid.

The orthodox Christian

The ANC did not advocate any particular faith or religion, but treated all faiths with due respect. By the late 1980s Church leaders such as Bishop Desmond Tutu and Revd Allan Boesak were in the forefront of the anti-apartheid struggle. A young Anglican Church deacon had joined us in exile. Comrade Gqiba had abandoned his studies for the priesthood as OR had done in the 1950's and burial services were a mixture of freedom songs and prayer. Comrade OR quietly persuaded the deacon to complete his studies for priesthood and Gqiba was subsequently formally ordained at the Cathedral in Lusaka.

On the day when Revd Fumanekile Gqiba was ordained as a priest at the Lusaka Anglican Cathedral, the only face I recognised in the congregation was that of Comrade OR. I had attended the service because, as the son of an Anglican priest, I was equally keen to see that our chaplain was properly qualified. Revd Gqiba was later to become chaplain to the new South African National Defence Force in the post-1994 democratic South Africa.

I REMEMBER CHIEF

Sobizana Mngqikana

Oliver Tambo is often referred to or addressed as OR. I prefer to call him 'Chief' as I have done in all my interactions with him. Every time I hear the word 'chief', I remember Oliver Tambo. It's a term of endearment that has special meaning for me.

I do not claim to be an authority on Chief's legacy, but on the not infrequent occasions I interacted with him, I found him to be a remarkable person – a great leader who exuded authority, humility, compassion and empathy.

My first encounter with Chief was through Thabo Mbeki, South Africa's current President. I had recently arrived in the UK in October 1965 to take up a scholarship at the University College in London. I met Thabo at an ANC meeting called by Raymond Mazisi Kunene, then the ANC Chief Representative in London. Thabo was doing his Master's degree at Sussex University and had as his colleagues the Pahad brothers, Essop and Aziz. After a few pleasantries, Thabo and I agreed to meet to discuss and plan what role we, as the youth and students, could play in the liberation effort. The idea of the youth and students being organised had been mooted by Kunene. Our role was to concretise it. The potential composition of recruits was diverse and included exiled youth and students of the Congress Alliance – Africans, Indians, whites and so-called coloureds.

The first hurdle Thabo and I had to overcome in forming this organisation was that the membership of the ANC at that time was exclusively African. This novel idea of a racially mixed organisation under the banner of the ANC would require sanction from higher authority – the then ANC Deputy President OR Tambo, Chief.

It was to present and discuss the issue of the formation of an ANC Youth and Students' Section that I had my first encounter with Chief in early 1966. He was in London on one of his periodic working visits when we met. It was not to be the last meeting as Thabo and I reported to him on the progress and developments in our political work. As an open and concerned person he would ask us about our personal lives, our progress in our studies, etc.

I had read and heard about Oliver Tambo but never met him before. I knew that he was the head of the ANC abroad to coordinate the international struggle against apartheid. As an underground activist in East London, in the Eastern Cape, I had never met an ANC national leader, and I was petrified at the thought. Chief's demeanour, when we made contact, was to banish my fears forever.

Thabo led the discussion by reporting on the idea of forming an ANC Youth and Students' Section in the UK. Chief listened attentively without interruption. He congratulated us on the initiative and gave it his blessing. This demonstrated his ability to embrace change, creativity and innovation. He was not averse to new ideas and continuously worked to refine and improve the ANC.

This initiative we presented to Chief in 1966 was the precursor of the open membership of the ANC adopted at the Morogoro Conference of 1969. That conference tested Chief's leadership of the ANC and the organisation's reaction to change and innovation. As environmental and political factors change and new challenges emerge, leaders must continuously reassess their standpoints and meet these challenges. Some sections of the conference were against open membership of the ANC, preferring to maintain the status quo, content in the comfortable environment of constancy. Under Chief's skilled leadership the forces of change prevailed – membership of the ANC was now to be open to all races on the proviso of unqualified loyalty and subscription to the policy and principles of the ANC.

The rumblings of capitulation to anti-African elements at Morogoro found fertile ground in some ANC circles in London. The Morogoro decisions affected the ANC's London office functionaries. Raymond Kunene was replaced by Reg September as Chief Representative, and I was designated as the Deputy Chief Representative – changes which were misconstrued by some in London as a sell out of Africans.

I dared to ask Chief about the changes in the London office. Raymond Kunene had asked to be relieved of the position of Chief Representative so as to concentrate his energies on fund-raising for the ANC, Chief explained. Since Reg September had been acting as Administrator (finances and other matters), it was logical, for continuity's sake, that he assume the position of Chief Representative. In any case, Chief argued, it had been decided to open membership of the ANC to other races. The response was classical Tambo in terms of its honesty and demonstration of resolve and courage.

In South Africa a music DVD has recently been released that is dedicated to the memory of Chief. It is a beautiful piece of music composed and arranged by the gifted Victor Ntoni, a project initiated by Pallo Jordan. Many people might ask why a musical project would be dedicated to Tambo? What did he know about music? In fact, musical ability was one of those hidden talents that Chief had which very few people knew about. How many people know that he inspired the ANC's successful music ensemble Amandla, whose members were MK's cadres? As an accomplished musician and arranger, Chief would advise and help the ensemble in its repertoire, especially in singing African choral songs. These reminded him of his days as a teacher-choirmaster at St Peter's High School in the late 1940s and early 1950s.

The Chief's love and appreciation of music was limitless. It had been an annual practice for the ANC to commemorate 26 June as freedom day. In 1967 the mood was sombre as it was after the mysterious death of ANC President Albert Luthuli. The ANC declared a week's mourning following Luthuli's death. To commemorate freedom day and pay our respects to the late Luthuli a meeting was held at the ANC's London offices and addressed by Chief. As part of the proceedings the ANC Youth and Students' Section Choir (which included the bass voice of Thabo Mbeki), performed a musical item – Todd Matshikiza's classic 'Hamba Kahle'.

Chief responded typically to the performance by showering the choir with praises and commendation. He always gave credence and due where and when it was deserved. After the meeting he called me aside and asked: 'Bizo, how did you manage this?' He was intrigued and pleasantly surprised, almost shocked, he confessed, to see and listen to non-African comrades sing a complex African choral piece littered with clicks.

Subsequently Chief and I became music buddies as well as political comrades. Unbeknown to me, he had been working on his own re-arrangement of 'Nkosi Sikelel' iAfrika' – South Africa's current national anthem. He informed me that as a test he was planning to get a Welsh choral group to sing his arrangement of the national anthem. Later I was pleasantly surprised to hear Chief's beautiful arrangement of 'Nkosi Sikelel' iAfrika' played and recorded by the Soviet Red Army Orchestra.

Chief was wary of people not taking responsibility and instead passing the buck to him. On two occasions he thought I was reneging on my responsibilities. At the close of an ANC political meeting in Lusaka, I went to Chief and made some suggestion relating to the singing of the national anthem – introducing more dynamics and variation in contrast to the dreary, monotonous singing. His reply was: 'You should have stopped the singing and explained why and how they should sing the anthem', the unsaid rider being, 'why me and not you?'

On another occasion – this time in a political context – I experienced a similar response from Chief. The late MP Naicker (then the editor of the ANC's monthly bulletin, *Sechaba*) and I had been slogging late into the night drafting Chief's speech for a public meeting and rally to be held in London the following day. Chief was a perfectionist and kept chopping and changing the draft until he realised that we were tired and that he would manage to do the finishing touches. One of the speakers at the rally was to be Marcelino dos Santos, FRELIMO's Deputy President.

What MP and I overlooked was the fact that this was a solidarity rally rather than a conference-type of meeting where formal papers are presented. Dos Santos spoke first and his speech was spiced with slogans and revolutionary rhetoric. As I listened to the tone and manner of the speakers before Chief, I realised that the speech we had prepared was too scholarly for an audience that was more at home with sloganeering and agitation. It was too late to advise Chief to extemporise as he was far out on the podium. Chief's lament after the meeting was: 'You should have told me what format the meeting was to take.'

Another remarkable trait in Chief's leadership of the ANC was his realistic approach in handling problems and obstacles. Whilst internationalist in political outlook, he was cognisant of the limitations imposed on the ANC as a liberation movement. This was demonstrated when confronted with the Soviet bloc's military intervention in the then Czechoslovakia in 1968. The ANC had issued a statement signed by Duma Nokwe, the ANC's Secretary-General, in support of the Warsaw Pact intervention.

When I asked Chief about the statement, he expressed ignorance of it prior to publication and commented that he was not the only leader in the ANC. He did, however, feel that the ANC ought not to meddle in Cold War inter-state conflicts, especially if these had no relevance to South Africa. He cautioned the ANC not to punch above its weight.

He was to repeat the same reply when asked to account for Chris Hani's statement that the struggle may have to be taken to South Africa's white suburbs. Chief told the journalist that Hani was one of the leaders of the ANC and was entitled to his views. He recommended that the journalist should address his question to Hani himself.

To evaluate and appreciate Chief's accomplishments, we need to be aware of the obstacles and impediments he had to contend with. At the outset Chief's brief from the rest of the ANC leadership had been:

1) to mobilise the international community in its diverse formations – governments, political parties, churches, NGOs – in support of the struggle against apartheid South Africa, including isolating the racist government and its institutions;
2) the resuscitation of the internally depleted ANC underground structures; and
3) the intensification of measures to effect the armed struggle.

These were formidable tasks requiring committed and dedicated cadres, and that burden fell on Chief. Whilst Chief progressively garnered support, admiration and respect worldwide, he experienced setbacks and even active opposition to the isolationist policies against South Africa that he was advocating. The Margaret Thatcher–Ronald Reagan alliance's steadfast opposition to apartheid South Africa's isolation and the imposition of economic sanctions against that regime is well documented. Thatcher and Reagan branded the ANC as a terrorist organisation at the behest of Moscow.

Nevertheless, Chief's patient commitment to the just cause of South Africa's oppressed people was ultimately to be crowned with success. With every passing year the international stature of Chief and the ANC grew whilst the policies of the Reagans and Thatchers were discredited and undermined.

Whilst it is true that Nelson Mandela deserves credit for inaugurating the first democratic system of government in South Africa, it is equally true that he would not have been able to do so had Chief not paved the way before him.

One of the lessons Chief imparted to some of the activists in exile was how to work with solidarity organisations. We frequently had heated political discussions in the ANC Youth and Students' Section where some colleagues felt that the AAM was 'running the show' instead of the ANC. We consulted Chief on this issue and his wise words have remained with me. He stated that it was impolitic and ill-advised for us to be in the forefront in the UK mobilising support from the British public. The ordinary British person was more likely to listen attentively to a compatriot than to a South African. Above all, the more you make the ordinary British person lead a solidarity movement and campaign, the more enthused and committed he or she will become. Consequently, it was important to make the British own the solidarity movement although the ANC would provide political guidance where and when it was necessary.

One important quality that Chief displayed in his dealings with people is often overlooked – his boundless humility. He never flaunted his leadership status and always made others feel important, lending an attentive and compassionate ear even to those low-ranking members of the ANC who had fallen victim to arbitrary treatment at the hands of some functionaries of the organisation. These cadres were always assured of their grievances being addressed, which, in turn, inspired the confidence, admiration, respect, and loyalty that they accorded Chief.

When I wondered aloud why he should expend his precious energy on trivial things such as securing shoes or clothing for a comrade, Chief responded: 'Bizo, these are human beings and comrades who have needs like everybody else. We cannot progress in the struggle with disgruntled and discontented comrades. Such is a recipe for disorganisation, disunity and inevitably a dysfunction of the organisation.' Here Chief identifies himself as a servant rather than as someone to be served – a rare but important trait in a leader.

The last time I exchanged words with Chief was in 1989 in a Swedish hospital where he was recovering from a massive stroke he had suffered in Lusaka. Unfortunately, it took time for this exchange to happen as Chief's visitors were severely limited by the hospital. After much persuasion the visit finally materialised. I could not stop the tears rolling down my cheeks as I saw my leader and mentor incapacitated by his stroke. It was a painful experience. A visit meant to comfort Chief turned out to be one where he had the inner strength to comfort me. We reminisced about a wide range of things, music in particular, and deliberately downplayed anything to do with politics. As was customary, he wanted to know about what I was doing, how my family was, and so on. I left the hospital saddened but content that I had fulfilled my duty and paid my respects to the man for whom I had unreserved loyalty, and who had groomed and nurtured me politically. Sadly, it was the last time that I saw and spoke to Chief.

A FOLLOWER OF HIS OWN PEOPLE

Ruth Mompati
(extracts from an interview with Thami Ntenteni)

Thami Ntenteni (TN): When did you join the ANC?

Ruth Mompati (RM): I joined the organisation officially in 1952. But I was involved with the ANC before then. When I started teaching in 1945 I found that the local teachers' union was very active in terms of the rights of teachers, the conditions of teaching and the education itself. When I got married in 1952 my teaching post became temporary. As an African woman, if you got married, your post was immediately made temporary by the powers that be. So I moved from Vryburg to Johannesburg, which was where my husband came from. When I got there he was already a member of the ANC, and it became very easy for me to get involved in the ANC in Johannesburg.

TN: When did you meet OR?

RM: I met Oliver Tambo after I joined the law firm of Mandela and Tambo in 1953.

TN: So at the time when you started working for Mandela and Tambo, you were already a politically conscious and active person?

RM: Yes, it was after the Defiance Campaign and Mandela was banned. And at that time, the ANC was a very popular organisation because of the Defiance Campaign. And I was already a member of the Women's League.

TN: It is unusual to speak to someone who actually worked for both Mandela and Tambo at the same time. And in an office situation. What was it like working with them?

RM: In actual fact, I was not officially working with Oliver Tambo. I was Nelson Mandela's secretary. But I was also a secretary in the office. And so I also dealt with Oliver. There was another woman who was Oliver's secretary and she also worked in the office.

TN: How did you find OR at that time? Was he as prominent as he would be later?

RM: Oliver was a leader, even then. He was already the Deputy President of the ANC. He was the leader of the Youth League. And he was a very good lawyer. Both of them were very good lawyers. Oliver was quiet. He was a reserved person, but he was a very strong person. I got to know him because I dealt with him in connection with the various cases that came to the office. He was not restricted to Johannesburg and could travel outside the city, whereas Mandela was restricted. So Oliver took the cases of removal, of people whose land had been taken, people who had been removed from the areas where they had been living all their lives. He did those types of cases. And when he went to court, he dealt with cases as a man who had confidence. As a man who knew what he was doing.

TN: Was he strict in terms of the work that you did for him?

RM: Well, in a lawyers' office people's lives depend on the work that you are doing. Whether it is a criminal case, whether it is a civil case, it doesn't matter. You depend on detail and you depend on those people who work with you doing their best. You depend on them for support. So Oliver was very strict, but not in a way that made you nervous, in a way that made you do your best. We were not frightened of him, we respected him. And we were responsible for the work that we were doing. We had to do our part of the work so that he would be able to do his part.

TN: Did you consider him to be friendly? Was he easy to talk to?

RM: Yes, he was a friendly man. He was quiet but when you spoke to him, you realised that he was somebody you could talk to.

TN: At the time when Mandela and Tambo were charged with treason (in 1956), were you still working for them?

RM: Yes, I was. I arrived at the office in the morning, not yet aware that they had been arrested. But when I entered the building, Chancellor House, there was a young woman, a sister of one of my colleagues in the Women's League, who said to me, 'Sissie, Bertha is arrested.' But people were always getting arrested, so I didn't think it was anything unusual. So I said, 'Okay, Sissie, come, let's go up to the office. Mr Mandela or Mr Tambo, one of them will attend to you.' And we went upstairs. When we got up there, the phone started ringing. We got phone call after phone call about people who had been arrested all over the country. Soon we realised that this was the expected Treason Trial. Because the ANC was aware that there were going to be these arrests.

TN: What did that do in terms of the day to day running of the affairs of the organisation and of the office?

RM: At the time we had an attorney in the office who was working with Nelson Mandela. He was a junior attorney. And we had the two articled clerks, if I'm not mistaken. And all of the secretaries were still there. So at least we had the staff. We knew what to do. The articled clerks knew what to do. The junior attorney took some of the cases and other cases we gave to the advocates or we asked other lawyers to take them.

TN: So you managed to keep going until the leaders were released.

RM: Oliver Tambo was the first one to be released and he came back into the office for a while. But then Sharpeville happened.

TN: And Oliver had been given instructions to leave the country ... Did you know about that?

RM: As I've said, I was a very active member of the ANC. So I did get to know that Oliver had been given instructions to leave the country. In fact, I was responsible for doing certain things when his family left South Africa and went to Swaziland, and from there overseas.

TN: How soon thereafter did you go into exile?

RM: Well, after the offices of Mandela and Tambo had to be closed I left the country in 1962. Initially it was meant to be for one year of training, but then there were the Rivonia arrests (in 1963) and I couldn't come back. The ANC leaders decided that I would probably just be arrested and that would be a waste. So I stayed and worked in the ANC offices.

TN: What was it like at that time? I mean, you confronted such extreme difficulties. Didn't you ever get disillusioned?

RM: No, the frustration I faced was that I was a trained MK cadre and I felt the leaders should let me join the other MK cadres to infiltrate South Africa. But none of the people who were outside, with Oliver and the other leaders, none of them, at any time, felt that the road they'd taken, the decisions they'd made to fight for liberation were wrong. All we could see was the struggle before us. A difficult struggle, but a struggle that we were prepared to face. I knew that it was not my lot to live my life as a slave under apartheid. And I was free in Tanzania. We were living and working and teaching in a free country. And we had a very good leader in Oliver Tambo. Although he had a family, he had children, he didn't take any time off. He went around the world informing people about the ANC. So, we had that example of a man who was selfless and who was so dedicated to the struggle for liberation.

TN: But weren't there times when the future looked bleak? When what was happening inside South Africa – the ANC had been banned, the leaders arrested – made people lose hope?

RM: I understand what you are trying to say. But I and the others had come from South Africa. I'm not suggesting there was no one who broke down and left, but compared to those who remained, they were insignificant. What did I have to look at? What was happening to my comrades? My leaders were in prison. In fact, they were on Robben Island in who knows what kind of conditions. What was there to look back to? What was there that would tell me that if I stopped doing the things I'd been doing, you know, following the ANC, that I would lead a better life? There was nothing. In any case, I didn't want to live like a slave. I didn't want to live like a sell-out. So I saw no other route than the fight for freedom. And that is the example that I got from the leadership that was there. That is the example that I got from Oliver Tambo.

TN: Oliver is credited with having kept the organisation united through those difficult periods. And, the ANC is seen as a unique organisation because the experience of other national liberation movements, then and before, in other countries was of major disagreements and splintering, in part, maybe because of the difficult circumstances in which these organisations found themselves. But with OR at the helm, it seems as if the ANC did not experience those upheavals as an organisation. Even if there were disagreements, OR was able to hold the organisation together. How did he do this?

RM: When I went into exile, Oliver was working with a number of the leaders of the ANC. One of the things that we as new cadres got to see was the coordination and collective leadership of Oliver Tambo, who was our Deputy President then. He worked with the old leaders, the young cadres and other people who were scattered around the world. Oliver's style of leadership was a collective one, with many discussions. He made sure that whatever was agreed upon, was agreed upon by everybody. This was his strength. He wasn't interested in the fact that he was capable of making decisions on his own. He could have but he never did. I think that is how he carried the ANC and kept it together through all the years in exile.

TN: But surely there would still be people who would disagree? How do you get to the point where you say: 'Okay, this is the position now?' And everybody subscribes to that position.

RM: Let me give you an example of how it worked. There was a lot of discussion about cadres coming home. There was a time when South Africa was surrounded by free countries and cadres wanted to come back home and fight. So we had to discuss the issue. For a very long time we told them that at the moment we must wait and see what develops. Then finally we could go through Zimbabwe to do reconnaissance work. But the issue was discussed and properly planned. And it also couldn't be a discussion for everybody. As a member of the ANC you believed in its constitution and you believed in the organisation's leadership. You couldn't just act according to your own independent emotions or beliefs. If you were part of a particular committee such as the National Executive or the Women's League and you disagreed, you could put the issue on the table and say: 'I do not agree with this particular decision, the way you say you are going to implement it. Can you help me to understand and explain it to me?'

TN: And then you listened?

RM: Yes, you listened. And the greatness of our organisation was that you were allowed to voice your belief, to say what you were worried about, and to criticise if you thought that things were not being done properly. You were free to do that and you were responded to.

TN: Was OR instrumental in inculcating that culture of discussion and debate?

RM: Oliver was the organisation's leader but it was broader than that; it was the ANC's culture.

TN: So far we have talked about OR the leader, the politician, the President. The serious side of things. Were there any lighter moments? What were Oliver's other interests besides serious politics?

RM: He was very fond of and interested in most kinds of music. And if there were dances at the camps, he joined in and danced. Of course, he didn't stay as long as everybody else did. Because he was always busy, always had work to do. He also used to go to football. He was a person who could relax with his comrades. But unfortunately he mostly never had enough time to do that.

TN: Could he get angry?

RM: Yes. You had to be very responsible when you worked for Oliver Tambo. And cadres also had to be responsible. Sometimes he got very angry with the South African regime. And he would let us know that it was okay to be so angry; that it would make us be even more determined in our struggle.

TN: But did he ever get so angry that he lost control?

RM: I never saw him lose his cool. I saw him angry, but not to the extent that he couldn't control himself. And he expected other people to be the same. To control themselves even when they were angry.

TN: How did OR balance his responsibilities as a political leader, as a family man, as an ordinary person?

RM: Well, I don't think OR really had the time to be a family man. I think this is perhaps one of the things that must have made him sad. He was hardly ever at home; he was hardly ever in any place for a long time. But he spent most of his time in the camps and in the ANC offices. He hardly ever went to London, where his family was, for long periods. That is why we all felt such great admiration for Adelaide, his wife, who took over the family and brought up the children.

TN: So if we used the word 'family' in a broad sense, we could say OR's family was the ANC?

RM: Yes, OR's family was the ANC. His children were without their father because of the ANC. And one of the things that was very important about OR, was the way he could relate to young people. Relate to the cadres. Relate to their sufferings. Relate, sometimes, to their sadness, for example, the loss of a parent, when they were out there. He had to make sure that the young man or woman had come to terms with his or her grief. He did that. He took time. He showed, you know, that he cared. He showed that support to whomever it was who had received bad news from home. And you needed somebody who could really sympathise, somebody who could really relate to you in this sadness. And Oliver was able to do that. That is why it was very easy for the younger people to go to him with their problems and talk to him. He was able to cultivate trust. He made them feel he was their father, not their President. One time in Luanda I came to our residences and I found around six young people. I looked at them and I knew they had run away from home to come to be trained. First I greeted them and then I said, 'What do you want?' They looked at me and I said, 'Don't worry. You are going to school tomorrow. I'm going to take you away from Luanda, and I am going to take you to a college where you are going to study.' One of them said, 'I'm not going.' I said, 'But you are only a child.' He replied, 'Mama, when we are in South Africa, when they look at me, they don't see a child. They just shoot.' Then I said, 'I'm going to report to President Tambo.' They replied, 'President Tambo has already talked to us. And he didn't tell us he was going to take us to school tomorrow. He talked to us, and we understand him.' Actually, I laughed because it was true. Here I was coming and saying you are children, you are going to school tomorrow. OR didn't say that. He saw that they were children but he spoke differently to them. And I am almost sure that when he was through with those young people, they went to school.

TN: Did you ever sense a feeling of achievement on Oliver's part when negotiations for a democratic South Africa started?

RM: OR had a way of communicating with his counterparts on Robben Island. How he did it, I don't know. But he did. And before negotiations started inside the country, they had started outside. OR started preparing the way. He had meetings with all the heads of states we had supported and who had given the ANC support. He kept people informed all the time. And the interesting thing, what really touched all of us who were in the ANC leadership outside, is that OR called in all of us to inform us what was happening. He did not draft documents of how the new government was going to be run on his own. He called us all in to write down what we expected the new government to be like. Each one of us wrote about what and how it should be. Those documents were collected up by OR and when the final document came, each person could see that he or she had contributed, however little. I remember a number of us sitting together and looking at this final document, looking at it and saying, 'I can see what I wrote'. This was the strength of Oliver Tambo.

TN: Is there any area that I haven't touched on that you would like to talk about?

RM: I think it is important to discuss Oliver Tambo's relationships with the leaders of Africa. He had a very close relationship, a personal friendship, with President Julius Nyerere of Tanzania, who came to many of our meetings and get-togethers. And Oliver was just as close with President Kenneth Kaunda of Zambia, who also became his friend. Kaunda worked with us, and it was from Zambia that we launched our arms, that we sent our cadres into South Africa. In addition, OR worked very closely with leaders of other liberation movements. With Eduardo Mondlane of FRELIMO in Mozambique, with Agostinho Neto of Angola's PLA, with Joshua Nkomo and Robert Mugabe in Zimbabwe, and with others. He worked very closely with all of these men, discussing the various struggles and options. OR also had contact with other countries because he travelled so widely. He went to Cuba, to America, to Canada, to Italy, to France, to the Scandinavian countries. And international organisations such as the UN all had great respect for OR because he respected them and listened to them. Actually, I think that was the secret to Oliver's greatness: the fact that he listened. He didn't tell people what to do. He listened to them and then, if he felt that he didn't agree with them, he put forward his opinions. He asked questions so that people would explain. If he didn't agree, he said no, this idea, I don't agree with, but of course, these are your own plans and struggle. But for my country that would not work. For my struggle, that would not work. People would come to him for advice and they would walk away feeling they had given OR something. He made you feel you really had something to give. That is why he was such a great leader.

TN: Any last thoughts?

RM: I remember that when our leaders came out of prison OR acknowledged their leadership so selflessly. He made us all realise that these people had contributed more than anyone else. Actually, they had given most of their lives. And now they were coming back. He called a very big meeting in Zambia at which these leaders addressed the cadres. As far as OR was concerned, this leadership, the real leaders, were back and now he was going to step down and follow them. That is how selfless he was. He didn't see himself as a big leader because he had been in exile and had led the ANC from outside. No, he always saw himself as a follower, even a follower of his own people. Anyone who worked with him will always remember working with a man who never considered you to be beneath him. He always considered you to be a member of the ANC, a fellow cadre of the movement.

NO EASY WALK

Mosie Moolla

My first contact with OR was in the early 1950s. I had taken part in the Defiance Campaign of 1952 and had consequently been expelled from high school. I began to work for the national liberation movement on a full-time basis. Inspired, like many of my generation, to fight and struggle for a free and non-racial society, the examples of Nelson Mandela and Oliver Tambo, Walter Sisulu and Albert Luthuli, Yusuf Dadoo and GM Naicker as well as other giants of our struggle spurred us on to play our humble part in the great endeavour to transform South African society to a more just, free and humane one.

The names of Mandela and Tambo in particular began to capture the imagination of our people – not only as leading black attorneys but as champions of a cause for human freedom and dignity in a society steeped in racial bigotry and the oppression of its overwhelming black majority by a white minority racist regime.

To have a better appreciation and understanding of Oliver Tambo it is necessary to take into account the times he lived in and how they shaped him to become the leader of his people.

The decade of the 1950s saw the rise and clash of two contending forces or tendencies – call them nationalisms if you wish – in South African society. On the one hand was Afrikaner white power exemplified by the likes of DF Malan, Hendrik Verwoerd and JG Strijdom who were riding the crest of a wave after the defeat of the more moderate United Party of Jan Smuts in

the 1948 all-white general elections. The creed and vision of Afrikaner nationalism was to build a South African society in which white overlordship
would be permanent: the overwhelming black majority reduced to hewers
of wood and drawers of water serving their white masters. Their vision of
society was based on a patent injustice – the suppression and subjugation of
an entire people solely on the basis of skin colour. On the other hand we
witnessed the rise of African aspirations and organised resistance by a people who were oppressed, exploited, humiliated and dispossessed of their land
through the exercise of brute power. The gun held sway.

African opposition to racial tyranny and white overlordship began to
manifest itself in a more organised and coherent way. The campaigns of the
1950s began with the May Day general strike of 1950, the Defiance Campaign of 1952, followed by the two-year-long campaign of the Congress
of the People which culminated in the adoption of the historic Freedom
Charter on 26 June 1955 by over three thousand elected delegates. The various boycotts and anti-pass campaigns were clear indications that the people
had had enough. No longer would they be ridden over roughshod and their
meagre privileges and few rights trampled upon with impunity. The people had given notice that they were preparing to fight back and claim what
was rightfully theirs – their inalienable right to live freely in a democratic
and just society. The African giant was beginning to stir and unshackle itself
from its long-induced sleep – sending shivers down the spines of white oppressors.

The response of the repressive regime was typical. Increasingly dracon-
ian measures were adopted and implemented to stem the resistance movement. Notwithstanding the might and brutality of a police state the people
were not cowed or bludgeoned into submission. They fought back. Bannings, banishment, detention and arrests of leaders and activists only spurred
our people to greater resistance to oppression.

In December 1956 156 leaders and activists of the Congress movement
were arrested on charges of high treason and were taken to the notorious
Johannesburg Fort (a prison where in earlier times the great Indian freedom fighter and apostle of non-violence Mahatma Gandhi was also incarcerated for his campaigns of non-violent resistance). The Fort, now the site
of the Constitutional Court, saw the cream of our movement incarcerated:
Mandela, Tambo, Luthuli, Sisulu, Joe Slovo and his wife Ruth First, Rusty
Bernstein, Ahmed Kathrada, Helen Joseph, Lillian Ngoyi, and others. I was
one of the accused and together with a hundred-odd black co-accused we
were herded into two large cells (blocks) which were promptly designated as
the 'upper and lower houses of parliament' by the comrades.

During the day the accused were herded into one of the blocks where a 'joint sitting' of the 'upper and lower houses' would be held. These 'joint sittings' were extremely useful for they gave us the opportunity to get to know each other more closely and we utilised the time fruitfully by holding debates, lectures, discussions and cultural activities. For example, Professor ZK Matthews spoke on the African-American fight for full and unfettered freedom and equality based on his visit to the US; the Revd Calata gave an exposition of African folk music; Dr Arthur Letele spoke on indigenous medicine; and Debbie Singh discussed the history of the South African Indian Congress. These lectures were highly instructive and inspirational.

Before we retired to our respective blocks the days ended with the full-throated singing of freedom songs to keep morale high – after all, high treason was a capital offence in terms of South African law.

The impending Treason Trial captured the imagination and interest of millions of our people as no other event had done before. On the eve of our appearance at the Johannesburg Magistrates' Court we held a last 'joint sitting of parliament'. Instead of the normal ending of the day's work by singing freedom songs, a special choir (the Fort Choir) was organised and under the able baton of Comrade OR they sang the 'Hallelujah Chorus' from Handel's *Messiah*. It was a truly moving experience to hear the famous chorus (probably the only time in the history of the Fort) sung by a group of prisoners facing a possible death sentence if convicted.

We were later told by passers-by and black nurses from the nearby non-European general hospital that our songs had inspired them – particularly the magnificent rendition of the 'Hallelujah Chorus' which had many in tears. Among the choristers was Vuyisile Mini – a beautiful bass-baritone and composer of many of our freedom songs – who was later to be executed by the racist authorities on trumped up charges of complicity in the killing of a police informer. It is said that Mini went to the gallows singing, unbowed and with his head held high.

I refer to this 'special sitting' for it revealed an aspect of OR which many of us were unaware of – OR the musician and conductor. I can still picture him conducting the choir in a very professional way with the magnificent voices reverberating throughout the notorious prison.

The 'Hallelujah Chorus' was a fitting farewell to the Fort as we prepared ourselves for the coming trial. To this day Handel's immortal piece brings back memories of the Fort with pride and a tinge of sadness for that beautiful rendition which was sung with such gusto on that memorable evening over fifty years ago. And all credit goes to OR for having organised the Fort Choir on the spur of the moment and for creating an unforgettable experience.

It was against the backdrop of the 1950s that I came into contact with OR and other leading lights of the struggle. After the Defiance Campaign I was enlisted to serve on the Secretariat of the National Action Council of the Congress of the People in an administrative capacity. This led to my being in almost daily contact with OR and other leaders of the movement who were either banned or restricted from taking part in the activities of the ANC and allied organisations. Messages had to be relayed and instructions obtained. OR's signature had to be appended to various directives, documents, and appeals for transmission to the national, provincial, regional and local committees of the Congress movement.

I found my meetings with OR very instructive, educative and humbling. He was meticulous and very strict on the style and content of whatever directives or statements were issued under his name. He insisted that the t's be crossed and the i's be dotted and, as a trained lawyer, that the precise meaning of what was to be conveyed was clear and concise – there was to be no room for any errors or ambiguity. In later years this stood me in good stead as editor of the ANC weekly news bulletin – 'Spotlight on South Africa' – published from the headquarters of the External Mission in Dar es Salaam, Tanzania, during the 1960s and 1970s. I recall how on many occasions OR and I would be slogging away in our offices until late at night or the early hours of the morning – OR writing the leading articles for the bulletin and myself on the typewriter and cyclostyling machine. And even though this meant putting aside more pressing work OR never demurred from doing so. His editorials were concise little masterpieces that were widely used by the local and international media. The international anti-apartheid movement used them extensively to garner support for our cause. OR was very enthusiastic about our weekly news bulletins and looked forward to its publication. He realised the value of this humble publication as even the UN Special Committee against Apartheid began to quote extensively from it.

It was extremely heartening and inspiring to see OR work. He never complained, even after long and exhausting hours of work with no food or refreshments at hand. I remember the two of us leaving the office for the ANC 'residence' – in reality a sickbay for comrades – where, like others, we slept on the floor. Our supper was a few slices of buttered bread, some cooked vegetables and a cup of coffee or tea before we retired for the night's rest. There was never a word of complaint from OR for this 'special feast' at one-thirty or two in the morning. And even after an exhausting day's work he would be up at the crack of dawn to do his daily physical exercise to keep mind and body fit – another good habit that many comrades emulated.

I believe it was OR's uncomplaining nature that endeared him to hundreds of our comrades and to many others internationally who came to know him during the arduous three decades of exile. As a further example of this, although OR was asthmatic he never let the condition interfere with his work. And not once did I see him call upon people not to smoke in his presence despite the adverse effects this had on his general well-being.

There can be no gainsaying the fact that OR was one of the most erudite, eloquent and inspiring speakers of our movement. His incisive and persuasive gift of speech helped to rally millions of well-wishers and supporters to work resolutely and relentlessly for the freedom of South Africa.

An occasion worth remembering occurred soon after the Sharpeville massacre in 1960 when OR addressed a special session of the UN General Assembly. He spoke impromptu (OR at his best) detailing the evils of the apartheid system and calling upon the international community to redouble its efforts for the eradication of the racist scourge. He received a standing ovation from the gathering for his lucid, inspirational and impressive address.

The representative from apartheid South Africa, Foreign Minister Eric Louw, then challenged any delegate from Africa to do better than OR had done. In a typically arrogant and cynical manner he described OR's stirring address as the 'product of South Africa's Bantu Education system' – a despicable system of education which the world had condemned so vociferously over the years.

OR's ability to win over doubters and fence-sitters is the stuff legends are made of. Not only was he able to inspire by the sheer strength of his argument and conviction, but his insight and ability to look beyond the present and into the future won over many adherents to our cause. He could inspire the already converted to new heights of commitment and dedication to accelerate the process for a free and democratic society on the southern tip of the African continent.

When OR paid a visit to India in the 1980s to receive the prestigious Jawaharlal Nehru award for International Understanding and Peace I had the honour of accompanying him to meet Prime Minister Rajiv Gandhi. A known and committed supporter of our cause, Rajiv made it known that he was honoured to have met a great South African freedom fighter. Friends close to him later informed me that he displayed a renewed commitment to our cause. It was during his tenure that India raised the stakes and pledged to redouble its efforts to hasten the day for the liberation of the peoples of South Africa and Namibia. Thus it was that India established the Africa Fund. Another direct consequence of the OR–Rajiv meeting was the convening of an international conference against apartheid in the Indian capital attended by delegates from over ninety countries, and the establishment of the World Youth Action against Apartheid. Rajiv was also instrumental in getting Indian parliamentarians across the political spectrum to play a more prominent part in the anti-apartheid struggle at all levels, particularly with their counterparts in the Commonwealth and in Western countries.

When President Mikhail Gorbachev paid a state visit to New Delhi in the late 1980s he singled out the ANC Chief Representative for a word or two at the welcoming ceremony at Delhi airport. I distinctly recall President Gorbachev mentioning the ANC President's recent visit to the Soviet Union and how pleased he had been with it. He stated in Russian that OR's visit was 'atlichni' (excellent) and that Soviet support would be further enhanced.

Space does not permit me to elaborate on how OR was primarily responsible for the creation of a worldwide movement against apartheid – a truly unprecedented achievement in the annals of human solidarity. It was a movement that enjoyed the support of young and old, male and female, communist and non-communist alike, and it united labour, youth and women's movements in their opposition to the criminal and obnoxious apartheid system.

For over forty years OR worked relentlessly and resolutely for the destruction of the apartheid system. He spared no effort to accelerate the process and hasten the day of liberation – a consistent effort that eventually led to his failing health. He was able to hold together a disparate South African exile community and have them focus on the main prize – the liberation of our people from the shackles of white racist domination. In that he was eminently successful.

OR was firm and resolute on principle but flexible on tactics. He brooked no nonsense and made certain that tendencies inimical to the success of our struggle, which manifested themselves within the movement at various times, were firmly dealt with. He ensured that the demon of tribalism and racial bigotry would have no place in our struggle and he showed no tolerance for such destructive tendencies. Anybody perceived to be tribalist or with racist inclinations was given short shrift and was expelled from the ANC.

Oliver Reginald Tambo's contribution cannot be measured, but it is safe to say that it was immense. His life and work need to be recorded in detail so that present and future generations are made aware that the fight for human dignity and freedom was a long, bitter and arduous one. Indeed, there was no easy walk. People need to appreciate the sterling work done by the giants of our movement and the ordinary masses, who made tremendous sacrifices so that we may live in a free society.

OR was an outstanding human being, a great leader of our people and a person of whom we can all be proud. He needs to be honoured in many ways and, I believe, the greatest honour both present and future generations can pay him is to build upon his lifelong work – to ensure that racial and tribal bigotry will never again rear its ugly head and mar our beautiful land.

OR'S SECURITY UNIT IN EXILE

Tony Msimanga

I joined MK, the military wing of the ANC, at a fairly young age. The 1970s were a very politically volatile time in South Africa, and I was politically active on the dusty streets of South Africa's major townships of the former Pretoria-Witwatersrand-Vereeniging (PWV) area. I left South Africa for Lusaka, Zambia, by escaping to Swaziland, and then on to Mozambique where I stayed for a short while before proceeding to Angola.

I received my first MK military training in Angola. After spending some time there with other comrades we were instructed by the ANC to go and further our military and academic skills in Europe. After a military spell in Europe I was then deployed to Lusaka to become a member of the elite security unit that protected ANC President OR Tambo in the last ten years of his life in exile. My code name in exile was 'Gap'.

We dedicated our lives to protecting 'Chief', as we affectionately called him, and were ready to die for him as we knew that his safety ultimately meant the freedom for us to go back home. Our commitment, conviction and dedication in protecting OR meant real liberation for all South Africans at home and in exile irrespective of colour, creed and religion.

All the members of the elite security unit were highly trained and disciplined. They had acquired their military and intelligence training in Cuba, the former Soviet Union and other European countries. This had implications not only for OR's security but also guaranteed the survival of the entire leadership of the ANC in exile. Each member of the team was vetted by the ANC's Chief of Intelligence and Security. Mine was the security unit of the ANC which got direct orders from and reported back to the NEC.

In addition to ensuring OR's safety, the security unit was responsible for all household chores including washing his clothes, preparing his meals, guarding and driving him. Driving OR was a security priority. There was a car for the day and one for the night. The day car was known to most members but the night car was only revealed to a few, including the specific driver for a particular shift. The various houses in which OR lived were also a closely guarded secret in order to ensure his safety. Only a few members, myself included, knew the locations of all of the secret houses. Others would only know a particular house when driving OR there at a given time. These houses had code names and were provided by South African expatriates living in Lusaka or by Zambians who sympathised with or were friends of the ANC in Lusaka.

In the late 1980s Lusaka started to become unsafe with bombs going off during the night. This posed serious threats to OR's security. The various secret houses also became unsafe. President Kaunda's intelligence had gathered information that the apartheid regime had begun to intensify its quest to capture OR. During this period Kaunda offered to accommodate OR at the State House. Some allies of the ANC in Lusaka also had OR to stay during this time. Two out of many that come to mind are the Cuban Ambassador who accommodated OR in his residence and the current Vice-President of Zambia, the Honourable Rupia Banda.

Amongst the various safe houses, one codenamed 'Phiri' was the ANC's official residence and OR's favourite. It was situated in Chelsteen, one of Lusaka's elite suburbs, along the main road leading to the airport. The reason for OR's love for Phiri was the fact that the garden was full of trees and flowers. OR loved trees and he knew each tree that was planted in the yard. Sometimes he would say, 'I love these trees because they camouflage us so the enemy won't see us.' OR had a large number of chickens that he was fond of and that he kept at Phiri. In those days even if a unit craved chicken, it would not dare to touch OR's poultry.

OR treated his security unit like his family. We looked up to him as our father and in return he treated us like his sons. We ate with him and slept in the same accommodation as he did. We soon learned what he did and did not like. If you drove him slowly then he would want to drive himself as he preferred fast-moving cars. We needed to keep pace with OR, which was not always easy as he was a workaholic, extremely meticulous and neat, very strict with time and highly observant.

OR groomed and mentored this elite security unit which was full of youngsters except for the likes of Bab' uMshengu, Bab' uNxumalo and Bra

Shooter. Mshengu had lived with OR since the 1960s and he knew Chief very well. He knew when OR was sick or in a good mood or upset with something. Mshengu occupied one of the two upstairs bedrooms of Phiri with OR.

Bab' uNxumalo was a dedicated driver for OR for many years. He was diabetic and died in exile. Knox and I then took over the driving of OR.

Bra Shooter was the overall commander of the unit and was in charge of us in OR's absence. Bra Shooter was very short, very fond of his tobacco pipe and he also died in exile. Amongst these three senior members of the unit, Bab' uMshengu was the only one who lived to return to South Africa after 1990. Other members of this elite team were Jacky and Chris, who are now both deceased, Mzabalazo, Jomo, Godfrey, Knox, Kingsley, Banda and Distance (who was the youngest member of the unit) called 'Last born' by OR and the rest of the unit.

There were three important women who were not part of the unit per se but were key in giving administrative support to both OR and the unit. These were Rhoda, Dudu and Mam' uMasondo. Both Dudu and Mam' uMasondo died in South Africa just a few years before the advent of democracy.

I was very close to Chief who was not in any way a 'communist' or 'terrorist' as he had been labelled by the apartheid regime. He was Anglican and had nearly become a priest before becoming involved in politics. In fact, he ensured that all of us went to church, especially on significant days such as Good Friday.

The elite team faced many challenges in protecting OR, especially during PW Botha's reign. Under Botha's leadership the apartheid regime intensified its efforts to capture OR alive. The apartheid regime had successfully gathered intelligence with regard to OR's security. It had established that OR had a security unit of youngsters and that wherever he travelled he was always accompanied by two of them. They ridiculed us by saying that we were just skinny, young black boys who could be easily mopped up by their hefty and tall agents in seconds. Little did they know that we were highly trained and dedicated to protecting OR with our lives.

A plot was uncovered by the ANC's Department of Intelligence and Security. A plan had been devised by Botha's racist government to kidnap and ship OR, together with his two young security guards, to South Africa, around 1984–86. Apartheid agents were to wait for OR and his unit to travel to London as they knew where his wife and children lived in Muswell Hill. They would be kidnapped, sedated, put into coffins, and shipped to Pretoria as diplomatic consignments. Our unit had vowed to protect OR even if it meant dying for him on the streets of London.

One of the biggest challenges we faced was that we were not allowed to carry firearms in most European countries as well as in a few African states which were not sympathetic to the ANC cause. In many instances there was no back-up security made available to OR. Consequently, Europe was a major challenge for the team protecting OR, as was the UK. OR's house in London was a particular security nightmare for the unit. Every time we visited there, we found a handful of 'adopted' members of the family. The majority of these extended family members were young people not known to the unit but who were friends of Mam' uTambo. Some were refugees, others were stranded and some were seeking the help of Mama in terms of arranging scholarships or bursaries. The security team would ask that these people be expelled from the house for the security of the family. Mam' uTambo would refuse and say that they were all her children. In Lusaka we were in control of the situation, but not in London. Despite this, somehow we still managed to protect OR and his family.

Official trips of OR abroad and his accommodation in hotels posed serious security threats. OR only travelled with two people from his security unit (as opposed to the four considered the international norm with regard to VIP protection). OR would work until the early hours of the morning. You would be there guarding him and only go to sleep when you were certain that he was asleep. In the morning when he delivered his speech you would have to be there and be wide awake. I do not know how we fought fatigue, but perhaps we were able to cope because we were young and fit.

After OR suffered a stroke and relocated to a hospital in London, it became difficult to provide effective security for him. During his first few months in hospital the unit could not control or scrutinise the movements of the members of the public moving in and out of the hospital area where OR was as it also accommodated other patients.

OR's last years in South Africa no longer demanded an intense security plan. This kind of security shifted to other leaders such as Nelson Mandela, Chris Hani and other young leaders of the movement. Moreover, OR was ill and possibly no longer considered a serious threat to the apartheid regime and its agents.

Subsequently most of the members of OR's security unit returned to South Africa after the demise of apartheid. Now they are either in government, the private sector or running their own businesses. Apartheid and death stripped the country of a brilliant genius. It was indeed a privilege to have worked with an invaluable leader such as OR.

A TALENTED SON OF AFRICA

Sankie Mthembi-Mahanyele

Comrade Oliver Reginald Tambo, fondly known as Comrade OR, was one of the greatest leaders of our time. He led the ANC to a powerful and respected position on the global stage. He did not do this alone; it was a collective effort, but he became the face of the ANC and brought to the organisation his stature, power, dignity, integrity and deep respect for humanity.

One afternoon as we went about our daily tasks in the Information and Publicity Unit of the ANC in Dar es Salaam, Tanzania, Comrade OR stepped into our office unannounced. The surprise visit was welcome because it was not every day that a busy person such as himself had the time to visit a unit such as ours.

As he entered the ANC office in Dar es Salaam on that memorable afternoon, someone muttered 'Chief is here'. A sudden excitement engulfed us. It was the kind of excitement that wants to tear across your ribs and is difficult to control, but then you end up containing it because protocol requires you to.

Comrade OR greeted all of us with his customary smile, a thing most of us came to appreciate over the years. His genuine smile opened doors for the ANC and it ushered in many who became friends of the people of South Africa.

It was the first time I had met Comrade OR and, greetings over, we enjoyed the opportunity of sharing some valuable time with him as he briefed us on his recent travels around the globe, describing and dissecting the international political tapestry for us. He explained global politics at the time and its bearing on the South African struggle. It was important for the Information Unit to be able to locate the South African question within the bigger scheme of things in order to remain effective and have an insight into issues in order to analyse events and situations adequately. Policy was central to what we communicated and how we projected developments occurring on all fronts.

Comrade OR was not an imposing personality; he was approachable and accessible to all comrades. There was always an opportunity to communicate with him if one had a good reason for doing so. He was a permanently busy man, full of energy and zest. When he was working in Africa he spent much of his time on the ANC itself as an organisation. He would neither fish for news like a gossip nor discuss any of his colleagues with comrades in a disparaging manner. His interest was the steady, quiet growth of the organisation. Where there was a problem he addressed it squarely and firmly and he was able to resolve many difficult issues because he remained above the pettiness, gossip and backbiting that sometimes afflicts small, tight-knit communities.

These principles strengthened his authority and made him the last port of call in the event that structures of the ANC were unable to address a comrade's problem fully or if a comrade felt that the President had to intervene. It gave us a sense of security to know that OR was there.

ANC members were scattered all over the world. Exile means being away from home and not knowing when one will return. The exile regularly feels homesick. Caught in a life not necessarily of your own choosing, living in a culture very different to that one is familiar with, as exiles we drew comfort and inspiration watching Comrade OR travel the world and adapt to any situation.

Some ANC members were students, who guided by the movement's Representatives in various countries, embarked on the project of mobilising solidarity for the ANC and the struggle for freedom. ANC students were integrated into the work already being undertaken by the full-time activists and the Anti-Apartheid Movement: organising community meetings, addressing the churches, the NGOs, the progressive political parties, collecting food and clothes for those in Africa and the camps, and on drawing the governments in host countries closer to the ANC's cause.

The international Anti-Apartheid Movement played a significant role in the struggle against apartheid by offering the movement forums where the voice of the oppressed could be heard through the ANC.

Success did not come easily; changing the minds of millions of people all over the world required courage, determination, a clear programme of action and the clear enunciation of policies. Comrade OR was the champion who drove the programme even where the terrain was tough. He led a contingent of foot soldiers, the young and the old, and he had a way with language, choosing the right words to explain or describe a situation clearly. His dedication and commitment saw the ANC through some of the most challenging times in our struggle.

After a stint of training in various fields I met Comrade OR again at the ANC headquarters in Lusaka. His presence at the headquarters created a special vibe. It made everyone happy and he commanded massive respect wherever he went. He was very observant and sensitive and this made him a very caring person who displayed his concern for all comrades irrespective of their race, gender and ethnic background.

Ethnicity and race had been dealt with by the ANC in many meetings and conferences. The organisation, in word and deed, belonged to all South Africans. This was a central to the ANC's identity, what it stood for then and still stands for today. The movement's ethos on such issues was central to attaining our goals and objectives.

Comrades quickly learnt that OR did not entertain gossip. Should one person say something about another comrade in their absence, the two people would shortly find themselves invited to Comrade OR's office to verify the facts. This contributed to the ANC's stability and its ability to confront challenges maturely. It ensured that the ANC's self-image, despite the enemy's attempts by to label it an organisation of terrorists, was never sullied.

Sometime in early 1981, when Comrade OR came back to the headquarters after one of his travels, he found Lusaka unsettled because enemy agents who had infiltrated the ANC were disrupting the organisation. They had targeted a few comrades who were most amenable to rumour and tried to convince them that the military leadership was reluctant to intensify the struggle at home.

Comrade OR became a one-man commission and invited the rank and file to express themselves freely on whatever issue that bothered them. Comrades were invited to submit their verbal complaints to him. Through these one-on-one interviews he was able to demonstrate that the rumours being circulated about the ANC and its leadership were the deliberate work of enemy agents. This approach enabled the ANC to identify the real culprits. The apartheid state's agenda of disorder and disruption was brought to a halt and the people's movement was soon back on track.

Sometime in the mid-1980s Comrade OR led an ANC delegation to the Zaire. The delegation included the Treasurer-General, Thomas Nkobi and myself The objective of the visit was to hold discussions with Mobuto

Sese Seko and key members of his government. Zaire was one of a few African countries that was not committed to our cause. The ANC had to talk to both friend and foe, and particularly the latter, in order to win them to our side. Mobuto gave us a lukewarm reception and kept us in the OAU village but we were well taken care of by his aides. Though we waited for more than four days before he was ready to meet us, it was a good sign that he had agreed to see an ANC delegation. Our patience was running out but Comrade OR encouraged self-control because it was important that the ANC talk to Mobuto and, if possible, convince him to support us or at least adopt a posture of benevolent neutrality.

When he did finally grant us meeting, half the time Mobuto kept his face hidden under his traditional leopard-skin hat and had his eyes closed as Comrade OR spoke. We passed a note to Comrade OR suggesting that Mobuto was asleep and not listening to him. He wrote back, saying: 'I will continue talking until he hears us.' And, indeed, he did hear Comrade OR. The ANC delegation eventually left Kinshasa happy in the knowledge that we would be able to continue our work for a while with the help that Mobuto offered to us at that meeting.

Comrade OR was very particular about a dress code. He preferred us avoiding jeans at official occasions and he insisted that we always be presentable when we were at work or as we campaigned for change. I recall one occasion in Madagascar when an ANC delegation was on its way to visit senior officials of the government. A member of the delegation, evidently late rushed into the lift still trying to fasten his tie. Comrade OR asked him to go back to his hotel room and finish dressing and not in the lift. It was message to all of us that we should be punctual and be serious about our work. Comrade OR's argument was that people would listen to us and take us seriously only when we conducted ourselves in a manner that demonstrated that we respected the audiences and the people we were trying to win onto our side.

Caring for oneself became something of a deliberate effort and was part of the image we were creating. Apartheid had denied us basic human rights, but we made sure that the image of the kind of South Africa we were striving for should be projected through what we did and how we lived as the ANC. It was not easy. We worked tirelessly making no distinction among the days of the week. Sundays, Tuesdays, Christmas Day, Saturdays and Mondays flowed into a seamless web because there was always so much to do for the struggle.

Comrade OR was very aware of the energy of the youth and he insisted that we incorporated cultural activities to engage with issues.. The ANC's

cultural ensemble, Amandla, was born out of this desire to see the youth interpret South African culture through song, dance, music and poetry. Culture can be a powerful link between people of different languages and cultures. Music, drama, poetry and dance became popular tools of mobilisation
and communication with the world. Comrade OR inspired a well-packaged
musical revue, put together by Jonas Gwangwa, which drew the attention
of the world to the South African struggle and helped mobilise support. The
Amandla ensemble was a vibrant cultural troupe composed of highly talented young comrades. The energy and the power that came with their dancing were electric. It was extremely successful and traveled to many parts of
the world telling the South African story.

In the late 1980s on a visit to the Scandinavian countries with Comrade
OR, we had occasion to catch a connecting flight at an airport in one of
the countries in southern Africa. A big, well-fed rat sluggishly crawled past
us. Before it reached the rubbish bin it was heading for, it hesitated, turned
back in the direction it had come from, then half turned again in the direction of the rubbish bin. Some of those who witnessed the rat's confusion
were amused, but what struck Comrade OR was the tragedy of the disorder
and filth in an international airport. He looked at me and said, 'Ribbs when
we achieve our freedom we should make the best out of it, and never allow
ourselves to live in dirt, to allow the situation to deteriorate to such levels.'
He pointed to the rubbish bin, 'It is just not healthy and not dignified at all.'
He was upset and disappointed.

On that trip we met very senior officials of the governments of Sweden,
Denmark, Norway and Finland. The visit was to update the governments of
these countries and to consolidate the firm relations we had developed, particularly with Sweden's Prime Minister, Olof Palme, who had allegedly been
killed by the apartheid regime agents.

While we waited at the Stockholm airport on our way back to Lusaka,
via London, Comrade Lindiwe Mabuza and myself joked about our lives
and experiences in exile with Comrade OR. We described to him the hu-
mourous and comical moments occasioned by many different characters
from diverse backgrounds and experiences working and living together. OR
laughed so much that tears rolled down his cheeks. At the end he jokingly
pleaded that we should not include him among our list of comic characters.

In 1987 Comrade OR visited Nigeria to meet President Babangida. At
the time I was based in Nigeria and we had to meet OR at the airport, but
were refused permission to go up to the plane. It was a frustrating situation
but finally we were able to escort him from the airport. When we reached

the hotel we were told that there was no reservation for Comrade OR and therefore he could not be accommodated. But the bookings had been made and there was evidence of this. The ANC's Chief Representative realised that there was a problem and asked me to give him a chance to solve it. A room for Comrade OR's suddenly became available.

That visit to Nigeria was one of the most interesting for me. After OR's daily round of meetings we met in the evenings to plan for the next day. He talked to me about the difficulties we had in some areas, including about comrades who did not carry out their instructions to the full. We, in Lagos, had been waiting for months for supporting finance from one of our missions in Europe and nothing had been forthcoming. It was an extremely difficult time for the ANC's Nigeria office. My confidential talk with OR helped me to understand why it took so long to receive support even when headquarters had issued an instruction. Such moments with OR were rare and were regarded as a treasure and a privilege because we all understood how busy he was. The visit to Nigeria was a success. Political mobilisation continued and the West African communities were serviced through the Nigeria ANC Mission.

I will always remember Comrade OR as a humble, intelligent, talented, selfless, committed and determined leader. Not even once during the entire period that I knew him did I get the impression that he abused his leadership position. This was remarkable because he wielded enormous power over the years as Acting President and then President of the ANC. He used to remind us that Comrade Nelson deserved to be the President of the ANC; he was only Acting President because Nelson was in jail. It was only after pressure was brought to bear on him that OR agreed to be called President of the ANC, an action that paved the way for the organisation to participate in high-level meetings that eventually led to the birth of South Africa's democracy.

A GIANT OF A MAN

Godfrey Nhlanhla Ngwenya

The liberation struggle in South Africa produced many great leaders who sacrificed for the betterment of our society. We enjoy freedom today and as we continue striving for a better life for all, we recognise the contribution of great leaders. These include those who led the wars of resistance against the colonisation of our country: Shaka, Sekhukhune, Makanna, Makhado, Manthatisi, Moshoeshoe, Bhambátha, and many others who, against all odds, gallantly defended our land.

Then there are the leaders who founded the ANC in 1912. I often wonder whether the founders of this great organisation ever realised that it would produce world-class revolutionaries in the mould of Oliver Reginald Tambo.

Talking about OR, as we affectionately called him, is a huge and challenging task. How do you begin to describe that giant of a man; how do you begin to find the right words that will express your innermost feelings; how do you translate your thoughts into words?

The name OR Tambo started to mean more to me in 1967 when MK cadres fought in Zimbabwe alongside their Zimbabwean comrades from the Zimbabwe African People's Union (ZAPU), led by Comrade Joshua Nkomo. The ANC had decided to send its cadres through Zimbabwe into South Africa to intensify the armed struggle. Obviously the aim was not to remain in Zimbabwe but rather to create a route through that country by fighting. We managed to get some news about what was happening in Zimbabwe even though the racist regime suppressed all kinds of news that they perceived as subversive. OR Tambo was always mentioned as the Acting President of the ANC. Little did I know then that I was later to meet the man himself when I too joined MK.

As the struggle for freedom in our neighbouring countries (Mozambique and Namibia) gained momentum, the name OR Tambo became increasingly well known and linked to our own struggle within South Africa. In the face of brutal repression our people identified more and more with the ANC and songs were composed about OR and the struggle.

My first contact with Comrade OR was in exile, in Tanzania to be specific. We were housed in a flat like those Tanzanians lived in, although we learnt later that this was, in fact, an ANC office. OR looked so ordinary, more like the 'old-timers' we had left behind at home in South Africa. He freely mingled and interacted with us youngsters, who often appeared a bit wild and asked all sorts of provocative questions, even sugesting that he and the rest of the leadership were doing nothing whilst students and the people of South Africa were facing the brutality and might of the JB Vorster regime.

After OR had led a few debates and exchanges on the situation in South Africa, it dawned on our young and militant minds that the struggle to rid our country of the scourge of white minority racist rule was not as easy as we had thought. It was not simply a question of taking guns and going back to South Africa to shoot whites.

Shortly after our arrival in Tanzania, the country hosted a meeting of the Front-line States. We were surprised to see OR participate in that meeting, not merely as an observer, but as an equal who often addressed the heads of states on matters relating to the liberation struggle in Africa.

It was shortly after that meeting that we were informed we would be leaving for our long-awaited destination – Angola – where we would receive military training. It transpired that an agreement had been reached between two of Africa's great minds, OR Tambo and Agostinho Neto, that would enable the ANC to train its cadres in Angola. The two men were comrades that would enable as well as personal friends. Word had it that Neto had told OR: 'Look OR, we [Angola] are only a few months old and do not have the resources to assist you with the struggle of the people of South Africa against apartheid, but we can provide land that will afford you the time and space to train your people.' This was a great relief to the ANC and its liberation army, MK, and we immediately left for Angola. By this time OR was a household name, a respected and revered leader not only as Acting President of the ANC but also as de facto President of the people of South Africa.

I met OR several times during my training in Angola as he frequently visited us, as did our other military leaders such as Comrades Andrew Masondo and Chris Hani. What struck me about OR was his humility and confidence. Here was a man who had left his country in the early 1960s, yet he never wavered in his belief that South Africa would one day be free. The most amazing thing about OR was that he was easy for us ordinary soldiers to approach and we could discuss our struggles, even personal matters with him. Here was this man who struck fear into the hearts of racists in South Africa, here was this man who was a respected giant in the international arena, and yet he shared a meal with us ordinary cadres. No special meals were prepared for him and he slept in the same dwellings, often rudimentary underground bunkers, that we slept in. He was firm yet easy to work with, always ready and willing to listen to and resolve whatever problems we had. Some of our questions were sometimes immature, nasty and provocative. These were encounters that OR enjoyed for they afforded him the opportunity to understand and develop our young fiery minds.

My other interactions with OR occurred when I became the overall Commander of MK in Angola. OR was one of the few leaders who frequently visited 'his' soldiers. The modesty, simplicity, outreach and humanity of our Commander-in-Chief again overawed me. We kept up to date with the internal situation in South Africa as well as with international affairs. When MK was forced to pull out of Angola because of the agreement reached between the US, Russia, Cuba, Angola and South Africa, we followed OR's advice that it is sometimes necessary to move one step backwards in order to advance. This agreement was to pave the way for the independence of Namibia. We accepted the notion of pulling back to Tanzania and even further up to Uganda. It took the intellect of a leader such as OR to make the bold decision of pulling back beyond the equator as a tactical move that would benefit the struggle in South Africa. This was in spite of the fact that many thought it would be wiser to move closer to home. OR's decision later proved to be one of the wisest ever made by a leader of a liberation movement faced with the challenges of the time.

I met OR more frequently when I was co-opted to the NEC of the ANC. He was still the same simple man whom I had first encountered in 1976. His dedication was still evident and I could see even greater determination sparkling in his eyes. It was a sparkle that said to all we would achieve freedom in our lifetime. I am undoubtedly a better person today because of what I learnt from OR. During his term in office, every member of MK and the ANC felt his style of collective leadership. This rubbed off on the general membership and truly made the ANC a people's organisation. The ANC, like any organisation, had its own problems and there were times when divergent views resulted in fierce debates. I remember these instances as they always brought out the best in OR. Like a seasoned captain, he would steer the ship out of a threatening storm into calm waters.

I will always remember OR's visits to me when I was hospitalised in Moscow after being shot by UNITA (União Nacional para a Indepêdencia Total Angola) forces in Angola. UNITA was then used a proxy by the racist regime in Pretoria. The intensification of the struggle inside South Africa frustrated the apartheid regime so it had resorted to attacking our bases in Angola. I will forever cherish the time that OR spent visiting, as he would brief me on developments in the organisation, on our struggle inside South Africa as well as on the international situation. I remember that he had to leave Moscow in a hurry as he was expecting a message about the release of Nelson Mandela. That was in 1988 and already pressure to release Mandela was mounting on the apartheid regime.

History gave us Ghana's Kwame Nkrumah and Angola's Agostinho Neto. Mozambique produced Samora Machel, the Cuban revolution gave us Che Guevara and the Vietnamese had Ho Chi Minh. In Oliver Reginald Tambo South Africa has its own giant, a man who earned respect in the international arena, a man to whom the world listened. OR was respected in the UN, in the then OAU and, most importantly, in the rural and urban areas of our country, in our towns and townships. He played a significant role in laying the foundation for the final demise of apartheid and I was indeed privileged to have rubbed shoulders with this great statesman.

OR AND EKURHULENI

Thembi Nobadula

Wattville in Benoni, now part of Ekurhuleni, was one of the oldest town-ships in the East Rand and it was a highly politically charged area. When OR arrived there, in 1956 he immediately got himself involved in our lo-cal political activities and work in the community. This was a great morale booster for us township activists because OR was not only a member of our branch but also a member of the ANC's NEC. Oliver was the first African solicitor in Benoni.

Not long thereafter, the ANC leadership was rounded up and charged with treason by the apartheid regime. All this was happening while OR was engaged to be married to Adelaide. As the plans were so far advanced OR gave instructions to Bishop Reeves to marry him in prison if he was not re-leased before the set date – luckily he was granted bail before his big day.

In 1960 when the ANC sent OR abroad little did I know that our paths would cross again. OR did not settle in the UK, only his family did, but we were neighbours for most of the time firstly in Highgate and then in Muswell Hill where they lived until their return to South Africa after the end of apartheid.

OR got to work as soon as he arrived in exile. He initiated the forma-tion of the SAUF, comprising the ANC, the PAC and the South West African National Union (SWANU) which resulted in the expulsion of the apartheid regime from the Commonwealth in 1961. He also established ANC missions in many countries, beginning in Ghana, prompting the comment during the 1980s that the ANC had more embassies in democratic countries than the apartheid regime.

Although OR did not live in London he maintained contact with the UK. He would make stops in transit or when travelling on ANC business on invitations to address conferences around the world and at the UN, lobbying members of the Security Council to isolate South Africa.

OR was doing a very hard and taxing political job as Deputy President of the ANC. Initially OR was not attracted to the idea of an armed struggle, which he regarded as violence and OR said he would not be provoked to take that route. Some of those who were less patient argued that it was futile seeking a political settlement with the apartheid regime. But, dealing with a most vicious and repressive regime, he was reluctantly compelled to alter his view in that regard.

After Chief Albert Luthuli's death in 1967 OR became the ANC's acting President, a position he held until his health finally failed him.

Although Oliver was based wherever the ANC had its headquarters, his family always lived in the London Borough of Haringey, first in Highgate then in Muswell Hill, which honoured him by giving him the freedom of the borough in 1990. By this time he had suffered the stroke that left him partially paralysed, but I can remember him hobbling along the corridors of the Town Hall to receive this honour.

When news of his illness reached Adelaide in 1989 she did not know what to pack in her luggage as she feared the worst. Then a second message came that she was to meet the plane that was bringing him at Heathrow Airport, where he was flown in what was like an air ambulance with a doctor, courtesy of Kenneth Kaunda, then President of Zambia, one member of the NEC and a posse of protectors.

OR was taken to the London Clinic, near Harley Street, where he lay for some time. Very few people thought he would pull through. Slowly but surely he started to make minor improvements and eventually regained consciousness. Nobody thought he would be able to work again.

After some time his doctors felt he could go home and ordered him to take things easy. However, it was not long before OR had some of his staff from his ANC office in Zambia come over to his home in Alexandra Park Road in North London where he converted one of the rooms into an office and started to work again.

The stroke seemed to have affected his mobility more than anything else, but he would still join in all activities at home and in some public engagements. I remember when he met his old friend and comrade Nelson Mandela over Easter in 1990. The reunion was electrical.

It was a shame of life or fate that after all the years of struggle and sacrifice OR only managed to see the dawn of South African freedom and not the sun rise on that morning when South Africans of all colours formed those long queues to vote, many for the first time in generations.

We celebrate the fact that Johannesburg International Airport was renamed OR Tambo International Airport in October 2006. It is fitting for many reasons, but particularly because the airport is situated in Ekurhuleni and OR lived there before going to exile – and was laid to rest there.

RADIO FREEDOM

Thami Ntenteni

Leaders of the calibre of OR Tambo emerge from the midst of despair and human suffering, their consciousness formed and sharpened by their experience of human misery and degradation. Because they are by nature sensitive and compassionate, their consciousness refuses to accept the status quo and invariably their sense of justice revolts against the system. They rise above their own personal self-interest and they become the embodiment of the people's yearning for deliverance from the yoke of oppression. They become the personification of hope and resilience. They hold a steadfast belief in people's ability to transform their lives and they inspire people to adopt a new attitude to life.

As a leader and a committed revolutionary, OR inspired the generation of 16 June 1976 and the entire nation. Through force of example, he brought about a new consciousness, a belief that change was possible. When OR was once asked what sustained him and why he had chosen what seemingly was a thankless vocation by a journalist, his response was simple and yet profound. He said, 'We are the salt of the earth.'

Any struggle for national liberation, any struggle to restore the dignity of people and pull them out of the morass of human poverty and deprivation creates and nurtures cadres such as OR Tambo because they are the ones who teach and live by the ethos of the humanity that all of us profess.

The eruption of the June 1976 student uprising which started in Soweto and soon engulfed the whole of South Africa signalled a turning point in the struggle against apartheid. It precipitated the mass exodus of young people who left the country to join the ANC as well as the PAC in exile.

The generation of 1976 had confronted and survived the armed might of a regime that felt itself threatened by young people armed only with stones. Our approach to the revolution was a mixture of youthful adventurism, enthusiasm and a romanticised version of the struggle.

We were the hot-blooded youth, excited by the victory of FRELIMO in Mozambique and the imminent downfall of the Portuguese in Angola. We sincerely believed that all we needed were AK47s in our hands and the enemy would be vanquished. The power and confidence that comes with an AK47 was demonstrated and confirmed when we crossed into Lomahasha in Mozambique from Swaziland. Here we met with FRELIMO soldiers and saw their eyes glowing with the pride of their recently attained victory and their newly acquired sense of power. They told us stories of heroic escapades by FRELIMO soldiers and they allowed us to handle their weapons, albeit without the magazines.

It was in this frame of mind that we passed through Mozambique en route to Dar es Salaam. We imagined ourselves coming back home, guns blazing, destroying the enemy through our superior fire power and the masses of our people receiving us as heroes, liberators and conquerors.

It was understandable that our young and rebellious contingent of budding revolutionaries would demonstrate a certain level of impatience with the pace of the armed struggle. Many of us were disillusioned with the philosophical debates and endless political discussions about apartheid. The time for talking was over. It was now time for action. We wanted the ANC to expose us to the military skills, to the guerrilla tactics of Che Guevara. We had read Robert Taber's *War of the Flea* and we believed we were sufficiently equipped to confront the forces of oppression. Taber reinforced our sense of confidence and invincibility with the words: 'The guerrilla fights the war of the flea, and his military enemy suffers the dog's disadvantages – too much to defend, too small, ubiquitous and agile an enemy to come to grips with.'[1]

We knew very little about strategy and tactics. We were still to learn the theories of revolution, about the maturing revolutionary situation wherein the oppressor can no longer rule in the same old way and the masses refuse to be ruled in the same old way. We did not yet appreciate the balance of forces both internally and internationally that were so necessary for the successful execution of the struggle for national liberation.

Little did we know that within a very short space of time, we would meet with OR Tambo and all of our dreams would change, although the overall objective of liberation would remain at the core of our thinking.

My first encounter with OR was a profound learning experience. It formed the foundation of my ability to analyse situations and make an assessment of the political developments in the region. That learning continued throughout the years of my stay in exile and on the numerous occasions I had the opportunity to engage with OR.

On arrival in Dar es Salaam, Max Sisulu was assigned the task of identifying individuals within our group who would be sent to the Soviet Union to train as journalists to join Radio Freedom, the voice of the ANC.

Needless to say, there were no volunteers. How do you execute the revolution by talking on the radio? We were serious revolutionaries and now this ANC representative was telling us about radio.

The next leader to come and address us on the matter was army commander, Comrade Joe Modise. He also talked about the various forms of struggle, but still there were no takers.

It was late in the afternoon in the scorching heat of Dar es Salaam that Ntate Mashigo, our camp commander, informed us that the President of the ANC, OR Tambo, was coming to see us. The prospect of meeting this legendary revolutionary in person was nothing short of electrifying. We believed that the time had come to talk about serious matters of revolution. We expected Tambo to tell us how soon we would be sent for military training and how soon we would be infiltrated back into the country as guerrillas. As guerrillas we owned nothing and had nothing to lose except our chains.

OR arrived that evening, joined us for dinner, and the political discussions began. But the armed struggle, blazing guns and us marching victoriously into South Africa were far from OR's mind. Instead, he talked about mass mobilisation and the supremacy of the political struggle over the military. He painstakingly explained that the struggle in South Africa was a political one. The decision to take up arms was intended to advance the political struggle and was arrived at as a result of historical experience. While the people engaged in peaceful protest against the apartheid system and demanded to be treated with dignity, the enemy responded with violence.

He explained that we could never successfully execute the armed struggle without the support of the masses. But, because of the brutality of the system, the support of the people for the armed struggle could not be taken for granted. OR drew our attention to a fact that the system of apartheid had so dehumanised our people that their self-esteem was almost completely destroyed. He emphasised that a people with low self-esteem, dehumanised by apartheid, suffer from a paralysis of fear of the might of the system. On a daily basis, they see this apparent might of the system being unleashed at anyone who even dares to lift a finger, either in self-defence or in defiance.

This paralysis leads to a state where the people begin to doubt their own ability to act in their self-defence. It was the role of Radio Freedom to restore this self-esteem, this confidence that was a necessary condition for the people to rise against oppression. This would be done in combination with certain predetermined military attacks whose purpose was to serve as 'armed propaganda'. But for this armed propaganda to succeed, it had to be reinforced by the broadcasts of Radio Freedom with the intention of strengthening the resolve of the people to fight. This was the role that OR saw for Radio Freedom.

After this discussion OR asked to see those individuals who had been identified by Max as candidates for Radio Freedom. I was one of these candidates. Once again OR patiently explained what we were being called upon to do, the heavy responsibility of marshalling the people through radio to support the armed struggle. He said that it was our responsibility to keep people's hopes alive, to whip up their enthusiasm and to demonstrate the weaknesses of the enemy while at the same time demonstrating the strength of the people. Above all, the people had to know that the ANC was alive and well and preparing to engage the enemy, and that the ANC continued to lead the struggle of the people.

This encounter with OR changed the course of my life. It had never been my intention to be a journalist but now I pursued this career and was eventually appointed as the Director of Radio Freedom. Over the years, OR demonstrated in practice that he respected and held the work of Radio Freedom in high esteem. Whenever I met him in the corridors of the ANC office in Lusaka, he would ask me about the situation at Radio Freedom.

I remember that there was a time when we did not have transport to get to work. I did not think that this matter required the President's attention. We were raising the issue with Comrade Nkobi in the treasury, but it was taking a long time to resolve.

One day I happened to bump into OR and he asked me about the state of affairs at Radio Freedom. I casually said, 'Well, everything is fine, Comrade President, except that there is a small problem which we are dealing with and I am sure it will be resolved in time.'

OR immediately called me into his office, sat me down and asked about the nature of the problem. I explained that for a few months we had been without transport to get to work, that the matter had been raised with treasury and they had promised to look into it.

From that day onwards, OR gave instructions that his own car was to be assigned to Radio Freedom. We were fetched in the morning when we were going to work and we would inform the driver when he should fetch us after work as well as about whatever other errands we had to run in the course of our duties.

What is amazing about this gesture is that OR gave Radio Freedom priority over the use of his transport without regard to his own transport needs. He
may even have revised his own schedule so that we had priority over the use of
his car. This continued for about a month until a replacement vehicle arrived.

OR was never too busy to grant Radio Freedom an audience or an interview. But over and above this, he had complete faith and confidence in
the abilities of the individuals who were entrusted with the responsibility of
the radio broadcasting.

On one occasion I arrived at the office in Lusaka to find NEC members
involved in a heated debate about a programme that Radio Freedom had
aired. In this programme Radio Freedom had criticised one of the leaders of
a Bantustan. Some NEC members were angry because this Bantustan leader
was involved in discussions with the ANC at the time. It appeared that based
on the contents of the radio programme this Bantustan leader had questioned the bona fides of the ANC.

I was asked to explain the radio's position with regard to this Bantustan
leader and the programme that was the cause of so much anger. I explained
that the policy of the ANC as we understood it was against the Bantustan
policies of the apartheid government. In this context any individual who
was participating in these institutions was collaborating with the system.
Taken from this perspective our criticism of this Bantustan leader fell within
the realm of the policies of the organisation.

It was Comrade Joe Modise who subsequently explained the context and
I understood what the issue was about. As a consequence there was a proposal that somebody senior should be assigned to look at our scripts before
going on air.

I raised this matter with OR, pointing out to him that we were not opposed to our scripts being edited. But the suggestion that scripts must be
given to someone who did not work with us and who had other commitments besides radio was not practical because of the daily deadlines that we
had to meet.

OR listened attentively and then said, 'Don, what do you think is the solution to the problem?'

'Comrade President', I responded, 'anyone who is assigned to be an editor
of Radio Freedom must have as his daily responsibilities the work of radio.
That person must attend our editorial meetings, must be part of the debates
when we analyse situations and decide on the angle that will be taken. It is
only when that person is familiar with the thought processes and the debates
that we engage in that he or she would be in a position to understand the
reasoning behind certain decisions.'

Comrade OR simply said, 'Yes Don, I understand.' What he did after that
I do not know, but the subject never arose again. In addition, from then on
Radio Freedom was briefed more fully about political developments, in-
cluding matters that were highly sensitive and confidential.

This incident is important to me because it established and reinforced the
editorial independence of Radio Freedom. There are many critics who, even
without knowing how Radio Freedom operated in exile, are quick to dis-
miss it as a propaganda instrument in the hands of the ANC leadership.

Yes we consulted with the leadership of the ANC, yes our broadcasts reflected the position and the policies of the ANC. But on a day to day basis,
the editorial decisions of what went on air were solely the responsibility of
Radio Freedom operatives. In retrospect, I believe that this had a lot to do
with the kind of leader OR was.

Whenever we invited Comrade OR for an interview on Radio Freedom,
he would get a briefing from us. He would say, 'Don, obviously you have
been dealing with the subject on air. What have you been saying and why?'
I recall an occasion when we briefed OR about two Urban Bantu Councillors. It was a time of elections for the Urban Bantu Councillors and Radio
Freedom was urging a boycott of the elections. These two councillors were
campaigning in the same area in Rockville, Soweto. They had booked ad-
jacent halls. They then proceeded to put speakers outside the halls and they
began trading insults. When OR heard this, he made the theme of the discussion, 'A struggle for power among the powerless'.

These brief words encapsulated the futility of these elections. I have never
ceased to be amazed by the manner in which OR could grasp the salient
features of a subject and proceed to draw conclusions which seem very obvious but are very profound in terms of their meaning and content.

Comrade OR was a visionary and an eternal optimist. At no stage did he
lose his focus and his belief in the justness of the struggle against apartheid
and the ultimate victory of the liberation forces.

When the ANC was grappling with the implications of the Nkomati Accord signed between Mozambique and South Africa, and Swaziland was
coming under increasing pressure from the apartheid regime not to allow
itself to be used as a transit point for the ANC, a Swazi journalist came to
Lusaka to interview OR. I was asked to sit in on that interview and when it
was done, the journalist looked at OR with eyes seemingly full of pity. He
asked whether in the light of all the problems confronting the ANC OR
was still confident about victory, to which OR answered simply, 'Victory
amounts to the sum total of the resolution of problems.'

The year before the unbanning of the ANC, OR addressed the members of the ANC in Makeni, Lusaka. We knew he was not well and all of us, deep down in our hearts, felt that we could not face the future without him. It was as if he sensed this because his concluding remarks were both prophetic and reassuring. He said, 'Comrades, my health is no longer what it used to be; you are all aware that I am not well. But I want to promise you that whatever little breath is left in me, whatever little strength I still have, will be consumed in struggle together with you.'

At that moment, all the comrades who were there felt at peace, united in the resolve to continue the struggle and yet at the same time reassured that OR would forever be there to lead and guide us.

The last time I met OR in exile and was able to shake hands with him was as memorable as my first encounter with him. This was after the release of Nelson Mandela and the unbanning of the ANC.

OR had just paid a brief visit to South Africa and was accompanied by Nelson Mandela en route to Europe. They made a brief stopover in Lusaka. I had not seen OR since his address in Makeni, and I was anxious to be re-united with him. I had never met Nelson Mandela and I was excited and wondered what kind of a man he was. As journalists of Radio Freedom we were allowed into the VIP lounge where the two great leaders of the struggle for the liberation of South Africa were sitting.

I will never forget what OR did when we entered that lounge. He saw me and his eyes lit up as he struggled to stand up with the aid of his walking stick. Then he smiled and said, 'Hello Don, it is good to see you.' The gentleman sitting next to him, who happened to be Nelson Mandela, also stood up, shook my hand and said, 'Hello Don, it is good to see you.' It was as if Mandela had known me as long as OR.

OR was a great man, a visionary, an optimist, a leader, and yet he was so humble. It is an honour and a privilege that I have had occasion to bask in the sunshine of such great leaders and to drink from their well of wisdom.

NOTES
1. Robert Taber, *War of the Flea: The Classic Study of Guerilla Warfare* (London: Granada Publishing Ltd, 1965).

A FEARLESS FIGHTER
AND LIBERATOR

Sam Nujoma

I am humbled and honoured to recount my vivid memories of one of South Africa's and Africa's great patriots and revolutionaries, Comrade Oliver Reginald Tambo. I was privileged to share the same trenches with him, scientific guerrilla tactics, and platforms at international conferences at the UN and AAM rallies. We travelled far and wide with the view to mobilising the international community to support the just cause of our genuine freedom and independence and to isolate the minority white apartheid regime of South Africa. As a result of our joint patriotic efforts, we gained many friends who stood by us during the difficult days of our protracted armed liberation struggles: in Namibia, led by SWAPO, and in South Africa, led by the ANC.

During the liberation struggle I had the honour and privilege of knowing and working closely with Comrade Oliver Tambo. He dedicated his life to the dismantling of the minority white apartheid regime of South Africa. He will be remembered by current and future generations of Namibians, South Africans and the wider African continent as a fearless fighter and liberator who stood firm until victory was achieved. Sadly, he could not witness the hoisting of the new South African flag that symbolises freedom, democracy and a multiracial society on 10 May 1994.

After the Windhoek Location Massacre on 10 December 1959, we found it very difficult to have SWAPO's case defended in court in the then South West

Africa where there were only white lawyers who were not keen to defend Africans. Consequently, in January 1960, we hired a lawyer – Comrade Oliver Tambo – from the prestigious Mandela and Tambo law firm in Johannesburg.

On his arrival by air from Johannesburg, however, Comrade Tambo was not granted the necessary permit to enter South West Africa and he was detained at Windhoek's Eros Airport. We went to meet him at the airport and took him food. He was deported back to South Africa the next day.

The apartheid colonial regime in South West Africa would not allow Comrade Tambo to defend our case. Instead, it sent a white lawyer from South Africa to defend us. Contrary to the white apartheid regime's expectations, he eventually defended our case successfully.

After the Sharpeville massacre in March 1960, Comrade Oliver Tambo escaped from South Africa. He went to what was then Tanganyika where we were reunited. We were received and helped by President Julius Nyerere and other officials from TANU, the party that was to govern Tanzania following independence in 1961.

I proceeded to New York and Comrade Tambo headed for London. We met again a few weeks later in a free and independent Ghana, in Accra, at the Positive Action Conference hosted by President Kwame Nkrumah against the French government's testing of atomic weapons in the Sahara Desert at the time when the FNL of Algeria was fighting for its freedom and independence.

The same conference also condemned and denounced South Africa's apartheid policy and its refusal to place South West Africa under the UN trusteeship system. We met again in New York in September, and thereafter we jointly established our liberation movements' offices in Dar es Salaam, Tanzania.

Our friendship was anchored in the strong bonds of comradeship rooted in the historical fact that we were fighting the same enemy. On one occasion, I stood in for Comrade Tambo at the ANC Women's League Congress in Luanda where I addressed the ANC women on his behalf.

Another historic occasion occurred when the ANC had been unbanned and comrades who lived in exile started to return home. On his way back to South Africa after thirty years of leading the liberation struggle in exile Comrade Tambo made a stopover in a free and independent Namibia.

He landed at Eros Airport, the same airport where he had been detained in 1960 when he had come to defend us. This time, in contrast to his previous treatment, I accorded him a full Guard of Honour as is given to visiting heads of state.

In 1992 Comrade Tambo and I attended the reburial ceremony of the remains of the late Kwame Nkrumah, Ghana's first President, in the Kwame Nkrumah Memorial Park in Accra at the invitation of the then Ghanaian head of state Flight-Lieutenant Jerry Rawlings.

We were the only foreign dignitaries invited to attend this singular occasion and we addressed the solemn proceedings at the ceremony, recognising the bravery of the late President Kwame Nkrumah.

Comrade Tambo was a fearless freedom fighter, a comrade in arms, and a shrewd intellectual whose contribution to the liberation of southern Africa is unsurpassed. He cherished the idea of freedom. We can only reward him and his legacy by protecting and defending the hard-won independence, territorial integrity and sovereignty of our African countries. His entire life was selflessly dedicated to this cause.

Although he is no longer with us, Comrade Oliver Tambo still speaks eloquently to us from afar. We must continue to emulate his exemplary deeds that contributed immensely to the realisation of a democratic and non-racial South Africa.

To his revolutionary spirit and his visionary memory, we humbly offer our honour and respect.

THE HUMANITY IN EVERYONE

Stan and Angela Sangweni
(extracts from an interview with Thami Ntenteni)

Thami Ntenteni (TN): How long have you known OR?

Stan Sangweni (SS): We came to know OR in 1974 when we moved to Lusaka. I had just been appointed to the UN Economic Commission for Africa and posted to the regional office which was, and still is, in Lusaka. Our first contact on the socio-political level, was with the ANC. As it happened, we were looking for our nephew who had left South Africa, our home village Jobstown in Newcastle way back in 1962, when he joined MK. He was Walter Mavuso Msimang, but to me he was known as Muzi. We made contact withn Muzi and that was a reunion to to celebrate. And, of course, we also had to link up on the political front. Muzi was instrumental in facilitating our contact with the ANC, both organisationally and in terms of the individuals, the leadership and so on. One of the leaders that Muzi was instrumental in introducing us to, was none other than the President, OR Tambo. And our relationship grew intimate as we saw one another at meetings and at social gatherings.

TN: You say you met OR in 1974. What was the mood in the ANC then? And what was OR's demeanour? Because I suspect that the mood at that time would really be different from when we started moving with the June 1976 generation.

SS: That is a very interesting point you raise. We had come in from Swaziland where I had been employed by the then University of Lesotho, Botswana and Swaziland. I had been assigned to Swaziland since 1964. In Swaziland there wasn't any outward, overt political activity other than what you might have seen coming to the surface at funerals, when one of our South African people, particularly the ANC's, died. Then we arrived in Zambia where you had the ANC mission and office. It was a very vibrant office. The entire ANC leadership was based there although they moved in and out and OR himself was, of course, very mobile and always on the road. But there was a really vibrant ANC community in Lusaka. There were also other liberation movements. All of which really contributed to this vibrant political activity, long before 1974 I believe.

TN: Okay, let's come back to OR. You used the word 'intimate' to describe your relationship. Can you elaborate on this? And here Mma [Angela Sangweni], I would also want you to come in.

SS: The first thing that inevitably strikes you when you meet OR is his tremendous stature. You can't miss that. You are struck by him as an incisive, assertive leader of Africa. And yet, at every moment you speak to him, you interact with him. You have a feeling that this man is really talking to you. He is listening to you. He is identifying with you. It could be about anything: personal or political. To give you an example, we had a situation with my sister Lindiwe Mabuza (Lindi) and her daughter Thembelihle Msibi (Thembi). Lindi wanted Thembi to live with her, but the girl's father, Dr. George Msibi wanted his daughter to live with him. It was a very tricky situation given the circumstances of Lindi's participation and employment in the ANC and the position of Thembi's father in Swaziland. So, at the family level we had a problem and OR was able to come in and advise us on how to handle the situation. He persuaded us that we should let go of Thembi, the child of our sister. Let her go back to Swaziland to stay with her father.

TN: What was OR's approach to the problem? How did you come to see the situation in his way?

Angela Sangweni (AS): OR acted like a big brother to Lindi. He sympathised with Lindi's point of view. But he also saw things from Thembi's point of view, because she wanted to be with her father. OR came to the house to talk to Dr Msibi, who we had called from Swaziland, and to Lindi. At the time Lindi would not listen to us, but when OR came, he said: 'Look here

Lindi, this has to be settled this way.' Lindi wanted Thembi to go to Cuba but OR was able to convince her that Thembi should be given the choice to go and be with her father.

TN: From what you describe, each parent was thinking about their own situation and what they wanted and not about the child. Did OR bring about this focus on the interests of Thembi?

AS: You're correct. OR was the one who brought in the interests of the child. I think Lindi and Dr Msibi were just fighting for their own space to have their daughter with them. But OR showed them their child's angle. Although OR knew that many children were being sent to Cuba for political reasons, for studying and so on, he was able to make an exception here, and see what was in the best interests of Thembi.

TN: Let's now get back to the political situation. How did you see OR as a leader?

SS: As I said, I moved to Lusaka to take up a position with the Economic Commission for Africa. Our mandate then was to bring about cohesion in the countries of eastern and southern Africa. I remember OR's leadership in that context. We would have meetings in Lusaka, which I was very involved in organising. At these meetings the Heads of State would come to talk about critical issues confronting them. One of the critical issues was how to reinforce the Front-line States – Botswana, Zambia, Mozambique, Swaziland, and eventually Zimbabwe – against the powerful economy of South Africa. This was at a time when the ANC was neither a government in waiting nor anywhere close to being spoken of as a government. It was just one of many liberation movements. But without fail, whenever OR stood up on those occasions to speak, everybody would listen, and listen intently. If you had come in from outside this environment and were told that these were the Heads of State, you would say that OR was the leader of the Heads of State when you listened to him talking, addressing the issue politically.

TN: Did you at any point sense either a weariness or disillusionment on OR's part?

SS: There was no question whatsoever of OR or anyone with him becoming frustrated or disillusioned. I don't think those kinds of word existed in OR's language. Even down the line in the 1980s when we were relocated to Nairobi and I was with the Environment Programme, he still seemed like the same old OR, although he had grown in stature and age. He lit up and he continued to grow in strength.

AS: There was one thing about OR. He would always remain so calm even when emotional things were happening. For example, in Nairobi during the Decade of the Women conference in 1985, OR was addressing the delegation that came from South Africa. And then some unruly youngsters who were from South Africa but not with the ANC came in and attacked him. They were so rude and they used such bad language. OR remained very calm; he just went on with his speech. But Johnny Makathini, who was very emotional, had to be held back. Johnny wanted to box them. Something like this also happened in Lusaka when OR went to the University of Zambia to address the 1976 group. There were some people who came to the meeting who were very much against the ANC. Those youngsters were so rude. They actually started throwing leaflets towards where OR was sitting. But he remained very calm. He could see, I think, the foolishness of those youngsters.

TN: What about OR as a person? He was someone who shouldered all of these responsibilities, but did he have his lighter moments?

AS: The thing that always struck me about OR was that he could be a very simple person. Our house was one of the ANC's safe houses in Lusaka and there was all of this tight security around him. We would be told at the last minute that OR was coming. I remember the first time we were told OR was coming, we were so tense. Then, just before he arrived, our dog brought a smelly fish into our yard.

SS: It was a big fish and it was the stinkiest thing.

AS: The whole yard started smelling. We were so worried and embarrassed, but when OR arrived and we started apologising for the terrible smell, he said: 'I don't have a sense of smell. I can't smell anything.' So that was his simplicity. He would eat what was there. Our house was very simple and we just had one toilet which we all shared. One night OR was sleeping in our house and I went to the toilet. When I came back, I met him walking along. He had a handkerchief tied around his head with a knot, and he was holding his pyjama pants up; I think they were falling down. And he was walking to the toilet. That memory will remain with me forever because I didn't know that the President of the ANC could just be a simple, simple man.

TN: What kinds of problems did OR have to deal with?

SS: You know, it is amazing how we sometimes overlook the kinds of problems that leaders have. These might be related to the struggle or related to leadership or they might be personal, but they are problems all the same. I think that OR faced many different issues. He once told me a story about his relationship with Mwalimu Julius Nyerere, the president of Tanzania. Now Mwalimu undoubtedly had tremendous respect for OR. But OR once told me about this exchange that he had with on the question of the PAC and the ANC. Mwalimu had said: 'You know, you ANC people and the PAC must find each other. Africa is always talking about unity. Find each other so that we can operate as one front. This is the only way in which we can support you and help you.' I got a clear picture of these two giants, engaged with one another. OR told me that he ended up saying to Mwalimu: 'You know what, Mwalimu, we are outside here as refugees. We left our people in South Africa. We have a tradition in the ANC that there are fundamental decisions which can only be taken by our people who then give us the mandate. The matter that you are talking about now, of finding each other, with the PAC, is a fundamental matter. Very very deep. You can't comment on it as you sit here.' OR told me that he and Mwalimu never spoke about the issue again. The two of them spoke at length about various things, but never on that topic. There were other issues but mostly, I think, OR managed his problems and found ways of dealing with them. They never daunted him that I can recall.

AS: He could get very angry though. Especially when it came to keeping time, OR could get angry. One day he was at our house and his driver was supposed to pick him up, but he didn't come. [Whistle] He was so angry. Stan wanted to give him a lift, but OR said: 'No, no, no! I'm going to walk.' And off he went.

SS: Our house was some distance outside town where the ANC office was, but OR just walked.

AS: There were other things that OR used to insist had to be done properly. He was a perfectionist. And he could lose his temper if things weren't done in the way he wanted. One day he was at our house and he was meant to give a speech the following day. But his speech was not what he wanted and so he summoned people, including Comrade Thabo, to come and work on the speech. His secretary had to bring a typewriter to the house. Because the speech had to be just right.

TN: Did you continue to have contact with OR towards the 1990s?

SS: We did and we were in Nairobi then.

AS: We met OR once after his stroke. He came through with his son Dali. He was in a hotel and we all went to see him. OR was so different. It was very sad because he was no longer the OR we knew. He couldn't talk properly. I think that was the last time I saw him.

SS: But, I used to see OR at meetings in South Africa during the whole run-up to the 1994 democratic elections. He was ailing but he still made an important contribution.

TN: In conclusion, just very briefly, what makes OR great for you?

SS: I'm basing what I say on a very short period of time when we interacted with OR. I know that many South Africans made their contributions to the struggle, but I'm inclined to say that OR gave perhaps more than anybody. In his unique manner, under extremely trying circumstances, daunting circumstances, prohibiting circumstances, OR was able to vocalise, to articulate, the South African problem to the world out there. Whether you were thinking of the children, whether you were thinking of the women, whether you were thinking of the labourers, whether you were thinking of the various formations, students and so on, it was OR who was able to articulate the situation. And he did this in such depth and with such a truthful manner that nobody could doubt what he said. His integrity was above question. He dedicated himself to the cause of South Africa, the free democratic South Africa. Truly, that dedication sums up the greatness of OR.

TN: From your side, Mma?

AS: I think that politically OR was a giant. But the most important thing was that he could see the humanity in everyone. When OR talked to you, or to anyone, you thought that you were the most important person. He could relate to everyone and he made you feel important. And he didn't just do this to certain people; he did it to everyone. He was unique.

VISITS TO AUSTRIA AND WEST GERMANY

Tony Seedat

When Oliver Tambo visited Austria at the beginning of 1980, the Cold War was at its height and anti-communism was the name of the game. One of the points made against the ANC was that it included communists as members and, worse still in the eyes of some, as officials. Although there were very many liberal-minded and anti-racist people amongst Austrians and their leadership, Africa as a whole was unknown to them and many viewed the continent with a racist bias.

An example of this attitude had occurred during a previous visit to Vienna by Thomas Nkobi, the Treasurer of the ANC. Nkobi and I met with many high-ranking officials in the Church and the government. Amongst others we held meetings with the Chancellor of Austria, Bruno Kreisky, and Heinz Fischer (who today is the President of Austria). But when we went to see Bishop Sarkovsky he refused to offer us a seat in his office until we requested seats. It was one of the worst experiences of my life when Sarkovsky suggested to me that Nkobi and the African people needed generations of civilising before they would reach the level of the white man.

Unfortunately, sentiments such as these were not isolated and we encountered this kind of thinking and attitude when OR visited Austria. at the invitation of the Karl Renner Institute, which hosted an annual lecture attended by Austria's most prominent personalities. Oliver Tambo was to be the guest speaker. It was the first time in the Institute's history that a black man was invited to deliver this lecture.

One of OR's dilemmas was that he was addressing an audience that was, firstly, ignorant about apartheid and the evils of the system and, secondly, sceptical of a black organisation's ability to govern a country such as South Africa.

In his address OR briefly went into the history of the ANC and the century-long resistance to both colonialism and apartheid. He told people that apartheid was a crime against humanity and that it wreaked havoc amongst the black population. He touched upon the thousands of people arrested in South Africa every year (in addition to political prisoners) as a result of the country's inhuman system of population control. It was the brutal suppression of peaceful resistance to apartheid and the government's refusal to enter into any negotiations that had forced the ANC and others to take up arms. He explained that the armed struggle was a just struggle against a system that the UN had declared a crime against humanity. OR also argued that apartheid restricted economic development. A liberated South Africa could absorb massive amounts of foreign investment and consequently it was in the interests of Austria and Europe to rid the world of apartheid.

At the end of his speech, judging by the applause and questions, the audience had begun to view apartheid and South Africa in a new light. OR had been introduced as a lawyer and a practising Christian, and his speech had made a significant impression on both his audience and the Austrian public.

The upshot of this visit was that the Austrian government invited the ANC to open an office in Vienna, which the government was prepared to finance. But the ANC did not take up the offer as it was felt that Austria could be adequately taken care of from the ANC office in Bonn, West Germany.

When OR met with Chancellor Bruno Kreisky there was immediate mutual respect between the two leaders. One of Kreisky's concerns was the ANC's relationship with the Soviet Union and its 'dependence on them for military training and arms'. This was a concern common to most European parties and governments and the ANC's reply was logical and rational, but not necessarily accepted.

During our visit to Kreisky we asked him for material aid and support for our refugees in East and southern Africa. Kreisky asked his Personal Secretary to consider a sum of two to three million schillings. Tambo, not knowing the exchange rate at that time, very gratefully accepted the offer. When I intervened and asked Kreisky to consider increasing the amount to a sum of ten million schillings OR seemed to be embarrassed at what he considered my rudeness. Subsequently, when I explained to him that I had met Kreisky on several occasions and that, in fact, he had granted us a sum of seven and a half million schillings, OR forgave me my 'indiscretion' and promised never to question me on money matters again.

Football

I was surprised by the passion that OR showed for football. At the dinner table one Saturday evening some of us were discussing the English League football results. OR showed a keen interest in the game generally. In addition, he was a supporter of Liverpool Football Club and a very big fan of the footballer John Barnes. OR greatly admired Barnes's dribbling skills and surprised us when he described some of the greatest goals scored by this player. During a subsequent trip I took OR two videos of football matches in which Liverpool was involved. While watching one of the videos he behaved like any other football fan, clapping enthusiastically at good moves and accurate shots.

OR in Bonn

The ANC opened an office in Bonn, West Germany, in 1981, at the invitation of a joint parliamentary delegation visiting Lusaka in the late 1970s.

This office was situated in the same street as the South African Embassy. From the beginning the ANC was treated with respect and some of our partners in government were those who were dealing with the Embassy and the South African Ambassador. OR considered the ANC's official presence in West Germany to be very important as the Germans were one of South Africa's most important economic, political and social partners. There was even convincing evidence that the West Germans were involved with South Africa in the nuclear field. Through a system of foundations, churches, trade unions and NGOs, West German activities within South Africa were significant.

One of the Germans' most important goals was to develop alternatives to the ANC and strengthen those elements as well as trade union federations, which were regarded as 'not under the wings' of the ANC. In addition, the West German government invested a lot of money in trying to develop an 'independent' students' organisation. With their support they hoped that the BCM could possibly be an alternative to the ANC. The Bantustan concept and its leaders received financial and political support from West Germany in order to make them more acceptable internationally. Gatsha Buthelezi and high-ranking Inkatha Freedom Party officials were regular visitors and were hosted by the highest officials of government, political parties, churches and others. Trade union federations such as the Federation of South African Trade Unions and the National Council of Trade Unions, which were regarded as 'independent', also received funds and were regular visitors to West Germany.

Despite these activities, the Germans had to invite OR to their country because it was a time when there was heightened internal and international activity against apartheid. Literally millions of people acted in some form against apartheid all over the world. The German government was aware of OR's crucial role both inside and outside South Africa.

The West German President, Richard von Wiezsacker was a liberal and a humanist. He supported change, undefined change, in South Africa and his close contacts with the Church made him aware of the inhumanity of apartheid. But, like others, his main aim was to convince the ANC that any association with communists and the communist world would harm South Africa and Africa generally. The meeting with Tambo was definitely an eye opener for Von Wiezsacker. They met on a one to one basis behind closed doors and it was an opportunity for them to get to know one another personally. I don't think Von Wiezsacker had met a South African, black or white, who explained to him the inhumanness of apartheid and the form of resistance that was forced upon the people of South Africa. The resistance against apartheid included armed struggle. Von Wiezsacker's questioning of the apartheid system was converted into understanding the ANC's struggle and, more importantly, to supporting the disbandment of apartheid. OR's role in convincing Von Wiezsacker must be seen in the light of the great respect he commanded amongst the German people.

While in Germany OR met with Johannes Rau, who at that time was the Premier of North Rhine-Westphalia. Rau, who in later years became the President of Germany, was a Social Democrat. If I remember correctly, his nickname was 'Missionary'. During OR's visit to him all Rau spoke about was the Church and a black Christian he had met in his youth. This meeting confirmed, since I had met Rau on a few previous occasions, that he was very badly briefed on or informed about South Africa and the apartheid system generally. He refused to address our requests for material support for our people in exile in East and southern Africa. It was an altogether disappointing occasion, but OR, as ever, tried to be positive about the get-together. He suggested that it was important to have met the man who was the Premier of the biggest state in Germany, and that that fact alone was a slap in the face of the South African regime.

In his various addresses to German business people, politicians and members of NGOs OR spoke about the tragic consequences of the apartheid system on the vast majority of South African people, particularly the black population. He explained the hatred and animosity it was causing between people and he talked about the division even amongst Christians and the various Churches. He spoke about the Bible being used to justify apartheid and racism.

I am not sure that this part of his speech convinced the business people involved to withdraw their investments from South Africa. A different attitude was noticeable when he explained that apartheid affected economic growth and that if the resistance within South Africa continued to grow it would result in total chaos of the economy. He explained that a system based on the well-being of a small part of the white population and an even smaller number of blacks was a hindrance to the growth of the South African economy. A democratic South Africa was interested in opening the market to all South Africans and its desire was to attract foreign investments. The economy could grow and expand to the whole of southern Africa. The ANC, which represented the vast majority of people in South Africa, was not prepared to destroy the economy.

During all of OR's public and private meetings he pleaded for the release of our leaders incarcerated on Robben Island and in other prisons in South Africa. He spoke at length about the torture meted out to political detainees and prisoners and highlighted the plight of families of political activists who had 'disappeared' while in the hands of police. He thanked all those people – and there were hundreds of thousands of them – who petitioned and held vigils for the release of political prisoners, to save the lives of those sentenced to death, and to protest against people being murdered while being interrogated by the security police. He asked people to condemn cross-border raids and the murder of both South Africans and the citizens of neighbouring countries. He did not stop explaining and educating and pleading for change.

OR never understood how people could support apartheid and become its apologists. He couldn't understand why the ANC was branded as a terrorist organisation. He couldn't understand those who condoned apartheid state terrorism. He always spoke about Europeans as being our natural allies as they had experienced Fascism and many had perished fighting it. He couldn't understand Amnesty International (Germany) which explained that it could not support the ANC's campaigns to release South African political prisoners as these prisoners practised 'terrorist methods'. He held discussions with the official Church in Germany, which took a similar position, and he debated the statement, 'We are not in favour of apartheid, but we will not support your methods of struggle.' He couldn't understand the leaders of different organisations and parties who refused to sign petitions for the release of Mandela and others because a leading communist had signed the same petition.

Nevertheless, ever the optimist, OR was always of the opinion that some day people would understand and would join other international forces in supporting without any reservations the struggle in South Africa. It was a topic close to his heart and we often discussed it.

OR made a significant impression on his audiences throughout Germany. It was very interesting to see the reaction of the South African Embassy as it found it most difficult to counter his position. The impression he made was aptly summarised by the International Secretary of the Friedrich Ebert Foundation who said, 'This is the first time I've heard a black man present such a convincing case on behalf of his people.'

OR and trust

Sometime in the 1980s I received a phone call from a gentleman who was a member of the British Embassy in Bonn. He invited me for lunch. During our meeting he was very open about being a senior official in the Embassy and a member of MI6. He said that he had received a message from London which suggested that Margaret Thatcher, then Prime Minister, was proposing a direct line between herself and Oliver Tambo. When I suggested London or Lusaka as the appropriate office to handle this kind of issue he refused, giving the explanation that this might be viewed as a recognition of the ANC. He asked me to convey this message to nobody but Oliver Tambo.

When I spoke to OR he suggested that I accept the request and direct all correspondence or messages to him personally. He reminded me that as a representative of the ANC in a foreign country I was regarded as an ex-officio member of the National Executive. He said, 'You represent the ANC and we have every confidence in you.'

In terms of this trust and confidence, OR was not afraid to inform fellow comrades about the successes and the problems experienced by the movement within South Africa and in the countries we were active in. This sometimes included sensitive and very confidential matters.

Whoever travelled with OR was made to feel totally accepted as part of his team. He never made a speech or contribution without first discussing it with the people in his delegation. Any proposals regarding change or amendments to the content were considered with due respect.

Death of our daughter

While I was representing the ANC in Bonn, our five-year-old daughter, Ayesha, who had suffered from a complication from birth, passed away. My ex-wife Aziza and I decided to bury her immediately as is our custom. She was buried in Bonn within twelve hours of her death and I informed the ANC headquarters a few days later. When he received the news OR phoned me at midnight to convey his sorrow. Shortly afterwards he sent Mzwai Piliso to visit us and personally communicate OR's and the organisation's condolences. We were assured of every assistance that we might require.

Last meeting

It was at a conference in Johannesburg that OR and I met and embraced for the last time. My President had suffered a stroke and he did not contribute to the activities of the conference, but he was visibly happy to be home and to meet hundreds of activists he had not known.

When I spoke to OR he was with President Kaunda of Zambia and we sat together for an hour or more, recalling some of the problems we had encountered and discussed in exile. He had never doubted the justness of our struggle. OR and President Kaunda spoke about the enormous tasks and difficulties that the ANC and South Africa would still have to face and overcome, but OR had every confidence in the outcome. His words to me were, 'Comrade Tony, we have made it!'

For me OR is the greatest South African and, in fact, the greatest human being I have ever met. I loved and respected him unreservedly.

A CULTURE OF SERVICE
AND SACRIFICE

Reg September

I first became acquainted with OR (or 'Chief') in 1956 when we all met at the Treason Trial. The Western Cape had hardly ever played host to Africans of that stature. Those who governed had seen fit to declare the Western Cape a coloured preferential area and in the coloured community many were duped into believing they were in fact superior to those of darker skin. It was an extremely difficult time.

Before the days when people of colour walked urban areas with confidence, young black men who graduated in the Eastern Cape set their sights on Johannesburg. After all, that was the industrial hub, the mining centre, and the heart of African resistance. Among those who had aspirations to be part of that great hub were young patriots of the calibre of Nelson Mandela, Oliver Tambo, Walter Sisulu and Duma Nokwe, to name but a few. Many of us who did not come from the Eastern Cape had to wait until the Treason Trial to experience the privilege of meeting these men who were to play such an important role in shaping the future of our country.

It was during the Treason Trial that we had the honour and pleasure of being invited to OR and Adelaide's wedding. It was such a treat to see them dance, to be part of such an enjoyable yet solemn occasion. I was about 33 years old, and at times felt quite overawed by the whole scene: the wedding, the trial, the meetings, and the company. Such warmth, such comradeship.

In the fort itself, where we were imprisoned, we once heard a group of prisoners singing in an adjoining cell. It was beautiful to hear them sing 'Ten to Ten' – the story of a mother, a girlfriend, seeing off a young man on a train journey to the mines. Meanwhile OR had pulled together a choir of some of our own cell mates. On hearing the neighbours sing, he organised a joint session. God knows how he managed it. The professionalism with which OR got the choirs together was truly admirable.

I next saw OR when I reached Dar es Salaam on my way out of South Africa, escaping from the police. He was in charge of the External Mission, which faced the difficult task of arranging the reception for cadres who had come for military training, organising camps in different countries prepared to offer training, accessing food, facilities and clothes, and facilitating the return to South Africa of those who had been trained. In addition, our External Mission faced the huge challenge of building international solidarity, which had to be developed. The UN had to receive constant attention, as did friendly states, organisations and individuals. All of this took place under OR's leadership. He had to gather the most suitable comrades he could muster. The task before him was truly mind boggling.

While I was in Dar es Salaam, for about a year and a half, I saw OR when he was around. At times we lived in the same building. When he left before anybody else in the morning, I understood that he usually went to a place of worship. As he entered the office, he would greet each and every person by name, taking special interest in any newcomers. He was so respectful and so careful in his relationships with people. He was a deeply caring person, too. On one occasion I had to join his group on a visit to Zanzibar, and I did not have a jacket. He quickly offered one of his own for me to wear.

Over a period of time I came across OR at various ANC bases. On these occasions, those in charge of food appeared to be competing for the privilege of looking after OR. I can remember how they made sure that the best pawpaws or mangoes were set aside for him. It was the same when he visited a camp occupied by MK. You would see the young cadres taking extra care in preparing a special toilet for OR. If I say that people all had such a deep respect for him, which bordered on hero worship, I don't think I would be far wrong.

OR had to travel extensively, to meet Christian or Muslim leaders, communists and non-communists, people in the US, Sweden and Russia. He made sure that they all understood our difficult challenge, and he tried to provide a space for them all to render assistance in whatever way was suitable or manageable.

During my time as the ANC's Chief Representative in Western Europe, I had the honour of accompanying him on trips to Russia, Korea, India and

China. I witnessed first hand the exceptional care he took in preparing his speeches and statements. In India I sat in on a group preparing his speech with him. OR was meticulous in his choice of words. In fact, the task proved too much for me, and after a while I 'retired hurt' with exhaustion.

How OR coped with the ongoing stress and travelling I shall never know, but his health suffered as world leaders all clamoured for him to visit them. His asthma attacks were painful to witness and his feet became swollen as a result of his frequent travels. Once, when I was about to remove his shoes, he would not allow it since it would have been too difficult to put them on again. His driver, Nxumalo, who looked after him over a long period, took great care of him, but it was still understandable just how worried Adelaide must have been.

At meetings, OR gave everyone the opportunity to present his or her point of view and then would summarise a consensus at the end. I would describe him as the ultimate consensus man. 'Beware the wedge driver,' he would often say. And, of course, we were all in contact with people who held different points of view. Once I remember having been asked to communicate an idea for an attack that would have meant the loss of civilian life. He did not take much trouble to give a detailed answer. He was totally committed against the loss of civilian life. In a private chat, he always tried to articulate respect for other people. He would make certain that nobody ever spoke in a language that was not understood by all participants in a discussion. He was very strict about this, and would reprimand any transgression.

On one occasion, after a long night's meeting in Morogoro, OR took me for a walk. He conveyed a message which he had received from Nelson Mandela, who wanted to be certain that we all understood the difficulties that Winnie was facing, and that she needed the support of all of us. OR held my hand in a fatherly or brotherly way as he ventured into a couple of personal anecdotes, jokingly telling me of an experience he had had as a young man. His chief had insisted that he, OR, share the chief's liquor, something which OR never quite understood. Afterwards, when he tried to mount his horse, OR fell off. He had learnt his lesson the hard way. It was an experience that stood him in good stead for many years – I never knew OR to drink any alcohol.

In the UK, where I had the pleasure of seeing OR from time to time, people in the solidarity movement all listened to him most attentively. Canon Collins and his wife played a key role in seeing him through. We were all so grateful for the care which people of every level of political and social standing afforded to him.

At the end of OR's life, I felt humbly honoured to be among those who carried his coffin from his home. OR, one of the world's greatest revolutionary Christian gentlemen, often said that we had to cultivate a culture of service and sacrifice. He meant every word and lived it too.

IGNITING A PASSION

Wally Serote

The last time I saw Comrade OR alive was in Dawn Park on Easter Saturday in 1993. He arrived with Comrade Walter Sisulu, into a stunned, large crowd of people, who were milling in the street, hurt, sad and angered by the assassination of Comrade Chris Hani. When OR and Walter arrived, the body of Chris had been removed from the driveway where he had fallen when the assassin shot and killed him. OR climbed from the car that had been driven into the crowd. As soon as he emerged, followed by Walter, the crowd split in the middle, forming a natural guard of honour for them. They both sized up the crowd and were stern as they greeted.

Someone guided them to behind the van where Comrade Chris lay. Comrade OR ordered the white policeman who stood guard over Comrade Chris to uncover him. He looked at the face and, after a while, he made an angry sound, and ordered the policeman to cover Comrade Chris's face. OR and Walter walked into the house. From the time he climbed out of the car to the time when he got back into it and drove off, a great quiet – dignified, sad and angry – fell over the crowd.

The next time I saw Comrade OR was when he lay in state at the FNB stadium, where a few days earlier we had paid our respects as Comrade Chris lay in state.

The first time I met Comrade OR was in 1977 in New York at the UN when he came to address the UN Security Council. He was the first head of a liberation movement to do so. We walked in with the ANC Chief Representative, Comrade Thami Mhlambiso. I remember shaking Comrade OR's hand and noting with joy his Mpondo marks on his cheeks. I sensed, not being able to give a political interpretation to this unprecedented event, that besides the 1961 decision by the ANC to establish MK, and the 1969 Morogoro Conference which rededicated and replenished the ANC for deepening and escalating the imminent fall of the apartheid system in our country, OR's presence at the UN represented another turning point for South Africa.

Shortly after this event, I finished my studies and left the US. I settled in Gaborone, Botswana. In 1978, the ANC headquarters in Lusaka, Zambia, sent Comrade Ray Mokoena to meet with those of us who were suggesting to the movement that we wished to initiate a cultural front in Botswana. The cultural front would have an underground and an aboveground structure. The underground structure would use all means to contact and engage all South Africans active in the area for the purpose of the creation of a democratic arts and culture movement.

An underground unit, consisting of four people, reporting to Comrade Henry Makgothi, was formed in 1978 through Comrade Ray's and Zake's guidance. It was code-named 'Brother'. We made contact in South Africa and began to function. From 1979 to the late 1980s this unit listened every year to OR's voice on tapes that were also clandestinely distributed into South Africa. The taped January 8th message tapes reached us every January, and 'Brother' sat in an underground house quietly listening to Comrade OR's voice, engaging with the issues of struggle and revolution that he raised. Afterwards a political discussion ensued followed by an attempt to translate and transform the speech into issues, projects and programmes to be engaged by the arts and culture formation in Gaborone, and in the underground in South Africa.

One of the most difficult questions we had to answer was one that Comrade Makgothi had posed to us, seeking that we provide an answer to it through action and continuous discussion: 'How can arts and culture function in the underground?' The result was the formation of Medu Art Ensemble, which was spearheaded by 'Brother'. Medu consisted of an administration section, a newsletter, which we distributed clandestinely in South Africa, and the Theatre, Music, Literature, Photography, Film and Graphic Units.

As the head of both Medu and 'Brother', I was required to sit in the local Revolutionary Council, headed by Jerry Matsila (Victor Makhosini), which became Senior Organ and later the Regional Political Military Council. It was through these structures that I was exposed to the rich, dynamic, humane, progressive and civilised thinking, policies, strategies and tactics of the

ANC as I met, during sessions of these underground structures, both the political and military leadership of the South African revolution: Joe Modise, Chris Hani, Mac Maharaj, John Nkadimeng, the late Nate Motshabi, Thabo Mbeki, the late Cassius Make, the late Florence Mophosho, Gertrude Shope, Lambert Moloi and many other leaders in the political and military structures.

I recall that one of the greatest finds for me, in my interaction with these leaders, was my joy at the discovery that the most profound issues and moments in the revolutionary process could express themselves in the simplest manner. I was utterly engaged by this find in the revolution. I struggled to understand and interpret it.

I was conscious that Cassius was very senior (in the structures of the ANC). I was aware that whenever he came to Botswana, 'the Front', he was always extremely busy. All of the leaders like Cassius went an extra mile whenever they were at the Front. Cassius and I had an understanding between us that after all the formal meetings, he and I should meet on a one-to-one basis. He said that he wanted to learn about arts and culture. We did this between other meetings in and outside of Gaborone. I drove him around – dropped him here and picked him up there. At times we would drive long distances.

It was from these drive meetings that I began to come to grips with issues of armed struggle, underground work, mass action and international support for the democratic struggle in South Africa. It was through these meetings that 'Brother' suggested to Comrade Cassius that the Cultural Front in Botswana should organise a major cultural symposium and festival of the arts, so as to begin a debate, discussion and dialogue on arts and culture in South Africa. In addition, it was in these meetings that a marriage of arts and culture and issues of revolution were cultivated. It was from there on that 'Brother' made continuous reports to Comrade Cassius regarding the progress of the plans for the major arts and culture event. And then he came up with a suggestion: 'I think you must come up to HQ, to brief Chief and seek his guidance on this project.'

Eventually Comrade Cassius made it possible for me to land in Lusaka and have a meeting with Comrade OR. I had agonised, throughout my journey from Gaborone to Lusaka, on how to handle my brief to OR. I was conscious of the fact that OR was an extremely busy person with overwhelming responsibilities. I entered the office where I found OR seated behind a desk on which several files were piled.

OR had speaking eyes. He had a very warm smile but he could also be very stern. He was an intent listener. Face to face with all this, with me very curious about his Pondo marks and wanting to talk to him about them, but also carrying millions of questions in my head, I forgot to refer to my notes. I spoke off the cuff. It must have been one of the most jumbled briefs OR had ever received from a cadre. At one point, after I had been talking for a while, I stopped. I felt that I was wasting very valuable time.

OR watched me. He took his spectacles off, put them on the desk and listened. I tried to organise my thoughts. At the end, he asked a few questions: 'What do you want to achieve by all this? Who is coming to the event? How many people do you expect?' Finally, he said, 'Arts and culture is very important. It has the potential to unite all South Africans.' He thought a little further and then said that we were doing a very important job in the struggle. OR had lit a passion in me. If he said it was important, no one but no one in the world would ever be able to stand in our way.

I felt like a madman as I sat in the plane flying back to Gaborone. A passion had been ignited in me about the role of arts and culture in the revolution. We had a long discussion about this in 'Brother' and then began a series of debates, discussion and consultations in the Medu structures. These were followed by discussions with several other people in the country. In July 1982 the 'Culture and Resistance Symposium and Festival of the Arts' was held at the University of Botswana in Gaborone. About 2 000 people – black and white, men and women, South Africans from exile and from inside the country – convened for about five days. There were Europeans, Americans and Africans from other countries on the continent. In 1983, the ANC formally established its Department of Arts and Culture.

Comrade OR was a strong, firm and solid foundation for human integrity and dignity. His digity was relentless, contagious and very dynamic. Around him, there were the late Comrade Treasurer General, Thomas Nkobi, the late Secretary General Alfred Nzo. There were Comrades Thabo Mbeki, Mshengu and Gab. But more than this, there was the NEC of the ANC. Out of all these people, with OR at the helm, the ANC machinery purred and the struggle unfolded. The next time I came close to OR again was in London. He was staying with his family after he had suffered a stroke.

Following on from 'Culture and Resistance', we passed through 'Culture in Another South Africa', a conference held in Amsterdam during December of 1987, with Comrade Barbara Masekela heading the Department of Arts and Culture and organising the international aspects of the conference. I worked under Aziz Pahad to handle the underground coordination.

The ANC Arts and Culture policy was consolidated at the Amsterdam conference. A myriad of arts and culture formations had emerged in South Africa. They had as their foundation the structures of revolution, which were sprawled across South Africa. The cultural boycott had been intensified as a means to isolate the apartheid system. In 1987 OR came to London to meet with the anti-apartheid leadership and ANC cultural structures. Trevor Huddleston and Mac Maharaj were there and so were, I think, the South African Congress of Trade Unions and the SACP. We had been able to create a parallel power and governance structure to the apartheid system. There were various, non-racial, non-sexist and democratic formations which were challenging the power and authority of the apartheid system. These structures pushed to, among other things, 'open the doors of learning and culture for all', as the Freedom Charter states. As they interacted among themselves, these structures also sought to create a people's exchange programme among and between themselves and with their counterparts around the world.

When Comrade OR delivered his famous 'South Africa at the crossroads' Canon Collins lecture that Sunday in London he spoke about the importance of 'people to people' contact among democratic South African structures and the international community. A debate and discussion had been primed. A process enriched by the culture of liberation, the culture of negotiation, and of the armed struggle and the intensification of the mass and international struggle had begun.

The ANC's history as a liberation movement has contributed to producing an amazing variety of people. One of its most outstanding intellectuals, leaders, freedom fighters and statesmen is OR. On that Sunday in London he commented: 'The crisis which was in its early stage when Canon Collins joined us for the emancipation of our people has matured. The septic boil caused by the apartheid system has ruptured irrevocably and for all times. South Africa is at the crossroads ...'

OR came to London to inform South Africa and the world that a new era had dawned in South Africa. We all may have heard OR speak, but many of us did not understand the meaning and implications of what he said. Even today, in 2007, the mass movement in our country is still grappling with the 'crossroad' which OR identified and analysed for us nineteen years ago. We the cadres in 'Brother' consulted with OR throughout the time he was in London as we were organising another major cultural event in 1990. 'Zabalaza: Arts and Culture and Festival Programmes' was a direct follow up to 'Culture and Resistance' and 'Culture in Another South Africa'. A non-racial, non-sexist and hopefully democratic contingent from South Africa arrived in London. They represented all regions and art forms including a possible handpicked group of cultural administrators to be trained. We attempted to do a 'people to people' contact between the South African contingent coming straight from home, and their counterparts in London. This event coincided with the first visit by Nelson Mandela to the UK after 27 years of imprisonment.

'Arekopaneng' ('Let us unite', in Setswana) cultural group consisting of people from Medu Art Ensemble, South Africans and some British and Africans from other countries, organised and, through Zabalaza, hosted this massive arts and culture training and festival programme. The highlight of this event was when we organised for those from South Africa to meet Comrade OR, and listen to and discuss issues with him. The ten or twelve ANC regions in South Africa which were represented by the contingent of cultural workers, resulted in our having to organise five consecutive days of meetings with OR at his home.

On each day, OR insisted that the South Africans first had tea and cake with him. During this time he asked people's names and surnames and familiarised himself with where they came from. Then came the formal part when he listened as the cultural workers related relevant conflict situations and other issues. OR sought the views of those who were working in London and he asked other questions. Throughout he listened keenly and would then briefly give his views. Finally, we would distribute copies of his book, *Oliver Tambo Speaks*, and he would autograph these slowly and with great care. At times there were about twenty books to sign. He was using his left hand as his right hand had been incapacitated by his recent stroke.

In 1993, the Department of Arts and Culture of the ANC, now based in Johannesburg, South Africa, organised its final conference, the 'Cultural and Development Conference'. We consulted closely with OR, who had agreed to be the chief convener of the conference, at a time when there were very serious threats to the democratic cultural movement from the strong and moneyed liberal movement in South Africa. The Department of Arts and Culture organised for various formations of this movement to meet with OR at his office in 'Shell House' (the ANC's former headquarters building) in his position as the national Chairman of the ANC.

I am not quoting him verbatim. The gist of what was recurrent in his response to the various presentations by the different participants was: we must integrate the grassroots into the cultural process, we must insist on being non-racial, non-sexist and democratic. We need to transform apartheid cultural structures. We must learn from the international community. Africa expected us to learn from her experience, as she expected free South Africa to become fully involved in continental affairs, armed with that experience. I have, in my mind, the memory of a smiling, almost mischievous, expression on OR's face.

Like millions of South Africans, when Comrade OR died in 1993 I was first lost, then very, very sad and then very, very angry. Then I realised that we must build the ANC as it is the only hope that millions of South Africans have.

I often think about OR and I have great joy in my heart about him. I hope that in whatever work we do, we will respect his integrity, dignity, sacrifices and his love for South Africa, Africa and humanity. Now and again I have a sense that our leader, our comrade, our friend, our chief, Comrade OR, is still present – stern, listening intently, pondering, smiling his most beautiful smile. I remember once saying to him that his Pondo marks on his cheeks made him most handsome. He replied, '... they are mine, they are mine ...' and gave his smile.

THE ROLE AND PLACE
OF WOMEN IN SOCIETY

Gertrude Shope

I knew Oliver Tambo as one of the leaders of the ANC, at the time when he was Secretary-General of the organisation. Shortly before the 1960 State of Emergency was declared in South Africa, Tambo was elected Deputy President of the ANC, and then sent into exile to create the External Mission and to drive the struggle from outside the country. His role involved briefing the UN, OAU and other world bodies on the political situation in South Africa, as well as soliciting moral and material support for the oppressed majority. I got to know him better when I too went into exile, especially during the 1970s after I returned from Eastern Europe where my husband, Mark Shope, represented the English-speaking African countries at the World Federation of Trade Unions (WFTU) in Prague, then Czechoslovakia. I assisted Florence Mophosho with the ANC Women's Section, as it was known in the External Mission, at Morogoro, Tanzania. Later our office moved to Lusaka, Zambia, where the ANC had its headquarters. On Comrade Tambo's advice, we formed a Secretariat of the Women's Section that took charge of all issues pertaining to women. It was during this time that I worked more closely with Oliver and gained a lot from his experience and unselfish mentoring.

As a person, Oliver was humble in character, very down to earth and always ready to assist, including in our personal lives. During the course of our struggle, many things happened that affected us both as individual families and as an organisation. Oliver played the role of father in the absence of our

parents. I recall times when some of our colleagues got into domestic conflict with their partners, resulting in tensions that could affect our work as a
collective. At our request, Oliver would readily intervene and calm down all
tempers. Furthermore, he understood the various needs that people had and
he would assist where possible. When Lyndall, my daughter, married Tebogo
Mafole, one of our cadres in Lusaka, Oliver asked Adelaide, his wife, to assist
with the attire that Lyndall would wear on the day. It was a duty that Adelaide carried out wholeheartedly and efficiently. She also helped to organise financial donations for the Women's Section when we prepared for our
conferences.

An additional responsibility that Oliver took upon himself was to be
present whenever a cadre had to be buried, with the occasional exception
when he was far away and out of reach.

Even when challenged and placed in danger, his concern was to put the
people first and himself last. I remember that in 1982 a large number of
cadres were massacred in Maseru, Lesotho. The ANC felt duty bound to
go and bury them and a delegation led by Oliver went up to Maputo. The
atmosphere was very tense in the whole southern African region and some
people tried to discourage Oliver from attending the funeral in case the
apartheid regime brought down his plane or attacked Lesotho again. But
Oliver was insistent on attending. His argument was that the bereaved had
travelled from South Africa and the ANC in South Africa had also sent a delegation including Victoria Nxenge and Father Xundu. In addition, Leabua
Jonathan, Prime Minister of Lesotho, needed him for moral support. There
was no way that Oliver would abdicate his responsibilities.

In the end, we were told that Oliver would lead the delegation from Lusaka. Kenneth Kaunda, then President of Zambia, offered to release his plane
to transport the ANC delegation and the various diplomatic representatives
of countries who were attending the funeral. The Lesotho government was
very honoured by OR's attendance. Comrade Tambo was taken to the government guest house. We all stayed in one hotel and room service provided
all our meals. Arrangements were made in the evening to have a briefing session with our people from South Africa who had come for the funeral. As
sad and tense as the occasion was, the funeral's organisation and attendance
gave Oliver great strength and he delivered an inspiring address. This in turn
motivated Leabua who spoke very well on behalf of the host country.

As we left Maseru, heading back to Lusaka, Leabua sent a small plane carrying two women passengers, employees of the Lesotho Foreign Ministry.
They found us in Mbabane as we were finishing the soft drinks we were
offered whilst the plane made a short stop. They came into the plane and

walked straight up to Oliver, telling him that they had accompanied our plane to Swaziland. Now that our plane was about to depart, their duties included seeing it off, flying back to Maseru and reporting to Prime Minister Leabua that the duty which Oliver had come to perform had been fulfilled, and they had seen him off safely home. This was a great honour to Oliver and a sign of appreciation from the government of Lesotho.

Oliver first formally introduced the subject of the place of women in society at the close of the first conference held in Luanda by the ANC Women's Section in the External Mission. In order for me to give a proper interpretation of the concern, the mood and manner in which this challenge was squarely presented as the responsibility of women themselves, I choose to quote from his closing address to the conference. He said in part:

> The meeting of the Women's Section which commenced on September 10, 1981, with an opening address by Comrade President Sam Nujoma, President of SWAPO of Namibia, has now completed its business. I believe it is the general consensus among all the participants that a fair and objective assessment of the meeting would be best conveyed by two words only: supremely successful. This would be a reference to the businesslike manner in which the proceedings were conducted; the serious atmosphere in which discussions were held; the fierce concentration with which speakers addressed the topics presented for discussion; the prevalence among the participants, individually and collectively, of a sense of mission inspired by a constant awareness of the national and international challenges posed for the women of South Africa, and the ANC women in particular, in this decade of the eighties, the Decade of Destiny. To have held a successful conference is to have put substance into our verbal expressions of gratitude to the MPLA Party of Labour, the government and people of Angola, and especially to the Organisation of Angolan women (OMA), who made the meeting possible in the first instance.
>
> To have held a successful conference is to have vindicated the confidence and trust which the international community has in the ANC and its Women's Section – confidence and trust reflected in the generous financial and other material donations without which the meeting could have remained a remote dream.
>
> To have held a successful conference at this critical moment in the southern African situation is to have focused the attention of everyone in South Africa on the presence in Angola, in this very

month of September, of two types of South Africa: the one type concentrated in the south of Angola, the other assembled in Luanda – the question being: Which of these two is the true South Africa?

Which one represents those forces which the people of South Africa must and will destroy and annihilate? Is it that unsightly army of marauding murderers in southern Angola, or is it the glorious band of [the] ANC in Luanda?

On the other hand women in the ANC should stop behaving as if there is no place for them above the level of certain categories of involvement. They have a duty to liberate us men from antique concepts and attitudes about the place and role of women in society and the development and direction of our revolutionary struggle. In fear of being a failure, Comrade Lindiwe Mabuza cried, sobbed and ultimately collapsed on top of herself when she learnt she had been appointed ANC Chief Representative to the Scandinavian countries. But looking at the record, could any man have done better or even as well?

The oppressor has, at best, a lesser duty to liberate the oppressed than the oppressed himself. The struggle to conquer oppression in our country is the weaker for the traditionalist, conservative and primitive restraints imposed on women by man-dominated structures within our movement, as also because of equally traditionalist attitudes of surrender and submission on the part of women.

We need to move from revolutionary declarations to revolutionary practice. We invite the ANC Women's Section, and the black women of South Africa, more oppressed and more exploited than any section of the population, to take up this challenge and assume their proper role, outside the kitchen among the fighting ranks of our movement and at its command posts.

To have held a successful conference now is to have paid a worthy tribute to 25 years of heroic struggle by the women of South Africa.

But in assessing this conference as a great success we are making a preliminary judgement; we are talking about the immediate past rather than the future. It is the testing period ahead, it is the rugged and boggy terrain of implementation now opening up before us, which will decide the correct place of this conference in the history of our struggle.

The mobilization of women is the task, not only of women alone, but all of us, men and women alike, comrades in struggle. The mobilization of the people into active resistance and struggle for liberation demands the energies of women no less than of men. A system based on the exploitation of man by man can in no way avoid the exploitation of women by the male members of society. There is therefore no way in which women in general can liberate themselves without fighting to the end of the exploitation of man by man, both as a concept and as a social system.

If we are to engage our full potential in the pursuit of the goals of our revolutionary struggle, then, as revolutionaries, we should stop pretending that the women in our movement have the same opportunities as men. There is little evidence of it, if the high calibre of the women meeting here today is anything to go by. For this has been a meeting of women who are worthy of Lilian Ngoyi, and her great impact on the struggle.

Our struggle is, therefore, local, regional, continental and global. It is against this background that we must see the glorious challenge we face, the enabling task assigned by history to the people of South Africa, to the women of our country, to her youth and to her workers: We are called upon to save Africa, to defend her independence, and contribute towards world peace by seizing power in our country. We have the capacity; if we do not, let us develop it. We have the strategies: if they are wrong, let us correct them.

In our opposition to the regime whose preoccupation is the domination of black peoples everywhere, we are a united majority in South Africa comprising not only the oppressed and exploited masses, but also people from every racial group. These include that brave brigade of women known as the 'Black Sash' – veteran fighters for justice and peace; they include thousands of white youth and students who are convinced that the regime is digging a mass grave for their future; they include a growing number of white democrats, true patriots of our land; they include white members and leaders of the religious community, who have come to appreciate the essential justice of the cause we fight for.[1]

Prior to this occasion, Oliver had encouraged the Women's Section to organise workshops where male and female cadres would all participate in discussing the role and place of women in society. At one point, he instructed the ANC legal team and the Women's Section to prepare and hold a joint workshop on the subject. This workshop went a long way to shedding light on the need for the role and place of women to be recognised.

Under Oliver's guidance, we learned to understand the importance of working together as a collective with women freedom fighters of other liberation movements, especially the women of SWAPO, in Namibia, as we were both oppressed by the same regime and our goal was one – the liberation of our countries.

In the same vein, he encouraged us to work closely with women of the host countries where we lived. We shared each other's rich experiences and exchanged valuable ideas, which had a major impact on our work as a collective. We organised joint activities for international events such as International Women's Day (8 March) and International Children's Day (1 June), and also held joint meetings as we prepared for big conferences such as the 1985 'End of Decade for Women' conference in Nairobi. We gathered to strategise with women of our host countries so that with their support we would all speak with one voice, especially in support of the liberation of southern Africa. We arrived at a collective decision to stage a walk-out from the 1985 conference in the event that Elize Botha, the apartheid First Lady, forced her way into the women's conference to represent women of South Africa.

Some delegates from developed countries such as the US did not support the idea that women from liberation movements be allowed to relate how the political situation in their countries affected their emancipation and development. As far as they were concerned, this conference was to deal only with the question of the equal status of women and men in society.

However, with the support of friendly countries such as Zambia, Tanzania and some countries from eastern and western Europe, we proceeded with our preparations that were meant to present apartheid and colonialism in southern Africa and the Middle East as a crime against humanity. We attended all preparatory meetings in Vienna and made our voices heard. Good advice came from our leadership that we should invite women's organisations from inside South Africa to attend the Nairobi conference. The WCC and Young Women's Christian Association (YWCA) assisted by sponsoring travel, board and lodging for delegates from South Africa, a gesture we highly appreciated. Other friendly countries sponsored the ANC delegates from their various places of exile.

The wisdom of Oliver Tambo could not have come at a more appropriate time. He and Sam Nujoma, President of SWAPO, held a short briefing session with the women in Lusaka just before we left for Nairobi. Shrewd analyst that he was, Oliver had thought of a strategy that was to place the ANC and SWAPO women high on the conference agenda, and give them prominence for many months to come. On the eve of this important conference, Oliver and Sam organised a press conference in Nairobi at which they briefed the world's press on the main purpose for which the South African and Namibian women had come to the conference. A number of questions were asked and clarified by our women.

As the sun rose to shed light on the first morning of the conference, delegates were abuzz with excitement and enthusiasm. The South African and Namibian women were in the headlines. Our presence and the purpose for which we were attending the conference were given favourable coverage. This annulled all the negative attitudes towards the participation of liberation movements. Instead, the issue now attracted attention and many people began to understand that women cannot claim or strive to gain full, equal status in a society where the people are still oppressed and colonised as a nation. At the height of this excitement, Oliver and Sam were already halfway to Addis Ababa to attend an OAU summit. Their input back in Nairobi made an indelible mark that the world found difficult to ignore. The press emphasised the need for apartheid and colonialism to be done away with once and for all. It was an affirmation of the moral high ground captured by Tambo the deep thinker and Tambo the strategist.

In his endeavour to accord women the opportunity to access various experiences and development possibilities, Comrade Tambo included women in his delegations to national and international conferences such as the Non-Aligned summits in Cuba and Zimbabwe, the conference on 'Women, Children and the Law' in 1987 and many other gatherings at the UN and OAU. Shortly before the ANC's return to South Africa, in May 1990, under the leadership of Tambo, the NEC issued a statement on the emancipation of women in South Africa. During the same period as the leadership went to Mitchell's Plain for talks with the Nationalist government preceding the negotiations on the Government of National Unity, Ruth Mompati was in the ANC delegation that came from Lusaka.

This ongoing involvement exposed women to a variety of experiences and equiped them to play a role in the reconstruction and building of the country, as they do so efficiently today.

NOTES
1. O. Tambo, 'Speech to the Women's Section of the African National Congress', Luanda, September 1981.

THE PICTURE ON THE WALL

Nomasonto Maria Sibanda-Thusi

I have a photograph of the late ANC President Oliver Tambo hanging near the entrance to my house in the north of Johannesburg. Whenever I pass by and look at this picture of Comrade OR, as we affectionately knew him, I always pause and smile as I feel in me a sense of satisfaction and fulfilment.

I wish I could tell him that today I am one of the few citizens of our beloved South Africa who has been given the honour and privilege of representing our democratic, non-racist and non-sexist country in a foreign capital.

I wish that he could hear me say, 'Comrade OR, you have always believed in members of the ANC and our people as a whole and yet your attention and commitment to women's emancipation was never compromised. You also stressed the importance of investing in the young generation and cadreship of the ANC. The Young Women's Section was therefore highly valued by you.'

When I pass his picture, I often say to him: 'Comrade OR, I am one of those members of the former Young Women's Section who has been recognised for the contribution, no matter how big or small, we have all made to women's liberation and equality for all our citizens.'

I look at his picture and say: 'Comrade OR, it's me, Nomasonto. You met me at the ANC Development Centre in Dakawa, in Morogoro, Tanzania. You were visiting the government and people of Tanzania and all ANC settlements in 1984. You came to Dakawa where I, together with other very capable and strong comrades, was assigned to ensure that this piece of land donated by the government and the people of Tanzania to the South African people, was developed to provide for the welfare, education and settlement of our people as they left South Africa due to the injustices of the apartheid regime.'

His picture reminds me of his smile and his attentive and noticing eyes as he watched my comrades and I spread out the plans for the development of the Dakawa centre on our small dining room table, showing him and the delegation the various phases of construction.

We were fearful of making a mistake or misinforming the ANC President. But for some reason, I felt surrounded by his strong trust and belief in me, as young as I was then, as I led the administration team through the presentation of the plans and all phases of the development of Dakawa.

I look at my picture and say: 'Thank you, Comrade OR, for helping me to administer the Development Centre with my comrades even when the ANC was experiencing trying times.' We had to prepare for an influx of our people escaping persecution during the mid-1980s, especially from the Front-line States. We had to deal with hazardous weather conditions, particularly during the rainy season, which was a real nightmare.

Comrade OR's guiding hand kept me going during those difficult and painful times when our young people and tested cadres of the organisation had to retreat to inland Africa – Tanzania. I vowed not to let Comrade OR and the organisation down.

The picture also reminds me of special moments when the ANC President spent some time in Stockholm, Sweden, in the late 1980s. I was privileged to be assigned by the ANC to work in one of its missions abroad and I was deployed to Stockholm. Thanks to the ANC, I was given a rare opportunity to see the world and interact with various cultures. I got to work very closely with members of the anti-apartheid movement in Sweden and elsewhere abroad.

I believe that the main reason I was able to experience this unique assignment was due to the leadership and vision of Comrade OR, who understood that the South African liberation struggle needed to move to the centre stage of world politics. It was then that I began to understand the role of multilateralism. I understood the impact that the international solidarity spirit could have in helping those who believed in their own liberation and equality for all in South Africa.

Comrade OR Tambo's picture reminds me of the opportunity that I had to meet Nelson Mandela soon after his release from Pollsmoor Prison when he came to visit Comrade OR in Stockholm.

As I glance at the picture again I smile and think about how blessed I am to have attended and participated in the ANC's very decisive and strategic conference that was held in Kabwe, Zambia, in 1985. Comrade OR led the conference and the ANC in a manner not seen before. I got to understand and experience the guidance of Comrade OR, and his shaping of me and other young cadres of the organisation present and beyond. He made us appreciate that the NEC of the ANC was ready to expand and include the diverse leadership of the movement. The picture on the wall reminds me that Comrade OR saw the leadership of the ANC in its diversity; he saw people endangering their lives in pursuit of our national liberation. Equally he was of the opinion that the ANC's diversity should be reflected in its own top leadership structure, the NEC. Consequently, I always look at his picture and say: 'Thank you, Mr President, for watching over me and my family as you remind me of where I come from in terms of my serving the government and the people of South Africa.'

Comrade OR, every day that I see your picture it reminds me of your humble and humane manner of being. You taught the ANC membership to work in unison and speak with one voice. And quietly, as I pass your picture, I feel great and lucky to have seen you, worked with you, and experienced your wisdom while you were alive, although it still feels as though you are with me every day, as you are with many others who knew you well.

'I DID NOT CHOOSE MYSELF'

Adelaide Tambo
(extracts from an interview with Lindiwe Mabuza)

Lindiwe Mabuza (LM): Well Sissie [literally, 'Sister'; Adelaide], let's start with the whole question of the renaming of the airport, the Johannesburg International Airport to the OR Tambo International. When our Minister of Foreign Affairs was speaking in Glasgow recently she said that Oliver Tambo was South Africa's gateway to the world. And now we have the gateway of the world into South Africa named after him. How do you feel about it?

Adelaide Tambo (AT): What I honestly and truly feel about it, is that it was about time. Papa [Oliver Tambo] gave each and every inch of his life for the liberation of this country. At great expense to his health. And our people, everybody who was with us in exile, knows that.

LM: When you say he gave every bit of his life, I remember a conference in Kabwe in 1985. At the end of the conference, he addressed all of us and said: 'Comrades, my health has not been the best of late, but what is left of it will be consumed for the struggle.'

AT: That's very true. And he said it time and time again. And it ended up by taking, literally consuming, him. Let me tell you a story. I took Papa to East Germany and the doctor said he needed a pacemaker. In my profession, I had not had the pleasure of nursing people with pacemakers. So I said to

219

this doctor, 'What I would like to know are the repercussions of having a pacemaker?' I had a string of questions to ask about the quality of life people could enjoy if they had a pacemaker and so on and so forth. Anyway, OR had a pacemaker put in and within three days he was okay and came back home. I was very pleased. But the doctor had said, you must come back and have regular check-ups. Three months later Papa was in Zambia and I was in London. I looked at my diary and I saw that it was time for Papa to have a check-up. And I said to him, 'I'm coming to fetch you to take you to Germany for your general check-up.' And he said, 'I would love to see you, but I'm not so certain about going to Germany. But do come.' And then when I got there, it was about the time of the Harare Declaration.

LM: I think it was being prepared then.

AT: Yes. And Papa said, 'I can't go with you.' So I said, 'Hey, do you remember what the doctor said about the seriousness of having check-ups?' He replied, 'No dear, I can't. I am preparing an important document, and I have been to African states discussing this document with the heads of states, and I truly cannot go to Germany now. Perhaps afterwards.' And then I said, 'Papa, when it comes to things like this, there is no afterwards. When the time comes for you to have a check-up, you must have a check-up!' And he said, 'You know, I did not choose myself.'

LM: Meaning, choose his role?

AT: Yes. He said, 'I did not choose myself. I did not choose the part that I play in the struggle for the liberation of my people. And that comes first.' The truth of the matter was that most of his political colleagues were on Robben Island in jail. Each time I complained about anything, he said, 'No, there is one thing I must not do. I must not forget that my colleagues are in jail. And they depend on me to lead the struggle so that they can come out of that Robben Island.' When the Boers mowed down 27 of our people who were in Lesotho, I called him . . .

LM: That was in 1982.

AT: Yes. I knew a family there, that was also killed in that raid. And I called Papa and I said, 'I understand you want to go to Lesotho?' And he said, 'Yes, I am going to Lesotho.' So I said, 'Please Papa, don't go. The Boers will shoot down your plane as it crosses South Africa.' He replied, 'Listen, I was talking to Samora Machel just a few minutes ago, and he was saying the same thing. But you know, those people are in Lesotho because of me. And now, when the Boers have attacked them and mowed them down, I must now sit back and say I can't go to Lesotho to go and bury them because there is a likelihood that I might be shot down. That's cowardice of the first order. I am going to Lesotho. I'm going to be with the relatives of those people who were killed in Lesotho. This is the only decent way of doing it.'

LM: And to Lesotho he went.

AT: Yes, to Lesotho he went.

LM: Sissie, can we go back to OR Tambo International? There is a child of the Tambos', a young man who has become a hero because of his dedication in this campaign to have the airport's name changed. I'm talking about the Mayor of Ekurhuleni, Duma Nkosi. Can you say something about what he means to you now?

AT: Duma is the Executive Mayor of Ekurhuleni. He is, I must say, like my son. He is the one who suggested that the airport should be named after OR. And initially most, I'm not being racist, but most white people did not want that. I understood their reservations; I know the part that Oliver played in the political struggle. He fought apartheid vigorously, and I think there was a time when the ANC had more embassies abroad than the South African government. And you know, having been born in South Africa and having grown up here, I can say that South Africans as a whole, black and white, don't take defeat very easily. But Duma was fiercely determined to have the airport renamed, and he and his committee eventually succeeded.

LM: Let's get to uButi – you know I always called him Buti because he wasn't anything else but that – as a husband, as a father. A husband who was not there all the time. A father who was not there all the time. And yet, you brought up the children together. How was that possible?

AT: [Laughing] Well, you know, we only saw him about twice a year for an extended visit. But if he was on his way from Lusaka to the UN, he would spend one night. And on his way back from the UN he would spend the night and leave the following day for Lusaka. When I told the children that he was coming, they would get so excited; they would all rush home to come and spend the night with him. But it would never happen. The whole of the ANC in London would be at the house. They all had things to discuss with him. And he would be in the lounge with these people talking about different things. I would give my kids food, and give everybody food, and they would go into the TV room. I would say, 'Papa, the children are waiting for you.' But I remember Gill Marcus saying to me, 'But Adelaide, he is also our Papa. And we are also part of the children waiting for him.' And that was true, but the tragedy was that our kids would not have had an opportunity to talk to their father. Before Oliver went to bed, he would wake them up, trying to catch up with them. But the only real communication between him and the children was letters.

LM: Sissie, you said Gill Marcus said we're his children too. Indeed, people like the current President, and the Minister of Foreign Affairs and the Minister of Arts and Culture, they were literally like your children.

AT: Yes, it's very true. I remember when Thabo came back from his military training. He said, 'I am very happy to be back. But there's something I've got to do.' So I said, 'What?' And he said, 'I want to marry Zanele.' I said, 'But you've just arrived. You haven't told me about what you were doing, where you were.' I asked him if he had permission from the movement to marry her and he said, 'No. If Old Tata and the leadership tell me that I can't marry Zanele, I'll remain a bachelor all my life. I will not marry anybody.'

LM: That generation, the young people of the time, were doing military training but they were also learning some values as the future leaders. What values would have been important at the time? What things would have made them strong in their determination to be part of the liberation struggle and to carry on?

AT: First of all, they needed truly and honestly to love their country. To love it so much that they were prepared to lay down their lives for it. To be convinced that they were doing the right thing.

LM: Sissie, uButi was part of a formidable leadership from the Communist Party, from the ANC, from the trade unions. Names such as JB Marks, Moses Kotane, Johnny Makathini, Moses Mabhida, Florence Mophosho, Joe Slovo and Kate Molale. And they bound the ANC together. How was it possible in conditions of exile? And what were the really critical factors in achieving that unity?

AT: Let me say in the first place that the ANC had no allies in the country. The first ally of the ANC was the Communist Party. And it supported the ANC not only by word of mouth, but in actions too. And JB Marks and Moses Kotane were members of the Communist Party as well as many others whose names I cannot remember now. During the meetings of the Communist Party and the ANC, a lot of discussions took place. We didn't want an alliance that would be there today and not tomorrow. We knew that we would walk a long road together – through good times and through difficult times – because we had one aim. And that was to defeat the enemy. A united front was formed. So then the next step was that our people must be scattered to the African countries and other countries that are sympathetic to the struggle of South Africa. People had to write their names and the names were put in a hat. Write your name, put it in a hat, and the countries were also written down. And then you put your hand in the hat and bring out your paper and it says London. And you go to London. When it says Egypt, you go to Egypt, the US, and so on. And so people were distributed all over the world.

LM: Tell me a little bit about uButi's relationship with Olof Palme, the Prime Minister of Sweden who was assassinated in 1986.

AT: Olof gave his full support and he also had the support of his wife, to help South Africa, to help Oliver, to win the struggle. And I have to say that I wonder if all his help to the ANC did not perhaps contribute to his assassination. He was a very honest, truthful, reliable man. And a lot of people in the world must have known that when he said he was going to support the ANC, he meant it truly and honestly. And then of course there were people such as Pierre Schori and the old man Ernst Michanek who were also supporters. Most of our young men had left home, especially some of the older ones, without having a penny to support their parents. And Michanek made it possible, working with IDAF and Canon Collins; they made it possible for the ANC to send money to the parents of these young men and women.

LM: And there was also money for the legal defence of political prisoners. You mentioned Canon Collins, of course. And another very special friend of yours was Archbishop Trevor Huddleston. This leads me to ask you about your relationship with OR. It was founded on a deep spirituality. Say something about that.

AT: You know, we did not meet in church, but in the ANC Youth League. When I was still a student at Orlando High I gave a speech at the launch of a new branch of the Youth League and Oliver, as President of the Youth League, was there and he gave a speech too. I think I started my speech by attacking the fact that we had the Native Representative Council in parliament. I said that I couldn't understand why other people were representing us when we were still alive. Why couldn't we do it ourselves? The following day I got a letter from Oliver in which he congratulated me on the way I had spoken. It was the start of a great correspondence.

LM: So you met in the struggle. But I had started asking about the depth of your spirituality as a family.

AT: Oliver was an Anglican and I was a Catholic. And I had a friendship with Nelson Mandela. After church on Sundays I used to see them at the Blue Lagoon.

LM: It was a restaurant in Johannesburg – one of only two black restaurants at the time.

AT: And then I was also doing some studies in Diagonal Street. And Oliver used to collect me there after my studies. I got impatient with our relationship at times. In Johannesburg, the boys used to come clear and say, 'Ek notch jou. I love you.' Now here was this man who did not say 'I notch you'. And one day I just said to him, 'When are you going to propose to me?'

LM: Just like that? That must have shocked him.

AT: Anyway, he was Anglican and I was Catholic. And I told him that I wasn't going to change my religion. And he said, 'There is no reason why anybody should change the way they want to worship their God.' Those were his exact words. Then we went to go and see Father Maldoon about the issue. He said, 'Hmm, of course you can't get married. You [Oliver] should do the honourable thing.' And he gave Oliver the rules, and spoke about how any children would have to be brought up as Catholics. Oliver said, 'I can't make decisions like that. I can't make decisions for children who are not even born yet.' It was his lawyer logic coming through. After we left I decided that Oliver must get my family together. My uncles and my aunties. And the struggle fathers too. Ahh. To my horror, they did not support me. They said: 'How can you even think of that? Is it the man who is marrying you or are you marrying the man? It is not African tradition that a woman marries a man. It is the man who marries the woman.' So I did not have support from my family.

224

LM: And so Oliver's side won.

AT: Yes, he won. And I must say that I was really angry. I went back to the Helping Hand Club where we used to go and I told Winnie [Madikizela Mandela] that in that case I was not going to get married. And Winnie said, 'You can't do that. People are going to think that he dumped you.' Oh my gosh. Anyway, we were going to get married on 22 December. And then Oliver was arrested on 5 December. I got a call at 6:00 a.m. on 6 December and was told that Oliver had been arrested on a charge of high treason.

LM: Together with 155 others, the so-called treason trialists.

AT: People were asking me if we were going to postpone the wedding. Everybody was worried that maybe Oliver would still be in prison, but I said that I was prepared to put on my wedding gown and get married in prison.

LM: That would have been a first.

AT: Anyway, they released him on 21 December. On 22 December Oliver went to the office to check on the work there and then we went to Vereeniging. On our way back, we got arrested.

LM: This is on your wedding day?

AT: Yes! There we were in the pick-up van and Oliver said to this policeman, 'Why am I arrested?' And he replied, 'Because you don't have a night pass.' But as a lawyer Oliver was exempt from that. We were with our best man, Yengwa, and he was also arrested. Eventually, after picking up several more people, we got to the Germiston Police Station. Oliver took out his exemption and he said, 'I want to know why I am here.' The policeman checked that the exemption was in order and then Oliver said, 'Let me speak to counsel.' And our lawyer spoke very strongly to the policeman. He said, 'If you do not release these people, I'm suing the government', and so on... Is this really the kind of thing that you wanted to hear about?

LM: Yes, it's amazing. You know, I've never heard this story.

AT: So then we were waiting there, and the policeman spoke to Oliver. All of a sudden he was very polite and humble. And he said, 'It's all right. I apologise and you may take your fiancée and your friend and go.' It was the first time I had heard a Boer say: 'I apologise.'

LM: Finally, Sissie, no liberation movement before the ANC had done so much work in the cultural sphere. Under OR's leadership there were poems written. The first Chief Representative of the ANC to London, Raymond Mazisi Kunene, was a great poet. And the ANC women put together a book of poetry as well as a book of short stories. But perhaps the most well known contribution to culture was the creation of Amandla. Can you say something about what that group did for you. I think your son, Dali, was responsible for them coming to the UK, wasn't he?

AT: Yes. Dali formed Artists against Apartheid and he called Harry Belafonte to come from the US and to open Artists against Apartheid. That's how the artists got strongly into the liberation struggle.

LM: And later in the US they formed Artists and Athletes against Apartheid. uButi was also a consummate lover of music, a producer of music, a maker of music. I remember how he changed the words of 'iPoni', the Xhosa choral piece.

AT: He said that he didn't want MK to sing words that were meaningless to the nation. That was the reason why he changed it.

LM: And then he also took the ANC anthem, 'Nkosi Sikelel' iAfrika', rearranged it, and it was sung, conducted by him in Lusaka for one of the OAU summits. And at the end of the anthem, all those heads of states were on their feet and I understand that President Kaunda asked for an encore. An encore of the anthem – that was OR's power, his gift.

AT: I think I might still have that music. Because OR wrote it, you know.

LM: There is so much more that we could talk about, especially with regard to the role of women and OR's position on women. But anyway, Sissie, I want to thank you so much for sharing your stories and your time with us. It has been wonderful talking to you.

Top: Samora Machel welcoming OR to the 4th FRELIMO Congress in Maputo, 30 April 1983.

Above: OR with Tanzania's Julius Nyerere (centre) and Namibia's Sam Nujoma at the Front Line Summit, Dar es Salaam, Tanzania.

Left: OR and Nelson Mandela.

Top left: OR meeting Fidel Castro at the 6th Conference of Heads of State of non-aligned countries, Havana, Cuba, 1979.

Top right: OR and Yusuf Dadoo. Dadoo was instrumental in the establishment of the South African United Front (SAUF), which brought together the ANC External Mission, the PAC, the South African Indian Congress, and the South West African National Union (SWANU).

Below: OR and Olof Palme at the People's Parliament Against Apartheid in Stockholm, 21 February 1986.

Top: OR with Archbishop Trevor Huddleston and Brian Filling with Abdul Minty behind, at the rally on Glasgow Green, 12 June 1988, which sent off 25 marchers to walk to London to arrive for Nelson Mandela's 70th birthday on 18 July.

Above: Brian Filling addressing the rally on Glasgow Green, 12 June 1988.

Left: OR listens as Albie Sachs addresses the crowd at the second National Consultative Conference of the ANC in Kabwe, Zambia, 16–22 June 1985.

Top: OR, Morarji Desai and Indira Ghandi.

Above: OR, Alfred Nzo and Joe Slovo in conversation.

Top: OR with Pearl Robinson and Johnny Makathini (at that time head of the ANC International Affairs) at a meeting of the New England Circle/Global Citizens Circle on 30 October 1985.

Above: OR with Thabo Mbeki, Zodwa Sisulu, Themba Vilakazi, Aggrey Mbere and Zwelakhe Sisulu at the same New England Circle/Global Citizens Circle meeting in 1985.

Left: OR with Edward Kennedy at the State House in Lusaka, Zambia.

Left: OR dancing with an unidentified companion.

Below: Adelaide Tambo with Tselane on her hip, and Dali looking on, at their Muswell Hill home.

Above left: OR and Johnny Makathini on a visit to China.

Above: 'OR was one of the kindest and least boastful men I have encountered, and yet, you could tell when you were with him that there was steel within ...' Gillian Slovo.

Left: OR, Paul Boateng, Princess Zenani Dlamini (daughter of Nelson Mandela and Winnie Madikizela-Mandela), and Ken Livingstone at the unveiling of the statue of Nelson Mandela on the South Bank in London, 28 October 1985.

African National Congress (South Africa)
Office of the President
P.O.Box 31791, Lusaka, Zambia. Phone 211169 Telex 45390

Friday 84.

Dear Thandie,

1981 – Year of the Youth

Just in case I don't see you before you take off, I want you to know how grateful we are to you for stepping out of your job to help our Movement in the difficult situation in which we find ourselves. The Amandla tour, tly of Nigeria must be a staggering success, if it takes place. But if it takes place and is not a success, then the failure & the political as well as financial loss will be staggering. So, my sister, your trip to Nigeria is a soldier's march to a battlefield. When you get there, fight the good fight with all your might in the interests of all your people. We have great faith in your abilities. Amandla. OR.

P.S. Before you leave, arm yourself with all possible telephone and telex numbers — Lusaka, London, New York. so that in case I need you can contact us. As you will be aware we are ignorant of what is happening there and will want to be kept informed of progress. Between Tuesday evening and Saturday afternoon next week, I shall be in London (Tel. 883-3209) The best time to call is in the morning, before 8 a.m. London time. OR

A letter from OR to Thandi Lujabe-Rankoe, discussing her trip to Nigeria to try to persuade the Nigerian government to allow the Amandla group to perform in that country.

THE ANC INCARNATE

Ben Turok

Oliver and I were sitting side by side on a couch in his house in Muswell Hill. Adelaide had phoned me an hour before. 'He is here, and will see you at eleven, come.' And there I was, sitting intimate with one of the world's most famous personalities. Oliver had greeted me with his usual bright smile, a hug, and a moment of great warmth, which passed quickly. But his eyes were tired; there was the usual slightly sad smile around his mouth, and as we talked he had that habit of looking past you with his eyes darting here and there, so that it was impossible to read his reaction to what you were saying.

'What do you want to see me about?' he asked.

'Adelaide wants me to write your biography.'

'Why?'

'Well, I suppose she wants the world to know who you are.'

'But why?'

'Oliver, you are the most famous of all liberation leaders.'

'Maybe . . . so?'

'Well, even the comrades in the ANC don't really know you as a person.'

'That's not true. They meet me frequently in the camps and in our branches around the world.'

'Yes, but they don't know the whole person.'

'Why should they anyway?'

'Oliver, they have the right to know just who you are!' I said with great passion.

'No, I have failed the movement; we are not where we should be.'

Shocked by this extraordinary statement, I fell silent. There was no more to be said, but nevertheless I added, 'So you refuse? I will not do this without your approval.'

'Let me think about it.'

'All right, but if I don't hear from you I shall take it that you are not opposed.'

He smiled sadly but said nothing.

Then Oliver collected his winter coat and we walked to the door. I saw him a little way into the street and he walked off slowly, in deep thought, a man with a very heavy burden weighing him down.

When I got home, I phoned Adelaide to tell her what had transpired. She said, 'He's silly, he is so stubborn, go ahead.' But I decided to give Oliver some weeks to reflect on the proposal. In any case, I was busy editing his speeches for a forthcoming volume. For some years Adelaide had been collecting his speeches and she presented me with several dozen, which I had to sort into some order and then edit down to a reasonable form.

Most of the speeches had been made at international meetings of the UN or similar forums, but others had been delivered at ANC meetings. Seretse Choabe, who had often travelled with Oliver to these events, told me how these speeches came to be constructed. Oliver always had a team of three or four advisers who travelled with him on these occasions. On the evening before the event, the group would meet under Oliver's direction and he would set out the broad parameters of the speech. Each adviser was then allocated a section and would start work. They would work through the night. Oliver would go to sleep, but he would be called in every few hours to consider a draft, and the final version would generally be ready by early morning. He was enormously fussy about every turn of phrase and was hard to please. By breakfast, the speech was ready, and he would be taken to the meeting to deliver it.

The publishers gave me a tight deadline, which I met, and they produced five thousand copies. However, no sooner did I get a copy, then I received an irate call from Alfred Nzo, Secretary-General of the ANC, who was in Lusaka. He asked about the book and insisted that I immediately courier him a copy for inspection. A few days later, he phoned me to say that there was one piece that had to come out of the book. It was a report of a speech by Oliver that I had found in *Sechaba*, the official organ of the ANC, which I had edited for two years in London. In it Oliver apparently had made some unfortunate reference to the Zimbabwe African People's Union Permanent Force (ZANU PF), which would cause a diplomatic incident. The publishers had to pulp all the copies and reprint.

Then I had to consider what to do about the biography. After many discussions with Adelaide, we decided to go ahead with interviewing all those who knew Oliver over the years. I did so and collected some wonderful material dealing with many different facets of the man.

What emerged was a profile of someone who was universally loved and admired, often for very different reasons. This was because Oliver kept various roles and values in distinct compartments, rarely allowing overlap between them. This was why Christians with deep faith were able to relate to him in a special way as one of their own. After all, it was almost an accident that he was not a man of the cloth.

The lawyers who had to be consulted on so many technical matters to do with international law also felt at home with Oliver, who had practised law for some years and retained an acute legal brain.

Diplomats and international political figures saw in him a man of enormous diplomatic experience due to his very many interactions with heads of state, senior diplomats from the most powerful countries, and many others. Indeed, it was in this area that Oliver shone most, since he caught every nuance of international politics and every speech reflected this.

As the leader of the ANC he came to represent unity of purpose as no other leader could. He was patient with the critics within and without the organisation; he arbitrated in disputes; he insisted on discipline but not in an abrasive manner. He consoled those who were suffering trauma. In short, Oliver steadily grew not only to represent the ANC but also to be the ANC incarnate.

Of great importance internationally was that Oliver always insisted on non-racialism in all the structures of the movement and he conveyed this attitude in all his international dealings. As a result, some of the most biased and bigoted Western leaders and diplomats came to respect this impeccably mannered personality who could by no stretch of the imagination be seen as anti-white, or indeed anti-anything other than the apartheid regime.

At the same time, as Commander-in-Chief of MK, it was Oliver's responsibility to reflect the militancy of the armed struggle. It was not an easy task for him, and at times he did not relish the role of armed revolutionary. At other times, however, the terror unleashed by the apartheid regime at home, and the bloodshed of the raids into Lesotho and Botswana, for example, so incensed him, that he seemed to be on the verge of calling for an eye for an eye.

Oliver's relations with the Communist Party were intriguing. Although he shared many of the senior structures with members of the SACP, he never left anyone in any doubt that he would not identify with communism as an ideology or its organisational practices. But he managed his differences with great subtlety and in a way that generated no heat.

Finally, Oliver as human being was someone whom everyone treasured. His kindness and consideration were extraordinary in any circumstances, but especially in the harsh environment of exile, with all its difficulties and tensions. You never lost the sense that a contact with Oliver was an experience to be cherished.

And so it was that I felt a deep chagrin, as I was beginning to shape the biographical material I had received, that I received an instruction from Lusaka that the NEC had decided that the work on Oliver's biography should not go on. Adelaide had given me three bags of letters and documents, which I had to return, but I kept my tapes and notes. We had to wait until Luli Callinicos produced her biography for a serious portrait of this remarkable man.

★ ★ ★

I need to go back some years to my first close meeting with Oliver Tambo in Dar es Salaam. On my escape from South Africa in 1966, I collected some maps and information about the route from Lusaka through Botswana to South Africa. The idea was to return underground in order to rejoin the movement there. But I could only report on my information to Oliver when I arrived in Dar es Salaam a year later. We went for a walk on the beach where I reported my instructions from home, but he dismissed the idea as it had been tried and proved unworkable.

Subsequently, two years later, I arranged a meeting with him to say that I had decided to take my family to the UK and that we were travelling by an East German freighter. I would survey the Eastern Cape coastline from the ship to look for possible landing sites for guerrilla groups. He was delighted, gave me his personal code and arranged through the embassy in Dar es Salaam that I was to have full access to the ship's charts and binoculars in order to study the terrain on the coast.

I concluded that there were indeed favourable areas and I produced a report that I handed to Joe Slovo when I reached London. I heard nothing more, but met Oliver again in London to discuss the landing possibilities, which were then communicated to the Revolutionary Council in Lusaka.

From then on I received periodic calls from Oliver to visit him in London on his brief transits through the city. Although he had many important contacts in London, Oliver could only ever stay for a few days at a time. During one of his visits I was told that he was meeting with top executives of British banks. I gathered that they wanted some assurances that this President of what Mrs Thatcher had called a terrorist organisation was actually a responsible and serious political leader.

At my private one-on-one chats with Oliver, I was able to get some insight into what was happening in Zambia and Tanzania, information I needed as the de facto editor of *Sechaba*, the official organ of the ANC, where I worked full-time during 1969–71. However, our meetings were much more a matter of my briefing him on our own organisation and the various tensions that pervaded the ANC. These tensions centred on the different roles of the ANC office, the Branch, the Revolutionary Council which had a separate office in Goodge Street, the Communist Party headquarters (also in Goodge Street), and, finally, the AAM. Oliver wanted to be informed about all these matters, though he rarely intervened directly. His style was to discuss things with individuals he could trust, give his views, and leave it to the local people to sort out. The only time he did become involved was with what became known as the Group of Eight, led by Alfred Kgokong (Themba Mqota), who took an Africanist position within the ANC, and who were later expelled for contesting the policies of the movement.

After I left the ANC to take up a teaching post at the Open University, I was less closely involved in the day-to-day work of the organisation, although still a member of the Branch Committee. In 1979, I was seconded to the University of Zambia for two years and soon contacted Oliver at his residence in Lusaka. He welcomed me with his extraordinary warmth and we soon got down to talking about the situation in the front-line. I was able to meet him from time to time, until one day I received a message that Oliver was on the move as there were fears of an abduction or assassination.

The next day he arrived without any ceremony to stay for a few days at our university apartment. He seemed extremely shy and reserved, but in a most pleasant way. That evening he approached me with a tape cassette in his hand, from which a piece of tape was extruding. He explained that he had recorded it in a cathedral in Rome and was very attached to the wonderful choral music. Try as I might, I could not get the tape back into the cassette and had to admit failure. He was disconsolate, but accepted without demur. I recalled that he had himself been a choir conductor at home and had always been enchanted by choral music. It was just one of the many facets of Oliver's remarkable life that I had come to have insight into as I researched his biography, a project, as I have already recounted, with a complicated history.

JURISTS AND LEGAL
ACQUAINTANCES

A MODEL FOR ALL LAWYERS

Geoffrey Bindman

I cannot claim to have known Oliver Tambo well. I met him on a few occasions in London during the 1980s when I chaired SATIS (Southern Africa – the Imprisoned Society). We were also together in 1987 at the memorable conference on the plight of children under apartheid that Trevor Huddleston, Glenys Kinnock and others organised in Harare.

Despite only a small number of face to face meetings, Oliver's reputation and charisma were such that I felt immense warmth and admiration for him as a man of integrity, strength and humanity. With quiet authority he played a dominant role in the liberation of his country.

Like his close comrade Nelson Mandela, Oliver was remarkable in his ability to maintain an attitude of calm understanding. He never lost his belief in the equality and fundamental goodness of humanity in spite of the humiliations to which he and so many of his people were subjected. Like Mandela he recognised that the overriding aim of a peaceful transition to democracy on the basis of equality required the suppression of those entirely justifiable impulses to hatred and revenge. He realised that a new South Africa must find a place for all those who lived in it. It was this sense of human dignity as a universal attribute of all that led him to challenge separatist tendencies within the ANC and the liberation movement generally. He was well aware of the dangers of internal conflict and how difficult it could be to avoid a violent outcome to the liberation struggle.

My own admiration and respect for Oliver were partly fuelled by what I knew of the difficulties and humiliations he endured in the practise of his profession, which happened to be the same as my own. It now seems unimaginable that under apartheid black attorneys were not permitted to sit alongside their white counterparts in the body of a law court during a trial, but were forced into a segregated corner of the room where they could barely hear or be heard. This form of discrimination may seem relatively mild in comparison with many of the brutal manifestations of apartheid, but the selective ill-treatment of lawyers in court has a special kind of symbolic viciousness in its distortion of fundamental legal values.

As a black attorney Oliver Tambo had to overcome other humiliations. Albie Sachs has spoken of his own early career at the South African Bar when among his contemporaries was the late, much lamented, Chief Justice Ismail Mohamed. Though one of the outstanding young advocates of his day, publicly complimented by the judges of the Appellate Division when he appeared before it in Bloemfontein, in the Orange Free State, his ability to practise in the country's highest court was severely hampered by discrimination. The judges doubtless did not consider it relevant to mention the huge additional burden faced by non-white lawyers in South Africa's highest court: they were not allowed to remain in the Orange Free State overnight. Consequently, while an appeal was going on Mohamed – and any other black lawyers who had to appear in that court – had to travel out of the Orange Free State to a neighbouring province each evening, and then back again each morning.

As attorneys the discrimination suffered by Mandela and Tambo and their black colleagues was in one respect arguably worse, because it took place inside the courtroom itself.

As a white lawyer brought up and practising law in England I have always felt enormous respect for those South African lawyers who upheld the rule of law when so many of their professional colleagues sided with the oppressors. This courageous minority of the profession continually confronted and overcame daunting obstacles in seeking justice for their disadvantaged clients.

There is much scepticism among the public at large about the legal profession and the ethical standards of its members. That attitude doubtless derives from the perception that lawyers are the agents of the rich and powerful, and that they are motivated by greed and personal ambition. Yet the public and the media often overlook the existence of lawyers who are the exact opposite of this stereotype. These lawyers believe that justice is their calling and that it is their duty to serve the ideals of equality and the cause of the oppressed. Oliver Tambo was a shining example of this kind of lawyer.

Although he gave up practising law at an early age as he took on a growing leadership role in the liberation movement, it is plain in retrospect that his achievements in that role must have owed much of their precise focus to his legal training and experience.

The most remarkable and admirable feature of the new South Africa has been the peaceful transition from an authoritarian racist regime to a modern democratic society based on constitutionality and the rule of law. The embodiment of the ideals of the Freedom Charter in a just and practically effective constitutional framework can certainly be traced back to the example of Oliver Tambo. In a recent interview in *The Guardian* newspaper (28 August 2006), Albie Sachs, one of the main architects of the constitution and a judge of the Constitutional Court, affirmed his debt. Though Sachs says he has grown to dislike the idea of role models, he identifies Oliver Tambo as the man who inspired him as a civil rights lawyer.

When I look back on the life and work of Oliver Tambo, it is striking to observe the consistent humanity of his vision, and its reliance on the highest ideals of ethical conduct. It is also evident that his vision was firmly grounded in the practical values of the rule of law. His life is truly illustrative of the best of the legal profession and will remain a model for all lawyers.

ARCHITECT OF
SOUTH AFRICAN DEMOCRACY

George Bizos

Oliver Reginald Tambo, Duma Nokwe, Godfrey Pitje and others were excellent teachers by profession whom the apostles of apartheid haunted out of their chosen career for fear that they were abusing their position to teach their students to aspire to greater heights than those determined by their oppressors. Little did they foresee that at least the three of them, inspired and helped by the wise man of the ANC Walter Sisulu, would become lawyers. Freed of the shackles of tight control and fear of dismissal by the Department of Education they intensified their participation in the ANC Youth League, participated in the Defiance Campaign and represented communities and individuals in court. Even though there was little room available to get justice, particularly in political trials, the mere fact that a black man was represented by a black lawyer was a negation of the myth created by most whites that black people were inherently inferior.

In the early 1950s, directly opposite the main entrance of the magistrates' court in Johannesburg a sign appeared on the windows of the first floor of Chancellor House. In large black capital letters with green and yellow outlines it read: 'MANDELA AND TAMBO – ATTORNEYS'. Most white attorneys and advocates, policemen, prosecutors and magistrates asked what these 'Natives' were doing in the centre of the city. The self-appointed guardians of legal ethics complained that the large letters were contrary to the practice of discouraging advertising. When some of them learned that the colours were those of the ANC they resented the fact that Mandela and Tambo used their political profile in order to get work.

I had first met Nelson Mandela at the University of the Witwatersrand (Wits) in 1948. He qualified three years before me. Nelson, Duma Nokwe and I were attorneys' clerks together and we all became friends. We saw one another during the day in the corridors of the courts and at Wits in the late afternoon when we attended lectures.

I asked Duma about Nelson's partner. He told me about Oliver's background as a teacher. How the two of them (Duma and Oliver) had both decided to do law and had received so much assistance from Walter Sisulu and the newly qualified attorney Nelson Mandela. Duma and Oliver were both active in the ANC and the Youth League, helping the national leadership in secretarial and organisational matters particularly in relation to the Defiance Campaign. Duma agreed to arrange for me to meet Oliver in his office. At the time, there was not a single tearoom, café or restaurant where Africans could sit with whites to have food or refreshments. We met in Oliver's office. The waiting room and passage were full of clients waiting to see one of the partners of what had become within a very short time the popular firm of Mandela and Tambo.

The passing of the Bantu Education Act in 1953 was an anathema to both Oliver and Duma. There was no attempt to hide the reason for enacting the law. Dr HF Verwoerd told parliament:

> The Native must not be subject to a school system which draws him away from his own community and misleads him by showing him the green pastures of European Society which he is not allowed to graze ... (if he) is being taught to expect that he will lead his adult life under the policy of equal rights he is making a big mistake.

There could not have been a greater insult, particularly to the two highly qualified teachers who had been prevented from continuing in their chosen profession soon after the Nationalists came to power.

The ANC in the Transvaal and elsewhere decided to call on parents to boycott the new schools. Thousands of pupils did not turn up on the first day and Verwoerd lost no time in announcing that those who had stayed away would never be admitted to any school. Soon top schools teaching black pupils closed down. Schools for the Bantu had to be registered. For Verwoerd's department, failure to register was a criminal offence as was teaching at an unregistered school.

Mandela and Tambo were too busy to do all the work that came their way and they requested counsel to do much of it. Duma and I were asked by Oliver to investigate what could be done to bypass the provisions of the Bantu Education Act. Father Trevor Huddleston, a mentor and close friend of Oliver's, also wanted to know how the provisions of this 'tyrannical Act' could be circumvented.

In consultation with ANC committees we advised the teachers who had lost their jobs to ask Huddleston to lend his name to 'Cultural Clubs' to draw the affected scholars into groups to be 'taught', mainly by teachers who had been dismissed by the Bantu Education Department.

Our research into dictionaries and decided cases led us to formulate a definition of a 'school' as 'an establishment at which formal imparting of knowledge took place'. The police were quick to arrest and charge 'teachers' whom we referred to as 'Club Leaders'. We successfully argued that the absence of suitable premises, chalkboards, desks, textbooks and even writing materials clearly proved that these were not 'schools'. They did not have to register. It was not an offence to gather and speak about various issues. Highly trained educationists had been requested by Father Huddleston, Oliver and Duma to prepare notes for the club leaders on various subjects. These were not to be widely distributed so that they could not come into the possession of the police and be used as evidence in court.

It was not an easy programme to put into operation. There weren't sufficient funds to pay the club leaders. Discipline and particularly regular attendance were difficult to enforce. Some of the parents of the excluded children were able to afford to send them to schools in neighbouring Botswana, Lesotho and Swaziland.

Charging people with a criminal offence because they may have been surreptitiously educating excluded students attracted the attention of both local and foreign media. The habitual acquittals of the accused led the prosecution authority to devise a plan to put an end to them.

A case was brought against a teacher before the magistrate in Benoni near where Oliver was living. To our surprise, instead of the usual policeman going in to the witness box a young man came to say that some six months previously he had joined the South African Police Force. He was instructed to wear a worn shirt, short trousers and tennis shoes, to go to the local 'Cultural Club', pretend that he was one of the excluded boys and say that he wanted to attend the school. He described the daily routine and spoke of the notes used by the teacher, which were hidden whenever a police vehicle approached. He handed in some of the notes that he had managed to persuade the teacher to give to him and which he had passed on to the police. The teacher was upset by the young man's betrayal. He told us that he had spoken the truth and that we should not cross-examine him. He wanted to know from us whether the police were entitled to set a trap and shook his head in disbelief when we told him there was nothing to prevent them from doing so.

The next witness was an inspector of schools who spoke highly of the quality of the notes that were used. He told the magistrate that at the next inspectors' conference he would recommend that they should be used in schools within his area.

The 'Cultural Clubs' had to be disbanded. Oliver Tambo, as a senior office bearer of the ANC who had led the movement into the boycott of the new school system, was criticised for its failure, as was the ANC as a whole. But Oliver persisted in the view that the decision to do so was correct. Accepting the introduction of Bantu Education without any form of protest would have been worse.

It was not easy for African lawyers to decide as a matter of principle what ought to be done in their personal and professional lives. Although Duma Nokwe, the first African to be admitted to the Johannesburg Bar, was welcomed by the leaders of the profession, the supporters of the apartheid regime threatened that if he came into the Bar common room they would report the matter to the group areas inspectors to charge him and the Bar Council with the offence of allowing a native into a place where seating was available for refreshments. The Bar Council told Duma that he was a fully fledged member but that he would have to make a decision for himself as to whether he would risk prosecution if he insisted on his rights. Duma consulted Walter Sisulu, Nelson Mandela and Oliver Tambo. There was a difference of opinion. Nelson and Duma thought that he should take the risk. Oliver however agreed with Walter who said that the African people had been trying for a whole generation to have an African advocate; the opportunity should not be lost for the sake of a cup of tea.

However, both Mandela and Tambo were not prepared to accept discrimination in the courtroom. One of Mandela's clients had made a successful application for the recusal of the magistrate for making it difficult for Mandela to conduct his case for no apparent reason other than that he was black.

Additional magistrate F A H Johl of Boksburg told Oliver that he had arranged for two tables in his court, one for Europeans and one for Non-Europeans. As Oliver was Non-European, he must sit at the small table reserved for him on the side. Oliver was shocked by this insult. Although his manner was gentler and quieter than that of Nelson when he appeared in court, this was too much even for him.

He asked the magistrate whether attorneys, black or white, male or female, were of equal stature and standing in the eyes of the court. How would a client feel, he asked, if his legal representatives were obliged to sit at a separate table because of their colour? Would the client not feel that because his legal representative was treated differently, he, the client, might not get a fair trial?

Unlike the magistrate before whom Nelson had appeared, Johl was calm and superficially polite. There was nothing like that in his mind, he assured Oliver; he had merely arranged his court in this way. He expected Oliver to obey his direction to sit at a separate table reserved for Non-Europeans. Oliver asked for a postponement to consider his position. He made it clear he was not prepared to sit at a separate table and would not conduct the trial under such circumstances before this magistrate. The scene was re-enacted when he appeared for another client during the same morning. That case was also remanded to another date. Oliver was not available and so he asked Godfrey Pitje to appear for the second client.

Godfrey Pitje had been a senior teacher and became an articled clerk in the office of Mandela and Tambo. Because of his academic qualifications he was entitled to appear in the magistrates' court. The magistrate sent the court interpreter to tell Godfrey to sit at a small table that was reserved for Non-Europeans. Godfrey was older than both Oliver and I and he confidently told the interpreter that he knew where to sit. The magistrate told him to move from the table reserved for Europeans to the one for Non-Europeans. He refused to do so and was convicted of contempt of court and fined. His conviction was upheld by both the Provincial Division and the Court of Appeal in Bloemfontein. A fellow clerk, Douglas Lukhele, suffered the same fate in an Orange Free State court where the policeman acting as a court orderly forcibly removed him from the courtroom.

But Oliver was prepared to accept humiliation in the interests of his client, particularly when the matter was one of life and death. He telephoned me on a Saturday morning to tell me that a young man convicted of murder in the Orange Free State was to be executed by hanging on Monday morning. The man's trial and sentence had been completed in the absence of a would-be co-accused who had not been apprehended until after his trial and sentence were completed. The condemned man insisted that his fellow accused, who was about to be tried, had informed him in prison that he would be exonerated. It was too late for any investigation to be made and the courts were most reluctant to grant orders postponing executions.

I telephoned Sydney Kentridge who was a friend, my senior and one of the top lawyers at the Johannesburg Bar to ask him whether we had sufficient cause to ask for a stay of execution. He told me that it was not for me or Oliver to decide and that we should make the application. We hurriedly prepared a short affidavit by the father, informed the registrar of the court that we were coming and gave notice to the sheriff who was to carry out the execution. We arrived at the Palace Justice in Pretoria. I introduced Oliver to the registrar. He told us that Judge Toss Bekker on duty would not come to the courthouse but we should go to his home. The registrar was quick to add that only counsel were allowed to go to judges' homes and not attorneys. I knew Judge Bekker to be a humane and enlightened man who would not have had any objection to an African attorney coming into his home. We followed the registrar to the judge's home. On the way I asked Oliver whether or not we were to accept the so-called practice invented by the registrar. His answer was that in matters of life and death we should avoid issues which were less important. He remained in the car. I followed the registrar into the judge's study where we found the sheriff and the Secretary of the Department of Justice.

The judge read the short petition, looked at me and said, 'It's very thin isn't it Bizos?' I agreed.

'Then why did you bring it?' he asked.

'I could not reconcile my conscience by not bringing it,' I answered.

'Why then do you want to put it on my conscience?' Bekker asked.

'Because you are a judge,' I replied.

The judge thought for a while, then turned to the Secretary of Justice and asked, 'What can you do to help us resolve this matter?' The Secretary said that he kept the warrant of execution until the last moment. He had the authority to keep it back. He assured the judge that he would not hand it over to the sheriff until the new trial was completed. The judge thanked all of us and told us that his wife had been preparing tea for us. She brought a large tray with four cups and a platter of crumpets. We indulged in small talk whilst Oliver was sitting in the car at the judge's gate, anxiously waiting to hear what the fate of the condemned man was to be.

Oliver, Nelson and Duma were accused in the preparatory examination on a charge of treason on which they were arrested at the end of 1956. The preparatory examination commenced in 1957 and their legal practices were severely affected. Duma, who unlawfully shared chambers with me and who received numerous briefs from Mandela and Tambo, was no longer able to do work for them. Both Nelson and Oliver could only attend their offices on weekends and on those occasions when the preparatory examination was adjourned.

In their absence, their clerks Mendi Msimang, Godfrey Pitje and Douglas

Lukhele ran Mandela and Tambo's practice. I was asked by both partners to be of whatever help I could to their clerks. I did many cases myself and asked colleagues to do the same.

Mandela and Tambo's occupation of their premises was unlawful both in terms of the Group Areas Act and the Urban Areas Control Act. Inspectors from both departments visited the premises and threatened prosecution if they did not vacate them. Jules Browde, a friend of both men, and particularly of Nelson, intervened on their behalf and obtained extensions of time that enabled the practice to continue without any criminal prosecution being brought.

At the end of the preparatory examination all the accused were indicted before a Special Court in Pretoria on a charge of treason. As a result of successful attacks against the validity of the indictment a group of only 30, including Nelson and Duma, of the 156 were charged. The charges against Oliver and the 120-odd others were temporarily withdrawn pending the decision in the main trial. This was a welcome respite that enabled Oliver to continue with his legal practice.

Then, in the middle of the main trial, on 21 March 1960, the police killed 69 unarmed people outside the Sharpeville police station and wounded hundreds of others. The reaction of the oppressed people of South Africa and the international community led to the declaration of a State of Emergency and the banning of the ANC as an unlawful organisation. Those on trial and many others throughout the country were detained at the Pretoria Prison.

Oliver Tambo was asked by the leadership to leave the country to avoid detention and to lead the struggle from beyond its borders. He did not come or telephone to say goodbye. Instead, Adelaide came to our home and told us that she had been asked by Oliver to contact me and ask for help for her and the children to follow him into exile.

Oliver and I did not see or speak to one another for over twenty-five years. He became the head of the ANC in exile and was branded by the apartheid propaganda machine as a leader of a communist and terrorist organisation. These allegations against Oliver were hardly believable in the light of the acquittal of the accused in the Treason Trial in June 1961, the description of the Freedom Charter on which the charges were mainly based as no more than a socialist document, the forthright statement from the dock by Nelson Mandela, and the evidence of Walter Sisulu and Govan Mbeki in the Rivonia Trial.

I did not have a passport for many years and could not travel. In addition, it would have been dangerous for me to attempt any direct communication with Oliver. We were, however, more or less aware of what each one of us was doing. This came about not only as a result of what was in the public domain but through those of our friends who did visit him and by those who came back into the country who were arrested, charged and whom I defended. Although the prison authorities thought that no information of what was happening in and outside the country got to Mandela and other prisoners, the transistor radio tuned to Radio Freedom in Zambia, local and foreign newspapers and magazines kept the prisoners well informed.

I would convey information to Nelson Mandela on my visits to Robben Island but he would also tell me what was happening outside. Before anyone in South Africa knew who had made the keynote address at the Mozambican Independence Celebration, Nelson told me that it was Oliver, which he saw as a positive sign of the respect for the ANC by the African states.

By the mid-1980s the UDF's campaign of ungovernability, the External Mission's success in isolating apartheid South Africa from the rest of the world together with the increased membership of MK and the independence of Mozambique and Angola led PW Botha to make conditional offers to Nelson Mandela for his release. When Mandela, Sisulu, Kathrada and Nhlaba were moved to Pollsmoor Prison, Nelson was isolated from the other three. He became ill and was operated on. Winnie Mandela and the UDF leadership informed Nelson that the external wing was concerned that he might make some technical concession that might embarrass him and the movement.

Nelson was visited in hospital by Justice Minister Kobie Coetsee who made a tentative suggestion that negotiations might commence not only for Nelson's release but also to put an end to the conflict.

Nelson called me to his ward in the hospital. He asked me to meet Coetsee and tell him that I was going to go to Lusaka in Zambia at Nelson's request to report to Oliver on the developments and assure him that he was in control and that he would do nothing which might prejudice the struggle without consultation with Oliver.

Coetsee had arranged for us to meet on the plane as if by chance. The plane could not land in Johannesburg because of fog and was diverted to Durban. We talked for about five hours. Each of us tried to gain useful information from the other. He wanted to know details about the life and beliefs of both Nelson and Oliver and I tried to disabuse his mind from what his party said about the two men.

At the Lusaka airport I was met by ANC members before clearing customs or collecting my luggage. They appeared to have free access to the whole airport. I was introduced to the hotel receptionist as an important guest of the ANC and was asked to remain in my room until they returned.

Within an hour Oliver was at the door. We spent six hours together until past 3:00 a.m. when the guards sitting outside the room knocked on the door for the second or third time and announced that it was dangerous for Oliver to be in the same place for such a long time. He was glad to be assured that Nelson was well and in control, that he had sent me to report on what was happening, and agreed that it was important that the preliminary negotiations should not become public, not even to the ANC NEC. If Oliver wanted to discuss the matter with anyone, it should be confined to Thabo Mbeki. Both Mandela and Coetsee feared that if there was a leak there was a danger that people on both sides would sabotage the efforts.

We arranged that I would be fetched the next morning to be introduced by Oliver to President Kenneth Kaunda. I was taken to the well-guarded presidential palace to the guest cottage in which Oliver was living. I was enthusiastically received by President Kaunda. I conveyed Nelson's regards and gratitude for what Kaunda was doing in assisting the South African struggle. He wiped tears away with his white handkerchief and said, 'Tell my friend Nelson that none of us in Africa feel free whilst he is in jail.' We went back to the cottage for lunch. One of Oliver's assistants came in with a small transistor radio for Oliver to hear the 1:00 p.m. news. He was sent away but came back a few minutes later and whispered to Oliver who was obviously flabbergasted. In a shaken voice he told me that Olof Palme, the Prime Minister of Sweden, a close friend and great supporter of the struggle, had been murdered. The assistant was asked to make arrangements for Oliver to go to Sweden for the funeral. He pulled himself together, told me that he had to leave and that he had arranged for me to be taken to the airport. Then he unexpectedly appeared at the airport to ask me, for security reasons, not to disclose the fact that he was living within the presidential palace.

I reported to Nelson that Oliver was happy that he should continue with the talks. I asked Judge Johan Kriegler to facilitate an appointment with Coetsee so that I could report to him that Nelson and Oliver were prepared to start negotiations. The National Party's hopes that they could isolate Nelson from Oliver and the external wing of the ANC were obviously not proving to be successful. Nelson had earlier prepared a statement that was read by his daughter Zindzi at Archbishop Tutu's Nobel Prize celebration in Soweto, saying that there were no differences between him and Oliver and emphasising that the relationship between the two of them was such that if Oliver could, he would substitute himself as a prisoner.

Thereafter Thabo Mbeki and representatives of the government established communication channels and meetings were held between leading Afrikaners and members of the ANC. Despite P W Botha's reservations, it became public knowledge that negotiations were taking place.

The suggestion I had made to Coetsee that the government should make a start by releasing Govan Mbeki on the grounds of his age and health was done. When FW de Klerk took over, Walter Sisulu and the other Rivonia Trial accused were released. Meetings of the ANC legal and constitutional committee were taking place even before the ANC was unbanned. In February 1989 a conference was held near Oxford and another at Columbia University in New York in September at which in-depth discussions took place as to the nature of the Bill of Rights and the constitution that should be put forward by the ANC.

Although Oliver did not attend these conferences personally, the NEC in exile was represented by Albie Sachs and Kader Asmal who informed us of the leadership exercised by Oliver and that a Bill of Rights and a constitution that were good for all South Africans should be written.

Oliver Tambo left South Africa as a fugitive. While in exile he held together the liberation movement as a united force; no other movement in exile managed to remain as united as the ANC. This must surely be the best part of his legacy. He returned to South Africa in a frail state, but when I visited him he was so looking forward to the day on which the people of South Africa would cast their votes for the first time. Sadly, he was deprived of this opportunity himself.

THE PEACEMAKER

Sydney Kentridge

In the early 1950s, when I was a young advocate at the Johannesburg Bar, I would from time to time be briefed to appear in minor criminal cases in the Johannesburg Magistrates' Court. Occasionally the brief would come from a firm of attorneys called Mandela and Tambo. There were very few black attorneys in South Africa at that time, so I was intrigued to meet the two partners in the firm. Our meetings were short and businesslike, and quite unrelated to any political issues. I had, of course, heard of the ANC, but I had no knowledge of the ANC Youth League, still less of the part played in it by what has been called 'the great triumvirate' of Walter Sisulu, Nelson Mandela and Oliver Tambo.

My impression of Oliver Tambo then was simply of a pleasant young man who combined a rather old-fashioned courtesy with a thoroughly professional approach to his calling as a lawyer.

As has been told many times over, Nelson Mandela became something of a public figure in the course of the Defiance Campaign of 1952 and the trial that followed it. Oliver Tambo remained very much in the background, escaping public notice and, possibly, the attentions of the police. In any event, I became acquainted with Tambo the rising ANC leader only some years later, with the commencement of the Treason Trial of 1958–61.

In late 1956 the police had arrested 156 members of the Congress movement, including most of the leaders of the ANC, on a charge of high treason. Among them were the President of the ANC, Chief Albert Luthuli, and Oliver Tambo, by then a figure of note on the ANC Executive. After a year-long preparatory examination the state decided to prosecute only 90 of those arrested. Following legal arguments at the beginning of the trial, and the rulings of the three judges appointed to preside over the trial, the number of accused was reduced to 30. They included Walter Sisulu and Nelson Mandela, but not Oliver Tambo or Chief Luthuli.

Although all of the Treason Trial accused were on bail, they had to travel day after day to and from Pretoria, most of them from their homes in Johannesburg or Soweto. A good deal of the day to day direction of the ANC during the whole drawn-out period of the trial therefore fell on Oliver Tambo. One of his responsibilities was to keep in touch with Chief Luthuli, who was restricted by a government banning order to a small rural area in northern Natal. Another was to liaise with the team of defence lawyers who were representing the accused at the trial.

It must be explained that the prosecution's case of treason was based on the allegation that the common objective of all the parties to the Congress movement (and of the ANC in particular) was to overthrow the state by violence. The accused disputed this vigorously. Up to that time the ANC's policy had been a policy of non-violence. But the prosecution had produced several ANC documents and reports of speeches at ANC meetings which were, to say the least, ambiguous, and which required cogent explanation. I was one of the junior counsel for the defence at the trial. It was my good fortune to be deputed to consult with Oliver Tambo on these controversial issues, and consequently to spend many hours discussing them with him. As our discussions developed I came to realise the intellectual and moral stature of the man.

Oliver (as I came to call him) took me through the history of the ANC and the development of its policies, from the 'African Claims' document of the mid-1940s to the Freedom Charter of 1955. He left me in no doubt of the genuineness of the ANC's policy of non-violence. It was a policy in which he believed deeply, and which the ANC maintained until circumstances after its banning in 1960 drove it into militancy. His own adherence, for as long as possible, to the doctrine of non-violent resistance seemed to me to spring both from his deep Christian faith and from a hard-headed practical assessment of the forces of the apartheid government and the ruthlessness of that government.

If there was any one measure of the government which roused him to real bitterness it was the Bantu Education Act of 1951 which had the avowed object (according to Dr Hendrik Verwoerd) of downgrading the education of black children. Oliver, a graduate of Fort Hare University, had himself been a teacher in a well-regarded high school for black pupils run by the Anglican

Church. Under the Act such schools were closed down. The ANC Executive had resolved on a campaign calling for a boycott of Bantu Education schools. Both Nelson Mandela and Oliver, while feeling bound to accept the Executive decision had, I gathered, been sceptical of the merits and prospects of the campaign. In the event it was a complete failure. Oliver felt that education was vital for the future of his people, and what he had seen of the actual operation of Bantu Education had driven him almost to despair.

In the Treason Trial the prosecution were laying stress on the communist affiliations of some of the ANC leaders. Marxism had no attraction for Oliver but his viewpoint was that the ANC was not merely a political party: it was a national movement that could accommodate communists, socialists, nationalists, believers in God and atheists, provided only that they were committed to the fundamental objective of the ANC – a non-racial, egalitarian, democratic South Africa.

During the long years when he led the ANC in exile Oliver Tambo was sometimes referred to within the organisation as 'the peacemaker'. I understood why.

(A footnote: At the end of the Treason Trial in March 1961 the judges held that the prosecution had failed to prove that the ANC and its associates in the Congress movement had conspired to overthrow the state by violence. All of the accused were acquitted.)

THE QUIET SOUTH AFRICAN

Albie Sachs

At school I used to hate being told that 'manners maketh the man'. It was not that I had developed feminist ideas by then, but I resisted the notion that the merits of peoples should be judged by how correctly they spoke and how well they conducted themselves. Years later, when I heard Oliver Tambo speak in London on two memorable occasions, I had to rethink the matter. It was not only what he said, but it was the manner in which he said it . . .

My friend Wolfie Kodesh, a well-known member of the South African exile community in London, who loved hinting that he was sitting on a se-cret, had told me that I had to attend an ANC meeting at Friends House in Euston to be addressed by Oliver Tambo. Filled with anticipation, sitting at the back of a large and well-filled hall, I jumped up with the crowd to ap-plaud OR as he arrived. He joined in the singing of our anthem and began to address us. So far nothing unexpected.

I always had mixed feelings when OR spoke. Part of me wished he would be more fiery, that he would arouse us with muscular, emotional language. We needed to feel our courage soar, to be reassured not only of the justness of our cause, but of our collective invincibility. When some speakers wish to be especially forceful, they raise the volume of their voice, gesture em-phatically and rely on dramatic pauses. Not so OR. Yet, another part of me responded to his quiet and carefully articulated way of communicating his thoughts. He looked even more serious, at times almost unbearably so, when he had a special point to make. (I was later to discover how thoroughly he worked on his speeches, how determined he was to get every nuance absolutely right, so that his presentation would more than make up in care and precision for what it lost in energy and emotional flow.) The gravitas would be enormous. You felt that truth was being conveyed openly and honestly in its most direct form. The emotion lay in the thought, not in the power of the delivery. So, in a firm, resolute way OR revealed the secret that Wolfie had been holding close to his chest (not so close, I mention, as to prevent you from knowing that he was privy to something momentous).

In tones even more measured than usual, OR announced to us and to the world that a group of ANC guerrillas in the Albert Luthuli Detachment of Umkhonto we Sizwe, the armed wing of the ANC, had some weeks before crossed the Zambezi River into what was then called Rhodesia. Their objective was to pass through the territory ruled by the racist minority regime of Ian Smith, so as to get to South Africa and develop the armed struggle on our soil. For some weeks they had managed to avoid detection, but eventually Ian Smith's soldiers had been informed about their presence and battle was joined.

The audience was rapt and, as I recall, the speech went as follows: 'Our comrades skilfully took up positions and were able to out-maneouvre the enemy. In the firefight which followed, lasting a number of hours, many of the enemy were killed and wounded and the survivors fled from the scene.'

We jumped up and cheered. The moment we had been waiting for had at last arrived.

This was 1967. We had been through a terrible decade since the Sharpeville massacre and the banning of the ANC and PAC in 1960. The formation of Umkhonto we Sizwe ('the Spear of the Nation') or MK had led to acts of sabotage against apartheid targets. Repression had been ferocious. People were tortured to death. The underground leadership was captured at Rivonia and sentenced to life imprisonment. Supporters of white supremacy were gloating that apartheid was there to stay. Now, with the announcement of the launching of the Luthuli Detachment, the initiative would be in our hands. We had no doubt that as soon as the freedom fighters got back to South Africa, the masses would rise up and overthrow the racist system. We cheered and cheered.

OR continued his speech: 'And as they fled, the enemy left five bodies on the scene . . .'

We cheered even louder.

Then suddenly a very well-elocuted voice from the back of the hall shouted out: 'That's murder!'

We all looked around in astonishment. Who was this person who dared to challenge what our President was saying, who had the effrontery to impugn the justness of our struggle?

The voice repeated: 'That's murder! That's murder!'

We looked to OR to see how he would react. He was clearly taken aback. He paused for a moment and stepped away from the microphone. Then he came forward and said in a quiet, soft, troubled voice: 'Yes, we have become killers. This is what the situation in our country has led us to.'

He went on to explain to the heckler how patiently the African people had struggled over the decades for their rights, how eagerly they had sought the negotiation of a non-racial democracy. And whenever they had come up with new initiatives for peaceful change, the response had always been the same, greater and greater repression. The deep sadness of our country, he told us, was that for all our longings for peace, the rulers had left us with only one option, and that was the use of violence in order to achieve our freedom. We did not have the vote. Our organisations were illegal. Our newspapers were closed down. Our leaders were in jail. There was no other way.

'The tragedy of our country,' he told us, 'is that our finest and most honourable children are being forced to turn themselves into killers. We believe in peace, and yet we are becoming killers.'

A tape recorder might have captured the words differently, but this is how I remember them. I also recall sharply the impact they had on me. I was amazed. I had expected a powerful and indignant response from a revolutionary leader. Instead came this softly expressed and heartfelt statement, something reflective and true to OR's nature, taking the interjection seriously and responding to it.

I have never forgotten that moment. Perhaps in part OR was sensitive to the fact that the meeting was being held in a hall belonging to a pacifist organisation, not exactly the place to announce to the world a new phase in the armed struggle. But there was something more. He, the leader of an organisation dedicated to the revolutionary overthrow of a ruthless and unjust system, was baring his innermost sentiments, and doing so in a way that carried total conviction. It was the manner as much as the matter that madeth the person.

This was a time when the most heroic figure in our imaginations was the freedom fighter with gun in hand. I had been active in a youth movement and then in the underground opposition to apartheid. We never thought of guerrillas as killers, let alone murderers. While not retreating in any way from the ANC's position on the need for armed struggle, OR was pointing to the inevitably tragic character the use of violence would have. He was thinking not only of the innocent people who always get killed in a war, but of the cost to the freedom fighters themselves, not just through loss of life and limb, but through the inevitable damage to their psyches. To pick up a gun to shoot fellow human beings, whatever the cause, whatever the necessity, is a serious thing, he was saying. You do so only when there is absolutely no other way, when you choose your targets carefully and in a principled manner to achieve a clear political objective, when you stop as soon as you can and never cease exploring other ways of achieving your goals. And yet still you grieve at what you are doing.

Many years later, once more in Wolfie's company, I found myself listening to OR in another great London space – St Paul's Cathedral. There he was, up on the pulpit, preaching to the (mainly) unconverted. Canon Collins, the Dean of St Paul's, had invited OR to give a sermon. Loyal to a person, we exiles had gathered, believers and non-believers alike, to ensure a good attendance. I remember thinking to myself at the time what a smart move it had been on OR's part to get a spot in such an august place to proclaim the good news of our struggle. And I recall being moved by the passion, grace and fluency with which he orated.

On the way out I made a clever-clever remark to Wolfie: 'OR spoke with such conviction that you could almost think he believed what he was saying.'

'Oh, but he does,' Wolfie answered with the assurance of someone in the know. 'There's nothing more he would love to do than be a minister in the Anglican Church.'

Once again I was flabbergasted. The stereotype I had of a revolutionary leader was quite different. I could understand a liberation theologian becoming a revolutionary leader; I couldn't image a revolutionary leader becoming a cleric. And yet, far from being disappointed by the discovery of OR's passion, I felt elated. I knew that at the core of his faith was a set of principles very close to the humanist and rationalist values which I liked to think animated me. And I was not surprised when sometime later when OR wished to prepare a speech for a world congress of religious leaders, it was to me that he turned for support rather than to the Religious Desk of the ANC.

I'm not sure exactly why the bond between us grew so strong in the years that followed. Our backgrounds both socially and politically could not have been more different. I think that part of the rapport came from the fact that we shared something major in common – we were both soft people in a hard struggle. Every movement needs those who are tough and those who are tender. Yet as OR showed, and before him Albert Luthuli, it is often the tender who survive the longest and remain the truest to their beliefs. Perhaps it is because they are more supple and adaptable in character, more sensitive to the people around them and more eager to learn from new experiences.

Whatever the reason, OR's quiet, schoolmasterish and lawyerly manner, his gentle style of speech, his warm, embracing smile and sense of interest in all those who came into contact with him, was ultimately to give him a stature more enduring than that enjoyed by any of the bold and charismatic leaders of his generation, a stature equalled only by that of Nelson Mandela.

The Oliver Tambo of London and the Oliver Tambo of Lusaka were not two different people, one diplomatic to please a British audience, the other fiery to inspire soldiers under his political command. OR was OR, always the same, always militant in his beliefs, yet always dreaming of negotiations when circumstances were right and always certain that South Africa would one day become a country that belonged equally to all who lived in it. If his spirit lives on today, I know where to find it: it is in a document that is as beautiful, as progressive, humane, and as calmly and carefully articulated as any in the world – the Constitution of South Africa.

A VIGILANT GUARDIAN

Michael Seifert

As I waited in Addis Ababa airport at some ungodly hour between flights from London Heathrow to Kilimanjaro to attend the historic ANC conference at Arusha, in December 1987, a voice from across the lounge called out, 'Michael!' I turned and saw Oliver Tambo – his arms outstretched, beaming at me. We embraced; he enquired about my mother, Connie Seifert, and then hurried off to be met by Ethiopian government officials who whisked him to a meeting of the OAU. He would arrive the next day in Arusha for the ANC conference.

I have related this anecdote because it encapsulates several aspects of the character of OR. After a gruelling flight at an unsociable time of night Oliver appeared to be as fresh as a daisy. He knew me – but not that well – and yet he recognised me, remembered my mother and embraced me with great warmth. Over the years, I have met many people who showed a deep love of humanity in general, but were somewhat deficient in their affection for and interest in individual human beings. Oliver was someone who loved both humanity and individual people. It is not surprising that when Trevor Huddleston returned to visit South Africa it was Oliver Tambo who, despite serious ill health, went to greet him at the airport along with other members of the ANC.

A man of truly awesome intellect, OR was never in my experience arrogant – intellectually or otherwise. While he didn't suffer fools entirely gladly, I rarely heard him speak sharply or rudely to anyone – although a gentle, even mocking humour was often apparent.

OR left an indelible impression on the numerous people he met during the years of exile. These included people at all levels of society in the UK, from Church leaders and senior politicians to local activists. His influence on these people was indeed profound, and through them he had an important if indirect influence on the political and moral life of the UK.

As Acting President (and later President) of the ANC it would, of course, have been totally inappropriate for him to have intervened directly in the domestic politics of the UK or, indeed, to have commented on them publicly. Furthermore, the ANC maintained a representative office in London – staffed by competent personnel and headed up by a senior person. It was the task of this office to liaise and work with local activists in various political parties, churches and all other areas of civil society – including, of course, the anti-apartheid movement.

On the occasions when I heard OR speaking in public in London he invariably held his audience spellbound. This was not so much by virtue of oratorical pyrotechnics as by his calm logic and the enormous moral authority and dignity that permeated everything he said. People knew they were in the presence of someone whose integrity was absolute.

The nature of OR's influence in the UK stemmed to a large extent from the extraordinary nature of the politics of the ANC itself which were brought into our lives by the considerable numbers of South African activists who sought refuge in the UK, particularly (following the Sharpeville massacre) during the 1960s.

The country which these early exiles (including the Tambo family) came to in the 1960s was in many ways different from today (at least on the surface) – although some aspects of UK life at that time must have been only too depressingly familiar to the exiles. For example, it was unremarkable to see small advertisements for rooms and flats which carried a perfunctory qualification 'No Blacks' or – if the landlord considered him- or herself more liberally minded and cultured – 'Sorry, No Blacks'. Long leases drawn up by perfectly 'respectable' solicitors contained restrictive covenants prohibiting sub-letting or assignment to non-white lessees. Overt, unrepentant discrimination was the norm in all areas and walks of life. For example, the armed forces had an open colour bar until the late 1960s and a promotional ceiling for much longer.

The struggle against racism in the UK – which is still, of course, as necessary as ever – was spearheaded in those days as one would expect by local activists – both black and white. However, there can be little doubt that colleagues from overseas – from the Caribbean, the Indian subcontinent, Africa, etc. – were of central importance. Amongst the influences from abroad, in my experience the South Africans were outstanding as they brought an illuminating political vision and well-honed political skills at building alliances around the most progressive positions. These political skills had been laboriously and painfully developed by the ANC over many decades since its origins in 1912. Paradoxically, they were brought to a peak of brilliance during what most people would regard as the barren years following Sharpeville and Rivonia when the leadership was either in prison or in exile.

There can be no doubt that OR was the truly great figure who synthesised everything that was positive in the politics of the ANC – adding that touch of magic of his own. For example, the clear policy and ideological guidelines hammered out by the ANC at the Morogoro Conference at the end of the 1960s were brought into the UK in the early 1970s by the South African exiles. This helped progressive people in the UK to address issues of race and class in a new, clear headed way. Joe Slovo, speaking in 1983, was convinced that 'there were moments at that Morogoro Conference when the very future of our whole movement seemed to be in jeopardy. But it was JB Marks's skill as Chairman and the greatness of Comrade President Tambo which pulled us through and laid the basis for what we are today'[1]. What emerged from Morogoro was a brilliant synthesis of the experiences of the ANC over the previous decades, summed up by OR as follows:

> And who are the black in South Africa? They are the people known and treated as 'Kaffirs', 'Coolies', and 'Hotnots' together with those South Africans whose total political identity with the oppressed Africans makes them black in all but the accident of skin colour … This type of black man in South African is rare today [1971]. But he will grow in numerical strength ….[2]

The vital importance of this formulation for the future history of South Africa speaks for itself. However, in addition, the politics of the ANC as produced and articulated by OR were of great importance in major campaigns in the UK. For example, as National Secretary of the Angela Davis Defence Committee in the UK I was involved in putting together a very broad alliance encompassing every shade of non-racist political opinion together with all the significant anti-racist and non-white campaigning organisations. Of the fifty of more organisations affiliated to the Campaign Committee I personally found the membership and participation of the London-based members of the ANC to be invaluable. For clarity of thought and strategic maturity no one could match them – in particular the Pahad brothers, Aziz and Essop, who played a major role in the campaign. There were, of course, as in any broad committee, strongly held and vigorously argued differences of opinion, but the ANC representatives carried such authority and spoke with such clarity that they usually tipped the balance in favour of uniting around our common goals. This was in no small measure due to the ethos and strategic genius of the ANC itself – as exemplified by the greatness of its President, Oliver Tambo.

Once I got to know OR, it was not difficult to see why the top leadership of the ANC (particularly Nelson Mandela and Walter Sisulu) chose him to go abroad in 1960 to carry the message of the horrors of the apartheid system and regime to the outside world and, after the Rivonia Trial, to lead the ANC and rebuild its shattered ranks from the External Mission. His success in both spreading the message and in rebuilding the ANC must have surpassed the wildest hopes of even those of his comrades who held him in such high esteem. His ability to hold together such a disparate group of strong-willed individuals was based on an authority that stemmed from respect for the sheer integrity of the man.

I found OR to be a man of considerable personal charm and modesty but fiercely proud when it came to the ANC and its true history and the honour of his position as President General. An illustration of this was when OR was potentially to be libelled in a UK television programme purporting to deal with the crucial period of South African history following the Sharpeville massacre. He consulted me as the London lawyer to the ANC and we were able to obtain a copy of the script before filming was concluded. I instructed Tony Gifford as counsel and we met in his chambers. The nub of our complaint was that the programme depicted OR's departure from South Africa as him running away to escape danger rather than the truth, which was that he was ordered to go abroad by the NEC as the person best able to set up, organise and lead the External Mission. My admiration for OR soared to new heights when it became clear during our meetings that he was not mainly concerned about his personal reputation (although, of course, that troubled him), but more about the effect these lies would have on the ANC and the anti-apartheid movement in general. He insisted that the historic record must be put straight. Fortunately, this incident occurred in the mid-1970s at a time when – largely thanks to OR's inspirational leadership – the ANC had achieved a degree of respectability among some leading media executives in the UK. Armed with Tony Gifford's written opinion, we were able to lean heavily on the programme makers who, under our guidance, rewrote that part of the script, and who, at our insistence, made a substantial donation to the AAM.

What really impressed me about OR's conduct during this whole episode was his determination to see that the truth prevailed – a vigilant guardian of the true history of the ANC – and his relative disregard for his own personal position – other than as it affected the dignity of the movement as a whole.

I am sure that I am not alone in feeling that recollections of Oliver Tambo and the UK are not complete without talking about the warm hospitality of the whole Tambo family. Sunday lunch with Oliver, Adelaide, the children and grandchildren in their welcoming house in Muswell Hill was always something to look forward to. As much as everything else, it was always great fun as was the ceremony of negotiating with Adelaide as I left with lashings of food to tide me over the next few days. In addition, it was always remarkable to see how someone with the weight of such awesome responsibility as Oliver carried could completely relax and enjoy the company of his family and friends. It was on occasions such as these that one could see how vital family life (albeit so often disrupted by the requirements of the job) was to Oliver. In this, as in so many other things, he was an inspiration to his comrades and to those of us in the UK who were privileged enough to get to know him.

NOTES

1. F. Meli: *A History of the ANC* (Baton Rouge, Indiana University Press, 1989).
2. *Oliver Tambo Speaks* (Heinemann, 1987)..

INTERNATIONAL FIGURES

HEROISM OF AN
EXCEPTIONAL ORDER

Emeka Anyaoku

Voltaire memorably said that to the living we owe respect, to the dead we owe only the truth. In life Oliver Tambo compelled respect and I'm sure that in death he would insist on nothing less than the truth.

Oliver Tambo belonged to a remarkable generation of South African leaders on whom history was to place a stern destiny. It entailed the sort of choice that history rarely calls upon leaders to make. In the case of Oliver and his circle the choice was either to leave their people in perpetual thrall to apartheid slavery or risk everything to bring an end to that slavery. The challenge called for heroism of an exceptional order and it was this challenge that Oliver Tambo, Nelson Mandela, Walter Sisulu, Govan Mbeki and many others embraced. But even within this remarkable circle of leaders, Oliver Tambo was a leader apart.

My first encounter with Oliver was in 1964 in New York when he came to address the UN Special Committee Against Apartheid. At the time I was a young diplomat at the Nigerian Mission to the UN and chairman of a sub-committee of the Special Committee responsible for petitions to the Committee. It fell to that sub-committee to decide whether Oliver Tambo should be allowed to address the Special Committee as the representative of the ANC. The sub-committee decided unanimously to allow him to address the full committee. This was not his first appearance before a UN committee. The year before he had addressed the Special Political Committee of the

UN on the Rivonia Trial. I had been present as Nigeria's representative at the meeting, and his address was an impressive performance. This time he devoted the substance of his speech to the need for international action for sanctions against the apartheid regime. In its intentions and in its practice the apartheid system had brought down a permanent veil between the black majority and opportunity in all its forms. The steady and relentless degradation of black life had to be stopped if South Africa was to avoid catastrophe. Oliver ended his speech with the following moving words:

> No one can doubt any longer now that life for the African in South Africa is not life. If it is, it is worth nothing. But we promise in that event that no other life in South Africa is worth anything – white or non-white. Let the United Nations and the world, therefore, save what it can – what it cannot, will either be destroyed or destroy itself.

After listening to his speech I began to reflect on what sort of man he was. There was a certain degree of diffidence in his manner. I got the distinct impression that here was someone who had thought through the views he held and in whose mind there were no cloudy patches. His style was more like that of a university don than that of a politician out to sway an audience. His first approach was to the head, not the heart. He spoke like a man who felt responsible for every word he uttered. Luli Callinicos, his biographer, has spoken of his self-contained air and his calm, inner stillness. In fact, as I got to know Oliver better, I came to the conclusion that no man ever wore a great destiny with more humility and dignity or style. All these initial impressions were to be confirmed later when the Tambos moved to London and I also relocated there when I joined the Commonwealth Secretariat in 1966. It was in London that Oliver and I began to work more closely together.

Oliver left South Africa in 1960 at the behest of the leadership of the ANC. The net of the apartheid regime was then closing in on the movement's high-ranking leaders. The ANC had already been banned and had been compelled to operate underground against ever mounting odds. Morale was high within the movement, but the determination of the apartheid regime to dismantle it was equally resolute. If the entire leadership was captured and incarcerated, it would set back the cause of freedom by many decades. This consideration lay behind the decision to send Oliver out of the country so that he would establish the ANC's External Mission. The task was twofold: to keep alive the goals of the movement within the country, and, externally, to mobilise international support and solidarity.

In terms of the External Mission's mandate, the times were particularly propitious. The process of decolonisation in Africa had begun to accelerate. In 1960 alone, nearly twenty African countries achieved independence, making Africa's voice increasingly audible in international forums. At the UN, newly independent African states began to work in concert with other member states from Asia and Latin America to complete decolonisation on the continent and to bring an end to the white settler minority regimes in southern Africa. The same process of decolonisation had inaugurated the beginnings of fundamental change in the Commonwealth. It had already changed from being the British Commonwealth of Nations to simply the Commonwealth of Nations, a new model Commonwealth that would lead the world in the campaign against apartheid.

In 1961 South Africa became a republic and applied to continue its membership of the Commonwealth on the basis of the Indian precedent. But the regime did not reckon with the mounting international anger over its apartheid policies. Led by then Canadian Prime Minister John Diefenbaker, an overwhelming majority of Commonwealth governments opposed South Africa's application. The republic was compelled to withdraw its application and therefore its membership of the organisation.

It has become conventional to say that South Africa withdrew from the Commonwealth but the truth of the matter was later put more accurately by Sir Robert Menzies who was Prime Minister of Australia at the time and a staunch friend of apartheid South Africa. 'The decision', Sir Robert wrote in his memoirs, 'was one of expulsion, not in form, of course; but in fact and in substance, it could have no other meaning.' With the establishment of the Commonwealth Secretariat in 1965 and a further expansion of membership from the newly independent states of the Caribbean and the Pacific, the Commonwealth would become the focus for the anti-apartheid campaign.

The 1960s were a period of consolidation for the anti-apartheid organisations then springing up in Britain. At the forefront of these were the IDAF and the AAM founded by Canon Collins and Father Trevor Huddleston, both of whom Oliver regarded as father figures. By this time Oliver and I had come to know each other well. The Commonwealth had also begun to make the apartheid issue its central concern. Not everyone appreciated the reason for this, but within the association itself the view was that the continuation of apartheid was wholly incompatible with the essence of the Commonwealth. The Secretariat received visiting representatives of the ANC and the other liberation movements of southern Africa.

I would periodically meet and brief Oliver Tambo on the trend of events as they affected South Africa and he would in turn apprise me of the evolving situation in the region generally, but especially in South Africa.

Between 1963 and 1975, the apartheid regime appeared to have gained the upper hand. It had imprisoned most of the top leadership of the liberation movement and was successfully attracting a considerable amount of external capital and an inflow of migrants from western Europe. The regime also seemed to be successful in projecting itself as anti-communist at a time when the Cold War was at its height. It was a particularly difficult time for all those working to end apartheid. But in 1976 the Soweto uprising began to change all this. The brutality with which the regime tried to suppress what was basically a protest of schoolchildren exposed its true nature to the watching world. In the process the regime also revealed its fragility, a revelation which had implications for external investment.

Many within the Commonwealth had already been calling for sanctions as the only peaceful means of resolving the situation in South Africa. In the wake of Soweto, the Commonwealth imposed a ban on all sporting links with South Africa – the Gleneagles Agreement of 1977 – and stepped up the campaign for economic sanctions. Oliver and I talked extensively at his Muswell Hill home about the outcome of the London Summit and the implications of the Gleneagles Agreement which he warmly welcomed.

Gleneagles was significant if only because of the importance of sport in South African culture, but many in the Commonwealth had become convinced that the real objective in terms of ending apartheid was the imposition of economic sanctions. That opportunity came with the appointment of the mission of the EPG, a decision made at the Commonwealth Summit held in The Bahamas in 1985. The outcome of the EPG mission was to mark the turning point in the long-running international efforts to end apartheid; I therefore crave the indulgence of the reader as I sketch in the background to that decision.

Ever since the expulsion of South Africa from the association in 1961, every subsequent Commonwealth Summit had placed the apartheid issue at centre stage in its deliberations. From the 1970s the demand for wider international pressures, including economic sanctions, had been a constant theme. Commonwealth leaders had also come to the view that the instability in the region stemmed ultimately from the persistence of the apartheid system in South Africa and that only with its eradication could southern Africa be restored to peace and stability. Then, in 1984, the townships of South Africa rose in revolt. From Lusaka, Oliver Tambo appealed to his risen compatriots to make the country ungovernable. The black majority had regained the political initiative.

In October 1985 Commonwealth leaders met in Nassau, The Bahamas. The overwhelming mood was for economic sanctions. The only dissenting voice was that of the British Prime Minister Margaret Thatcher. She informed the meeting that she had it on authority that President PW Botha was prepared to negotiate with the representatives of the black majority and on that basis she encouraged her colleagues not to press ahead with sanctions but instead to encourage negotiations. The majority of Commonwealth leaders entertained serious doubts about the sincerity of the regime. In Africa, the Pretoria regime's word was practically synonymous with deceit and bad faith. Nevertheless, the meeting decided to appoint a panel of distinguished Commonwealth personalities – what would later be popularly known as the Eminent Persons Group – to go to South Africa with a view to facilitating negotiations between the regime and the representatives of the black majority. The EPG was led by General Olusegun Obasanjo of Nigeria and Malcolm Fraser of Australia.

On my return to London Oliver and I discussed the events at Nassau, the appointment of the EPG and what Commonwealth leaders expected of it. He welcomed the idea but with some reservations. Like most people with some knowledge and experience of South Africa, his concerns centred on the sincerity of the regime, especially President PW Botha himself. He pointed to Botha's record, which was one of unswerving support for apartheid. Botha set the tone of policy and led the most hardline elements within the government. If it was true that he had indicated a willingness to negotiate, that could only be to buy time to enable the regime to recover from its current difficulties and not because he was prepared to negotiate meaningfully, let alone surrender power. The ANC would nevertheless cooperate fully with the EPG if only to expose the regime for what it was.

Oliver's judgement was to prove prescient.

After an extensive round of negotiations in South Africa with political parties, the business community, church leaders, trade unions and other civil society organisations, the EPG appeared to be making progress. Some even spoke of the possibility of a breakthrough. It was at this point that the regime chose to scuttle the initiative by bombing three neighbouring Commonwealth countries: Zambia, Botswana and Zimbabwe.

The story of the EPG mission has been in the public domain for some time now. In addition to the EPG's own report which came out in 1986 within days of its return from South Africa, we now also have Nelson Mandela's memoirs and a host of specialist studies on the subject. What is perhaps less well known is what Oliver Tambo told the EPG when he met them in Lusaka on 17 May 1986. General Obasanjo did most of the talking on behalf of the EPG and he was particularly concerned to draw out Oliver on the viability of the ANC's armed struggle. General Obasanjo said that he had

had an opportunity to see the capability of the South African army from a professional angle. There could be no question of comparability between the resources and professionalism of the SADF and MK. In the circumstances he wondered whether there was much point in the ANC insisting on the continuation of its armed struggle.

Oliver's reply was illuminating. Slowly and in an unusually deliberative manner, he explained that at no stage had the ANC entertained the illusion that there would ever be parity between them and the enemy. If they had had to wait for anything like parity with the enemy before embarking on the armed struggle, they would never have launched it. From the very beginning the ANC accepted the inequality as a fact of life; but they knew that they had one thing which the regime lacked. The regime's army fought to defend privilege and material interests. There was nothing noble in anything that the regime stood for. In contrast, the ANC was fighting humanity's own cause and that gave them courage to endure hardship and risk life and limb. Then he came out with a memorable clincher: 'this is what puts us beyond death'. That meeting gave the EPG, and indeed the international community, a rare insight into the mind of this great man.

Oliver Tambo brought great qualities to the leadership of the South African people's struggle for freedom. Firstly, he brought dedication and a methodical approach to the prosecution of the struggle. There is a story in his biography by Luli Callinicos that brings out this point well. In 1958 in the course of one of the countless stayaways to protest against the injustices of apartheid, one of the comrades suggested a permanent stayaway in order to achieve freedom, 'We must stay away for ever until we are free', to which Oliver replied: 'You know, you come from Rustenburg. You have a piece of land there. When you are ploughing it, you always take an acre at a time. You plough it. You take another acre. That is *sekindima* – one by one. You can't say now this strike must go on forever until we are free. What are we going to eat?' Oliver was clearly committed to the cause but he pursued the struggle in a manner that was informed by an unfailing sense of realism.

Oliver led the ANC in exile for over thirty years. In the course of that period the movement faced serious obstacles. There were the challenges to his leadership in the mid-1960s and the accusations that the military struggle had made no headway. There was the rise of the BCM led by Steve Biko in the 1970s which seemed for a while to look like eclipsing the ANC internally. There was the challenge of finding placements for the thousands of schoolchildren who left South Africa in the wake of the Soweto uprising. There was the Nkomati Accord of March 1984 between Mozambique and South Africa and the expulsion of ANC cadres from Mozambique. All of these developments in combination could have been enough to bring about the break up of the exiled movement. The fact that Oliver Tambo was able to keep it united against all these odds must be one of the greatest tributes to his leadership qualities.

In his foreword to the Callinicos biography, President Thabo Mbeki made the same point in the following words:

> More than any other, it was Oliver Tambo who kept our movement together through his skilled and sensitive leadership of the ANC during its thirty years of illegality and exile. It was during these trying times of struggle and sacrifice that Comrade OR became our exemplar, both to those in exile and to the millions of members and grassroots supporters at home, including political prisoners.

The point could not have been put better.

Every revolutionary struggle, especially when it assumes the character of an armed struggle, always poses a serious moral challenge for the revolutionary combatant. In the words of Victor Serge, a witness of the Russian Revolution, 'it is the problem of combining the greatest practical efficiency with respect for the man in the enemy; in a word, of war without hate'. And even when armed hostilities have come to an end, there is a further concomitant challenge; and this second challenge was brilliantly formulated by Albert Camus as the question of the age: 'How cease to be victims without becoming executioners?'

To its eternal credit, the ANC always insisted that its war was against an oppressive system and not against individuals, let alone against a race. In keeping with this position, the movement took every possible care to train its fire on the institutions of apartheid and those functionaries sworn to ensure its smooth running. This was ANC policy. But it was the exceptional merit of Oliver Tambo that this ethical position, so full of humanity, but so difficult to execute, was nonetheless upheld in practice in the heat and dust of war. It should also be said that the acclaimed success of the policy of reconciliation that followed the end of apartheid was enormously facilitated by the principled leadership with which Oliver directed the anti-apartheid campaign.

His accomplishments were truly remarkable, all the more so given the paucity of the resources that were at the disposal of the movement. Hardly any of these achievements would have been possible without the support of his dear wife and lifelong companion, Adelaide. Against all the odds, she established a home for the family in London, became its sole breadwinner and was both father and mother to their children during Oliver's protracted absences. But Adelaide's contribution to the cause was wider and deeper and history will no doubt accord her due recognition. In 1998, when as Commonwealth Secretary-General I was given the uncommon privilege of addressing a joint session of the South African parliament, I considered it an additional honour that it was Adelaide who as a member of parliament was called upon to introduce me.

Finally, Oliver derived unfailing strength and inspiration from his faith, which was integral to his being. If the struggle for freedom had not claimed Oliver, then the Anglican Church would almost certainly have claimed him for the ministry. His faith bred in him a steadfastness to truth, justice and fellow feeling. It enabled him to deem as a certainty the defeat of apartheid and in the process to become more resolute, disdaining hardship and danger and ready to suffer extremities. In a very real sense, Oliver's faith enabled him ultimately to contribute decisively to 'moving' the mountain of apartheid.

I recall visiting him at a London hospital where he was receiving treatment after a stroke in 1989. The doctors had given strict instructions severely restricting the number of visitors he was to receive, apart from his wife and children. Only Trevor Huddleston and I were allowed to see him. On one of those visits I found his daughter, Tselane, sitting by his bedside and reading to him some of the speeches he had delivered in the past. Those readings brought back to life something of the old Tambo, the fighting Tambo, and I have no doubt that they went a long way to rallying him.

The stroke that he suffered brought to an effective end Oliver's leadership of the liberation struggle. Nor would he live to take his place at the rendezvous of victory. But he had already accomplished his life's work. For the best part of half a century he had toiled unstintingly to bring his people out of the bondage of apartheid slavery and he died knowing that this was as good as achieved.

Oliver Reginald Kaizana Tambo's place in history is secure. He was a great South African and an even greater son of Africa. More than this he belonged to all humanity. As he himself said, the campaign against apartheid was humanity's own cause. By playing such a pre-eminent leadership role in the defeat of this evil system, he contributed decisively to the removal of one of the greatest blots on our common humanity. That was what made his life such a blessing and a benefaction.

REFERENCES
L. Callinicos, *Oliver Tambo: Beyond the Engeli Mountains* (Cape Town: David Philip, 2004).

OUTSTANDING SON OF AFRICA

Paul Boateng

The image of Oliver Tambo viewing the sculpture of Nelson Mandela on the South Bank in London sums up the man for me: that unique combination of focus, strength and humility. The 1980s saw Oliver Tambo come to represent for us all the dedication of the movement in a crucial stage of the struggle. He came to the Greater London Council's Festival Hall in October 1985 to unveil the sculpture with Madiba's daughter, at the height of his formidable powers of intellect and organisation. I remember him demonstrating towards her the compassion and kindness that was so characteristic of him and which contributed to the refuge that he and Mama Tambo, who worked so hard, provided to all comers at their home in north London, a home created by Adelaide that Oliver seldom had time to rest in himself as he drove himself tirelessly for the cause. He travelled ceaselessly to build the solidarity movement and to wage war against apartheid. He recognised that it was the churches, the trade unions, the artistic community, young people, progressive local government and the opposition in parliament who represented the true spirit of Britain in the fight for a free, non-racial South Africa. He reached out to join hands with us all, uniting under the banner 'Free Nelson Mandela'. This statue was erected in their name. The statue and the London anti-apartheid declaration that preceded it were, incredible as it now seems, at the time politically controversial and the subject of frequent attacks by the Right. Oliver Tambo made time to be there on that day with Ken Livingstone and myself as it was unveiled. This great man who I originally met as a boy in Ghana during the first years of his exile has been a source of lasting inspiration. He lives on in our memories as an outstanding son of Africa and as a father of a nation. We in London are proud to have had him amongst us.

THE PATIENT LEADER

Lynda Chalker

From the day I began my Foreign and Commonwealth Office (FCO) 'life', I had a strong personal wish to build bridges between the UK and Africa, as well as with our European partners. The increasing frustration of black South Africans with the apartheid government was watched with growing alarm, and bringing the different groups closer seemed to me to be the number one task.

I had a lot to learn in my new role as Minister of State in the Foreign Office. I had rather limited experience of Africa, having visited only nine countries there since 1980. South Africa began to form more and more of my daily reading, but I had no real wish to travel to Pretoria as long as the apartheid regime remained. My need to help bring about change grew strongly, especially as I frequently began to travel across the continent as a Foreign Office minister. Our diplomats had their own quiet contacts with many exiled South Africans who visited London, as well as the activists studying and campaigning in Britain, but this was not ministerial territory at all. The most important of these exiles in Britain was Oliver Tambo, who had a modest home in Muswell Hill that he visited from time to time.

On my very first FCO ministerial visit to Kenya, Uganda (with new President Museveni sworn into office just days before) and Tanzania, I became acutely aware of the urgency of the 'building southern African bridges' task for Geoffrey Howe and myself. Hardly a meeting anywhere in Africa went by without a strong reminder from those whom I met that Britain was not doing enough to end apartheid. We knew the system was wrong, inhuman, vicious and destructive, but the UK seemed to be almost silent on the sidelines, whilst other nations spoke out strongly, even though to little lasting effect.

Whilst the Foreign Secretary and our officials understood the urgency and complexity well, a fair number on the Conservative benches and in the country could not see beyond the threats of violence from the ANC, the PAC and others. However, there were many Conservatives who knew that unless we stepped up our bridging role, we would have to answer for our seemingly over-quiet opposition to the apartheid system. The irony of it all was that our Prime Minister Margaret Thatcher found the apartheid system abhorrent. She said so often, but it was not until much later, in 1987, that the media began to report her view that 'apartheid had to be brought to an end'.

By April 1986 my knowledge of Africa and even South Africa was growing. We were particularly well served by many officials in the FCO who specialised in African politics and economics. Consequently, we were alerted to many protest actions, both violent and non-violent, as well as to the apartheid government's vicious measures against protest that never even made our newspapers, let alone reached our television screens in the UK. Friends in the academic world left me in no doubt about the changes in South Africa that had to come, and as fast as possible, before violence destroyed many good lives on all sides. There was also some thoughtful media coverage in Holland and other European partner countries. My responsibilities for the whole of Europe meant being frequently forced to defend Britain's position in capitals. I did so without feeling that we were doing enough as a government to influence change in South Africa, through those with whom we could talk. In reality, there were not nearly enough such people with whom we could have constructive discussions.

In April 1986, the German Foreign Minister, Hans Dietrich Genscher, received Oliver Tambo in Bonn. In addition, there had been meetings with our Dutch colleagues, although not officially at Foreign Minister level in Holland. The pressure to meet at ministerial level was evident, expressed informally as well as formally, in the margins of European Foreign Ministers' meetings. Once we knew that Oliver Tambo would be in London in the spring of 1986, I began to try to work out how to meet him. I knew that the Prime Minister was unlikely to encourage such a meeting, but, however difficult, it was essential that we tried. The office would use its channels, but it was necessary to ensure that the messages would not be blocked, unbeknown to us. Consequently, one or two friends made sure that our wish to talk was known to Oliver Tambo himself.

In early June the situation in South Africa was worsening, with raids on the ANC in Zambia, Zimbabwe and Botswana by the South African government forces, and then a significant bomb blast in Durban, which killed three people and injured many more. These items were making the UK press, and we were being asked in parliament, both across the Despatch Box and in corridors, when the government was going to take action to stop the bloodshed and the widening of the gulf between the South African government and the ANC. Geoffrey and I were deeply concerned to find an effective way to get through to the South African government in response to their increasingly repressive actions, led by President PW Botha and his Foreign Minister Pik Botha, as well as to try to make ongoing contact with the moderates in the ANC, whose leader was truly Oliver Tambo.

At every turn we were trying to establish our firm stance on the need for dialogue and our opposition to violence from wherever it came; our action needed to be stepped up and fast. On 11 June 2006 the Foreign Secretary gained the Prime Minister's agreement that I should meet Oliver Tambo, just as the SADF raids and the ANC bombing moved into a more violent phase.

My first meeting on 24 June with Oliver Tambo, the quiet and patient President of the ANC, was a moment of hope. He was accompanied to the Foreign Office by the ANC's then Director of Information, Thabo Mbeki, and Aziz Pahad, another member of the ANC Executive. Our meeting in the Foreign Office was calm, serious and thoughtful, despite the need for me to present a very firm case. At no stage was it angry, despite the heavy pressure to abandon violence, especially that perpetrated against innocent people. It was critical for both the South African government and its ANC and PAC opposition to begin somehow to build a dialogue.

I began the meeting by stressing the UK government's deep concern over escalating violence in South Africa and more recently in the neighbouring states. The remains of the burnt out buildings and personal effects after the SADF raid on the outskirts of Gaborone were mind searing. The British government understood the anger and frustration in townships in South Africa, but the spiral of violence would only lead to further violence and thus delay the achievement of change. This meeting was the first chance to declare just how abhorrent the UK government found apartheid and to explain what we were doing in the Commonwealth and with our European partners to hasten its end. I was able to underline the government's wish to exchange views with the ANC, but was careful to explain that such meetings did not mean a 'recognition' of the ANC, the specially phrased words used to avoid any read-across to the IRA.

Oliver Tambo could not have been more thoughtful in his responses nor more pleasant. He was particularly glad to come to the Foreign Office and speak to a member of the government, which he said, 'he knew to be trying to get change'. There was everything to be gained from exchanging views and seeking a way out of the great problem. He emphasised that the previous refusal by the UK government to deal with the ANC was interpreted by black South Africans as an expression of hostility. He carefully explained the non-violent roots of the ANC, but how its policy had developed as a reaction to the brutality of apartheid. This stance would end when the apartheid system was removed.

We had a very full dialogue about the violence that very morning in Johannesburg, and about those who were possibly responsible for it. He did not know who was accountable, but even assuming it was the ANC, it was a response to the continuing State of Emergency and the endless repression. Our discussions about violence took up more than half the meeting and I left the ANC leaders in no doubt about the strength of our concern, but also the need to find a way out of the spiral of violence.

Understandably, Oliver Tambo urged that the UK should threaten sanctions, for he believed that such a serious move by Britain would force the South African government to respond. If Mandela and other political prisoners were released from jail, this would enable the black leadership to plan the future peacefully. I discussed why we did not believe sanctions would force the hand of the South African government. Tambo explained the willingness of black people in and beyond South African borders to endure any further hardship that these could cause, and that he did not believe that Afrikaners would hold out until their economy was destroyed. There had to be a way to get President PW Botha to accept reality. Tambo felt that any talking that the British government could do had to be combined with economic pressure. Throughout the meeting, Tambo reminded me of my late father, who had died just days before on 12 June. Tambo did not jump in on the arguments, but patiently heard me out, and he encouraged dialogue and debate in a similarly thoughtful way.

The value of our exchange of views was strongly felt by both sides. The ANC, Tambo said, was not seeking recognition but dialogue. He felt deeply that the UK could play a decisive role. I undertook to report the detail of our discussions to the government, and we parted hoping that we could meet again. It had been a very important hour or so for me and my officials, for this was a man who sought solutions, who disliked violence, and believed in dialogue. Mbeki and Pahad were largely silent in our meeting, but their eye contact and facial expressions convinced me that Oliver Tambo really was the patient leader, often having to rein in others in his movement.

The Foreign Secretary left the UK for South Africa in mid-July, for the EPG visit to South Africa. He had already had some useful days in the Front-line States and had written to Tambo in advance of that visit, in the hope that they might meet in Lusaka or even in the margins of a European Union or other meeting. Geoffrey Howe's Lusaka meeting that summer did not happen because Oliver Tambo, or almost certainly his advisers, were suspicious about the increasing contact. Geoffrey's visit to Lusaka, Harare and Maputo had reinforced his view that there was a vital need for more contact with the ANC for the situation in South Africa could not continue and a way had to be found to lead to a non-racial, fully representative society as soon as possible. (Geoffrey describes this in his memories of Oliver Tambo.) Geoffrey wanted to take every possible chance to advance dialogue. The two of us were determined to achieve another meeting and consequently Tambo's visit to Chevening on 20 September was a real watershed, even though our contacts for a further year or so were often almost as difficult to achieve.

Most of my meetings with members of the ANC were unofficial and hardly recorded. They took place wherever we could meet on my African travels. Despite frequent attempts for official meetings in 1987 and 1988, I was firmly discouraged from having such meetings. In fact, a three-country visit to Angola, Botswana and Zambia was firmly 'postponed' in 1988, but at least officials quietly built up their links. The Krugersdorp car bomb and other violent actions had made ministerial contact impossible at that time.

Sadly I did not meet Oliver Tambo again until 1989 when we were in Lusaka for special development meetings. Even that encounter was brief and unofficial. But in the interim, the very dialogue we had so long sought was inching its way forward in South Africa. Wherever we met politicians, the numbers wanting to resolve the situation were steadily increasing. I found my meetings with Roelf Meyer, the forward-thinking minister in the National Party, probably the most helpful of his group. By 1989 talks between some in that party and the ANC and others were occurring more frequently, though they were unreported. When I met FW de Klerk, I could sense that talks were happening in private. There are many unsung heroes and some better known campaigners such as the determined Dame Helen Suzman, who were making a difference in thinking circles and through different religious groups across South Africa. All shared the positive view that the influence of Oliver Tambo, as well as the madness of apartheid, were slowly bringing this terrible chapter in South Africa's history to a close.

In February 1990 I was attending the meeting of the European Union Ministers of Development with the African Caribbean Pacific Ministers group in Lusaka, when I had some advance warning of change in South Africa. There can have been no better place to celebrate the news from FW de Klerk that Nelson Mandela was to be released, the ANC and other black political parties were to be unbanned, and the State of Emergency to be ended. That was a night I shall never forget, when we could rejoice with those who had worked for so long to end apartheid. I could only guess, as he was not there, what Oliver Tambo must have been feeling.

My next meeting with Oliver Tambo was sadly after he had suffered a major stroke. By then Douglas Hurd was our Foreign Secretary, and Robin Renwick our much respected Ambassador in South Africa, who had played a major role in achieving change from behind the scenes. From the time of Tambo's illness until long after his recuperation in London and Sweden, we had little contact. Others in the ANC were carrying the banner. On a short stopover in Uganda following a meeting of the ANC National Consultative Council in late 1990, Tambo made friendly comments to the then British High Commissioner about going to South Africa for the Independence celebrations. Relations were certainly much warmer.

The final private meeting I had with Oliver Tambo was on 11 June 1991 at his home in Muswell Hill before he left London for the ANC National Conference in July. He was excited to be returning to South Africa, was cheerful and confirmed the determination of a majority of the ANC to press on with negotiations. He was well aware of the need to support the political process with economic advancement and had spoken at the OAU summit in Abuja, which instituted a process for gradually lifting sanctions in response to events in South Africa. He was very grateful for and surprised about the extent of British aid to South Africans.

My memories of this gentle but fair-minded man are very special. He made a great effort, even when recovering from his stroke, to find out all he could about the current thinking. Officials told me frequently that he was a force for good and a clear thinker who would always try the peaceful route. That was certainly my experience, and the ANC must miss his influence even these days, as so many of us in Africa will always do.

THE UNDERSUNG HERO

Peter Hain

In those heady hours and days after Nelson Mandela walked out of prison in February 1990, who did he salute so consistently? His – and the ANC's – President, Oliver Tambo.

The hundreds of millions who watched on television might have been forgiven for wondering why. Who was 'his' President? The name Oliver Tambo did not trip off the tongue of a world enthralled by the courage, the resilience and, above all, the dignity of the man who had spent nearly ten thousand days of his life in gaol in the fight for freedom.

But Mandela knew what all those who were involved in the decades of struggle inside and outside the country had done: that his own freedom, and that of his people, owed as much to Oliver Tambo's leadership as President of the ANC during thirty years of exile as to anyone.

That anyone included my family and I. Fighting apartheid had become a major, everyday activity in our household in Pretoria from 1958, when I was eight years old, the eldest of four children. My parents had become very concerned over the proceedings that saw ANC leaders and fellow comrades arrested, and which led to the Treason Trial. A young white South African couple with no tradition amongst friends or family of radical activity, they broke with white relatives and their peers to join a thriving branch of the non-racial Liberal Party in the unofficial headquarters of apartheid Afrikanerdom – Pretoria – and became increasingly heavily involved.

The Treason Trial continued in Pretoria that year. The accused, most of whom were being bussed over from Johannesburg each day, were provided with lunch by local sympathisers, including my parents, which was when they first met Walter Sisulu and Nelson Mandela. Oliver Tambo was not there as the charges against him had been withdrawn two years earlier, so they did not meet the third man in the triumvirate that had emerged from the ANC's radical youth wing and was then leading it.

A fellow activist friend of ours, Margaret Legum, did however. In the mid-1950s, not yet 21 and just before leaving to go to Cambridge University, she went to visit the then ANC President, Chief Albert Luthuli, at his home in Natal, to be briefed on his views on what was really happening in the country. He was very informative, but said: 'You must meet my friends Nelson Mandela and Oliver Tambo', and gave her an introductory letter. She took this to the law office they ran in Johannesburg – the first black legal firm in the city. There she met Oliver Tambo. Despite his workload – there was a long queue waiting – she was immediately taken to see him. She was impressed by his manner; he was very welcoming, relaxed, gentle and interested, giving 'this young white girl' his full attention, which she never forgot.

By the time of the Sharpeville massacre on 21 March 1960 I was ten, and we were accustomed to Special Branch surveillance and raids on our home. A State of Emergency was declared on 30 March and thousands of ANC and other anti-apartheid activists were detained throughout the country, including the Liberal Party's National Chairman Peter Brown and the Chairman of my parents' Pretoria Branch, John Brink.

Soon afterwards, in a Special Branch raid on our home, statements by people wounded at Sharpeville – taken in Baragwanath Hospital in Soweto the day after the shootings – were seized and never seen again.

Around this time, the ANC learned that it was to become a banned, and therefore illegal, organisation. It decided at an emergency meeting that – with leaders such as Mandela and Sisulu still on trial in Pretoria, Oliver Tambo, then Vice-President, should go abroad as the organisation's 'roving ambassador'. He left at once, without a passport, through Bechuanaland (Botswana) and on to Tanzania, where he set up an ANC post in Dar es Salaam.

Although this was a critical move to keep the ANC alive, with its leadership under Tambo intact in exile, in a sense this made him the 'forgotten man' of the ANC within South Africa's wider politics, and especially amongst local activists, such as my parents, who were outside the ANC.

In June 1960 my mother, now the Pretoria Branch Secretary, was advised to leave immediately as her name had been seen on a list of people to be arrested. We arrived home from school to be told we were going on a sudden holiday. She loaded us into our car and we left on the eight hundred mile drive to our grandparents' home in Port Alfred, on the Eastern Cape coast. As the oldest, age ten, I was told the real reason for our travels, and my pleasure at going on holiday by the sea, instead of to school, was tempered by the fear that we might be caught.

Fortunately, all went well. My father joined us later – he had been asked to check on the state of the Liberal Party in the Eastern Cape and Natal as, under the State of Emergency, it was a criminal offence to divulge information on detainees and there was difficulty in communicating between areas.

Although the State of Emergency was lifted at the end of August and detainees released, the ANC together with the PAC remained banned.

Partly because of this, black membership of the Pretoria Branch of the Liberal Party, now the only legal anti-apartheid group left in the city, boomed. Branch meetings held in our living room were jam-packed and lively. As children we were alone amongst our white school friends in having non-whites as equals, not servants, in our home. Elliot Mngadi, later the Liberal Party's National Treasurer, recalled an early occasion when he told me: 'It was the first time I had ever come through the front door of a white man's house.'

In the meantime, Oliver Tambo had based himself in London with his family, gradually extending the ANC's reach across the world. It was he who walked the corridors of power from Washington to Moscow to lobby against apartheid on behalf of the ANC. It was he who charmed the corporate world as much as the trade union conferences. It was he who went to Scandinavian capitals and returned with vital resources to keep the ANC alive for the liberation struggle. It was he who spoke at rallies by anti-apartheid movements all over the globe. Tambo called himself 'Acting President' because he saw Nelson Mandela as the President-in-waiting to whom he would defer, but then in 1977 the leaders on Robben Island confirmed him as the ANC's President.

The Treason Trial had ended in March 1961 with all acquitted, the judges having found that the prosecution had failed to prove that the ANC was 'communist', or that it had adopted a policy to overthrow the state by violence. Nelson Mandela immediately went underground and Walter Sisulu returned to house arrest.

Also in March there was a Commonwealth Prime Ministers' conference in London that South Africa's Prime Minister Hendrik Verwoerd, the chief architect of apartheid, attended. He applied for South Africa's continued membership as a republic (it had become one in a whites-only referendum in 1960), but so great was the criticism of apartheid that he was obliged to withdraw his application and South Africa left the Commonwealth. My parents, along with their comrades, had campaigned against the application and, in London, Oliver Tambo – who had been lobbying behind the scenes – claimed the exclusion as a victory.

Back in South Africa, in May 1961, the government imposed a twelve-day detention without trial law. Nelson Mandela, still underground, called for a stay-at-home in protest against all racial laws. In support of his call, my parents and two other members were putting up posters in the township of Lady Selborne when the Special Branch arrested them. I was woken up in the early hours by a family friend and told, 'Your parents have been put in jail.' They were detained for two weeks, then released on bail on a trumped-up charge that was finally unconditionally withdrawn after two court appearances.

During the early 1960s Oliver Tambo was not only concerned with mobilising international political and diplomatic support. He also oversaw the establishment of ANC guerrilla training camps in Tanzania. And he made sure the arms found their way to their destination and into the hands of the ANC underground military wing, MK. Denied the right to operate peacefully and politically by being banned, Oliver Tambo implemented the ANC leadership's decision to adopt guerrilla tactics that were financed and directed from abroad.

When, in December 1961, MK began a campaign of placing incendiary bombs in government offices and other key state installations such as electrical sub-stations, we were amazed when some were put in Pretoria offices – even the government cabinet minister complex in the Union Buildings – in which all the staff, including cleaners, were white. Then Peter Magano, our local ANC contact, commented: 'Don't forget the messenger "boys" are still black.'

Early in 1962, Nelson Mandela, still underground, secretly went overseas and joined up with Oliver Tambo in Addis Ababa. Tambo had already established ANC offices in Ghana, England, Egypt and Tanzania. News of some of Mandela's meetings abroad began to filter back home, causing excitement amongst my parents' political friends. But soon after Mandela's return in August 1962, he was caught, arrested and later brought to trial at the Old Synagogue in Pretoria. My mother, covering it for the liberal magazine *Contact*, was often the only person in the whites-only gallery. Mandela would enter each day, raise his fist in the ANC's salute to the packed black gallery, then turn and do the same to her. Nearly thirty years later, when she and I met him in the House of Commons, she said, 'I don't suppose you remember me.' He gave her a great hug and replied, 'How could I forget!'

But, like so many other anti-apartheid activists (black and white) in South

Africa at the time, my parents found the noose of the police state tightening around them. My mother was eventually issued with a banning order in September 1963 and my father a year later. Amongst other restrictions, these prevented them from being politically active. From then on, from the age of fourteen, I became increasingly involved in a liaison role, passing messages to individuals such as journalists and other banned people, and so they were able to continue much of their anti-apartheid work 'undercover'.

Over five days in July 1964 many members of the African Resistance Movement (ARM) were arrested. Although our family opposed their strategy of limited armed action, some were our friends in the Liberal Party, including a close one, Hugh Lewin, from Johannesburg. They were all given prison sentences and one, Eddie Daniels of Cape Town, sent to Robben Island. They had all come to feel that the sabotage of power pylons, electricity substations, and so on was the only way forward. Another friend involved was John Harris. He had placed a bomb in the concourse of Johannesburg station that fatally injured an elderly woman and disfigured her granddaughter, and was found guilty of murder, even though he had telephoned the police beforehand telling them to clear the concourse. He was later executed in Pretoria Central Prison – the first white to be hanged for his stand against apartheid.

The early 1960s were to usher in the darkest days of apartheid, with most internal resistance repressed or crushed, Mandela, Sisulu and their comrades on Robben Island, but with Oliver Tambo keeping the struggle alive from abroad. From then until his return to his homeland in December 1990 for the ANC consultative conference, he lobbied the UN in New York and he sought help from behind the Iron Curtain, spending much of his life on aeroplanes.

Our family had meanwhile been forced into exile in Britain in 1966 when I was sixteen, and my parents soon became involved in the AAM in London. By 1969 I was on the National Committee and particularly concerned with campaigns to prevent all-white South African sports teams playing in Britain. The most important of these was the successful Stop the Seventy Tour (STST) campaign that I found myself leading. Formed to prevent the proposed tour by a South African cricket team in 1970, it was the first such campaign to use non-violent direct-action tactics to disrupt physically, and was so successful that these tactics were copied internationally, and helped deliver a worldwide ban, not just for apartheid cricket and rugby teams, but right across sport.

In all these campaigns, we received the active support and encouragement of Oliver Tambo (and his lieutenants such as Thabo Mbeki), which he gave to all anti-apartheid activities. He did this not with any great charisma – that was not his style – but with quiet and steely persuasion. I do not remember him ever electrifying an anti-apartheid audience with rolling rhetoric at our meetings in London. But I do remember him captivating listeners with compelling power.

I also remember him working in London with many other key figures in the struggle, amongst these the indomitable Executive Secretary of the AAM, Ethel de Keyser, and her indefatigable successor Mike Terry. Tambo also closely supported activity by others, including the champion of Steve Biko, Donald Woods, whose escape from South Africa in January 1978 and subsequent international campaigning in support of the ANC, especially in America, contributed so much in the late 1970s and through the 1980s to undermine apartheid's iron grip.

Those of us who were deeply involved in anti-apartheid campaigns were always aware of Oliver and he was held in deep respect. His face did not festoon posters; his image did not inspire T-shirts. But we knew all the time of his leadership and his tireless work. Perhaps tellingly, his wife Adelaide, herself a notable contributor to the freedom struggle – and especially to equality for women – always referred to him in his absence as 'The President'.

However, the frantic travelling and stress of thirty years at the helm left Oliver in ill health and, when he died from a stroke in 1993, it meant that he was tragically not alive to see the first democratic South African elections in 1994, though he knew by then that freedom and victory were near.

If we accept that the end of apartheid eventually came through a combination of both international pressure and internal resistance, then Oliver Tambo's guiding hand was the common one for both. He carried the torch when his fellow leaders in prison could not.

Whereas Nelson Mandela during 27 years in prison was the icon and inspiration of the struggle, Oliver Tambo, free outside, was at once the careful organiser, the suave-suited diplomat, and the tough guerrilla commandant. He was indeed the undersung hero – but never undersung by Mandela or the rest of us involved in the eventual triumph of freedom and democracy that he did so much to secure.

A GENUINE MEETING OF MINDS

Geoffrey Howe

One great sadness in my life is that I only ever had one real meeting with Oliver Tambo. That most memorable event took place on 20 September 1986, during my fourth year as Britain's Foreign and Commonwealth Secretary, in my official country residence, at Chevening in Kent. The venue was chosen not, as some people thought, to 'raise the status' of the encounter but, at Margaret Thatcher's specific request, to make it seem *less* important than if it had been held at the Foreign Office itself.

'The meeting lasted almost two hours', says the Foreign Office note of our discussion, 'the atmosphere was candid, open and good . . . The exchanges were courteous as well as frank and Tambo's personal distaste for violence came through.'

He seems to have taken a similarly positive view of the occasion. For when, a week or two later, he ran into a British diplomat at a National Day party in Botswana, we heard that he had spoken 'warmly about his meeting with the Secretary of State at Chevening. The whole atmosphere and setting', he said, 'had impressed him greatly. The sight of sheep grazing quietly outside the windows had made him feel really at home.' Understandably enough, our diplomat responded to Tambo by expressing the well-intentioned hope 'that the next time he went to Britain to have a talk with the Secretary of State perhaps he could stay overnight at Chevening'.

How I wish that that could have been so. We had struck a rapport with each other. He was indeed, as I had been told, a man who used real words and gave real answers. And most importantly, he was, in my judgement, genuinely seeking a non-violent path into the future.

That was only one of the reasons why I wanted to see Oliver Tambo again. During the months and years that followed, many others (besides myself) devoted much time and energy to the attempt to arrange another meeting between the two of us. But, alas, it was never to happen. And why, you may ask, was that? The account that follows may give some indication of the answer.

There were several reasons, of course. From Britain's point of view, the foremost continuing obstacle was our principled reluctance to have *any* direct contact with *any* organisation, which was in *any* way involved in, or responsible for 'terrorism' of any kind – but particularly if it was directed against civilians or other innocent third parties. Margaret Thatcher herself was particularly committed to this view.

Against that background, it can, I hope, be appreciated that any decision in favour of a meeting between the President of the ANC – by then clearly committed to 'the armed struggle' – and the British Secretary of State simply had to be regarded as an exceptional event. If it were to happen, it would do so only within the framework of gradualism that we evolved – with contacts starting at official level and, if those went well, gradually moving upwards.

Our meeting was not the first discussion at ministerial level (in the British government) in which Oliver Tambo had taken part. That had occurred only three months before (on 24 June 1986), when he had met the Minister of State, Lynda Chalker. In her notable contribution to this book, Lynda describes the occasion – only the first of several such meetings for her. It was fortunate indeed that arrangements for this had been put in place *before* the 'terrorist' bomb explosions, which happened to take place in Johannesburg on that very morning.

The fact that, even in those circumstances, the Chalker/Tambo meeting had passed off without destructive criticism in the UK appeared to pave the way to my meeting with Oliver Tambo. But, as will be seen, it came very close to proving impossible.

For these events were taking place at the start of the six-month period during which Britain held the presidency of the European Community (EC) – and when I was, for that reason, President of the EC's Foreign Affairs Council. It was a moment when 'the South African problem' was at the top of every international agenda. Just twelve months before, when violence (from both sides) was mounting in South Africa, the Commonwealth Heads of Government meeting, in Nassau in October 1985, had commissioned an EPG to attempt a mediatory mission to the country. By June 1986 that EPG had concluded that 'there was no genuine intention on the part of the South

African government to dismantle apartheid . . . and no present prospect of dialogue' on that subject.

One catastrophic episode had decisively driven the EPG to that conclusion. It had actually occurred during their very last visit to South Africa – namely a series of unprovoked raids by South African armed forces across the borders of Zambia, Zimbabwe and Botswana.

Public opinion across the world had been deeply shocked by this. Margaret Thatcher herself was very bitter about what she perceived as PW Botha's perfidy. Both the European Council of Ministers (at the end of June 1986) and the Commonwealth Heads of Government (meeting about a month later in London) decided to consider further action. Against this very discouraging background, I was commissioned, as President of the EC Foreign Affairs Council, to take a fresh, mediatory mission to South Africa (and the Front-line States) – above all to press the South African government to change position decisively: to unban the ANC and other organisations; to release Mandela and other detainees; to make a serious start on the abolition of apartheid; and to forswear violence. This was, it should be noted, exactly the same case as that which Margaret Thatcher and I had pressed upon the two Bothas (PW and Pik) more than two years previously, in June 1984 – to their dismay and even surprise, but without success – when we had met them both at Chequers, the British Prime Minister's official country residence.

At that time, as right up to the end, there was just one (important) difference between our position and that of most (though certainly not all) of our partners (in Europe as well as in the Commonwealth). Although we had joined in vigorously enforcing many important sanctions – from the oil and arms embargoes to the Gleneagles ban on sporting contacts – we remained firmly opposed to the imposition of comprehensive economic sanctions. This was because of our own experience – in the Zimbabwean context – of their complete ineffectiveness against the Smith regime. The population of Rhodesia may have suffered – but its unlawful governors not at all.

Against that background, there was one special message that we wanted to get across to *both* sides in South Africa (to the ANC as plainly as to the South African government) – and that was the totally negative effect of violence. And particularly if it was directed, in its practical effect, whatever the intention – against civilians and other innocent third parties. This too was a topic on which we believed our own experience – of 'terrorism', in many different settings – enabled us to form and retain a carefully considered (and enduring) view of its ineffectiveness – indeed of its counterproductive effect.

As I returned to London, on 24 July 1986, from my two exhausting and apparently unfruitful missions to almost every Front-line State, as well as to South Africa itself, there had been only one complete gap in my schedule. For the ANC – along with almost every other African organisation – had flatly refused to meet me. As Oliver Tambo explained to me when we did eventually meet, that was because they did not regard my mission as sincere or genuine – but rather as a device to conceal (but to maintain) the UK's refusal to take the fight against apartheid seriously.

This was one of the crucial misunderstandings between us when Oliver Tambo and I did meet. And it was a misunderstanding of our position that he shared with most of the rest of the world. For it was a misunderstanding that we had fatally created for ourselves.

It was not without good reason that I eventually gave to the chapter in my memoirs, *Conflict of Loyalty* (Macmillan, 1994), which is devoted to South Africa the title 'Arguing about South Africa'. The fact is that there was, from beginning to end of our six years in foreign affairs joint harness, a sharp difference in emphasis between the Prime Minister and myself – and, of course, my ministerial colleague, Lynda Chalker.

On the surface at least, we were all agreed on the essentials. But there was a sharp difference in the vigour, style and tone with which we condemned apartheid in all its manifestations. Likewise, in the clarity and conviction with which we made the case against comprehensive economic sanctions. And, finally, there was an obvious gulf between the terms in which we sought to condemn or react to the exercise of violence by either side in South Africa. As a result, our Prime Minister was often perceived as regarding comprehensive economic sanctions as more offensive than apartheid itself. So too with her view of 'the armed struggle', which led her (in October 1987) to denounce publicly the ANC as 'a terrorist organisation', notwithstanding the fact that we ourselves were at the same time and continuously urging the South African government to unban the organisation and to release its leaders.

Against that background, and in the light of the ANC's refusal even to meet me during my South African missions, it was remarkable that the Prime Minister agreed to the single meeting between Oliver Tambo and myself only a few weeks later. It was the inescapable topic – the impact of violence on the future – which was at the core of the ensuing discussion between Tambo and myself. There was a genuine meeting of our two minds, perhaps because we had both been trained as lawyers.

Tambo was persuaded, I believe, to accept the seriousness and sincerity of our condemnation of apartheid as an intolerable, and ultimately unsustainable, system of government. So too, our clear understanding of the impatience and

anger of South African blacks. The South African government, he also accepted, had been left in no doubt of our condemnation of human rights abuses
and of the violence employed in upholding the apartheid system.

We fully appreciated the length of time the ANC had held back from violence. In this context, as Tambo himself explained (and as I readily accepted),
he clearly regarded the armed struggle as a strategically necessary last resort.
At which point I reminded him that 'terrorism' in any form – particularly if
linked, as was then happening, with 'necklacing' – was bound to have a profoundly negative impact on public opinion in the rest of the world.

It was Oliver Tambo's clear understanding of this point – and his presentation that the armed struggle had become the only weapon ultimately
available, in the face of the violence with which apartheid itself was being
enforced – which most persuaded me of the need for our dialogue to be
continued. Above all, I thought it was necessary for this balance of the arguments to be fully grasped by Western leaders and not least by our own Prime
Minister. For it was Margaret Thatcher's voice, perhaps above all, that was
most likely to open more minds with the South African government itself.

Before I close, it is worth trying to explain why there was – and had been
– such a continuing divergence between Margaret Thatcher's approach and
my own – supported as I was, not just by my robustly perceptive ministerial
colleague, Lynda Chalker, but also by virtually all our advisers and colleagues
in the Foreign and Commonwealth Office. The explanation, I believe, may
be quite simple – and that is that our own Prime Minister was the only one
of us who had lacked any great experience of the facts of contemporary African life. For my part, I had spent almost two years in the army (1947–48)
in Kenya and Uganda, serving with African soldiers, who had themselves
fought against the Japanese in the Second World War. Twenty years later,
back in the UK, I had been a member of a legal team, which prepared Britain's first anti-discrimination legislation, the Race Relations Act of 1968.
And not long afterwards, in 1975, my wife and I had been able, on a fact-
finding visit to South Africa (originally as guests of the South Africa Foundation), to make a brief (and unauthorised) visit to Soweto.

Our guide (and driver) was a black community leader (I remember only her
Christian name, Constance). My most vivid recollection is of the way in which
she had to turn our car away down side streets whenever we saw any South African military or police vehicle approaching. The real tensions of apartheid were
conveyed to us in those few minutes: the fears and hatreds of a system in which
the upholders of the law were almost entirely drawn from a community other than the one they sought to police; and in which, even in our company, our
driver was obliged to behave almost as an alien in her own country.

But let me return to the closing years of my time at the Foreign Office. We were able during that time – and, not least, thanks to our then Ambassador to South Africa, Sir Robin Renwick, with whom Margaret Thatcher had worked closely in other contexts and in whom she had much confidence – to persuade the Prime Minister herself to undertake more than one successful journey to Africa. In the spring of 1989 she held an important meeting at Nyanga (on the Mozambican border) with Presidents Mugabe and Chissano. And on 1 April of that year (the date of Namibian independence) Margaret Thatcher, then in Windhoek, was able to play a crucially important part in helping the UN authorities to head off a serious conflict between the Namibian SWAPO troops of Sam Nujoma (the future Namibian President) and the SADF. Foreign Minister Pik Botha was fortunately also on hand to help in the same delicate task.

It was in this much more positive context that Margaret Thatcher's basic commitment to the anti-apartheid cause came at last to be expressed and understood more clearly and frequently than ever before. For almost the first time it was at last becoming clear that the stateswoman who had led international opposition to comprehensive economic sanctions was speaking with even greater clarity against apartheid itself.

At long last (and although they probably didn't know it – and had never met each other) Oliver Tambo, the non-violent supporter of the armed struggle and Margaret Thatcher, the vigorous opponent of economic sanctions, were seen and heard to be singing from the same hymn sheet. The tide of history really had begun to change.

PW Botha, who had suffered a stroke in January 1989, remained in office for only a few more months. In August of that year – just one month after I had been removed from the Foreign Office – he was succeeded as President by FW de Klerk. Fifteen months later, in November 1990, I was to leave government altogether, but I had been able to meet Nelson Mandela on his first visit to London in the summer of 1990 and again when I was one of the Commonwealth observers at the first Johannesburg meeting of the Conference on a Democratic South Africa (Codesa) in December 1991.

But I was, and I remain, very sad that Oliver Tambo's path and mine were destined never to cross again – and am correspondingly grateful for this opportunity to pay tribute to the outstanding wisdom, restraint and balance that he undoubtedly contributed to the ANC and to the part which it played in the transformation of South Africa during my lifetime.

BEYOND THE UNITED NATIONS' SPEECHES AND RESOLUTIONS

Enuga Reddy

I recently collected together my correspondence with Oliver Tambo in order to send it to the Tambo Collection, now temporarily at the William Cullen Library at the University of the Witwatersrand.

The correspondence was quite extensive as I used to write detailed letters to Oliver, at some risk, since I became Principal Secretary of the UN's Special Committee against Apartheid in 1963, informing him what we were doing at the UN and what we had in mind, and seeking his guidance as I felt that UN action should always be in harmony with the views of the liberation movement. I received replies from him unless we were due to meet soon or he could convey his views through his colleagues. There was frequent correspondence until the late-1970s and it continued until the mid-1980s when the ANC was given observer status in the Special Committee and I could travel more often to Europe and Africa and meet with Oliver.

Looking through the correspondence revived many memories of the problems we encountered in trying to make the UN go beyond speeches and resolutions to ensure effective support to the liberation struggle in southern Africa, and especially of the friendship, thoughtfulness, integrity and statesmanship of OR.

I decided to type a few extracts from the letters and share some insights in terms of the preoccupations of the UN, the liberation movement and the anti-apartheid groups in those days between the Rivonia Trial (1963/64) and the resurgence of the struggle in the 1970s.

From London, January 1964

The Christmas holiday has brought a temporary lull, particularly because of the absence of any significant developments in SA. Now, however, programmes for the new year have been worked out and are in the process of execution. Reports on activities flowing from these will soon be forthcoming ...

Alan Paton is reported to have welcomed the establishment of a group of experts.[1] Other influential circles have also reacted very favourably to the idea. In part this is out of respect for the UN and the Scandinavians, and an expression of support for any move that has as its target the apartheid policies of the South African government. In part this reflects an attitude of mind towards the South African situation which lacks the sense of urgency which underlies demands for sanctions. People who are sacrificing or are willing to make sacrifices to end apartheid immediately react to the idea of a group of experts by asking: 'What exactly are they supposed to do?' This has turned out to be a difficult question ... Of course I respect every one of the names so far mentioned, but I do think the UN ought to exercise great care in its use of such terms as 'experts' for they necessarily relate to the scale or standard of values which it observes and employs.

The establishment of a UN Relief Fund for South African families of apartheid victims has aroused considerable interest here and enquiries are being persistently made as to what progress has been made in the matter, and also what machinery has been set up for administering it.[2]

From London, 30 January 1964

Many thanks for your notes. I'm delighted to learn you will be coming through here ...

I am glad to note your reactions to the team [Group of Experts on South Africa]. I was already in the middle of an article in which I was not being very (merciful?). But I shall now take a softer line.

Instructions have been given for appointments to be made for you as soon as you advise the office of the date of arrival.

Finally, there are many organisations and people who are interested in handling the Relief Fund. Some are good organisations and I think all are manned by honest people. But not frequently you find people who are driven by ambitions rather than the zeal to serve ... Should you have to give any guide as to the machinery, I trust you will bear in mind the necessity of keeping the Fund outside of any area of conflict or rivalry, which would tend to give it a party-political complexion.[3]

My wife has very much improved – Thanks.

Regards to the family.

From London, 14 February 1964

... It was a great privilege for us all to have you in London for a few days, and you helped to place the United Nations' resolutions in perspective ...

I expect to be leaving for Africa quite soon, but it should be possible for me to keep in close touch with the United Nations.

I hope you had a successful time in Geneva, and I wish you all success with your vast work at the United Nations.

From Dar es Salaam, 6 May 1964

Many thanks for your letter and for informing me of the impending meeting of the Security Council ...

As it is, the probabilities are that I shall not come personally and may have to ask Mr [Robert] Resha from London to attend. We are short of funds and are rapidly approaching a situation when it will be difficult for us to do the things we feel should be done.

I have received a very nice letter from Mrs [Alva] Myrdal and will be writing to her. I have also received a copy of the Experts' report, which is in many respects a happy surprise, considering my apprehensions last year. Of equal surprise is the importance which the sanctions conference[4] and its deliberations and conclusions assumed, after a small and faulty beginning some time last year. With the interest which the Special Committee has taken in both the sanctions conference and the Experts' report, a powerful case for action by the Security Council can be made out, and would be the weightier if debated while these issues are hot, fresh and topical. On the other hand, however, any proposal for action must be based on events in South Africa. One of these events is the Rivonia Trial. I hope a formula can be found which enables the Security Council, in its discussions and decisions, not only to take into account the Experts' report, the sanctions conference findings and the report of the Special Committee, but also to accommodate the results of the Rivonia Trials and the impending executions of Mini and others.

We are giving this aspect some thought and hope to be able to make a feasible suggestion.

On the question of pressures, my view is that we must press for the kind of action which the situation demands and cast the burden of inaction on the big powers. At this time, with the mood that has been inspired by Mandela's statement, this is a burden they would not find it easy to accept. Let them offer compromises because it is they who are at fault by reason of their involvement. Last year things were made very easy and comfortable for them in the compromise resolutions adopted. This year they should be called upon to indicate where they now stand, since apartheid, especially with the rising numbers of executions and the Bantu Laws Amendment Bill, is mounting an offensive against us and world opinion. Besides, rightly or wrongly, the African states started off with strong demands. It is of course necessary to be realistic, but it would be a mistake to demand less, for if South Africa persists and the big powers in the West continue to resist action, a stepping down on demands could be the beginning of a complete withdrawal, ending in the disbandment of the Afro-Asian forces as far as this issue is concerned.

From Dar es Salaam, 18 May 1964
We thank you for your letter of 12th May, 1964, wherewith you enclosed a press summary of the meeting of the Special Committee.

We very much appreciate your sending us this summary, and are gratified by the efforts of the Special Committee to direct the attention of the United Nations to the need for immediate action against the policies of apartheid which, given a little more time, will set the world on fire. The threatened execution of the leaders of our people is a pointer to the vital importance of the time factor in the South African situation. We are happy to note that the Special Committee sees this so clearly.

From Dar es Salaam, 15 October 1964
… We welcome the statement issued by the Special Committee on Apartheid on the case of Mini and others. In our view the Committee discharged a very important duty to all concerned when it warned of the dangerous implications of South Africa's habit of killing our people under the pretext that they have committed a crime. Nothing that the South African government's courts do or say can ever alter the fact that the criminals are those who are perpetrating or assisting in the perpetration of the heinous crime known as apartheid. South Africa will surely find some day that it has taken one life too many from those it has learnt to decimate with impunity.

Thanking you and your Committee on behalf of my organisation and people …

From Dar es Salaam, 11 February 1965
It was a relief to me to note that the element of time did not remove the effect of the [Christmas] card I sent you.

I have been following the events in the General Assembly over the financial crisis. It is to be regretted that important and urgent questions have had to be shelved for lack of a satisfactory formula.

The response to the appeal for relief [for families of political prisoners] is indeed disappointing. The burden placed on emerging countries is a heavy one and I am persuaded to agree with your suggestion to Canon Collins.

The mode of contact which could possibly yield results would be a visit to Sweden. It is difficult to say how soon this could be arranged.[5]

The cost of sending children of prisoners to school would, in the context of the UN budget, be negligible. I should favour their being recommended for scholarship grants by individual governments or semi-governmental bodies. In the meantime, however, we shall ascertain what is being done about their applications and furnish you with particulars.[6]

I read Ambassador Marof's[7] powerful reply to Muller. I'll get you a copy of the songs.

Your visit to East Africa is long overdue I should think. Let us know when you expect to be here ...

From Dar es Salaam, 17 January 1967
NEW YEAR MESSAGE
At the beginning of the New Year, I would like to send cordial seasonal greetings to all friends of our cause, and particularly to our friends in the UN Special Committee on Apartheid.

Those of us who are engaged in the struggle for justice and for the destruction of racial oppression in our country are deeply grateful for all the help that is being given, both materially and morally, in our fight against a ruthless tyranny.

At this time of joy, there is much for us to sorrow over in our country, and unhappiness for many persons and families in South Africa who are bearing the brunt of apartheid oppression. But we are also conscious of the generous help which is being given by our friends, to alleviate hardship, to give legal assistance to those being persecuted for their resistance to apartheid, and to enable us to go on fighting in good heart.

For this we are especially grateful to the UN Special Committee on Apartheid and all its devoted workers. The Special Committee on Apartheid has engaged in many worthy ventures on behalf of the struggling masses of South Africa and I would particularly like to commend support for the Campaign for the Release of Imprisoned Politicians in South Africa; this is one project which we can never abandon, and which we must continually be working on. There can be no letting up until the men who are condemned to spend their lives in prison because they fought injustice are free: this is the duty which we owe to them and which we cannot abandon, and so I am especially glad to commend this project to which Defence and Aid International are now giving a great deal of their support and attention.[8]

The fight for freedom must go on until it is won; until our country is free and happy and peaceful as part of the community of man, we cannot rest. And so, at the beginning of a New Year, I greet you all and wish you well and say: Thank you, and forward to the freedom of our country.

From Morogoro, 21 April 1967

I owe you a thousand apologies for the delay in replying to your letters. I have been plagued by the thought that I deprived you of a Christmas day by writing rather unrestrainedly on a matter which, as I found out from your explanations, I had not all the facts. I hope a brief cable I sent you immediately on receiving your letter sufficiently indicated my full and unreserved acceptance of your explanation ...[9]

I would strongly advise you against your taking any precipitate step.[10] I need hardly say that there is so much at stake in the field in which we are involved that drastic decisions should follow painful, painstaking, and hard assessing and re-assessing of all the facts, and taking that decision only which in the final analysis must serve the ultimate cause. I don't have to say that I hope these things will be sorted out quickly and to the satisfaction of all concerned.

I look forward to three great events:

(a) Meeting Ambassador Marof;

(b) Meeting you;

(c) Attending the Seminar on Southern Africa.[11]

From Lusaka, 31 August 1967

This is a short note to apologise to you for my failure to return to the UN Seminar in Kitwe as promised. We had a very short time together on the night I was in Kitwe, and as you may have noticed I was tired and exhausted. I had looked forward to the end of the Seminar when we would have had time to examine a wide variety of problems of planning action for the future under more relaxed conditions.

But perhaps you understand now why I could not stay at the Seminar and why I was unable to come back later.[12] The situation in Rhodesia seems to be taking a turn for the better from the point of view of those who support and work for the African cause in that country. But as indicated in our many memoranda, and as was borne out by the very subject matter of the Kitwe Seminar, Rhodesia is an indivisible part of southern Africa, hence the predictable involvement of South Africa in the battles which our Freedom Fighters are waging stubbornly and courageously in the bushes of Matabeleland. Soon the whole area, and I repeat, the WHOLE area of southern Africa, will be caught up in the crisis. Unfortunately what happened at Wankie was the beginning of a racial war which may escalate into an international conflagration. Certainly for us the alternative to war disappeared when South Africa rejected the solution so ably and effectively advocated by the ANC under the leadership of the now late Chief Luthuli. With his death on July the 21st this year the last hope for South Africa went.

As usual I am hoping to get out of here and go round the world begging for moral and material support for our struggle. But as usual also, I am likely to stay pinned down to the day to day problems imposed on us by apartheid, racial discrimination and colonialism in southern Africa.

I hope you were satisfied with the results of the Seminar and that the decisions taken will form a basis for future action by the UN. With some luck I might see you this year.

From Lusaka, August 1969
Many thanks for your letter of July 3 – quite a long time ago, because I have been away.

About mid-July, when I was preparing to go to Sweden, I learnt from Raymond [Kunene] that the Swedes would not be ready to go ahead with the [Luthuli Memorial] Foundation on the date proposed. I have not heard from either Raymond or Robbie [Resha] since, but I wish to thank you for your ideas in the matter, and, needless to say your sense of involvement. I have been under somewhat heavy pressures lately – and still am. The result has been that it has not been possible to keep pace with all projects and developments. But the clouds should disperse soon, leaving a reasonably clear sky under which to think, work and get things done.

I shall keep you informed of developments on the Foundation project, and I retain the hope of landing in the UN corridors later in the year. In this connection, however, I believe I have two leading figures recently come out of SA – Dr WZ Conco is already in London and I notice has given evidence in Geneva;[13] and the other is under a Deportation Order requiring him to leave Swaziland by the end of this month. He is Mr MB Yengwa, a lawyer, who offended the Swaziland government by giving help to the dependants of jailed victims of apartheid.

Robbie has been having passport problems. I do not know if these have now been resolved. The delay in his getting to the US has been frustrating, like much else that is happening.

From Lusaka, 20 August 1969

I had fleeting talks with Mr Zoubeidi, whom I was regretfully unable to help as much as I should have liked to.[14] Worse still, I could not personally meet the Sub-Committee. I had to be away on a mission I could not cancel. The ANC delegation which met the Sub-Committee was not of the usual ANC level, all being new in this kind of operation. I must confess I had not had time to study your voluminous correspondence and out-pourings of your very active intellect, and could not – indeed had no time, to brief our group. I handed them the papers to enable them to use them as best they could. I am hoping and expecting Alfred [Nzo] will be prepared in Dar.

Tonight, on arrival from 'outer space', I found, and had dinner with, Bensid and Alo.[15] I came away quite excited over the prospects for the Luthuli Foundation. They will report fully to you, unless I find cause to write to you before they return to New York. I cannot write now because I am waiting to hear from Robbie [Resha] and Raymond [Kunene] who have a report to submit to me on this project. In any case, until your brief holiday is over, I do not want to 'burden' you – although I suspect you suffer from a feeling of mental 'weightlessness' when you do not have a South African problem to solve or an anti-apartheid offensive to mount.

I am at present attending to certain vital things that have to be done, all of which are as difficult as they are urgent; but as soon as I can find adequate breathing space, I shall follow up the many ideas you have, and perhaps Robbie will come armed with these. In the meantime, accept my expressions of very deep appreciation of your work and your infectious devotion and commitment to the liberation struggle in South Africa. Your personal contribution is most remarkable for its quality and quantity. It will not be long, I think, before we evolve a machinery that will maximise its effectiveness.

And now, my brother, let me bring this hurried note to a close with my very best wishes for a restful holiday and, after it, fruitful and rewarding service.

From Lusaka, 25 January 1970

This is no more than a note to thank you for your letters and documents, in particular the 'Notes and Documents' series as well as Chief Luthuli's statements.[16]

I can only say you are doing excellent work and to express my profound appreciation of your initiative and that of members of the Unit. Needless to say, the material is both interesting and of immense value for our work.

I have been unwell in the past ten days and still am. This is in part the result of rather strenuous meetings we have been having of our National Executive and Revolutionary Council. But I expect to show sound health soon. Then I shall devote some thinking on what we can and should do to complement and maximise the initiatives that have been forthcoming from the United Nations. As you will surely agree, it is absolutely imperative that we confront apartheid at its base in an effective manner if work done at the international level is in the long run to yield any fruit. This is why I have lately featured so little in international work. Yet I am attracted by the possibilities of some of the United Nations decisions. I seem to feel, reading the resolutions, that something immensely meaningful can be done, and it is to these possibilities that I intend to direct some hard thinking.

When shall I ever see you for exchanges? I suppose not before some government agrees to give me an air ticket enabling me to visit a few countries and places, which I want to in order to ensure firm support for our immediate plans. It's time racism got it in the neck, is it not?

Sorry I can't write further. I'm beginning to feel the strain. Bye-Bye, now.

From Lusaka, 3 April 1970

I have an extremely peculiar case to handle and I would like you to give more assistance. Somewhere about 1961 – I should say about the middle of 1961 – the Secretary-General received a letter purporting to have been signed by Chief Albert Luthuli in which he was expressing support for apartheid, for Bantu Education and so on. As I recall, the Secretary-General, no doubt stunned by this document, passed the letter to some of the African Representatives, among them, I think, Quaison-Sackey. The letter was suppressed and in the meantime we were contacted about. We naturally declared it a forgery. Later that year Chief Luthuli visited Oslo and I believe he then wrote to the Secretary-General, stating that he had written no such document.

We now want this document or a photostat of it and we want it most urgently. Please do everything you can to trace it, and if you have any news, cable or send an express mail to me at the above address.

I do not have the time to tell you the fantastic and incredible developments that have led to the frantic hunt for this nine-year-old document. But you will get the story in time. Meanwhile, please get cracking. Time is against me and I am only just recovering from three weeks of asthma, during which I could not do a stick of work.[17]

From Lusaka, 10 July 1970[18]

... A South African young man, at present teaching in Zambia, wants to study law ... I came to meet him personally. It is as a result of the profound impression he has made on me that I am now trying, in turn, to seek advice by way of assisting him towards fulfilment of what turns out to have been a lifelong desire and ambition, namely, to serve his people in the field of law ...

... Mr X is not a member of the ANC, or indeed of any South African political organisation, and yet I have been moved to support him fully in his desire and aim. Several cases of non-ANC persons seeking assistance of one kind or another, including the matter of scholarships, have been brought to my attention from time to time, and wherever I could I have readily helped my fellow countrymen, notwithstanding their being members of what we call rival Parties in some instances. But in none of these cases have I discovered such a deep-seated but silent and noiseless commitment to the cause of one's people as I did in the case of Mr X ...

May I conclude by saying that if I had my way, I would spread carefully selected students over a worldwide network of educational institutions, and assign to them courses of study which combine to provide our people with a full spectrum of experts covering every sphere and aspect of the political, economic, social, cultural and military life of a normal state. But then I do not have my way, neither does the ANC. In the meantime, the UN can help – and it does ...

From Lusaka, 16 November 1970
Many thanks for your letter of the 26th and for the enclosed form.

The Unit's publications are very good indeed and we highly appreciate the work being done by the UN in this field.

I have made up my mind to prepare a Paper as requested and have selected for my topic, 'The Roots of Apartheid and Racism', in which I have regard to 1971 as the International Year of Action to Combat Racism and Racial Discrimination. In this connection I enclose a brief outline of the Paper, which serves merely to indicate what I have in mind at the moment ...

I notice that there is a fee payable in respect of this Paper. In my financial circumstances this is more than welcome. But I am at a loss to understand why, for the purpose of doing a Paper for the Unit on Apartheid, I have to tell the world that I obtained a Science Degree with a distinction in Mathematics, or give my employment record from month to month and year to year, complete with the name of the Supervisor.[19] If it is in exchange for this detailed personal information that the fee is paid, or if the payment rests on the condition that I disclose all this information, then, on principle, I would not accept payment; but I will certainly prepare and let you have the Paper for use by the Unit as it deems fit. The UN, I believe, has all the information about me which, in my view, it reasonably needs for the purposes of identifying the author of the Paper in question.[20]

From Lusaka, 11 November 1970
In the middle of July I went to the UK. Before leaving I wrote you a letter, seeking your assistance and advice on behalf of a prospective applicant for a UN scholarship. I have been looking through all the letters I have received from you since. There is no reference to this matter. On the other hand many of my letters from abroad get intercepted by someone and I am constantly finding that letters have been written to me which I have not received. This has in the past happened to one or two letters you wrote me. It is therefore possible that you have written to me. It is also possible of course that something went wrong in the despatch of the letter to you. For that reason I am sending you a copy of the letter, which I have signed to enable you to act on it if the need should arise.

Please do what you can if you have not done so already ...[21]

From Lusaka, not dated (early 1973)
Let me thank you for your note which I received on arriving back here from a five-month 'tour' of Europe and Africa.

Alfred [Nzo] will by now have cabled advising that should the Special Committee finally agree or decide to invite us, I shall be available and I look forward to seeing you and numerous old friends and acquaintances ...

From Addis Ababa, 29 May 1973
I can see you've fully recovered from the Oslo flu [pneumonia] and have got plunged into work.

I have been all too mobile since Oslo.[22] London was no exception. In the next few days, I'll be better able to sort myself out properly, especially in regard to work in Europe. It is clear that is where effort should be concentrated ...

In regard to the other place you suggest, we need a discussion. I can foresee problems in the method you have in mind. I hope to drop in on the Geneva meeting on my way to London for a meeting there. This means we should meet in Europe somehow in the course of the next three weeks ...

Now let me wish you sound health and all success in your work. Look forward to seeing you soon ...

NOTES

1. The UN Security Council decided in December 1963, on a Nordic initiative, to ask the Secretary-General to establish a small group of experts to examine methods of resolving the situation in South Africa. The Expert Group was set up in January 1964, with Mrs Alva Myrdal (Sweden) as Chairperson and Sir Hugh Foot (UK) as Rapporteur. Oliver, who was in New York from October to December 1963, had serious reservations about this move. I agreed to serve as Secretary of the Group – in addition to my responsibilities as Principal Secretary of the Special Committee against Apartheid – and kept Oliver informed of its work. Eventually, when the Group reported in April, Oliver expressed full satisfaction.

2. In December 1963, the UN General Assembly invited governments and organisations to contribute to relief and assistance to families of persons persecuted by the South African government for opposing apartheid, and requested the Secretary-General to seek ways and means to provide such assistance. It did not, at that time, set up a UN fund for this purpose.

3. Oliver was always firm that assistance should be provided to all political prisoners and their families, irrespective of their affiliations.

4. International Conference on Sanctions against South Africa, London, April 1964.

5. The Special Committee sent an appeal to governments in November 1964 to contribute to the Defence and Aid Fund (D&A) and other agencies assisting political prisoners and their families in South Africa and refugees from South Africa. There was no response for two months except for a grant of US$5 000 to D&A by India. Canon Collins and I contacted Sweden before the letter from Oliver arrived and, in January 1965, the Swedish government announced a grant of US$100 000 to D&A and US$100 000 to the World Council of Churches. Substantial contributions from Nordic countries, Netherlands, etc., followed.

6. We were soon able to arrange grants for the education of children of prisoners through the D&A; grants for correspondence courses for prisoners through D&A and the National Union of South African Students; and UN scholarships at university level for the education of South Africans abroad.

7. Achkar Marof (Guinea), then Chairman of the Special Committee against Apartheid. I had requested the texts of freedom songs composed by Vuyisile Mini.

8. The International Defence and Aid Fund for Southern Africa (IDAF), led by the Reverend Canon L. John Collins, set up a World Campaign for the Release of South African Political Prisoners in South Africa – initiated earlier by the Anti-Apartheid Movement – with Dennis Brutus as Director. The Special Committee, which had given great attention to this matter since 1963, welcomed the Campaign as a means to promote greater public action.

9. This concerned the question of grants to IDAF after it was banned in South Africa in 1966. I explained to Oliver that the UN was providing funds to Canon Collins through a new trust he had set up and working out procedures for confidential direct grants to IDAF.

10. I was disturbed that my appointment of a South African to a junior position in my office (after consultation with Oliver) and my proposal to appoint an ANC member to a senior position (on the recommendation of the ANC official in charge of the UN) had been questioned in the UN and that Mr Y, an ANC member in a responsible position, had approached an African official in the UN with an unfair adverse report to block the appointment. I wrote to Oliver, and informed the Chairman of the Special Committee against Apartheid, that I would offer my resignation from the UN if there was any doubt by them of my honesty and integrity. (Mr Y was expelled from the ANC some years later for other reasons.)

11. International Seminar on Apartheid, Racial Discrimination and Colonialism in Southern Africa, organised by the UN in Kitwe, Zambia, in July–August 1967.

12. Oliver left the Seminar as the ANC and ZAPU guerrillas were moving into Rhodesia early in August.

13. Before the Ad Hoc Working Group of Experts on South Africa of the UN Commission on Human Rights.

14. I had sent a number of personal letters and notes to Oliver through Mr Ridha Zoubeidi who was going to Lusaka with a Sub-Committee of the Special Committee.

15. Algerian and Nigerian representatives on the Special Committee.

16. I had published a collection of Chief Luthuli's statements in the 'Notes and Documents' series of the UN Unit on Apartheid.

17. I could not trace any letter from 1961. But in April or May 1963, a forged letter purportedly from Chief Luthuli was received, opposing sanctions against South Africa. A copy was sent to Oliver and soon after the Secretary-General received a letter from Chief Luthuli. I sent Oliver the particulars.

18. This letter was an enquiry about a UN scholarship for a South African to study law. The name is omitted, but extracts are reproduced to show how Oliver used to recommend people from outside the ANC, even those from other organisations, for assistance.

19. I had requested Oliver to prepare a paper for the Unit on Apartheid and had arranged a fee. He had prepared a paper in 1968, but since then the UN Secretariat had issued new instructions that consultants preparing papers had to fill in the detailed form used by applicants for a job in the Secretariat.

20. I then prepared a short biography of Oliver and obtained approval from the Secretariat. But he was unable to prepare the paper because of the pressure of work.

21. The reference was to the letter of 10 July which I never received. As soon as this letter was received, I took immediate action.

22. International conference on southern Africa in Oslo in April 1973.

A GLOBAL STRUGGLE
FOR HUMAN RIGHTS

Bengt Säve-Söderbergh

In 1962 Oliver Tambo visited Sweden for the second time. He had been invited to speak at the annual gathering organised by the Swedish Social Democrats on 1 May. He arrived the day before without any specific plans of how to spend the evening before the big rally. Olof Palme, a young adviser to the then Prime Minister Tage Erlander, heard that Tambo would be free and invited him to his home to spend some time with his family. That evening the two got to know one another and became close friends for the rest of their lives. Some years later Palme succeeded Tage Erlander as the Prime Minister of Sweden.

I know that Palme respected Oliver Tambo and what he was fighting for. Tambo's strong commitment and perseverance, his low-key way of talking, sharing information and arguing all impressed Palme. Olof Palme followed all events related to southern Africa and was extremely well informed. He wanted Sweden to play as active a role as possible. He deplored that this struggle for decency and for elementary human rights ran the risk of becoming a victim of the Cold War conflict between East and West. For too long major Western powers did not quite see the struggle against apartheid in its own right. This only changed in the mid-1980s when opposition in South Africa had grown very strong and the East-West climate began to warm up.

In February 1986 a conference called 'The Swedish Peoples' Parliament against Apartheid' was organised in Stockholm. Palme and Tambo were both invited to speak. At the conference Palme, among other things, said the following:

> What we are now witnessing in South Africa is a vicious circle of increased violence in defence of a system that is already doomed. It is only short-sightedness, a disinclination to see reality as it is, that makes the white minority cling firmly to power through continued oppression of its own population and terrorism towards neighbouring countries. The white people must be aware of their own interests in negotiating a peaceful solution, while such a solution is still at all possible.

On this visit Tambo and Palme had a long conversation which I had the privilege of listening to. They talked about the escalating opposition to the apartheid regime in South Africa, which was about to make the country ungovernable. As in every one of their previous conversations they shared a strong conviction that 'a system like apartheid cannot be reformed, it has to be abolished'. Despite the violence that was taking place in South Africa at the time, this conversation took place in a different atmosphere. Both of them expressed views that now, after so many years and decades of resistance and protest, real change might be possible. They had started seeing the end of a long tunnel. One result of the meeting was an agreement that Sweden would finance a project about planning for a post-apartheid South Africa. Unfortunately, this was to be their last meeting.

One week later Olof Palme was killed in a street in Stockholm while walking home from a cinema with his wife. Oliver Tambo reacted with deep sorrow and sent a message, from which I quote:

> We have received with extreme shock and heartfelt grief news of the death of our dear brother, the Prime Minister of Sweden. We had come to know him as the leader of the Swedish people and an international statesman, but also as one of us, a fellow combatant who made an inestimable contribution to the struggle for the liberation of South Africa.

Tambo led an ANC delegation to Stockholm for Palme's memorial service. Oliver had many close friends in Sweden, who were attracted by his personal warmth as well as the cause to which he devoted his life. He certainly contributed strongly to the fact that so many Swedes became involved in the fight against apartheid. I was one of those people and had the privilege of meeting Oliver many times over the years of Swedish support to the struggle against apartheid. Oliver paid regular visits to our country, often in the company of other leading personalities in the ANC. They kept us updated on what was happening in southern Africa.

As time passed Swedish involvement and support expanded. In addition to government, a large number of organisations and individuals got involved. The breadth of this has been documented by Tor Sellström in several volumes published by the Nordic Africa Institute.

In August 1989, when I was State Secretary in the Ministry of Foreign Affairs, I received the sad message that Oliver had suffered a stroke and needed extensive medical treatment. The Swedish government immediately offered him this care at a Swedish hospital, which he accepted. At the hospital he became very good friends with the staff as well as with many other patients. His humble personality and warmth made a lasting impression on them just as he had impressed other people in Sweden over the decades of his visits here.

This final visit lasted for several months and coincided with dramatic developments in South Africa. In late October Walter Sisulu and seven other close ANC friends and partners were released from prison. By early February 1990 they came to Sweden, primarily to see and report to Oliver. During their visit the announcement was made that Nelson Mandela was to be freed after so many years in prison. Just a few weeks after his release he arrived in Stockholm and at the old Haga Castle the two friends met after having been separated for 27 years. It was a moment full of great emotion, tears and happiness after so much suffering, so much cruelty under apartheid, and so much resistance against this evil system.

A new era was about to unfold and in this country, far away from South Africa, we were witnesses to this historic meeting between the two giants. Conviction and dignity was about to win; so-called realism, with which the world had been fed, was about to lose. The victory of Oliver and all his friends in South Africa has served as a great inspiration for people around the world.

When Oliver passed away in 1993 a memorial service was organised in one of the churches in Stockholm. Those friends and admirers who could not be present at the funeral service in South Africa filled up the church. Speeches remembered this great man, a humble and soft-spoken gentleman who had been key to putting an end to an awful system. In doing so he made all our lives richer.

In Sweden people are proud to have played an active role in the transformation of South Africa. Today many of our citizens visit South Africa as tourists or for business. South Africans and Swedes have contributed to the transformation of each other's countries over many years. It is a partnership that continues to this day.

But we must not forget history. We have an obligation to keep the memory of such outstanding leaders as Oliver Tambo alive. He was a hero who always gave us hope, particularly in times when short-term prospects looked grim. Many Swedes would like to consider him 'one of us'. With Oliver we became partners in a global struggle for human rights.

SCANDINAVIAN CONNECTIONS

Pierre Schori

In the beginning, there was Oliver Tambo.

In global affairs, given the imbalance between the 'haves' and the 'have-nots', it is the North that usually impacts on the South. Too often, the Northern impact has been accompanied by a condescending 'we know better' attitude. In the worst case, it took the form of brutal force, masked as a crusade for Civilisation or Christianity. Desmond Tutu got it right when he said: 'First, they had the Bible and we had the land; we ended up having the Bible and they the land.'

But interestingly, it was during the bloody and sacrifice-filled struggle against colonialism and apartheid in southern Africa, that the high North got its first demonstrations and lessons of the opposite, the South impacting on the North. From the South we learnt the price you have to pay for human dignity and freedom. Our teachers were exceptional and convincing, engaging us in a lasting relationship of great value in this era of globalisation and interdependence.

In that beginning was Oliver Tambo.

He was the first leader of a Third World liberation movement to visit Scandinavia. Over the years Oliver – together with Thabo Mbeki and Billy Modise, the ANC representative in Sweden – used his extraordinary diplomatic skills and warm personality to contribute to giving the ANC a hegemonic position in the strong Swedish anti-apartheid and international solidarity movement. In the process, while crushing the propaganda illusion of racial supremacy, he also created understanding of and solidarity for other liberation struggles.

Oliver Tambo was thus instrumental in launching the biggest, longest and most successful solidarity engagement ever undertaken by Sweden.

The ANC Deputy President first visited Sweden in April 1961, invited as co-leader of the SAUF, together with Nana Mahomo of the PAC and Jar-iretendu Kozonguizi of South West African National Union, by the Swed-ish South Africa Committee. On 1 May 1962, he was invited by the Social Democratic Party to address the Labour Day demonstration in Gothenburg together with the Finance Minister Ernst Wigforss. The year before, sixty thousand people had marched on 1 May under a banner with the text 'Ver-woerd Commits Murder on Africa's Soil'.

The banner reappeared in 1962, but was seized by the police for 'defa-mation of a head of state'. Sten Andersson, later to become Foreign Min-ister, was arrested with two women carrying the banner and brought to court. The court proceedings, attended by a large number of anti-apartheid activists, ended in an anticlimax, when the court learned that Prime Min-ister Verwoerd was the South African head of government, not the head of state. Acquitting the accused, the court actually 'took into consideration that Sweden at the United Nations consistently had voted in favour of the res-olutions that condemned racial discrimination in South Africa'.

The next year, as Duma Nokwe, the ANC's Secretary-General, launched a boycott campaign against South African goods on behalf of Swedish youth organisations, he marched under the same banner, this time twice as big. As a consequence of the campaign many Swedes stopped buying South African products.

In August 1962 Oliver was received officially by Sweden's Prime Minister Tage Erlander. Three years later, in 1965, he came back on 1 May to march under the red flags with the Prime Minister.

Oliver used his frequent visits to work on the Scandinavian governments, public opinion, political parties, churches and trade unions. He successfully met with the Social Democratic Prime Ministers in Sweden, Denmark and Norway, as well as with the powerful trade union confederations of those countries.

The first recorded direct financial donation to the ANC by any Swed-ish political organisation was the modest sum of 3 000 Swedish Krona giv-en by the Social Democratic Youth League in 1964. It was 'to be used in an appropriate way in the struggle against the Verwoerd regime'. At the time, the ANC was in desperate need of financial aid and it appealed to the OAU Liberation Committee for funding, but the result was a meagre US$4 000 in six months of 1967/68.

Over the years Sweden's official government-supported solidarity grew to become one of the most significant to the ANC. Counting only the support granted directly by the Swedish government, at the time of the 1994 democratic elections in South Africa, it had in current figures reached a total of 900 million SEK. To this should be added the official support to the ANC via the UN system and other multilateral organisations.

This cooperation between Sweden and the ANC, an organisation that the Swedish authorities regarded increasingly as a government-in-waiting, was founded and sustained on the ANC side primarily by Oliver Tambo and Thabo Mbeki.

Oliver noted on 5 March 1981, when meeting with then Prime Minister Thorbjorn Falldin, that Sweden's assistance to the ANC exceeded that from any other country, including the Soviet Union and the German Democratic Republic. It also had the benefit of having no strings attached.

By comparison, Oliver did not visit the Soviet Union until April 1963, and the first – and last – meeting between the ANC President and the Soviet head of state, Mikhail Gorbachev, took place only in November 1986. And Oliver's first official visit to France was not arranged until 1984, when Régis Debray conveyed my request to François Mitterrand for the visit of 'a good friend'. In January 1987 the ANC leader was finally received by US Secretary of State George Schultz.

'There was thus a difference of some twenty-five years between the first Swedish contacts with [the] ANC at the highest level of government and corresponding contacts between [the] ANC and the Soviet Union, France, Great Britain and the United States, all permanent members of the UN Security Council.'[1]

Sweden's official solidarity with the ANC and other liberation movements in southern Africa incensed the apartheid regime. In October 1969 the South African Broadcasting Corporation called Sweden, 'the most strident enemy in Europe of white-ruled Southern Africa'. The country was subsequently labelled 'the terrorists' biggest source of income'.[2] And in April 1987, *The Citizen*, under the headline 'Sweden again' declared 'the Swedes should stop mucking about in a sub-continent in which they have no real stakes', and added that Sweden could 'go to hell'.

As Under-Secretary of State for Foreign Affairs I had the pleasure of responding to *The Citizen* in a speech on 5 May 1969, in which I commented:

We can take this, since the suggestion comes from a government

which has created a hell on earth for the majority of its citizens ...
On May Day, Mr Oliver Tambo was in Stockholm. We are pleased
to be able to note that our contacts are with the representatives
of a democratic and free South Africa, not with Mr Botha and his
entourage.

Oliver found a like-minded ally and lasting friend in Olof Palme, whose
very first political act was to donate blood, in the late 1950s, for a fundraising
campaign organised by the National Union of Swedish Students, in support
of South African students who had been expelled from the University of
the Witwatersrand. From that moment Olof engaged in a lifelong crusade
against apartheid and colonialism. The last speech of his life, on 21 February
1986, was at the 'Swedish People's Parliament against Apartheid'. With Oliver
at his side, the Prime Minister's final words were: 'If the rest of the world decides that apartheid is to be abolished, then apartheid will disappear.'

One week later Palme was assassinated as he was leaving a cinema in
Stockholm. Oliver later wrote about his Swedish friend in the foreword
mentioned below: 'There is more to life than the way one dies. It is the way
one has lived one's life.'

Oliver returned to Stockholm in March 1990, this time to see an old
friend, Nelson Mandela. It was Mandela's first of three visits before he was
sworn in as President of South Africa in May 1994. Staying at the state house,
Haga Palace, Mandela was reunited with his old friend and close comrade
after 28 years. The two had met previously in 1962 in Africa. Mandela notes
in his memoirs: 'Seeing my old friend and law partner was the reunion I
most looked forward to. Oliver was not well, but when we met we were
like two young boys in the veld who took strength from our love for each
other.'[3]

There was always an aura of deep, warm humanity around Oliver Tambo.
He inspired and created concrete solidarity that helped to liberate the un-
free and enlighten the already free. He laid the foundation to a North–South
bridge decades before the end of apartheid, which will inspire new generations of human rights activists.

Oliver was probably the last foreign leader who saw Olof Palme alive.
In August 1986 Oliver wrote the foreword to a book of poems written by
Lindiwe Mabuza, the ANC representative in Sweden at the time, which was
dedicated to the slain Prime Minister. In one of the poems, Mabuza wrote
the following lines about Palme, which could equally have been about Oliver:

Now you are gone
And you are now
And tomorrow.

In the beginning, there was Oliver Tambo. And he changed everything.

NOTES
1. T. Sellström, 'Sweden and the Liberation Struggle in Southern Africa'. Nordic Africa Institute, February 2002.
2. *Die Vaderland*, March 1974.
3. N. Mandela, *Long Walk to Freedom: The Autobiography of Nelson Mandela*. (Johannesburg: Macdonald Purnell, 1994), p. 564.

MY ABIDING MEMORY

David Steel

My contribution to this splendid volume will of necessity be brief. I cannot claim to have known Oliver Tambo well, but during my four years (1966–70) as President of the AAM I had the pleasure of getting to know him among the many South African exiles in London – including Ruth First, Albie Sachs, Ethel de Keyser, Abdul Minty and, of course, Oliver himself. We shared platforms at rallies, notably in Central Hall, Westminster. He was a moving and earnest speaker, not a ranter, not a demagogue, but gentle, forceful and persuasive. My one regret about that period is that because of my inflexible weekend discipline of going back to my family and constituency in Scotland I declined Oliver's invitation to his daughter's wedding, which was by all accounts a wonderful occasion when I would have got to know him more informally in the heart of his family.

But my abiding memory comes from a different period. In 1986 I was invited to give the annual freedom lecture at the University of Cape Town. This was my third visit to South Africa, meeting as many anti-apartheid activists as was possible at that time, amongst them Desmond Tutu, Alan Paton, Helen Suzman, Allan Boesak, Beyers Naudé and Gatsha Buthelezi, although the government refused my request to visit Nelson Mandela. The Progressive Party members of parliament Colin Eglin and Peter Soal hosted my visit and made all the arrangements.

After the South African visit I went on to meet with Presidents Masire in Botswana, Mugabe in Zimbabwe and Kaunda in Zambia, all of whom I already knew, to discuss the continuing cancer in South Africa.

At that time Oliver Tambo was running the ANC from the liberation

313

centre in Zambia's capital, Lusaka. I recall Kaunda telling me that war would break out over South Africa.

Prime Minister Margaret Thatcher had described the ANC as a terrorist organisation and banned any ministerial contact with them, though officials were allowed dialogue. And so it came about that at that time I was the only party leader to meet with the President of the ANC and his assistant – in the unlikely setting of the British High Commissioner's elegant drawing room in the Lusaka residence. Since Oliver and I knew each other we quickly got down to a couple of hours of serious discussion on how to combat apartheid in South Africa and indifference in Britain. Oliver was full of realism and a proper perspective on the difficulties ahead, but he was also firmly determined.

After his unusual guest had departed I asked His Excellency: 'Who was that bright young man with him who joined so freely in our discussion?'

'Ah,' replied the diplomat, 'very bright indeed – you may hear more of him. His name is Thabo Mbeki.'

AN INNER COMPASS

Per Wästberg

When I saw Trevor Huddleston in London not long before his death, he said: 'Very soon I am leaving you in order to talk to Oliver again.' To remember Oliver Tambo, particularly for a project such as this, is to get the chance to recall his voice and his typical gestures, the man that he was.

My memories of Oliver stretch from early 1959 to 1990 when he was in hospital in Stockholm. I have sometimes made diary entries, but still I find him hard to catch in words. His warm, unobtrusive personality lacked the charisma of Nelson Mandela and Julius Nyerere. He was not in the least egocentric, embodying his movement and the best part of it.

Oliver's many talents excluded the rhetoric and histrionic side common among politicians. He seldom made an exaggerated pronouncement for the headlines. He had a firm will, an inner compass that told him where to go and made him consider the best route, not always the straight one, and he was helped by his humility and good humour.

In March 1959, I met Oliver in his office near West Street, Johannesburg. The ANC was to be banned shortly thereafter and Albert Luthuli deported to his rural home district. The ANC called a private conference at Gandhi Hall. On a Saturday morning, the police were first on the spot with dogs, teargas, guns and cars for transporting the arrested. A thousand people packed the hall. I remember being appointed as a delegate from a friendly nation and seated below the posters on the platform: 'Friendship between the races'; 'Democracy is indivisible'; and 'Pass laws fill the prisons'. An old Zulu priest opened the meeting with the as yet unofficial anthem 'Nkosi

Sikelel' iAfrika' ('God bless Africa'). And then he told the story of the merciful Samaritan.

I identified almost helplessly with the well-behaved crowd that soon would be lost to a Christianity too cowardly to take a stand. Oliver read a message from Luthuli and continued himself until a few white faces down in the hall made him stop: 'We welcome Mr Paterson and Mr van Reyn from the Security Police. Since this is a private meeting, I presume we should count them as delegates.'

Patrick van Rensburg, who had left his post as the South African Consul in Leopoldville (Kinshasa) in protest, sat beside us. Lilian Ngoyi, the only woman on the ANC NEC, spoke on the women's campaign against passbooks and raised the loudest applause.

It was moving to see people demonstrate for the simple right to choose their homes and remain with their families. Each speech ended with an appeal against violence. When the police stopped the meeting, the thousand participants sang 'Mayibuye iAfrika' ('Africa, come back to us'). Oliver put his hand on mine – the first time I felt that typical gesture of his – and said that such is our life here and you will see worse things if you stay. I did – until I was deported two months later.

In August 1961 Oliver visited Sweden for the first time. I interviewed him on Swedish television's only channel and we dined with a few influential political writers. He struck me as a warm Christian on his way to wearing himself out on journeys all over the globe.

In 1962 Oliver spoke at the May Day rally in Gothenburg and had a long talk with Olof Palme. It was the beginning of a warm relationship. In other countries with diplomatic relations with South Africa, the ANC representatives were seen as non-governmental intruders, but in Sweden the ANC, not least Oliver, were treated as true spokesmen and a future government for their country.

In early 1969 the Swedish parliament decided to give humanitarian assistance to the liberation struggle in southern Africa. Sweden became the first country in the West to support openly, politically and economically, the ANC. It was controversial, since Washington and London regarded the ANC as a terrorist organisation.

The commitment did not rest with the government alone. Through writers, churchmen and intellectuals, and through many visits by Oliver Tambo, an opinion against apartheid permeated Swedish society. A successful boycott of wines, fruits and other commodities had started in the mid-1960s, and from 1979 the law in Sweden forbade investments in South Africa.

In 1975 I remember Oliver fêted in Stockholm like a visiting statesman and the ANC receiving a million pounds in extra funding. At that time Oliver told me how in Moscow he had happened to come across Harry Oppenheimer, the South African mining magnate, in the dining room of the Hotel Metropol. It was the Brezhnev era when the Soviet Union boycotted South Africa and provided the ANC with weapons but, as the second biggest player in the gold field, had secret talks with Anglo American to keep the gold price up. The guerrilla leader and the world's richest gold mine owner faced one another and Oliver ventured ironically: 'Plenty of South Africans here?'

Oppenheimer looked around suspiciously: 'Really? I don't think so. Perhaps only the two of us ... Well, we live in interesting times,' concluded Oppenheimer, and hurried away.

Oliver combined a sharp intellect with a capacity to listen to the other side's arguments. He strove towards consensus when reaching decisions and was intensely devoted to keeping together the ANC despite sometimes-serious rifts.

Canon John Collins of St Paul's Cathedral referred to Oliver as his African son. In the early stages the ANC had no funds and Canon Collins made money available from the British Defence and Aid Fund that soon became IDAF. I worked for IDAF for over twenty years, which meant spending a month or two each year in 2 Amen Court with John and Diana Collins and a group of eager, secret workers.

When he was in London Oliver turned up at Amen Court every second day, embracing John with Russian hugs and kisses. Hand in hand they walked into the library and talked in very low voices. They were spiritually close. At John's funeral in St Paul's Cathedral in January 1983 Oliver read the tale of the merciful Samaritan. He had flown in from the funeral of the many people murdered by South African forces in Maseru, Lesotho, where he had consoled the surviving with the humility and strength of mind that only he could show.

'You have not slept for two days; you must not tear yourself apart,' said Diana Collins.

To which Oliver replied, 'The oldest son must bury his father and I am John's oldest African son.' He also complained, 'I was born to become a priest and talk to people of love and reconciliation.'

After a stroke in 1989, Oliver was treated in Ersta hospital in Stockholm. I remember reading *The Guardian* and *The Weekly Mail* aloud for him there. When Mandela was freed in early 1990, his first European journey was an unofficial one – to see his old friend Oliver.

Extracts from my diary

'1970: At the IDAF annual meeting, [I had a] long private talk with Oliver about the training camps for Umkhonto in Tanzania and Zambia, the education schemes in agriculture, sociology and political science. He is enchanting, warm-hearted, so human and broadminded [even though] ... acting under a hardly bearable pressure.'

'1972: Olof Palme's state visit to Zambia. I went along as the Prime Minister's unofficial adviser on Africa together with Anders Ferm. At President Kaunda's banquet, Ferm and I were seated at the main door, the others on the platform. At our side were two huge black men who said, "'What have you got?'"We realised they were "gorillas" and Anders and I, being the youngest in Palme's group, were taken for his bodyguards. Mysteriously, we stroked our empty inner pockets, and made Kaunda's guards uneasy. At coffee, we joined Agostinho Neto and Oliver for talks into the night, and the feeling of informal mutual understanding was strong.'

The following year, the UN declared apartheid a crime against humanity. Some time afterwards, at an IDAF annual meeting in Oslo with Kader Asmal, Moses Gairoeb, Marcelino dos Santos, Agostinho Neto and Herbert Chitepo, Oliver told me how Zambian police informers had betrayed ANC infiltrators on their way to South Africa. They were shot swimming across the Limpopo River. On another occasion, a boat with a group of invaders to the desert coast of the Northern Cape was set alight, killing everyone on board.

'1973: Oliver attended the funeral of his often controversial colleague in arms, Robert Resha, in St Paul's Cathedral. Afterwards, we gathered in the home of John Collins who had had a crate of burgundy stolen in 1939 but, the thieves getting scared, left it behind a hedge. John discovered it after the war. At solemn occasions, he opened a bottle. But Oliver, tolerant of his friends' lack of discipline, did not drink.'

One midsummer, the UN Apartheid Committee met in Stockholm. Oliver was the main speaker, and John Collins joined us for Alva Myrdal's government dinner at the Foreign Office. Oliver was constantly on television, and we then went into hiding at my country house where I remember Oliver dreaming before the hand-painted wallpapers from 1770 and the lions of the sandstone fireplace from 1630: 'What will remain of the old South Africa, black and white, when the new South Africa is born?'

'1978: Oliver in Stockholm reminded me that the following year was twenty years after our first meeting in Gandhi Hall. We went through the streets of Stockholm hand in hand, while he told me that in Africa and England he seldom slept in the same bed for two nights. South Africa's destabilisation policy in the Front-line States was his principal concern these years. The defenceless states were at the mercy of South African agents, spies and murderers.'

Oliver was the main speaker at the Social Democrats' May Day rally in Stockholm one year, and I broke my intention not to join party demonstrations in order to be at Oliver's side and then interpret his speech for ten thousand listeners.

In February 1986, there was a so-called Peoples' Parliament Against Apartheid in Stockholm, in a very big and packed hall. The main theme was how to abolish apartheid. I sat behind Olof Palme and Oliver. Palme started his speech sounding tired; obviously someone in the Foreign Office had written it. Suddenly he threw the manuscript away and talked off the cuff. Besides a boycott of oil, air communications and weapons, he suggested strict economic sanctions. Only the multinational banks could wipe out the racist regime. It was a surprising speech; no Western leader had ever dared to take such a firm stand. Oliver's speech, I remember, sounded a bit pale after that. When I sat with Oliver and later that day with Thabo Mbeki, I found them overwhelmed by the angry force of Palme's commitment. Ten days later, Palme was shot dead.

On the day of Palme's funeral, 15 March 1986, I attended a luncheon for the guests, who included Willy Brandt, Rajiv Gandhi and, of course, Oliver Tambo. On our way from the funeral, we passed the place of the murder, in the very centre of Stockholm, and among flowers that the city inhabitants had put on the pavement was an olive branch sent by the Palestinian school children in Nazareth.

A further eight months later the US Congress passed legislation implementing mandatory sanctions against South Africa; new investments and bank loans were banned and air links between the US and South Africa were cut off.

In Harare in 1987 I attended a 'torture conference'. A number of black South Africans, mostly women, travelled there by bus to meet the ANC's leadership in exile, particularly Oliver and Joe Slovo, for the first time. After the terrifying eyewitness accounts of how children were treated in prisons, there was a closed meeting for only South Africans to hear and see their leaders. Oliver appointed me an honorary South African, and so I became the only outsider at that historic occasion. I think that none of the participants had ever met people of the stature of Tambo and Slovo; they were legends who were met with songs and applause.

'2 February 1990: Walter Sisulu, Govan Mbeki and Joe Slovo were in Stockholm when FW de Klerk announced that Mandela [was to] be released. Sisulu immediately drove to Oliver at the Ersta clinic [where Oliver was receiving treatment] and sat with him for hours. He told me they held each other and laughed to bridge an absence of three decades. Oliver had, with great effort, insisted that he would like to return to his country, and nothing else – it was an order! And he had pointed to a corner of his room where his suitcase stood packed and ready for his native land.'

RELIGIOUS CONNECTIONS

SOCIAL HISTORIAN AND
THEOLOGIAN

Brian Brown

Whom do we regard as the true representatives of the South African Church
– Verwoerd, Vorster and Botha or Tutu, Chikane and Naudé? The South African paradox is that apartheid was both implemented and resisted by those
to be found in church on Sundays.

Throughout his formative years, Oliver Tambo was able to view the
church with favour. When his father, Mzimeni, embraced the Christian faith
of his mother, it was inevitable that the young Tambo would be baptised.
First-generation believers generally reveal greater zeal than those who are
de-energised by centuries of tradition.

Methodist and Anglican Church schools provided Tambo's primary education in Pondoland, Transkei, until he departed for St Peter's Anglican College in Johannesburg. In a sea of black educational impoverishment, the
Church school was an island of excellence.

This schooling meant that Tambo was unusually well prepared for the
intellectual and political challenges that followed at Fort Hare University
in Alice. In Beda Hall, the Anglican hostel, he was Head Student. He both
lived and promoted his faith, joining the Students' Christian Association
(SCA) and teaching Bible classes in neighbouring villages after Sunday worship. Fellow SCA member and Bible class teacher Nelson Mandela writes
of their early relationship: 'From the start I saw that Oliver's intelligence was
diamond-edged, he was a keen debater and did not accept the platitudes that

so many of us automatically subscribed to . . . it was easy to see that he was destined for great things.'[1]

It was this belief in principles rather than platitudes that led to Tambo's expulsion from university; he instigated a student class boycott in support of a democratically elected Students' Representative Council.

Tambo acknowledged and valued the spiritual principles imparted to him from infancy. They would nourish and sustain his life. More than that, they explained it. When he returned to Fort Hare University in 1991 to be appointed as its Chancellor, he paid tribute to missionaries from Scotland who pioneered its tradition of mutuality and inclusiveness. He challenged staff and students alike; this tradition, destroyed by apartheid, was to be restored and emulated in the new South Africa.

The influence of the Church went way beyond Tambo's years of formal education. Although ambivalent towards the Church as an institution, particularly where it lacked a radical edge, he was acutely aware of the crucial support given by Church persons. In his early years of exile John Collins, Canon of St Paul's Cathedral in London, befriended him. Collins raised vast sums of money for political trials in South Africa, starting with apartheid's notorious 1956 Treason Trial of Congress leaders, and continuing as the IDAF until it was needed no more. In those early years Tambo also met Revd Michael Scott, head of the Africa Bureau in London. Scott was tireless and passionate in making representations to the UN on behalf of southern Africa's disenfranchised, Namibians in particular. Then there was Tambo's St Peter's mentor, Trevor Huddleston. In 1959 Chief Albert Luthuli, as President of the ANC, made an appeal for an international boycott of South Africa. Huddleston had returned to Britain on the instructions of his religious superiors and was able to take up the boycott cry. The AAM was born, and would become a leading support base for Tambo in Europe.

Tambo was to discover that the Church, rather like the curate's egg, was 'good in parts'.

Tambo the communist

The demonic genius of apartheid's propaganda machine, operative from 1948 for over forty years, was to categorise all of its opponents as communists. Prime Minister PW Botha could claim 'ours is a struggle of the Christian Western Civilisation against the powers of darkness and Marxism, and not just a black/white struggle'.[2] Successive leaders of the regime had offered to be a bulwark against 'godless communism'.

In 1960, when the bannings of the liberation movements took place under the Suppression of Communism Act, Tambo and the ANC's officers became 'statutory communists'. By so doing, the regime saw that the debate was removed from the issues of justice, human dignity and freedom and was placed in the domain of Cold War ideology. The Church was not always helpful in this battle for understanding and truth, and matters were made complex by persecution that the Church suffered behind the Iron Curtain.

In the 1980s, the BCC took every opportunity to 'demythologise' the ANC with regard to its communist/violent labelling. Nevertheless, more should have been done to get alongside and understand Tambo's ANC in the first two decades of his exile. Most faith communities in this era sought a false neutrality, choosing to endorse neither the legitimacy of the apartheid state nor that of the ANC. By contrast, the communist world had been both vocally and financially supportive of the ANC's cause from the earliest days of Tambo's exile.

Tambo's sense of gratitude, fairness and inclusiveness did not help his cause in Western capitals. He refused to rubbish his communist comrades. Addressing Church leaders at a WCC gathering in Lusaka, Zambia, in 1987, he told of how Communist parties and Socialist countries had been 'firm and reliable allies in the common struggle for the liberation of our country and people. Instead of being criticised and denounced for involving themselves in the struggle against apartheid, they should be congratulated, as should people of other persuasions, such as Social Democrats and Liberals, who have also joined in the fight against white minority domination.' In a more mischievous mood Tambo asked, 'why are the limpet mines used by the ANC never simply mines, but of Communist or Soviet origin? And why are Pretoria's guns, used to kill in townships, or Namibia, or Angola, never of Western origin but simply guns?!'[3]

However, loyalty did not lead to emulation. At the same Lusaka Conference, he promised that the ANC would 'resist all attempts to inject any anti-religious nations into our midst. Indeed, proceeding on the basis of old traditions within our movement, we are in the process of establishing an interfaith chaplaincy.'[4]

For Tambo, southern Africa's freedom was indivisible. Time and again he would share public platforms with the leader of SWAPO, Sam Nujoma. Nujoma was a liability with regard to the promotion of the ANC's cause in the West. As the conflict in Namibia and Angola escalated, so Cuban forces become involved in greater measure. Western capitals made the linkage: Cuba = Communist = SWAPO = ANC!

The London-based Namibia Communications Centre was established in 1984 by Protestant and Catholic Churches in Europe and North America to counter the myths so prevalent in sections of the British media. In particular, this Church agency sought to ask why the SWAPO liberation movement was often depicted as being anti-Western and anti-Church given that it drew its support from an overwhelmingly Christian Namibian people who related readily to Western Church bodies.

A BCC delegation visited the occupied territory and reported that: 'The presence of Communist military advisers in southern Angola is often portrayed as legitimising the presence of South Africa troops in the area. There is insufficient discussion as to whether the West's failure to unequivocally condemn South Africa's illegal occupation of Angola, from an illegal base within Namibia, does not encourage or even necessitate alliances with communist nations.'[5]

Tambo the violent

In conversations with Church representatives, Tambo would remind them that the Church was not a pacifist body and neither was the British government. His sense of frustration when dealing with much of the British establishment is well illustrated by comments made by a member of parliament when Tambo was testifying before the Foreign Affairs Committee of the House of Commons: 'This Committee totally condemns the use of violence to settle political disputes, and that is the view not only of this Committee but the view of the entire House of Commons and every party in it.'[6]

Tambo would later enquire: 'How do you handle such assertions?'

The British had waged war upon war to 'settle political disputes' in which millions of people (combatants and civilians) had been killed. By contrast, the ANC had been non-violent for some fifty years. Only in 1961, after it had been banned and when the apartheid army was deployed in the townships, did the ANC embrace violence. And then with such caution that: 'Violence has been largely confined to attacking economic installations, pylons and so on – very few casualties in comparison with the massive casualties we have sustained from the apartheid system ... we have virtually been non-violent now for about 30 years.'[7]

In South Africa, Beyers Naudé's Christian Institute (CI) had begun to talk of apartheid's 'institutionalised violence' in the 1960s. The WCC also saw it this way and in 1970 launched its highly controversial Programme to Combat Racism. The ANC and the PAC, in common with other groups of racially oppressed around the world, were to be the recipients of Church grants. Tambo had promised to ensure that the grants would be used for purposes unrelated to the work of MK, but his assurances did little to assuage the cry that the WCC was backing violence. Though causing deep divisions within the Churches, usually along racial lines, the grants concentrated the mind of the Churches on the nature of violence. It became axiomatic to talk of the primary or instigating violence of apartheid and the secondary or responsive violence of the oppressed.

These interpretations of violence as institutionalised in the structures and dehumanising laws of apartheid had enormous consequences for the Churches. A resolution passed by the SACC in 1974 condemned the hypocrisy of deploring the violence of guerrillas, 'while preparing to defend our society with its primary, institutionalised violence by means of yet more violence'.[8]

Although many Church leaders conceded that the ANC's violence was responsive, some still urged Tambo to have his movement lay down its arms. Tambo remained unequivocal: 'It seems to us strange reasoning that we, the victims of violence, should be asked to respond to the continued terror of the Pretoria regime against the peoples of Southern Africa by committing ourselves to cease our armed resistance, whether temporarily or permanently.'[9]

Tambo the theologian

In his relationships with the Churches, Tambo was both social historian and theologian. Addressing Church representatives in Holland in 1980, he showed how the Church had been a co-oppressor by virtue of its role, though not its intent:

> In the period of imperialist expansion, the Church accepted as legitimate the concept of a civilising mission, and for that reason justified the imposition of white colonial domination over many peoples ... The Church continuously refused to recognise the fact that the fulfilment of its black congregations lay in their liberation both from colonial domination and from what the Church describes as sin.[10]

He perceptively anticipated the debate that would consume the Churches, particularly those of Evangelical and Pentecostal persuasion, in the 1980s. Should the Church engage in the social gospel? Should it call for repentance from both personal *and* social sins?

Significantly, at a conference in Rustenburg, South Africa, in 1990, many Church leaders participated in public penitence. Typical of the responses was the *mea culpa* – 'our silence was in fact sin, and our failure to act decisively against all forms of apartheid made us party to an inhuman political ideology'.[11] Tambo lived to hear many, however belatedly, give up their assertion that Christianity had nothing to do with politics.

A further theological insight of Tambo's, one that has received little recognition, was his belief that the ANC helped to pioneer ecumenism (Church unity) in South Africa.

For this to appear credible, we must recall that the first three Presidents of the ANC, starting from 1912, were Church leaders, and that the third President, Methodist minister ZR Mahabane, was also the pioneering President of the Interdenominational African Ministers Association of South Africa. Mahabane saw that a divided black Church meant a divided and reduced resistance to black oppression; his Association addressed the denominational divisions of the white-led Churches:'Given our historical experience, which has made the ANC play the role of virtual incubator of the ecumenical movement in our country, certainly among black Christians, it is natural that we should make this call for Christian unity in the struggle against racism.'[12]

Tambo's theological insights also allowed him to anticipate the significant 'apartheid is a heresy' debate within the Church. In the 1980s, voices within the Church began to say that apartheid was institutionalised sin and its theological justification a heresy. Given the decades-old religious undergirding of apartheid by the Dutch Reformed Churches, this re-evaluation was of huge significance in encouraging radical, non-violent change in South Africa.

Tambo had long deemed apartheid to be evil *and* heretical; he said it claimed a divine mission to exercise dominion over the black majority, denied that all were created equal and, by appropriating to itself the right to subdue black people, appointed itself to a station in the universe higher than God himself: 'Apartheid transforms the Creator into a handmaiden for the fulfilment of its own diabolical aspirations.'[13]

Tambo and Church relationships

On 14 March 1982, the London office of the ANC was bombed (as the Truth and Reconciliation Commission would subsequently reveal, by Pretoria's agents). The ANC was homeless. Tambo made a direct approach to the BCC for assistance. Three days later the ANC's Communications Department was accommodated in the BCC's offices. The BCC's press statement was one of critical solidarity:

> While reserving a right to be critical of certain aspects of the policy of this and other liberation movements, the BCC has long identified with their just cause of ending apartheid by giving full rights of citizenship to all South Africans. To that extant an attack

such as this on them is also felt to be an attack on us. During this time of uncertainty, the BCC wishes to offer some interim office accommodation to the ANC, as an expression of our solidarity.[14]

Only days before the bombing, Pope John Paul II had received Tambo and Nujoma in Rome. Speaking after that occasion, Tambo saw it as unsurprising that those who opposed a racist regime, which was condemned by the Bible, should be received: 'And if those who call us terrorists are to be believed, then it must be shocking that the Pope can meet us. But I think he understands that justice is on our side, and the methods we're using to vindicate justice are justified.'[15]

Many organisations claim to have initiated the 'breakthrough' of enabling the ANC to dialogue with its opponents. Another claim now follows.

Christian Concern for Southern Africa was a small London-based organisation that out-punched its weight. With a membership of concerned Christians, rather than Churches, it had the freedom to act without customary institutional restraints. Consequently, in 1984, assisted by others, it sought to bring together the ANC and representatives of the most powerful opponents of sanctions.

Tambo was asked if the ANC would participate in a residential conference at which the South African (SA) Foundation would be present, together with representatives of British industry. The SA Foundation existed for the primary purposes of promoting trade and resisting sanctions. Moreover, Malcolm Rifkind and Chester Crocker, Ministers with responsibility for southern Africa in the UK and US respectively, would be asked to attend or send representatives with position papers. Both administrations had demonised the ANC and resisted sanctions.

Considering the years of opposition and rejection, it would have been understandable had Tambo declined. But, in a world where leaders so often prefer 'war to jaw', Tambo was a remarkable exception. He sent Seretse Choabi, Director of Luthuli Services for the ANC and a former prisoner on Robben Island, as Chief Representative. At the Royal School of Church Music in London in November 1984, representatives of big business, governments, Churches, campaigning groups and the ANC met face to face over dining and debating tables. Significantly, Choabi concluded his presentation by stating that the Mass Democratic Movement in his country *wished* to talk, but 'they arrest them and lock them up; and yet South Africa is presented as part of the free world, the defence of South Africa against communism. That is insane!'[16]

The above events had great significance. It was a help to Church leaders in

South Africa to declare that in the Vatican, London, and elsewhere the ANC was being addressed as the significant representative of the aspirations of the oppressed. The Churches and the ANC needed each other in this search for peace with justice.

Tambo and the Achilles heel

The ANC's call for immediate, comprehensive, mandatory sanctions took a long time to be embraced by the Churches.

In 1976 the CI's monthly publication, *Pro Veritate*, bit the bullet with two headline-grabbing editions. Earlier editions had argued for a more just economic system and had been banned. It didn't require great wisdom to know what the regime would do if foreign investments in South Africa were condemned as 'investments in apartheid'. Nevertheless, the CI made this condemnation, and the editions were banned.

No reasons were given by the regime when the CI was itself banned in October 1977, together with the leading BC organisations. While there would have been many, the disinvestment call had been crucial. Pretoria knew this to be its Achilles heel.

Initially, Churches resisted the call for sanctions; they hoped that moral persuasion would prevail and bring incremental changes to the system. But by the late 1970s, Pretoria's intransigence had called into question the efficacy of persuasion without pressure. The BCC, in its third, book-sized report on South Africa in fourteen years, asked its Assembly of 1979 to consider the resolution 'that the Churches should seek from any British Government a commitment to support, or at least not to veto, proposals in the Security Council for sanctions against South Africa so long as the majority of the people are denied an effective voice in national decision-making'.[17]

Significantly, one of Tambo's statements on sanctions was included in the report: 'The Investor is the ally of our oppressors, a beneficiary from our misery. We want all foreign investors to get out of our country ... See that your country, your church, your university, your union, withdraws from firms with interest in South Africa.'

During the 1980s the BCC saw virtually every member Church come to support the call for targeted sanctions, financial ones particularly. The BCC also sought to promote the chief representative of the ANC. It wasn't easy. Margaret Thatcher was Prime Minister and as she did not deal with 'terrorists', there was no invitation for Tambo to visit No. 10 Downing Street. This rejection made Pretoria feel more secure and less likely to consider fundamental change.

To challenge the demonising of Tambo, he was invited to meet the leaders of the mainline Churches in Britain and Ireland. They met in the BCC's London headquarters, with Archbishop Robert Runcie, the Anglican and BCC leader, presiding. Tambo spoke for over an hour and then fielded questions. It felt rather like an old-time testimony meeting. He told of his early days in London. On going to St Paul's Cathedral for a weekday Communion Service, he was surprised to be one of but a handful of worshippers. He had not anticipated the depths of British secularism. He told of the tension between his sense of vocation – to serve as an Anglican priest – and his sense of duty – to serve his oppressed fellows.

Many in the gathering were aware of how Tambo had succeeded Chief Albert Luthuli, the first of South Africa's four Nobel Peace Prize winners. Few had known how much Tambo had been influenced by Luthuli's Christianity, integrity and simplicity, and fewer still that he'd aspired to be a priest, but had instead honoured the mandate given to him by the ANC.

Some heads of Churches might have come to the meeting expecting a diatribe of hate. Instead, they met a man imprisoned by his Christian hope, a man generous and forgiving of his enemies, and understanding of (without condoning) the impoverished British response. His was a heartfelt plea for understanding, but essentially it was a plea to end the pain of his oppressed.

The BCC's Africa Secretary undertook the courtesy of seeing Tambo and his colleagues out of the building. On returning, the room was enveloped in an astonished silence. Runcie broke it, saying, 'Thank you for allowing us to meet a remarkable terrorist.' The meeting exploded in laughter. Every Church leader was aware that Runcie had intentionally both referred to, and repudiated, Thatcher's assertion of Tambo as a terrorist. Runcie would come to say that 'If South African Christians cry out, we cannot shut our ears; if they need support we cannot turn our backs; if they are being hurt we must be ready to share their suffering.'[18] Naturally, his dear friend Desmond Tutu would have been the most influential of those South African Christians, but Runcie had heard Tambo's cry.

As the 1980s saw the Mass Democratic Movement increase its resistance, and apartheid's oppression increase commensurately, the BCC focused on South Africa. A visit to South Africa in 1985 by representatives of the British Churches resulted in a report entitled *Whose Rubicon?* Just before their arrival in the country, Prime Minister PW Botha had made a speech in which he proposed no change of any significance in his government's policies: 'I believe that we are today crossing the Rubicon, there can be no turning back.'

The Church delegation responded: 'We have learned during this visit that PW Botha has not yet come to his Rubicon, but the black people of South

Africa have crossed theirs.'[19]

Church consensus was complimented from the mid-1980s onwards by a remarkable coalition of Churches, trade unions, political parties (with the exception of the Conservatives), the AAM and other campaigning bodies, and development agencies. The Bishop of Coventry, Simon Barrington-Ward, chaired this Southern African Coalition and the AAM and BCC serviced it.

The debate was no longer about the validity of sanctions but rather the unwillingness of Western powers to implement them. At the instigation of the Churches, this Coalition met in conference on 29 February 1989 – the first anniversary of the arrest of Church leaders marching in protest on the South African parliament. Its conclusions and recommendations would be ratified by the following BCC Assembly. Significantly, the Assembly highlighted the economic crisis, which, coupled with the people's unstoppable commitment to liberation, was causing Pretoria to think the unthinkable. It resolved that UK banks should 'respond to the appeal of South African Church leaders in connection with the 1990 negotiations for rescheduling South Africa's debt, by making no new loans to South Africa while insisting on the rapid repayment of existing debt'.[20]

The Assembly sensed that apartheid's end was in sight. Tambo had graciously assisted the Churches to contribute to that end. Though his enemies had tried to take Tambo out of the Church, they failed to take the Church out of Tambo.

NOTES

1. N. Mandela. 1994. *Long Walk to Freedom* (London: Little Brown and Company).

2. WCC Information Report No. 14, 1982 (Geneva, Switzerland).

3. WCC documentation, *Dialogue with Liberation Movements*, Lusaka, Zambia, 1987 (Geneva, Switzerland).

4. WCC documentation, *Dialogue with Liberation Movements*.

5. BCC Report, 1982. *Namibia – A Nation Wronged* (London).

6. House of Commons. 1985. Evidence Before Foreign Affairs Committee (London).

7. House of Commons. 1985. Evidence Before Foreign Affairs Committee.

8. B. Spong and D. Mayson. 1993. *Come Celebrate! 25 years of the SACC* (Johannesburg, South Africa).

9. Canon Collins Memorial Lecture. 1987. *South Africa at the Crossroads* (London: British Defence and Aid Fund).

10. WCC consultation. 1980. *The Church and our Struggle* (Geneva, Switzerland).

11. The South African Council of Churches Press Service, 1990 (Johannesburg, South Africa).

12. WCC consultation. 1985. *The Church and our Struggle* (Geneva, Switzerland).

13. WCC consultation. 1985. *The Church and our Struggle*.

14. Ecumenical Press Service, March 1982 (Geneva, Switzerland).

15. WCC Information Report No. 14.

16. CCSA. 1984. *The Policies of Western Governments towards South Africa* (London).

17. BCC. 1979. *Political Change in South Africa – Britain's Responsibility* (London).

18. BCC and Christian Aid. 1989. *Standing for the Truth, Britain and South Africa* (London).

19. BCC and Catholic Institute for International Relations. 1986. *Whose Rubicon?* (London: Hudson Print).

20. BCC and Christian Aid. 1989. *Standing for the Truth.*

AN UNBROKEN FRIENDSHIP

Trevor Huddleston
(an address at the Requiem Mass of Oliver Reginald Tambo
at St Mary's Cathedral, Johannesburg, 30 April 1993)

> The light shines in the darkness and the darkness has not overcome it.
> *John 1.3*

To stand in this pulpit in this lovely Cathedral of St Mary's is, for me, an awesome experience. The memories it evokes go back half a century. It is thirty-seven years since I preached my farewell sermon in this place and fifty since I first met the subject of this Requiem Mass, Oliver Reginald Tambo. So it is not only that I am overawed by events: it is my sense of responsibility for the words I speak to you all. How can I ever do justice to the memory of one who changed the course of my life? How can I even begin to express what his friendship has meant to me since we first met in St Peter's, Rosettenville, when he was only twenty-six and I a totally immature and inexperienced thirty, sent by CR [the Community of the Resurrection] to Sophiatown and Orlando. And, in any case, how can anyone spell out the meaning of friendship itself? But I must try and I ask your forgiveness now for all inadequacies: 'The light shines in the darkness.'

In a letter Oliver wrote to me five months ago in reply to one of mine written as President of the Anti-Apartheid Movement concerning the difficulty and dangers of a breakdown in communication at the critical time, he wrote this:

I wish to address myself to the concluding words in your letter, namely: 'I know that I can write to you as I know that you will fully understand my motives for doing so.' . . . I modestly wish to stress that nothing is more precious to me than our unbroken friendship over fifty years. Your kind words can never be improved upon. Their wholesomeness is an embodiment of the truth as *we* know it . . . Your concerns, Father, are also mine . . . I cannot say how much we value your consistent support and clarity of mind about our political situation. It will remain a shining force of example long after we have gone. The immortality of it all will be emblazoned on the grave of apartheid . . .

Perhaps that quotation could be regarded as a form of boasting. If so, I do not apologise for there are certain things we have a right to boast of and a lifelong friendship is one! Indeed one of the great English saints of the Middle Ages, a mystic and a scholar, St Aelred of Rievaulx, dared to say: 'God *is* friendship.' A contemporary theologian writes:

If someone were to say to me, 'But as a priest, isn't God more important to you than any of your friends?' I'd have to say that God is above all and through all and in all, and it's in and through my friends that I think I have learnt and still do learn, most about God and receive most from Him. With every true friendship we build more firmly the foundations on which the peace of the whole world rests.

And that is exactly as I believe myself about my friendship with Oliver. What I am saying is that Oliver not only gave me this gift but also enabled me to recognise the fundamental truth about the consequences – political, economic, social, cultural and theological – of South Africa's ideological philosophy. Apartheid. I did not learn the meaning of apartheid by academic study. I learnt it in the streets and homes and schools of Sophiatown and Orlando. I learnt it from the people whose parish priest I was and for whom, under God, I had pastoral responsibility. I learnt it from the young and the old, from the family struggling to live when all the force of institutionalised racism was mobilised against them. When every effort was made to destroy and destroy and destroy their human dignity.

I was there, in Sophiatown, when the Minister of Native Affairs, in introducing the Bantu Education Act in parliament, said: 'We are telling the native he is being educated for certain forms of labour: there are green pastures

in which he has *no right* to graze.' And there, at St Peter's, was Oliver, an outstanding educationalist and teacher, wholly committed to providing young
and intelligent Africans with a future in which their gifts and talents could
be used for their *own* country. Of course I was in South Africa as a member
of the Community of the Resurrection which had worked in Johannesburg
since *before* the beginning of this century, whose chief work was in education and specifically in teacher-training, who had established the first Anglican college for the training of men for priesthood. Oliver was so completely
at one with the Community's ideals and practice that he felt a strong vocation to priesthood himself and – in 1955 – asked me to recommend him to
Archbishop Geoffrey Clayton for ordination. But, as you all know, in the following years came the Treason Trial and the long years leading to Sharpeville
– the banning of the ANC and the decision of Albert Luthuli to send Oliver
out of the country to hold together the ANC in exile.

It is difficult, even for myself, to recollect the major events of the liberation struggle in which we were involved. But I do remember the moment
when Oliver received his banning order and his movements were restricted, deciding that I had to appeal to the *outside* world and particularly to the
Church in my own country about its total failure to act against the Western Areas Removal Scheme and, of course, the Bantu Education Act. 'The
Church sleeps on', I wrote to the *Observer* newspaper:

> It sleeps on while 60 000 people are moved from their homes in
> the interests of a fantastic racial theory. It sleeps on while plans are
> being made and implemented; it sleeps on while a dictatorship
> is swiftly being created over all Native Affairs in the Union – so
> that speech and movement and association are no longer free. The
> Church sleeps on – though it occasionally talks in its sleeps – and
> expects (or does it?) the Government to listen?

So long ago. Forty years. Was it really like that? Standing here in this Anglican
cathedral today – recognising so clearly how in the past ten years the voice
of the churches has *been* the voice of liberation when every other voice was
silent and the release of political prisoners was so loudly demanded by the
Council of Churches that at last came the beginning of the end: the battle of
Cuito Cuanavale and Namibian independence. It was Oliver in those long
lonely years of exile, first in Tanzania, then in Zambia, who held the ANC
together: was ready, after the Soweto uprising, to receive that great rush of
exiles and – at last – to be recognised as the international statesman that he
was. During those years, as I well know, he depended on his wife Adelaide

for keeping a home for the children and for himself to return to on his many journeys. Without her and her courage and determination he could not possibly have achieved what he did. And of course, he could not have survived successfully the first stroke and the painful process of rehabilitation that that involved. Indeed those last three years were a triumph of faith and hope and love, and even a deeper understanding of friendship too. Poetry is the only medium I can use to bring together and to end these words of mine ...

> *Oliver!*
> O Captain! My captain!
> Our fearful trip is done.
> The ship has weathered every track,
> the prize we sought is won ...
> The port is near ...

Well – is the prize won? No doubt the coming few weeks will tell. But I am certain that this Eucharist, this thanksgiving for Oliver, is far more than a memorial. It is a *rededication – making hope a reality* for southern Africa, not tomorrow, but today. The best memorial for him is free and fair elections for a truly democratic constituent assembly in the shortest time possible. Let that great Christian political prisoner, John Bunyan, speak the last words: 'When the day that he must go hence was come, many accompanied him to the riverside into which as he went he said "Death where is thy sting?" And as he went down deeper he said "Grave where is thy victory?" So he passed over, *and all the trumpets sounded for him on the other side.*'

The light shines in the darkness, and the darkness *has not overcome it.*

SOURCES
R. Denniston, *Trevor Huddleston: A Life* (London: Macmillan, 1999).

UNDERGROUND LINKS TO RELIGIOUS GROUPS

Horst Kleinschmidt

My first meeting with ANC President Oliver Reginald Tambo came at an astonishing time in the history of the liberation struggle when the light of freedom at the end of the dark tunnel of apartheid seemed suddenly to be visible.

In the summer of 1977 a huge international solidarity conference took place in Lisbon, Portugal, in support of the oppressed people of Zimbabwe. Political slogans and heroic images adorned thousands of walls throughout the city as the country was bubbling with political activity in the aftermath of the overthrow of the oppressive Caetano regime in 1974, and further hastened by the wars of liberation fought by its colonial subjects in Mozambique, Angola and Guinea Bissau. The conference was called to galvanise support for the liberation movements fighting against the white minority regime of Ian Smith in what was once called Southern Rhodesia, today's Zimbabwe.

I had only recently been exiled and was now living in the Netherlands. On arriving in Lisbon I watched in awe how this huge manifestation of international solidarity of liberation movements and solidarity organisations and some governments came together in a commitment to the struggle for a better world.

The purpose of my journey to Lisbon was to hand over to President Tambo a letter from a loyal ANC cadre, at that time standing trial in Pretoria. The letter, written on various lengths of toilet paper, had been smuggled out of prison and then out of South Africa. I became the messenger due to my involvement, albeit at a very minor level, with those standing trial. The charge against them was their alleged aim to frustrate the planned 'independence' of the so-called homeland, Transkei. The accused were operating as part of the ANC's military wing, MK. The letter was addressed to Comrade OR and was written by Magalies Ramokgadi, accused number six in a trial that would come to be known as the 'Tokyo Sexwale and eleven others' trial'. Magalies had previously served ten years on Robben Island for defying the authorities when the ANC was banned and organising an underground branch of the organisation in Alexandra, just north of Johannesburg. During his detention then, Magalies was witness to the murder of Solwandle Looksmart Ngudle, the first detainee ever to be killed by the police. Ngudle's body had been thrown in Magalies's cell whilst his interrogators had taken off for the weekend. This had happened fourteen years earlier.

On his release after his first stint on Robben Island, Magalies immediately started work for the ANC again. Despite his age (nearly seventy) and having served ten years on the Island, his courage and commitment were undaunted. I met him in the Rocky Street house of Ama Naidoo, the courageous mother of five children who all dedicated their lives to the struggle. After working with Magalies for several months he advised me one day that we should flee South Africa immediately to avoid arrest. Without passport I skipped the border to Botswana and thus exile. At the very last moment Magalies told me he had been given orders to stay. Seven months later he faced the prospect of the gallows again, but after a lengthy trial was sentenced to seven years imprisonment. Now he wanted Oliver Tambo to know what had happened during their underground actions, what had gone right, what had gone wrong, and what was to be learnt. The toilet paper was the only paper he could obtain. His writing skills he attained through a prison correspondence course during his previous imprisonment. His commitment and courage were exemplary.

My contacts in the ANC facilitated me meeting the ANC President, Comrade OR (as he was respectfully referred to in ANC ranks). This initially filled me with fear and trepidation. In my mind I was going to meet the man who should have been the South African President. Uncertain about the correct etiquette I stuttered through the explanation and background to the folded sheets of paper I handed him. He did not immediately turn to reading the missive. As I was of recent refugee vintage, Comrade OR enquired at length about Steve Biko and the BCM 'back home', which was not yet outlawed. In a fatherly fashion Comrade OR calmed my nerves by holding my hand as he spoke. I recall his words to his advisers sitting with him: 'What is so special about Black Consciousness? Ever since we formed the ANC Youth League in the 1940s we were motivated by such consciousness. We should not fight them – they are part of us.'

Comrade OR was not the huge figure I had expected him to be. His diction was precise and the vocabulary he used extensive – like that of an English gentleman. I recall the spectacles he wore: hopelessly old-fashioned, with a pointy shape toward the temples of his face, creating an impish appearance. I always felt that his public relations advisers should suggest that he wear something more flattering. But the spectacles more likely reflected the character of Comrade OR. His demeanour was to frown on or shun outer trimmings that would seem alien to a cause aimed at ending the suffering of his people.

Within weeks after the banning of the South African Christian Institute and an array of BC organisations in October 1977, I was assisted by Johnny Makathini, ANC Representative at the UN in New York, to address the UN Security Council. The gist of my message to the South African government was: you have banned the legal opposition groups; their only choice now is to join those you forced into the underground a decade earlier when you banned the ANC, PAC and others. I added that my prediction was that the majority would now join the ANC. I had to choose my words about 'underground' and 'ANC' carefully and despite agreement with them, in order to ensure that it would not be easy for new charges to be laid against my colleagues 'inside'.

At the same time I informed the ANC about the true intentions of my colleagues 'back home'. Comrade OR took a personal interest in this matter and I had occasion to brief him on communications from the Revd Beyers Naudé (Oom Bey, as we referred to him), the banned Director of the now banned Christian Institute.

The ANC set up a task group to ensure that underground links to religious groups inside South Africa be developed. Through my 'handler', Aziz Pahad, I reported on the internal network that I kept secret communications with and simultaneously conveyed messages and requests from the exiled ANC to them. My reporting structure was direct and mostly immediate. When important issues arose, Pahad would take me to the man next in his line of command, now our President, Thabo Mbeki. When Mbeki thought it necessary, I reported on issues directly to Comrade OR.

In this way the ANC built one further flank of resistance in what we called 'internal reconstruction'. For several years I spoke to the banned Oom Bey once a week from a UK call-box, phoning him at call-boxes on street corners across the length and breadth of the magisterial district of Johannesburg, to which he was confined. According to an agreed roster, the times and call-boxes changed for each call. Code names and code words were extensively used. We also regularly microfilmed copies of *Sechaba* and *African Communist* and hid the film in gifts that unsuspecting travellers to South Africa would hand to Oom Bey. He had a contact at the University of the Witwatersrand who would print out the microfilm, copy the documents and distribute them.

Over the years I wrote several hundred 'situational' reports, many of which were for Comrade OR's personal attention. I found him always receptive and probing. He would listen with sympathy, even when decisions had been taken internally that could potentially benefit a rival organisation and not the ANC. For example, Oom Bey was prone to funding underground operatives other than ANC people. Comrade OR never took a hostile attitude or suggested that the ANC was being undermined by such action.

By the time the ANC was unbanned in 1990, I could say with confidence that not once did my many reports go astray and land up in enemy hands. Whatever some critics have suggested, the ANC intelligence machinery around Comrade OR was secure, whether in Lusaka or London.

I have no doubt that Comrade OR was receiving vast numbers of other reports from underground structures within the country. In this way he and the leadership around him were meticulously informed about situations and developments in the country and, in time, were able to feed information back and begin to orchestrate the national revolution into a cogent national structure. That he had his finger on the pulse of the internal situation could be seen in Comrade OR's statements, speeches, and notably his ANC anniversary speeches delivered on 8 January each year from Lusaka.

Clearly 1977 was a further crossroads for South Africa. The numbers of those who believed that apartheid could only be ended through organised revolutionary struggle had grown in tens of thousands.

At one point it was thought appropriate for the banned Oom Bey to flee South Africa and join Oliver Tambo in Lusaka to announce his and his followers' support for the ANC. Together with others in the ANC we made elaborate arrangements to get him out of South Africa. It was no mean feat given the terms of Oom Bey's banning order and the constant surveillance he was under, having to report to a police station regularly, not being allowed to leave the magisterial district in which he lived, having had his passport confiscated, and a host of other conditions. Secret arrangements, facilitated by the ANC's people in Front-line States had to be made. Operationally the plan had been perfected to fly Oom Bey to Maputo and then on to Lusaka where he and Comrade OR would hold a joint press conference. At the very last moment, however, the plan was called off. It was preferable for Oom Bey to continue his work from his home in Johannesburg.

The Cape leader of the Christian Institute, the Methodist Minister Revd Theo Kotze, who had also been banned, was obliged to flee South Africa in July 1978. Like most of us, he went to neighbouring Botswana and then onwards. On the staircase in an apartment block in North Islington I one day accompanied Theo Kotze when, by chance, Comrade OR approached from the opposite direction. I introduced the two to each other. Theo was hugely impressed with the fact that the ANC leader immediately knew who he was and took time to enquire about his personal circumstances and the situation he had left behind in Cape Town. Without fail Comrade OR showed kindness and consideration.

Archbishop Trevor Huddleston was of Comrade OR's generation and the two of them sustained a friendship over many decades. My awareness of this grew from the Archbishop's role as Chairperson of IDAF and my role as its Executive Director. I was much younger and acted as the Archbishop's aide and assistant during many journeys across the globe to raise awareness of the situation in South Africa, and to raise funds for the defence of those incarcerated by the apartheid rulers. This drew the Bish (as we called him) and I together and we became close friends. I greatly admired his sharp wit and wide knowledge of religion, philosophy, social questions and politics. Most of all, I admired him as a scholar whose analytical ability came with his disciplined mind – a product of the religious order he belonged to, the Community of the Resurrection, an Anglican monastic order.

Through the Bish, I became aware that Comrade OR at times desired a confidant and a friend outside of the close-knit circle of senior ANC cadres. This was especially true after Comrade OR suffered a stroke during the last days of exile when he already anticipated his long-awaited return to South Africa. During Comrade OR's recuperation in London he sought the company of the retired Archbishop on regular occasions. Although the nature of their discussion was never disclosed to me, I gleaned that Comrade OR was a fallible human being who needed assurance and support like any of us. Comrade OR had always been committed to Christianity and during his illness affirmed this, not least through his private meetings with his lifelong friend.

My remembrance of Comrade OR is of a man of immense modesty, shying away from material wealth and from personal glorification. I saw Comrade OR wearing the same solidarity shirts sent by the German Democratic Republic that everyone else in the ANC camps was wearing. Despite his age he braved the discomforts and dangers of living in the Front-line States, never spending more time in London than his official duties demanded.

He was impatient with inefficiency, dereliction of duty and laziness, and spared no one who let the movement down. The perennial shortage of finances and other resources meant that gifts in kind had to be carefully shared. Comrade OR was often seen to mediate perceived preferences that someone was accused of having. He never tired of meeting all ranks of ANC members, seeking to be briefed and to attend to the inevitable problems a movement without a home and spread all over the globe would have.

In 1987 IDAF, based in Islington, North London, was approached more frequently (indirectly, since IDAF was also a banned organisation), by South African lawyers who represented children and young persons who had been detained and incarcerated in jails without charge or access to family or lawyer. The reports spoke of these young people being tortured and abused by warders and prison inmates alike. At one stage there were regularly thirty thousand people held under the detention laws, a good third of them who were juveniles. Young people, as in 1976, were once more at the forefront of struggle.

I proposed to the Bish that IDAF should organise a conference where testimony of these happenings could be exposed and the resulting world-wide publicity could increase the pressure on the apartheid authorities even further. The Bish agreed immediately and requested me to organise this in Harare, Zimbabwe. We had a plan to bring as many witnesses out of South Africa as we could. Huddleston's love of children and his support of their rights had been central throughout his life.

The first thing we did was inform the ANC of our plan. Together we sought an appointment with Comrade OR. He gave us his blessings and in fact arranged that the ANC underground would ensure that people attend from every far-flung corner of South Africa. In all over seven hunderd people managed to cross the border and cram into Harare's Sheraton Hotel. The management complained that through their presence and the manifest poverty they displayed, we had reduced the five star hotel to one star status. The evidence from witnesses, courageous children and mothers as well as from lawyers, clergy and a multitude of activists over a five-day period in Harare was harrowing. The trauma inflicted on a whole generation of South Africans would remain a scar that could not easily be healed.

Comrade OR attended throughout and met individually with each and every person who came. He countered the anger, frustration, hurt and pain they had endured with a mixture of compassion and motivation not to give up, but to steel themselves for the final hurdle. I was impressed by his confident message of hope that liberation was no longer a distant dream.

He closed the Harare proceedings with his famous and historic speech in which he quoted the white Afrikaans poet, Ingrid Jonker:

> The child is not dead
> The child lifts his fists against his mother
> Who shouts Afrika! Shouts the breath
> Of freedom and the veld
> In the locations of the cordoned heart . . .
>
> The child is not dead
> Not at Langa nor at Nyanga
> Nor at Orlando nor at Sharpeville
> Nor at the police post at Phillipi
> Where he lies with a bullet through his brain ...

Writing this contribution has made me aware that it was difficult to get close to Comrade OR. Although we had built a relationship of immensely powerful trust, he remained a private person, both through his own conduct and through his office as President of a movement in which his senior officials filtered and controlled interaction with him. Nevertheless, Comrade OR represented for me the hope and aspiration of a new, fair and equitable South Africa in which poverty, ignorance, disease, colour and class would be removed.

REFERENCES

Ingrid Jonker, *Selected Poems* (London: Cape, 1968).

MY INESCAPABLE SOUTH AFRICA

Paul Oestreicher

As a seven-year-old child I fled with my Jewish-born father and my mother from Nazi Germany to New Zealand where I grew up. Twenty-one years later as a young priest in the East End of London I knew how much I had in common with those who had fled from apartheid South Africa. The poison of racism is the same everywhere. With head and heart I knew that South African exiles and I were on the same side. In the years that followed, Oliver Tambo and his comrades of the ANC were engaged in a struggle from which I would not and could not stand aside. Oliver's wisdom, humanity and dignity matched that of Nelson Mandela, the imprisoned leader whom the world would eventually recognise as the greatest statesman of our age. South Africa's freedom, which Oliver knew would come, was the fruit of many years of patient struggle. Our bonds were deepened by a faith we shared.

It was the Sharpeville massacre of 21 March 1960 that first made my blood boil. I still see the pictures of running people who were shot in the back. A group of us, all young curates, put our heads and hearts together and decided to pledge a regular part of our small salaries to help the victims. It was so little, but it forged our commitment. We sent the money regularly to Archbishop Joost de Blank who had appealed on behalf of the devastated families. Beginning with that commitment, South Africa became part of my life. Even as a student in New Zealand, editing my university's undergraduate newspaper, I had published the stirring story of Revd Michael Scott's battle against white racism in southern Africa.

345

Reading Trevor Huddleston's *Naught for your Comfort* and Alan Paton's *Cry, the Beloved Country* and, in the years that followed, the impressive literature of André Brink and others opened channels of understanding of the nature of apartheid's oppression. The constant challenge was to counter white racism in Britain, its ever-present sympathy for white kith and kin and its unthinking condemnation of 'black terrorism'. To speak and write, to open a window to others, seemed the most important thing to be done.

In all this Trevor Huddleston, when he returned to England, was my inspiration, guide and friend until his death. More hands-on were my regular meetings at Canon John Collins's home, which eventually became the powerhouse of IDAF, that incredible undercover legal lifeline for those fighting against enormous odds. There were long discussions about whether I should join the staff at 2 Amen Court as the Canon's assistant, but that, in the end, did not seem to be the wisest use of my skills.

From 1961, as a BBC producer, I was able to help keep the struggle against apartheid in the forefront of the Religious Broadcasting Department's output. Canon Roy McKay, the department's visionary head, was firmly on my side, but that was not easy in the face of an overcautious bureaucracy.

In 1964 I joined the staff of the International Department of the BCC. That meant I was part of an international Christian network centred on the WCC. The defence of its controversial Programme to Combat Racism later became central to our work. The BCC itself embarked on a thorough study of the South African situation in 1968. *Violence in Southern Africa*, the Mason Report, was published in 1970 and became an important educational resource. Its sober analysis convinced many doubters.

It was poignantly prefaced with this text by an unknown poet:

> Because my mouth is wide with laughter
> And my throat is deep with song
> You do not think I suffer
> Although I have held my pain so long.
>
> Because my mouth is wide with laughter
> You do not hear my inner cry
> Because my feet are gay with dancing
> You do not know I die.

The exiled Bishops Ambrose Reeves and Colin Winter became friends and advisers. Sharing the pain of their experience widened my knowledge, deepened my commitment and made me determined to see the country for my-

self. The BCC's contacts were mainly with the SAC and the Christian Institute led by that unique and counter-cultural Afrikaner man Beyers Naudé.

In 1968 I was appointed to lead a team ministry in the Diocese of South-
wark, with an understanding that I would continue my work in international affairs. Living not far from my Blackheath parish was a wonderfully
good-humoured priest who was the Director of the WCC Theological Education Fund. His name was Desmond Tutu. Desmond, his wife Leah and
their children became the living face of South Africa on our doorstep. John
V. Taylor, the prophetic General Secretary of the Church Mission Society
(CMS) also lived nearby. He foresaw Desmond's future and invited him to
preach at his consecration as Bishop of Winchester in Westminster Abbey. In
that sermon the glorious liberty of the children of God that Desmond per-
sonifies with such warmth shone through.

In 1975 I was elected Chairman of the British Section of Amnesty International. The denial of human rights in South Africa became even more
directly my business. Tragedy and death on a large scale were looming. It was
around this time that a young chieftain came to visit England to raise money
for a Zulu newspaper. For two weeks I was Chief Buthelezi's host. He stayed
at the Diocesan Retreat Centre of which I was chaplain, an association that
would have significant consequences many years later.

The year 1976 was marked by such tragedy and suffering in South Africa that Beyers Naudé invited me to see for myself and record some of the
stories of suffering and death. I briefed myself as best I could and took advice
from many, perhaps the most valuable proving to be from that wise liberal
opponent of apartheid, Sir Robert Birley. To learn more, he sent me to one
of his brightest South African protégés, Neville Alexander.

But how would I get into the country? Surely I'd be turned down. Using
my New Zealand passport, my application for a visa was predictably refused.
That fired my determination. I wrote to the Home Secretary, explained
the situation, and as Chair of British Amnesty with long years of residence
asked for a UK passport. With that, I needed no visa although I might still be
turned back on arrival in South Africa. I was, almost to my surprise, made a
British citizen in record time.

I gave my occupation, then still entered in every passport, as 'Clerk'. Would
an Afrikaans-speaking immigration official know that this was (as confirmed
on my ordination certificate) the old English word for a priest? I gambled
that he or she would not. Still apprehensive, I arrived at Jan Smuts Airport (as
it was then known). The desk officer consulted his book of undesirables and
found my name. He pondered: was this British clerk the same as that New
Zealand clergyman? There was a long pause. 'Are you really from Britain?

And you are a clerk?' He stamped my passport. I was in. So far, so good.

I was met by Beyers Naudé who had worked out a strategy. He feared that I would soon be identified and then deported so there was no time to waste. We drove straight to the British embassy in Pretoria and requested the Ambassador to write to the Minister of Justice with the news that the Chairman of Amnesty International in Britain had come to see South Africa for himself, something his government was fond of telling people to do. I would be happy to meet the Minister at his convenience. My expulsion, after a letter like that, would have triggered a diplomatic incident.

But would a British diplomat be prepared to get up the nose of a friendly government? I didn't think so. Put on a dinner party for me, yes. But not that.

Beyers Naudé knew better. The Ambassador wrote immediately, not to the Minister of Justice but to the Prime Minister. Had he been tipped off? Not until then did I remember Robert Birley saying to me, 'Our man in Pretoria was one of my boys at Eton. You can trust him.' Here was evidence that the fabled British old boy network has its merits. The Prime Minister offered me an appointment with the Chief Secretary at the Foreign Ministry. I fixed it for the last day of my planned visit. Along with that offer there was another which was unstated but which would soon be obvious. BOSS, the Bureau of State Security, would do its best to be my constant and vigilant companion.

Quite early on David Russell, later Bishop of Grahamstown, took me for a walk to the top of Table Mountain. For the first but not the last time I was struck by the breathtaking natural beauty of the country, such a contrast to its troubled society. This walk had its lighter side. Our corpulent tail found it hard to keep up with us. Compassionately, as befits two clerics, we slowed down. When David was later imprisoned, I felt that he and not I should wear a Russian Orthodox priest's cross which had survived with its owner for many years in Stalin's gulag. David accepted it as a symbol of the deep bond between prisoners of conscience the world over. I had been given the cross by the Russian priest while on a clandestine visit to him after his release.

For three weeks I met victims of the system, heard of beatings and torture and death. It was harrowing. The Christian Institute had put together a full and demanding programme for me. In Cape Town Helen and Theo Kotze, later banned, exiled and near neighbours in England, were good humoured and adventurous hosts. Archbishop Hurley gave me probably the most incisive and accurate analysis of South Africa's divided society. In his quiet determination and utter dedication to a more just future he made a deep impression on me, as did Helen Joseph with her tough and quiet dignity.

But most moving were ordinary black people who had suffered terribly yet showed no sign of bitterness. This was especially true of the women whose men were in prison or dead. Listening to them was both disturbing and inspiring. Cedric Mayson, later to join the ANC in exile and today the party's religious adviser, had a pilot's licence. At dead of night he flew me illegally to Kimberley to meet the banned and already ill but remarkably wise and kind Robert Sobukwe. Two unforgettable hours passed far too quickly. BOSS missed out on that excursion and on an unbooked commercial flight to Namibia, then still firmly in South African hands. My dossier of evidence was growing.

Donald Woods, that bold journalist whose eventual escape from South Africa made world headlines, lent me his car to drive to King William's Town and see something of rural South Africa. The fate of Steve Biko to whom Donald was so close, has haunted me ever since that long and lonely drive.

On my last full day in the country Brian Brown, administrator of the Christian Institute, went with me to the Ministry of Foreign Affairs. Brian was later banned, as was the Christian Institute. In exile he became my most valued colleague as Africa Secretary of the BCC. Chief Secretary Botha listened. He could not have liked what he heard. I asked him to pass my findings on to the Ministry of Justice: evidence of massive injustice. He had few arguments to counter what I had seen for myself. It was, in fact, the same message that a stony-faced Archbishop Michael Ramsey of Canterbury later gave to the Prime Minister – with no handshake for the photographers.

On my departure, the Christian Institute had summoned journalists to the airport for an impromptu press conference. Before leaving I was able to share something of what I had learnt with those still able to print uncomfortable truths, which they did the next day.

My walk to the plane was on a tightrope. Would I, as I'd been warned, be searched and lose all I was carrying, not just documents but a whole dossier of photographs by Peter Magubane for Eve Arnold of *Magnum*? My guardian angel worked well. Everything was saved. The pictures were published in New York as *Magubane's South Africa*, one of the finest pictorial records of apartheid society.

Until Nelson Mandela's release, a return to South Africa was now clearly impossible. Before things got better they were to get a lot worse. Theo Kotze, Cedric Mayson, Brian Brown and their families now joined the exiles. Beyers Naudé, though banned, carried on the struggle at home in a remarkable pastoral ministry to the many who saw in him a beacon of hope. The Christian Institute of Southern Africa Trust was set up as a modest British charity which Brian Brown administered and which kept alive the spirit of the Institute which had been a unique example of prophetic ecumenism.

As conditions in South Africa were steadily deteriorating, the government sent a new kind of ambassador to London. Denis Worrall was a brilliant communicator and had a liberal image. English, not Afrikaans, was his mother tongue. He presented a picture of South Africa to the British public that became less and less credible as the system became more and more repressive. In 1981 I rejoined the BCC as Secretary of its Division of International Affairs with Brian Brown at its Africa desk. Brian and I made a point of befriending the Ambassador. Not everyone thought that was wise but I have always believed in the importance of person to person dialogue with opponents. As the situation kept going from bad to worse, with Worrall on the BBC's *Today* programme saying the exact opposite, defending the indefensible, I wrote him a personal letter ending our relationship. There was no more point in talking. There was only one more thing he could still do to restore his integrity and to serve all the people of South Africa: he could resign and tell the world why. A few weeks later he did. I could hardly believe it. I am sure my letter was at most the straw that broke this camel's back. He had lied enough. Bit by bit the system was beginning to unravel.

When I did return, it was to a South Africa in the process of a painful rebirth. Nelson Mandela was free, Desmond Tutu was by now Archbishop of Cape Town and by far the most loved Anglican churchman the world had ever seen. Dr Mamphela Ramphele was Vice Chancellor of the University of Cape Town. It all seemed too good to be true but it was by no means clear that the journey to democracy would be smooth.

In Natal a bitter conflict between the ANC and Inkatha was close to civil war. Many lives now hung on how Mangosuthu Buthelezi would act. Would he join the new South Africa or hold out for a separate Zulu nation? Someone remembered that I knew him. I was asked, as the guest of the Bishop of Natal, to visit Ulundi, talk to Chief Buthelezi and join those trying to persuade him to put an end to conflict by joining a new freely elected government. I agreed, but I had no illusions about the difficulty of the task. Buthelezi made much of his Anglican churchmanship. I hoped he would trust me as an emissary of his Church. I made two separate visits, flown to Ulundi in the Chief's personal aircraft, and had long conversations with him. I was convinced that he could serve both South Africa and his own interests – as well as save many lives – by coming in from the cold, but his advisers were telling him something very different.

He listened. I think he respected me, but had he really understood?

Certainly this was only one very small part of a highly complex diplomatic process. I had no way of knowing that it would end well. Nevertheless, I felt it to be a great privilege at such a time of fear and hope in equal measure to be able to share in this important process of reconciliation.

Two conflicts had dominated the greater part of my working life. During the Cold War, building Christian bridges across the Iron Curtain was at the heart of my ministry. Alongside it was the struggle for a free South Africa. The Soviet Union and apartheid died more or less at the same time. After that, I felt almost as though I would have to re-invent myself. Amazingly I saw the Berlin Wall come down on television in Desmond Tutu's study in Bishopscourt, Cape Town. Amazingly too, the little Archbishop with a big heart had humanised this palace, an anachronistic survival of English ecclesiastical imperialism. Much more importantly he helped to humanise – through the Truth and Reconciliation Commission – one of the most remarkable political transformations in human history.

What I have gained from the privilege of sharing in that process is much greater than anything that I might have contributed. To have played a small part within the intricate global network that helped facilitate this transformation was an empowering experience. To be given the opportunity to tell my part of this story in honour of Oliver Tambo is reason to be deeply grateful.

HOSPITALITY AT MUSWELL HILL

Judith Scott

It was a cold and wintry day in London in the early 1980s. I had been attending a meeting at Christian Aid trying to mobilise a churches support network for South Africa. This was in response to the call from South Africa where so many people were being arrested. After my meeting I made for Bounds Green station and the home of the Tambo family where I had been invited to stay for the night. I always went to their home by a devious route knowing full well that it was under constant surveillance. As always, I was greeted with much warmth and hospitality.

The Tambos were first introduced to me when they left South Africa in the 1960's. It was through Revd Simeon Nkoane who was a friend of Oliver's and who was himself brought to the UK by the Community of the Resurrection. At that time I was living with my parents in South London. We already knew other South African exiles through my involvement with Christian Action (the forerunner of the AAM) and felt deeply the plight of Oliver, Adelaide and the family. When my parents and I first met them we felt their sense of isolation at being so far from home and in such a foreign land. We were able to call with some goodies from time to time in the hope that we could contribute in a small way to their general well-being. During these visits we were made to feel very special whereas, in fact, it was they who were special. Such hospitality was symptomatic of their warm personalities.

Not long after the Tambos arrived in the UK I married, moved to Cardiff and then to mid-Wales. Over the years we kept in touch and I became more and more involved in the struggle against apartheid. As the years went by I greatly valued my conversations and the wisdom of the advice from the Tambos. I recall a discussion following one of the indiscriminate bomb attacks by the IRA. At that time some in the UK were trying to liken the ANC struggle to that of the IRA actions and therefore to categorise the ANC as a 'terrorist' organisation. People such as myself were in constant arguments about this and so it was important for me to hear from 'the top' a confirmation of my conviction. I was told very firmly that the aim of the ANC was to target specifically the South African state and its agents and not innocent people. This view put so eloquently, and with such conviction, strengthened my resolve to continue to challenge those in the UK seeking to undermine the struggle against apartheid.

I knew of both Oliver and Adelaide's deeply held Christian beliefs. Indeed, that at one time Oliver had very seriously considered becoming a priest. This was a source of support and affirmation to me as my own Christian faith had been severely tested during my stay in South Africa in 1953. I had witnessed so much racism and inhumanity perpetrated by those who purported to be Christian. What a contrast to the warmth of the hospitality I received at Muswell Hill.

In the 1980s I visited South Africa fairly regularly to help Simeon Nkoane of the Community of the Resurrection who by now was Suffragan Bishop of the East Rand. I was appalled at the plight of the children in the townships and Bishop Simeon asked me to try to get some of the youth leaders out of South Africa to continue their education in the UK. Back in the UK I found that I was being criticised for 'bringing South Africans out of their own environment'. This amazed me considering the alternative for these young people in South Africa seemed to be almost certain imprisonment and possibly death. However, my confidence was shaken as to whether I was doing the right thing and so a visit to Muswell Hill was called for. I shared the comments I had received. I was greatly encouraged to be told very firmly that it was easy for people in the relative security of the UK to make statements like that when young people were dying in South Africa. I was encouraged to go ahead and get as many youngsters out as possible. So it was that The Bishop Simeon Trust came into being and continues to this day. I have my visits to Muswell Hill to thank for so much encouragement and sound advice. My abiding memory is of the generosity of spirit and deep humanity that pervaded Oliver's whole being.

RELUCTANT FREEDOM FIGHTER

Desmond Tutu

The pass laws in South Africa were a much-hated symbol of the inferior status of blacks in their motherland where they were really not even second-class citizens. In fact, they were not regarded as citizens of any sort. The Land Acts designated 87 per cent of the best land for the use of whites exclusively although they were but 20 per cent of the population. The vast majority, the blacks, had to make do with the remaining 13 per cent where they were expected to eke out a living on land that was hardly arable and which soon deteriorated from overpopulation and overgrazing. These were the so-called Native Reserves, which were really reservoirs to supply cheap labour to the white areas.

A few black men were recruited from the reserves to work in the white man's town but only as migrant workers who were screened by a rigid system of influx control. They lived an unnatural existence in single-sex hostels, prey to prostitution and substance abuse.

The pass laws were the means of maintaining this control. Some blacks were permitted to live with their families in segregated areas called locations and later townships, which almost always had no street lighting, running water, water-borne sewerage or paved streets. They were ghettos of squalor, deprivation and poverty, and because they were really dormitories for the white man's labourers, no black man had right of residence. No, we were tolerated by the grace and favour of our white overlords and the pass we carried from the age of sixteen indicated whether or not we had permission to be where we might happen to be. It was not like a normal identity document since it was a criminal offence not to have it on your person if you were black. If, for example, I left my office to buy a newspaper across the road and was accosted by a constable and asked to produce my pass and I told him I had left it in my office in my coat pocket, strictly speaking, I was liable for arrest.

The police carried out regular pass raids and they would often be seen herding a column of blacks handcuffed together because their papers were not correct.

My father, a school principal and a fairly important person in the black community, suffered the indignity of being stopped many times and asked for his pass. The irony was that he belonged to a small group of black men who carried not passes but 'exemptions' – declaring that they were exempted from the provisions of the pass laws. It was ironic that they had to carry an 'exemption certificate' to prove that they were a privileged group – show a special pass to show that you do not have to show a pass.

When I became the Dean of Johannesburg, a fairly senior position in the Church hierarchy, I still had to go to the pass office to have my document stamped to say I was properly 'influxed'. My wife's document declared that she was permitted to be in the magisterial area of Johannesburg as long as she remained married to me. She had no legal status in her own right. One day an apartheid government Cabinet Minister spoke more truly than he probably intended when he referred to our old age pensioner parents and grandparents as 'superfluous appendages'.

You can understand how the pass laws had become such a hated symbol of our daily humiliations when our dignity was trodden callously underfoot and our noses rubbed mindlessly and unfeelingly in the dust. The pass laws declared most blatantly that we did not have even the rudimentary right of freedom of movement in the land of our birth and contradicted a fundamental tenet of the Freedom Charter that had been adopted at the historic Congress of the People in 1955 in Kliptown near Johannesburg – that South Africa belonged to all who lived in it.

People bristled at the whole apartheid dispensation and found the pass laws an apt symbol of their subjugation and so concentrated their opposition on this pernicious aspect of apartheid, much as the Soweto and other high school students in June 1976 bristled at Afrikaans as a medium of instruction when, in fact, they were opposing the entire inferior Bantu Education system.

Both the ANC and the PAC decided to engage in the Anti-Pass Law Campaign in 1960. Volunteers were to leave their passes at home and present themselves for arrest at police stations. On 21 March 1960 a crowd a few hundred strong congregated outside the police station in Sharpeville about 48 kilometres to the south of Johannesburg. The police, greatly outnumbered, panicked and opened fire on an unarmed and peaceful crowd. Sixty-nine people were mown down, most shot in the back. The international community was appalled, foreign investments were withdrawn and there was a run on the South African currency. Prime Minister Hendrik Verwoerd was belligerent. He imposed a State of Emergency. The police detained several political activists in a countrywide swoop and both the PAC and the ANC were banned. The organisations went underground. Those of their members who were not detained and who could, skipped the country into exile to become the liberation movements that had reluctantly opted for the armed struggle because the apartheid government had become even more intransigent.

The Bishop of Johannesburg, Dr Ambrose Reeves, had been very active in the aftermath of Sharpeville, collecting damning evidence about the conduct of the police and the kind of ammunition they had used, and in ferrying the wounded to hospital. He was a huge embarrassment to the government who summarily deported him back to England. The Church of England handled him like a hot potato and did not, as many had hoped, give him a prestigious appointment for his courageous ministry and witness in South Africa. He ended up becoming General Secretary of the Students' Christian Movement (SCM) based in London. One of the last things he had done in Johannesburg was to accept Oliver Reginald Tambo as an Ordinand prior to his going to theological college to train for the priesthood. OR, as he was affectionately known, had wanted to be a priest after being a brilliant teacher and later the senior partner in the Mandela-Tambo legal firm.

The Church lost someone who would have been an outstanding priest when the ANC ordered OR to leave the country to head up its organisation in exile, oversee its military training and be its chief representative abroad. This was a tall order. It is a measure of the man that in a relatively short space of time, cadres were receiving military training in various countries, camps had been established and an orderly movement in exile came into being. OR had his work cut out to get the ANC accepted in fairly conservative European countries as a legitimate liberation movement that had espoused non-violent means to change apartheid but had been compelled by the intransigence of the apartheid regime to adopt the armed struggle. Most easily dubbed the ANC a terrorist organisation and Margaret Thatcher famously dismissed Nelson Mandela as a terrorist (although the Conservative Party has subsequently apologised for that insult).

OR was a self-effacing, modest and reserved person. I recall a typical story about him. He had prominent tribal markings on his face. In South Africa most of those who worked for municipalities as refuse and nightsoil collectors came from his part of the world. One day he went into hospital because a fishbone had stuck in his throat. A young, impertinent nurse, not knowing who he was, asked mockingly, 'Hey, Mr Dustbin Collector, didn't you know fish have sharp bones?' Apparently OR never let on who he was. I suspect that when she did discover his identity she would have wished the earth could open up and swallow her. Even if the story is an apocryphal one, it tells us volumes about OR's gentle, attractive character.

First meeting

I went to study at King's College in London in 1962. My family and I lived in Golder's Green, North London, and our apartment at No. 2 St Alban's Close was next door to the SCM headquarters where Bishop Ambrose Reeves had his offices. My wife and I met Oliver Tambo and Adelaide, his wife, when Bishop and Mrs Reeves invited us to a meal in their house. OR had a gentle smile and was very soft spoken. I am not sure that we met him again in the three years we lived in London, but we saw Adelaide frequently. She was a great help to us as a nursing sister because we had three young children and a baby on the way. She was like an older sister who was concerned about our well-being and comfort.

Now I know why I don't think I saw OR again in the three-year period. He was hardly ever at home. I have come to realise the enormous sacrifices he and his family made for our liberation. He had to attend to building up the ANC in exile. He had to travel around the world soliciting support for the struggle, persuading Western and other governments that the anti-apartheid movement was a struggle worth supporting as a genuine, noble and idealistic cause. He, and those who worked with him – Thabo Mbeki as his aide, and many others – did a splendid job judging from how the anti-apartheid movement became a global movement that galvanised so many. We were fortunate to have one of OR's best friends, Archbishop Trevor Huddleston, on our side. OR and Trevor were a formidable pair, but OR's commitments meant that his family hardly ever saw him.

Subsequent meetings

I became General Secretary of the SACC in 1978. From the outset I made it clear in public statements that whilst I did not agree with the ANC's methods, I supported the organisation in its goals to abolish apartheid and to establish a just, democratic and non-racial South Africa. I went on to say that I understood why the ANC had opted for using violence, but that the primary violence was the violence of apartheid.

I would not allow the apartheid government to dictate who my friends would be and so I announced that I would be ready to meet with the ANC leadership. In doing so I took the wind out of the sails of the South African government which would have loved nothing better than to show that the SACC was simply the ANC at prayer, and would have gleefully revealed any private contacts I might have had with the organisation. So mine was a pre-emptive strike. I always announced ahead of time whilst I was in South Africa if I was likely to meet any of the so-called terrorists. Despite all my own caution, I was deeply touched by OR's solicitude.

The Archbishop of Canterbury, Dr Robert Runcie, told me he would make a venue available for my meeting with OR at Lambeth Palace should we want it. OR inquired whether I really was sure I did want to meet him given the hostile attitude of the South African government to such encounters. I assured him I did want to meet with him whatever the South African government's reaction would be. We had a happy meeting and I found him a charmingly attractive personality. With his black-framed spectacles he looked more like an Oxford don, somewhat owlish, than would have been the conventional image of a freedom fighter.

The Anglican Bishops of the worldwide Communion meet at the invitation of the Archbishop of Canterbury in what are known as the Lambeth Conferences at ten-year intervals. In 1985 we convened in Lambeth Palace.

Archbishop Runcie had arranged for me to meet with the then Prime Minister Margaret Thatcher. I had a fifty-minute meeting in which I talked for twenty of those minutes and she used up the rest. I was trying to persuade her to agree to impose sanctions on the apartheid regime. She was quite charming, but the lady was not for turning. Despite the fact that she had imposed sanctions on Argentina during the Falklands War, she argued that sanctions were not effective, inflicting suffering on those we wanted to help, in this case, blacks. She was far more supportive of Chief Buthelezi who opposed sanctions too. At the end of our meeting she did not accompany me to the front door as she normally did with other guests to address the press gathered there. After all, as I indicated earlier, she did regard Nelson Mandela as a terrorist.

After this No. 10 Downing Street encounter, I had another meeting with OR, this time near the Oval in South London in the house of Martin Kenyon, godfather of our youngest child as I am godfather to his youngest. Martin knew most of the African political leaders whom he had met when they were either students or exiles or, more usually, both.

Before our meeting we started with the celebration of the Eucharist.

Thabo Mbeki who was accompanying OR did not attend, but paced up and down outside smoking his pipe until we had finished. OR was a regular communicant and deeply devout.

More and more significant groups in Europe began to change their views about violence and the armed struggle. I recall how the German Church leaders caused a stir when they announced their support for the ANC. One of them described the crucial meeting that OR addressed which had then led to their changed policy.

He told me that Oliver spoke quietly and persuasively. He told them about his own pilgrimage and that he had actually intended to go to seminary for ordination training. The German Church leader said you could have heard a pin drop as he described life in South Africa and all the efforts they had made to try to effect change non-violently, how Sharpeville had been the last straw and the ANC had been left with no alternative but to opt for the armed struggle. There was hardly any one in the German Church leadership who remained opposed after that deeply moving testimony.

It was an important coup for our struggle. The Commonwealth was poised to support the imposition of sanctions on South Africa. Mrs Thatcher was the major stumbling block. Its Secretary-General, Sir 'Sonny' Ramphal, did all he could to marshal support for sanctions and to legitimise the ANC. He hosted a glittering reception at Marlborough House for Archbishop Trevor Huddleston, President of the International Anti-Apartheid Movement, and for Oliver Tambo. I recall it as if it were yesterday. Archbishop Trevor spoke eloquently as always. Then it was OR's turn. He leant against the wall and removed his glasses, evoking very strongly again the image of the erudite but somewhat absentminded don. Then he said quietly, 'I am a terrorist.' The utter absurdity of the assertion showed how preposterous and devoid of any credibility it was. I don't know that he said much else after. Only the utterly stubborn and wilfully blind could persist in condemning the struggle that the ANC was waging as terrorism.

Conclusion

How deeply indebted we all are to a truly remarkable man. OR and I met again when I led a delegation of our Bishops as Archbishop to meet the ANC leadership in Lusaka, Zambia. He was a quiet presence as he presided over our gathering. He hardly spoke at all, letting his other colleagues and us hold forth at length and then at the end he gave a masterly summing up.

He was not phased by the fact that Nelson Mandela was the centre of attention and the celebrity par excellence. OR was properly self-assured and did not suffer from a sense of insecurity. After Madiba's release, OR urged him to use his celebrity status and charismatic qualities for the good of the cause. OR did not feel miffed that he was made to play second fiddle. Our debt to him is incalculable and we praise and thank God for this His good and faithful servant. Viva Tambo, viva the reluctant freedom fighter hero.

ARTISTS AND JOURNALISTS

'AN EXTRA DAY OF APARTHEID IS AN EXTRA DAY TOO LONG'

Victoria Brittain

I first met Oliver Tambo in New Delhi, during the Seventh Non-Aligned summit of March 1983, which I was covering for *The Guardian*. His first words to me were, 'Don't worry, my dear, if this interview is not printed; that is what we expect from the Western press.' That did something to lift the weight of responsibility which I had felt acutely as his assistant, Frene Ginwala, took me to Tambo's small hotel room, insisting along the way how very important it was that 'OR's views should reach the mainstream audience who read *The Guardian*.'

It was a very modest room, with only one chair, and I was taken aback to see Tambo perch on the bed next to me, insisting Frene take the chair. Like his reassurance about his words' probable non-appearance in the paper, the seating arrangements gave an endearing picture of a leader of a liberation movement unlike any other. Bodyguards, distracting aides taking notes, long waits and/or much rescheduling of meetings, was the normal experience for journalists trying to interview liberation movement leaders, not only in Africa. Tambo needed no such distancing mechanisms or self-aggrandisement to underline the heavy responsibility he personally carried. Nor had twenty years as a prime target for assassination by apartheid South Africa as he took over the exiled ANC leadership, with Nelson Mandela and so many others in prison on Robben Island, sown the seeds of paranoia which were so much part of the general febrile climate of the time and the area.

Tambo opened the interview with me by saying: 'In the 1950s Nkrumah used to say, "Freedom now", while we were more modestly saying, "Freedom in our life time".' Although Tambo was a lawyer by profession, he was a teacher and historian by vocation. Even to a class of one, he was instantly teaching, looking for the connections and context which would make you able to understand the enormity of the ANC's current task in the fight for justice in southern Africa. The link back to the high drama of the anti-colonial struggle, and the most charismatic and brilliant of Africa's then leaders, was a typical Tambo ploy to make you really think about the great historical upheaval which was the present goal, and which then seemed such a distant possibility.

Looking back twenty years Tambo remembered with a warm smile and evident pleasure, 'the deluge of the 1960s when liberation swept over the continent before grinding to a halt in the Portuguese colonies. Then of course came Namibia, and there we have stuck for much longer than we thought. But the occupation *will* collapse, and the impact on South Africa will be terrific.'

Those days of the early 1980s in southern Africa were drama underrecognised by all outsiders. They were marked by South Africa's undeclared, and barely reported, war against the Front-line States through its proxy armies of UNITA in Angola (which also had significant US support); Mozambique National Resistance (MNR), later known as Renamo; the Lesotho Liberation Army; the Matebele Brigade in Zimbabwe; and the *askaris* or 'turned' ANC members who were sent into Swaziland to kill ANC and MK cadres. South Africa's dirty war of assassinations across the region, and wider, was bleeding the ANC, though no outsiders knew then how badly. Inside the country young people were similarly killed, tortured, co-opted by the South African police counter-insurgency units. For all Tambo's restraint, it didn't take much empathy to read in his face how much of all this pain was his.

'White South Africa is fighting for survival with everything they have, and the first target is of course the liberation forces inside South Africa, and then extends beyond to the moral and political support in neighbouring countries.' Tambo explained the deal that South Africa had recently offered to countries across the region: expel the ANC and we will call off the guerrilla war:

> The South Africans offered these countries non-aggression pacts, by which they really mean they should hunt down the ANC within their territory. There is no aggression by any of these states

on South Africa . . . the South Africans know quite well that none of these countries are involved when we attack, in Pretoria for instance, hundreds of miles from the border.

He warned gravely of 'imminent raids' on the Front-line States that had refused the South African deal, citing the raids on Matola and Maseru in which 13 and 42 people had been killed. But just a year later, when Mozambique signed the Nkomati non-aggression pact with South Africa and the ANC was forced to leave Maputo, Tambo would have to lead the stunned ANC through a setback worse than even he had imagined when he talked to me about dark days to come.

Tambo spoke of the horrors exported by apartheid's destabilisation policy, as well as of the attempted dehumanisation of the majority at home. His soft voice was more telling than any rhetoric or emphasis, bringing into that small hotel room the violence on one side, and the heroism on the other, which he well knew I had not then seen for myself.

But it was when Tambo, the teacher, spoke of young South Africans that his eyes lit up, his famous smile grew, and he was in the element that most inspired him. The Soweto riots of 1976 had given the ANC new impetus, he said. 'The youth were catapulted into the struggle. Then they had to contend with a desperate attempt to divert them with scholarships [apparently a deliberate part of US policy], but large numbers took up arms and many are still coming out of the country – a struggle produces its own cadres.' He spoke of his great respect for the courage of the young and the spirit of self-sacrifice. He was far too modest a man to realise that to anyone who met him – and to millions who only heard about him – he was the incarnation of that spirit of self-sacrifice.

Outside the atmosphere of that room and Tambo's quiet preoccupation with his own people, the four main themes of the Non-Aligned summit were: disarmament, reform of the Bretton Woods economic institutions, a Palestinian homeland, and ending South African rule in Namibia. Majority rule in South Africa, for the rest of the world in 1983, was only a distant dream, or a mere slogan.

As a journalist who followed the grim events in the Front-line States and the rising tide of revolt inside South Africa, I saw Tambo many times in the dramatic days of the mid-1980s. He was always the same whenever I encountered him: warm, courteous, modest, a listener with the gift of making each person feel that his or her concerns and thoughts were important to him. Amazingly to me, Tambo always had time for a word in the corridors of the many Non-Aligned and OAU conferences where the fate of southern Africa was on the agenda as it never was in the Western press. Everyone else knew that he was the key figure in those rooms, but neither his face nor his manner ever gave the slightest hint of the weight of responsibility that must have been on him. These were meetings, such as the OAU in June 1983 in Addis Ababa, where the day started with a minute's silence for three ANC cadres hanged the day before, and the OAU Secretary-General Edem Kodjo called for Africa to get nuclear weapons to counter the threat of South Africa.

I used to watch Tambo sit so patiently through these interminable meetings which just might influence some people in some place to denounce apartheid, but I never forgot his words to me in New Delhi: 'The key is what people inside South Africa are doing. The way to persuade South Africa to listen to the rest of the world is greatly to step up the struggle inside.' The birth of the UDF, bringing together five hundred organisations, in early 1984, seemed to be just what he had been talking about to me the previous year. And in its leadership as well as membership it followed the strong commitment to building a non-racial new South Africa which Tambo's leadership held as an important part of ANC philosophy.

In Harare in September 1987 I saw Tambo literally swept off his feet by those very people from inside South Africa: UDF, church leaders, lawyers and children. The ANC's Conference on Children, Repressions and the Law in Apartheid was one of those key moments when the changing international climate about apartheid was palpable. It seemed like the expression of everything Tambo had taught me over the years: what mattered was what people inside the country were doing and, in particular, South African youth. South Africans from inside the country took Tambo, their President, their mythical leader, in their arms. But the elation was only one part of the mood of the moment. The conference had been postponed once because of fears of a South African attack, and all the leadership were deeply affected by the desperate sadness of the people from home, especially the children, who had taken the risk to come out. As one senior person put it, 'These days it is not easy being a South African leader; the burden of people's expectations gets heavier with every new phase of repression.'

Tambo sat to one side of the big conference centre, listening intently to every word of personal testimony from victims and the hardly less painful analysis from lawyers, doctors, priests and community organisers. His face became more and more grave as he listened. Every speaker started with a nod to him, and the words, 'Mr President'. The weight of the responsibility for these people, and the anguish he clearly felt, were in his own words to the conference:

... under that terrible order the children die, with bullets through their heads, welts on their bodies, hearts and brains stopped before they could attain maturity, because a person as ordinary as you and I, has inherited powers that go beyond all that is permissible in the conduct of relations among those we would all count as mortal.

A criminal tyranny that has the audacity to call itself a civilisation lives on across the borders of this country, Zimbabwe. It survives because humanity, and principally ourselves, has not yet said that an extra day of apartheid is an extra day too long ... We meet here today because we want to discuss the unspeakable plight of the black children in South Africa ... we meet because we recognise that our own lives have meaning only to the extent that they are used to create a social condition which will make the lives of the children happy, full and meaningful.

That was Tambo's public eloquence on behalf of the children he cared so much about. In private his tenderness to the wounded children and the distraught mothers was unstinting. For all of them, as for the exiled children in the ANC's school in Tanzania, or for the young MK soldiers training in Angola, Tambo personally was the incarnation of the ANC. Their trust in him was their trust in the organisation. For an outsider like me too, Tambo, with his dignity, his lack of pretensions, his straightness when you wanted to talk about difficult things, his warmth, his love of children, his selflessness, his tireless capacity for work, was the image of the ANC that has marked my life.

A REMARKABLE MAN

Evelyn de Rothschild

It is often difficult to remember on what date and at what time you meet a very remarkable man such as Oliver Tambo. He came to lunch at *The Economist* when I was Chairman and brought with him his team, including the now President Mbeki.

My memory suffices to highlight that Tambo expressed views on the tragic situation in South Africa in a manner which made me realise that he understood only too well that the solution would, at that time, take a great deal of patience – and that he might never see it. I was struck by his understanding and tolerance whilst at the same time appalled by the complete lack of dignity and understanding displayed by the South African government.

So although my memories are faint I can but say that this was a very remarkable man who in the end played a crucial part in solving the problem of apartheid and in bringing South Africa to its position today.

AMANDLA

Jonas Gwangwa
(extracts from an interview with Thami Ntenteni)

Thami Ntenteni (TN): When did you first meet OR?

Jonas Gwangwa (JG): Hmm . . . I had known of OR for a while, but I first met him when I was in New York. I went to New York in 1961 to study. I left *King Kong* where it was running in London and went to New York to the Manhattan School of Music. Then, in the summer of 1963 I went to London for a visit. I was meeting all the political exiles and when I was heading back to New York Mrs Tambo had a pair of pants she wanted to send to OR. He was in New York at the time, you see. So I took the pair of pants and when I delivered them that was the first time I saw OR.

TN: So there you were, carrying a pair of pants for the President of the ANC. What happened when you met him?

JG: Well, we started talking. He wanted to know what I was doing – studying music – and how I came to be settled in New York. We also talked about the struggle because I had my own ideas about it, and I'd had many people come to visit me after Sharpeville. My place was a meeting place for ANC and PAC students and we would talk about home and the struggle and everything. We came up with some wild ideas about flattening the country economically, introducing some counterfeit money or something. You know how patient OR was. He listened to me and then he started to explain and explain, and, of course, I came out of there an educated man.

TN: How did your subsequent encounters with OR unfold?

JG: Well, the second time I met him properly, was when I was summoned to Lusaka. I was living in Botswana because I had left the US in 1976. I went on a concert tour with Letta Mbulu, Caiphus Semenya, Dudu Phukwana and others in Botswana in 1976. And then in 1977, in Nigeria, I was also called in. And people came to Nigeria from all over the world, singers, dancers, musicians, poets and writers. You know, all kinds of disciplines. And we were there to perform. It was the first time for me and I didn't think it was going to work; it was a very big show. Anyway, we worked together and that was the prototype for Amandla. We talked about it, and OR passed by. I saw a little bit of him. After that first show, I was called to Lusaka to write down a memorandum for culture. The ANC wanted to develop a cultural policy. Again I met OR, very briefly, although I spent three weeks there with Lindiwe Mabuza drawing up the cultural memorandum. Then I was called to go to Angola to start Amandla. That's when I spent time with OR. We discussed music and culture and our relationship developed from there.

TN: I'm glad you have raised the issue of culture. Because most of the time we think of OR as a political leader and a political activist. We don't really get to explore this side of him, his outlook as far as culture is concerned. And how culture leads to the struggle for national liberation. I remember OR once saying that Amandla, musically, had done in a very short space of time, what the ANC could not have done, could not do, over a long period of time, through the speeches that it was delivering at the UN. Wasn't OR himself a choirmaster when he was a teacher?

JG: He was a conductor.

TN: So tell me more about the role of culture in the struggle?

JG: The thing is, when someone makes a speech it often only reaches a limited and selected audience, maybe a group that has been specially invited by an organisation. But when Amandla came, we had big, big concerts. We didn't only attract a few people who were aware of what was happening in South Africa or solidarity groups and the like. We attracted the general public. And the show was very relevant because it told the story of South Africa, the struggle as it was unfolding, beginning from pre-colonial days when the first settlers came to the country. Actually, we portrayed things before settlers came, how people lived and so on. That story mobilised a lot of people as did all the literature that we sold, *Sechaba*, *ANC Speaks*, and others. Sometimes it was difficult to get people back into the theatre after interval, you know, they were so busy buying those books. So the mobilisation went on, to the extent that, when we were in Brazil, for instance, we found that there was no ANC office. Amandla opened the office in Brazil, you know. When people are responsible they must act accordingly.

TN: Were you given much guidance with Amandla?

JG: No, not at all. I got a call to come to Angola and my wife arranged the ticket for me. There was some confusion over the ticket and the booking, but then I was ready and I went. But I hadn't been given any kind of briefing about what I was going to do. When I got to Angola, Mzwai Piliso (Head of Personnel in MK), stationed in Angola, was gone. And I asked the guys and commander Julius Mokoena, where is the group? They called the group and when they sang, I said to myself, 'Wow!' There was some serious talent, you know. But the songs were not well arranged and the dancers were poor. I didn't know what they wanted me to do but I decided that I was gonna build a show. I thought of all the things I'd been doing over the years. I'd learnt a lot from when I was doing *King Kong*, and I thought that I would try out all the things that I had learnt. I mean, OR was always collecting together dancers, singers and musicians, making up props and things, trying to have some kind of musical. We started doing a little sketch here and there. And it gradually grew over time, but there was no official briefing.

TN: Well, that's how the ANC operated at the time I suppose. To some extent it was an expression of confidence in your abilities. But what I'm trying to get a sense of is how OR related to Amandla. And how you related to him.

JG: When I arrived in Angola OR asked me what my needs were and he listened very carefully. He realised what it took to build the show. We needed costumes because the show had to be representative of the different black African groups in South Africa. And we needed the moves to be right. Then as we were going along, I started a band. There were some old beat up instruments there, a trumpet, a trombone. Now the band was growing and when we were on tour, we got more instruments. I ended up with a sixteen-piece band. Now there were musicians, there were singers, there were the actors, there were the poets, there were those doing stage sets, costumes and make-up. We all lived and rehearsed in this warehouse in Angola. And of course, there were always inputs and changes in the script. How about this or that? Amandla was always changing; every year it was different depending on what was happening in the struggle at home. And every time we came back from tour OR would call me to Lusaka to give a report. He would ask how it had gone; what else did we need? And he would offer advice on the show, on what to include.

TN: What are your impressions of the kind of person that OR was?

JG: OR was a very compassionate person. And when it came to the music, he was very serious. The music had to be relevant; it had to be representative of the struggle. Because Amandla was not only about entertaining; it was also about giving a political message and telling the international community that we had a vibrant living culture. I didn't just listen to OR's advice because he was the leader of the ANC. I listened to him because he was a musician and he knew what he was talking about. He helped quite a bit when it came to the choral part, and even with lyrics. He took some old classics and changed the lyrics to make them more revolutionary.

TN: If OR were alive today, what do you think his challenges would be?

JG: I think there are a whole lot of things that are happening now that OR would have been dealing with if he were alive. The tensions in the ANC, for example. He was the glue that held the ANC together. Even today I think that he would have been able to contain situations just by speaking to the people involved. None of us in this country really knows how this democracy works from the inside and so lots of mistakes are being made. Things will settle down, but OR could have helped this process because he was such a brilliant negotiator.

TN: OR might not be here now but he did, as it were, bring us home. Do you think, and this is obviously purely hypothetical, do you think that he would have felt that he had led a full life? Do you think he felt fulfilled as a person?

JG: As a musician I think he would have wanted to do more, would have wanted to have had time for something a little bit more relaxing. And I wish

372

that he had been around a little bit longer to see how the whole scene un-folded, just to see the results of all his hard work. You know how after an art-ist does a carving or a musician writes a song, they get the chance to sit back and appreciate their work, see how people react to it … In my view this is the kind of thing that OR didn't get to experience enough of.

A LONG WAY FROM GWELO

Michael Holman

They say no man can be a hero to his valet. By the same token, it would seem unlikely that a politician can ever be a hero to a journalist.

Just as the intimacy enjoyed by a servant sooner or later psychologically disrobes the master and exposes hitherto concealed flaws, so should a journalist's innate scepticism penetrate all pretensions. Above all, it should serve as armour against that dreadful possibility that one could end up admiring, and even – heaven help us – befriending, the man or woman we write about.

Some nevertheless break through this protective carapace, and find a place in one's heart. Alas, there was never the chance to find out if Oliver Tambo would have joined Nelson Mandela and Joe Slovo on my personal pedestal reserved for politicians I revere.

Tambo's disabling stroke came when the battle against apartheid was all but won, and thus his mettle was never tested to the full. We can never be sure that he would have made a success of the transition from opposition leader to head of government.

Nor did I know Oliver Tambo in the way I like to think I knew Joe Slovo, the SACP General Secretary and ANC guerrilla commander. We forged a friendship when we both lived in Zambia in the 1970s and 1980s, and the ANC had its offices in the capital, Lusaka.

I stayed in a cottage in the grounds of the Twin Palm Road home of Harry and Marjorie Chimowitz, the exiled South African couple who opened their home to Joe, Mac Maharaj, and so many others.

Joe would regularly drop in for a swim in their pool, or to watch football

374

on an old black and white television set in the lounge of the main house, his enjoyment of the game overcoming the erratic reception, the result of an uncertain relationship between the set and its aerial.

Oliver Tambo made regular visits to Lusaka, but not to Twin Palm Road. So I can offer no Tambo anecdotes from those years, nor claim to have shared a drink with him on the veranda of the Chimowitz's home. Indeed, I feel fortunate to be invited to contribute to this collection of tributes by many of his friends, for the truth is, I barely knew the man.

Yet I nevertheless hope that I qualify as a contributor to this celebratory volume on two counts. As a journalist, a good part of my career – first as the *Financial Times* Africa correspondent from 1976 to 1984 based in Lusaka, and then in London as the paper's Africa editor until 2002 – has been devoted to following the fortunes of South Africa. And that, of course, meant following the ANC under President Oliver Tambo.

The second reason is more personal.

I came to admire the man and the example he set, and the principles he stayed true to, for this helped to shape my own values. And this is an opportunity to explain how he came to play this role; and to say 'thank you' to a remarkable leader who had a crucial part in the forging of a democratic South Africa, and for which I believe he deserves more public credit.

★ ★ ★

I was brought up in what was then called Southern Rhodesia, the son of a South African mother from King William's Town, and a Cornish teacher who served in the Royal Air Force during the Second World War, based in Queenstown.

After a spell in Durban, the family moved north, and from the early 1950s we lived in the small town of Gwelo, now Gweru.

It was a golden period for us 'Europeans'. I was educated at Chaplin High School, where Ian Smith had been a pupil, a state school with all the facilities of a top English public school; as a Boy Scout, I roamed the countryside fearful only of snakes; and an illicit beer or cigarette in the school bus on the cricket team's trip to a border school called Plumtree was as close as one got to drugs.

Yet challenging the whites' sybaritic lifestyle of sundowners and servants, there came the rumble of African nationalism that was advancing south. The Belgian Congo was disintegrating, with Moise Tshombe seeking independence for the copper-rich province of Katanga, and white mercenaries were recruiting for his secessionist cause.

Most white Rhodesians, however, believed they could halt nationalism's march at the Zambezi River, sheltering behind what their minority government liked to call 'separate development' – apartheid by another name.

As a politically precocious Gwelo teenager, I lived in awe of a pantheon of politicians who led opposition to white rule: Nyasaland's (Malawi's) Hastings Banda, detained without trial in Gwelo's jail, which I would cycle past, marvelling that the man who vowed to destroy the Central African Federation of Northern and Southern Rhodesia and Nyasaland (and duly succeeded) was detained behind its whitewashed walls; Kenneth Kaunda, who led neighbouring Northern Rhodesia to independent Zambia; Julius Nyerere of Tanganyika, soon to become Tanzania's Prime Minister – 'Africa's evil genius' as Ian Smith, white Rhodesia's leader, later called him, in a back-handed compliment that Mwalimu relished; and Jomo Kenyatta, Kenya's first President.

All had an instinctive grasp of public relations. Banda had his dark glasses, pinstriped suit and flywhisk, a potent combination of Victorian values with a hint of voodoo. Kenneth Kaunda will be remembered for his ever-present white handkerchief, threaded through the fingers of his left hand; Kenyatta had his flywhisk; and Nyerere stood for modesty in his simple, open-necked safari suit never encumbered by a tie.

Missing from this group were men such as Albert Luthuli, Oliver Tambo and Nelson Mandela – partly because of my ignorance, and partly because they could not use those words, 'founding President', almost magical in their impact.

The triumph of Tambo and Mandela, the vindication of Luthuli was yet to come, and from my Gwelo perspective it seemed an impossibly long way off.

That era of relative calm was soon to be shattered.

In November 1965 Ian Smith unilaterally declared independence. Wars for the liberation of Angola and Mozambique intensified and the people of South West Africa struggled to become Namibia.

The 1974 coup in Portugal – colonial master to Angola and Mozambique for nigh on four centuries – was a seismic event for southern Africa. Lisbon surrendered its Africa claims. The guerrilla war in my homeland stepped up. By the mid-1970s white rule in Rhodesia was limping to an end.

In late 1979 I was at London's Lancaster House, helping Bridget Bloom, then the *Financial Times*'s Africa editor, report on negotiations that marked the conclusion of Mr Smith's costly rebellion.

It was during the Lancaster House talks that I went to interview the late Joshua Nkomo, co-leader with Robert Mugabe of Zimbabwe's guerrilla alliance, the Patriotic Front. When I entered his hotel room I barely noticed a figure sitting in the corner. Nkomo gestured towards his guest, who rose to greet me.

'Do you not know who this is?'

I took a further look. There was something familiar about him, but no, I could not place him. There was no Kaunda handkerchief, no Banda Homburg, no Kenyatta flywhisk, nothing that could jog my memory.

Nkomo gave a grunt of rebuke when I shook my head and introduced his guest: 'The next President of South Africa.'

I shook Oliver Tambo's hand, and apologised for my ignorance.

It was a long way from Gwelo.

★ ★ ★

More than three years later, in May 1983, Rhodesia's emergence as independent Zimbabwe had duly been celebrated. But the victory was a modest prelude to the battle to overthrow apartheid, which was now approaching its bloodiest stage.

The man I first met in London was due to hold a critical press conference at Nairobi airport.

A few days earlier a car bomb had created carnage in Pretoria, symbolising the ANC shift in strategy in the war against white rule. Seventeen people were killed and nearly two hundred were injured. The bomb, planted in a car in Nedbank Square, where the South African Air Force had its headquarters, went off at about 4:30 p.m., timed to cause the maximum damage at rush hour. Many of the wounded were dreadfully maimed.

Civilians, it seemed, had become fair game.

It was, declared Louis le Grange, then the Minister of Law and Order, the 'biggest and ugliest terrorist' incident since armed resistance had begun twenty years earlier.

These were grim days indeed. From white South Africa came the bully-boy threats, delivered by people who now are footnotes in the country's history, but who at the time had the power to put threats into practice with impunity.

While the ANC vowed to make South African black townships ungovernable, Pretoria's strategy was to defend apartheid on its neighbours' territory. Nowhere seemed safe. South Africa-backed UNITA leader Jonas Savimbi in Angola, took over from Rhodesia as the leading supporter of Renamo rebels in Mozambique, and did its best to make life uncomfortable for Robert Mugabe, Zimbabwe's first President.

Not even Botswana, as close to a model democracy as Africa offered, escaped unscathed. Violence seemed to have become endemic. Southern Africa was a region at war.

Were there to be a 'pain index', made up of people killed or wounded in battle, and of those who died as an indirect consequence of conflict – through food shortages, or for lack of basic medicine, or clinics destroyed, wells poisoned, bridges bombed, etc. – it surely would have peaked then. And for all the failures of today's southern Africa to realise ambitions and fulfil its potential, that pain index remains well below the horrific level of the mid-1980s . . . and notwithstanding the trials and tribulations of Zimbabwe, is slowly falling.

But I digress …

Back at that Nairobi airport press conference Oliver Tambo duly defended the Church Square blast. He accused the Pretoria government of driving the country's black community to violence, of using the South African military to suppress black political rights – and this was being met by what he called 'retaliatory violence'.

Yet for all the significance of his warnings, it was a disappointing performance. Something was missing. I did not expect a fire and brimstone denunciation of white rule and a belligerent defence of a policy that made civilians targets. That was not the style of the man. I certainly did not expect Oliver Tambo to follow the example of his friend and ally Joshua Nkomo, who would don an army uniform to emphasise his military qualities when he reviewed his guerrillas when they passed out from training camps in Zambia.

But as I listened to this 'gentle and gentlemanly' figure, as Patti Waldmeir, the *Financial Times*'s outstanding South Africa correspondent called him, it was clear his heart was not in the new strategy.

Two years later, the ambivalence came through again, this time when the ANC held an important strategy conference, its first since 1969, outside the small mining town of Kabwe. Delegates confirmed the drive to export violence from the townships to previously tranquil white areas.

After 'twenty fruitless years of selected sabotage', wrote Patti in her book *Anatomy of a Miracle*, the ANC warned of 'more bloodshed than ever before … blurring the distinction between "soft" civilian targets like supermarkets and schools, and "hard" targets like the military'.

For all the blood-curdling language, the threats still did not ring true. The ANC never did prosecute the civilian war with gusto. Its orders were contradictory. As Patti recounts, no sooner than Radio Freedom, the ANC radio station in exile, broadcast a call to black domestic workers to attack their white employers than Oliver Tambo would seem to retract it, warning against the ' "indiscriminate and senseless massacre of white civilians".'

At the time, I put it down to an inevitable gap between political rhetoric and pragmatic reality. Only as events unfolded did I belatedly come to understand what was happening. The war and its intensification was only half the picture. The other half, unbeknownst to me, was the early stages of a charm offensive, endorsed by Tambo and headed by Thabo Mbeki, which was intended to win over white South Africa.

Three years after the Pretoria bomb, in June 1986, a policy long in the making, and one that would have seemed inconceivable had a lesser man than Tambo been at the ANC helm, got under way.

At the Ford Foundation in New York, the first meeting took place between a representative of the apartheid establishment and exiled officials of the ANC led by Thabo Mbeki.

It was an extraordinary, seminal event, and the first fruit of a process that took leadership of utmost integrity to make credible. Not only was it an opening step in an attempt to bridge the country's racial divide; it represented a bridge within the ANC itself, between men such as the firebrand guerrilla leader, the late Chris Hani, intent on striking fear into white hearts, and Thabo Mbeki, wrapped in 'sweet reason and fragrant pipe smoke' as Patti put it, who preferred to charm whites all the way to defeat.

In short, Oliver Tambo had been riding two horses, one marked Reconciliation, the other called Resolve.

It might seem odd to suggest that during these bleak years the ANC matured under his leadership. After all, this was no fledging party. Founded in 1912, it was nearly as old as Britain's Labour Party; it supported votes for women before the franchise had been won by the suffragettes in the UK. It fought on when the National Party came to power in 1948, and survived the political trials of the early 1960s, when Nelson Mandela went to jail, and his friend Oliver Tambo went into exile.

Well ... if not matured, then it was certainly tested and not found wanting. Under Tambo's leadership, the ANC held its nerve, not deviating from its principles during the most demanding of times – never forgotten by those who survived them, all too often not appreciated by the post-apartheid generation of 'born frees' who have inherited the fruits of their parents' long struggle for democratic decency.

The rest, as they say, is history. Nelson Mandela became a hero for me and millions around the world, the iconic figure of the twentieth century.

But as I look back on the Tambo years, he grows in stature, for it becomes clearer that he laid the foundations of ongoing reconciliation that serves as a beacon in troubled times. I remember President Tambo for his courage in exile, his magnanimity as victory approached, the foresight with which he paved the way for modern South Africa, and for his steely compassion while pursuing an objective that seemed out of reach. Above all, he presided over a non-racial movement that was – and is – an inspiration to all who care about Africa.

On that joyful day of Nelson Mandela's inauguration as President in Pretoria in 1994, Oliver Tambo joined that pantheon of legendary African leaders who inspired a boy brought up in small-town Rhodesia.

I had indeed come a long, long way from Gwelo.

PAINTING A PORTRAIT

Gail Marcus

One day I received a phone call asking if I could paint a portrait of Oliver Tambo, which would be presented to him as a surprise present at his seventieth birthday party in London. As a South African artist living in exile in London, I was very excited and nervous about this request. Although I had seen Oliver Tambo at a distance as a speaker at various anti-apartheid meetings and rallies, and had done some quick ballpoint pen sketches of him, I had never actually met him.

The request was made at very short notice, about four days in all, and it took some time to find suitable photos to use as a reference. Consequently, I decided to use watercolour rather than my preferred medium of oil paint, which can take up to a year to dry. While I had used gouache, which is also a water-based paint, and most other painting media, I had hardly ever used watercolour, and was unfamiliar with the special problems and difficulties that it posed. There were several disasters before I managed to come up with something even reasonably satisfactory. Finally, in the nick of time, I managed to produce two portraits. When I took them in to those who had requested the portrait, they chose the painting that I had not photocopied, sadly leaving me with no record of the portrait.

The area of London in which Oliver Tambo lived was not known to me, and I arrived after the portrait had been presented. I was told that Oliver Tambo was very happy with it. I remember rooms crowded with people, noise, lots of talk, and moving from room to room, hearing speeches from the back of a crowd, and being offered food and drink, but I don't remember seeing the great man himself.

Until then, Oliver Tambo had been a legend known to me only from anecdotes by family and friends, and from the black and white photos of the 1950s. With his trilby hat and short stature, he reminded me of our family friend Casim Patel, a fellow South African and freedom fighter who knew Oliver Tambo very well.

It was Casim who introduced me to MB Yengwa, at an ANC bazaar in London. MB was a lifelong ANC member who had been part of the ANC Youth League, together with Tambo and Nelson Mandela, and was also one of the treason trialists. I asked MB if I could do a quick sketch of him. MB liked the sketch so much that he asked me to paint his portrait. While sitting for this picture, MB told me about an incident that had occurred when he and several other ANC activists, including Oliver Tambo, were arrested and thrown into the back of a police van, where they were forced to sit on the floor. The policemen who were guarding them began speaking to each other about how they had no time for 'these ANC people'.

'But there is one I really admire,' said one of the policeman. 'That is Oliver Tambo.'

'Oh,' said Oliver. 'Do you like him?'

'Shut up you!' shouted the policeman, and shoved him back into submission.

Somebody once told me that despite the large amount of gossip in exile politics, 'No one ever gossiped or had a bad word to say about OR, and that's really saying something.' He was universally loved.

While Oliver Tambo was President of the ANC, every January we discussed his New Year statement in our ANC units. These were speeches made each year on the anniversary of the foundation of the ANC, which provided a comprehensive analysis, motivation, and guide for the priorities and action for the coming year. One person would prepare and lead the discussion, which was often passionate and lengthy. Every word was looked at, questioned, argued over, and discussed.

I didn't get to meet Oliver Tambo until much later, in 1989 or 1990, when, as a member of the Regional Political Committee of the ANC, in London, I was invited to his house, along with the other members of the committee. Oliver Tambo had recently suffered a stroke. When Mandela came to London, following his release from prison, he told how Tambo, according to his doctors, shouldn't be alive. They had said he wouldn't recover, but OR, with his great fighting spirit, proved them wrong. Once he had recovered sufficiently to receive visitors, he had expressed a desire to be involved with what was going on, and invited us to come and talk to him.

We were greeted by OR and members of his family. I remember the look of pride on the face of his son, Dali, as his father came forward. This particularly struck a chord with me as only a few years earlier, doctors had told us that my father would never get better and needed long term hospital care. He too defied their prognosis and made a good recovery.

My first impression of Oliver Tambo was of his great kindness, modesty and simplicity, as well as his warmth. I was astonished. Here we were meeting a man who was loved and honoured by so many, and known around the world, but it was as if we were honoured guests. He greeted us all and we sat around a long table in the garden. Food was brought and photos were taken of us together with Oliver Tambo. He asked how we were, and spoke to us about everyday things. Finally he began to question us about our ANC activities in the region. He still looked quite frail and showed signs of the stroke he had recently suffered, but the questions he asked and the comments he made were probing and penetrating. The sharpness of his mind, his utter dedication, and sense of mission were evident, and he managed to impart something of that to us. I left with a feeling of joy after this meeting. I felt I had met with an extraordinary man.

Shortly after that, in 1991, Oliver Tambo returned to South Africa with his family. In 1993 I was visiting South Africa. A few days after my arrival, Chris Hani was assassinated, and I attended the funeral along with thousands of others. Just before I left South Africa to return to London, Oliver Tambo died. His funeral was on the day that my plane left for London, and as I was leaving from the airport, people from all around the world, including politicians of the highest calibre, were arriving for his funeral.

Shortly after my return I attended a memorial to Oliver Tambo that was held in London. His daughter Tembi spoke, and I was deeply moved when she said, 'Daddy always taught us that it didn't matter how rich a person was, whether they were black or white, what their religion was. All that mattered was that they were a good person.' This touched me to the core like a physical shock, because I, a white Jewish South African, had heard these same words from my father as I grew up in apartheid South Africa. It was this same attitude and outlook which ensured the unity of the ANC and its allies and enabled the peaceful transition to democracy in South Africa.

THE IMPORTANCE OF GOODNESS

Gillian Slovo

One of the most important things I discovered from knowing Oliver Tambo was that modesty and gentleness are no signs of weakness. OR was one of the kindest and least boastful men I have encountered, and yet, you could tell when you were with him that there was steel within. Perhaps it was his eyes, framed by those thick glasses, which had something to do with this. When OR looked at you, there seemed to be no hiding. He seemed to see you, clearly and keenly, and yet at the same time he also seemed to be able to give you all the benefit of doubt that you might need.

As a child, I didn't know OR as a political leader; I knew him as a family friend. And what I knew of him – of the way his gentleness always shone through – I also heard my parents and their friends repeat. In the sombre years of exile when every attempt by the external ANC to find a way back into South Africa seemed doomed to failure, there were inevitable disagreements and tensions. It was OR who stopped these disagreements from turning into splits; it was he who kept the organisation together. He was a Christian in the true meaning of the word: his calmness and his quietness came from an understanding and a belief that his organisation would not only survive but would also one day prosper.

I didn't see OR often but I heard of him, not least from my father, Joe Slovo, whose face would soften when he talked about OR.

I knew just how Joe felt when, in 1992, I travelled with my father and my partner to the University of the North. We were there to celebrate, with the students, the renaming of a hall of residence after my mother, Ruth

First. OR was also there. He had already endured the first of the strokes that would eventually kill him and it had been some time since we had last met.

I was upset by OR's obvious frailty. He was in a wheelchair and speech did not come easily to him. But I soon learned that his fragility, like his gentleness, was deceptive. When my partner, meeting OR for the first time, was introduced to him OR beckoned him down. Andy bent so as to hear better what OR had to say. OR took both of Andy's hands in his and, holding on to them, looked him in the eye and said, 'Are you a good man? And will you be a good man to her?'

And that, I think, says it all for me. OR was the reluctant leader whose task it was to preside over some of the most difficult years of the struggle. He had witnessed the loss of many brave young soldiers, and his health had given in before he could fully celebrate the victory that owed so much to him. Even so, he still stressed the importance of goodness, not out of a moral duty but because he believed in it and because it sustained him.

THROUGH THE EYES
OF A SCULPTOR

Ian Walters
(as told to Christabel Gurney)

Ian Walters saw Oliver Tambo through the eyes of a sculptor. 'His upright back and the way he held his head was a very powerful image.' When Ian first met him at his London home in Muswell Hill, Tambo had already suffered the stroke that partially disabled him in 1989. But Ian felt immediately that he had 'an intensity and a power' which was in no way diminished by his stroke.

When Ian gave up teaching in 1981 he decided 'to put [his] art at the service of the movement'. The biggest issue, he thought, was to do something about apartheid South Africa and so he went to the ANC office in Penton Street and was asked to make a sculpture of Nelson Mandela. This was not an easy assignment as no one except his fellow prisoners and jailers had seen Mandela since he had been locked away on Robben Island in 1964. Working from photographs, Ian produced an impressive likeness. The sculpture stands today on London's South Bank near the Royal Festival Hall, where Oliver Tambo unveiled it in 1985.

As Tambo travelled the world building support for the ANC, Ian conceived a new idea. For many years, he said, he wanted to make a sculpture of Tambo. When he heard that Tambo had fallen ill and was recuperating in a Swedish hospital, he thought he had lost the opportunity. Then he heard that Tambo had come back to London to convalesce. Ian contacted Mike Terry in the AAM office, Mike approached Adelaide and Oliver, and the result was the Muswell Hill meeting.

Tambo agreed that he would go to Ian's workshop to sit for a sculpture. During the sessions that followed the two men did not talk much as Ian was engrossed in modelling a likeness. But there was no need for conversation. 'I was concentrating on what I saw,' he said, 'and I put into the sculpture what I already knew about Oliver. There was a powerful presence that you can feel in the sculpture.'

On one occasion, though, Ian did enlist Oliver's help. It occurred to him that Oliver could exercise his right side, affected by the stroke, by reaching over to put some clay on his own image. Oliver felt the clay, stretched over and pushed it well into the model. 'So it built up,' said Ian, 'and Oliver had a hand in it.'

When the sculpture was nearly completed, some people felt that Tambo should be depicted as he had looked during the long years when he had held the ANC together under his leadership, rather than showing the obvious signs of his stroke. With Oliver's agreement, Ian created a second sculpture, showing Oliver as he had looked before his stroke. The result was the larger figure that now stands on the balcony overlooking the foyer in South Africa House, complementing the first image, which partners the sculpture of his friend and comrade Trevor Huddleston in the foyer.

Ian felt that creating a sculpture that shows Oliver Tambo's qualities of humanity, steadfastness and strength was one of the best ways to keep his memory alive. It was his dearest wish that a scaled up version of his work should be set up in an appropriate place in South Africa and he was working on a design for this when he died on 3 August 2006.

EUROPEAN POLITICIANS AND ANTI-APARTHEID ACTIVISTS

GLASGOW RALLY

Brian Filling

One of the highlights of my life in the anti-apartheid campaign was meeting OR Tambo and, especially, chairing the huge rally in Glasgow in 1988 at which he launched the Glasgow to London march calling for the release of Nelson Mandela.

Prior to that I had attended meetings and rallies addressed by OR over many years since my student days at the University of Glasgow in the late 1960s. In 1976 the Scottish Committee of the AAM had been established with John Nelson as Secretary and myself as Chair. We remained Secretary and Chair until the AAM was dissolved in 1994 with the first democratic elections in South Africa.[1]

From 1976 (and the Soweto uprising) the campaign never abated and although I don't think OR Tambo visited Scotland during the period, I felt I came to know him well through my attendance at meetings addressed by him in London and through my contact with others.

For example, Ruth Mompati (ANC Chief Representative in the UK) attended the Freedom of the City award to Nelson Mandela conferred in absentia in 1981 in Glasgow. I chaired the meeting following the ceremony at which the speakers were Ruth, Michael Kelly, the Lord Provost of Glasgow and Alex Ekwueme, Vice-President of Nigeria. Ruth and I became good friends. She had worked in the law firm of 'Mandela and Tambo' in the 1950s in Johannesburg and her conversation was peppered with references to OR. It was a wonderful occasion when I led a thirty-strong Scottish delegation to South Africa in November 1994, six months after the first non-racial demo-

391

cratic election, and Ruth, who had been elected as a member of parliament, joined us for dinner. In her speech in Cape Town that night she referred at length to the Freedom of the City event in Glasgow in 1981.

Another example would be that of meeting and working with Dali Tambo, Oliver and Adelaide's son, preparing for the tour of Amandla, the ANC cultural group. In preparation for the Scottish leg of the tour, Dali visited Glasgow to discuss arrangements. He stayed in my house and we got to know one another well. Dali, although very different from his father, spoke highly of him and worried about the hugely demanding life he led. Amandla played to huge audiences and the successful tour included a sell-out week at the Assembly Hall in Edinburgh during the International Festival.

Others who deepened my understanding of OR included Essop and Aziz Pahad. I met the Pahad brothers in the late 1960s and continued to work with them throughout their time in exile. Essop renamed St George's Place in Glasgow after Nelson Mandela in 1986, much to the annoyance of the apartheid regime, whose consulate was on the fifth floor of the stock exchange building in the renamed street. They refused to use the new address and instead transferred to a post office box. It wasn't too long before we had chased them out of Glasgow. Discussions with the Pahad brothers often included references to OR and his views on the latest political situation.

On another occasion, Zwelakhe Sisulu was the guest of honour at a dinner in the Ubiquitous Chip Restaurant, Glasgow, hosted by the Glasgow member of the European parliament, Janey Buchan, who was a veteran anti-apartheid campaigner. This was shortly after Zwelakhe's release from detention in the late 1980s. He had been held without charge for a lengthy period, tortured and was banned from undertaking his job as editor of the *New Nation* newspaper.

Zwelakhe was scheduled to speak at a lunchtime public meeting the next day in Glasgow, but had indicated to Janey that he needed to return to London earlier and so would have to miss the meeting. He had not specified the reason for having to return to London. Janey was very anxious that Zwelakhe remain in Glasgow for the lunchtime engagement and so created a seating arrangement at the dinner with me on one side of Zwelakhe and Archbishop Winning (later Cardinal) on the other. Her 'instruction' to me was that I should persuade Zwelakhe to remain in Glasgow and that he might listen to me because of my anti-apartheid credentials. I learned from the Archbishop that he had been given similar 'instructions'. Apparently Janey's reasoning to him was that the Catholic Bishops' Conference largely funded the *New Nation* and that Zwelakhe would therefore listen to the Archbishop.

As the meal progressed and Zwelakhe and I got to know one another (through discussing politics, connections, mutual friends and comrades), he disclosed that the reason for changing plans and leaving Glasgow earlier than intended was that he had the unique opportunity of meeting OR Tambo in London before returning to South Africa. We discussed OR and his role and the importance of Zwelakhe seeing him before he returned to the front-line of the struggle. Without hesitation, I acknowledged that meeting OR was far more important for the liberation of South Africa than an engagement in Glasgow the next day. I tried to ameliorate the consequences of this decision by proposing that we film Zwelakhe's press conference the following morning and replay the video at the lunchtime meeting. This became a topic of discussion for the whole dinner table and two offers of potential film crews were forthcoming.

Next morning Zwelakhe gave this amazing press conference in which he described his detention without charge, his solitary confinement and torture, and how as a banned editor he now found ways of associating with the paper by selling it on the street corner. The press conference was filmed in preparation for the lunchtime meeting when he would not be present.

Zwelakhe then went off to London to meet OR and the lunchtime function was held. A handful of people turned up and watched the press conference on screen. It was a great relief to me that I had not tried to persuade Zwelakhe to stay in Glasgow rather than see OR in London.

In 1987 I attended the world conference hosted by the ANC in Arusha, Tanzania. Oliver Tambo played a major role in the conference including delivering the keynote speech. Most of the British delegation were incensed by an article in *The Guardian*, which referred to old stagers, including Tambo, who were trailing round the world delivering tired speeches about a lost cause. My letter to *The Guardian* challenging this view of the situation and of the ANC leadership was not published.

However, the Arusha Conference was very successful and lifted the worldwide anti-apartheid campaign to a new level.

In 1988 the AAM in Britain agreed to launch a campaign to free Nelson Mandela at seventy years of age. A concert was held in Wembley stadium on Saturday 11 June 1988 and on the next day a demonstration and rally were held in Glasgow to launch a walk by twenty-five marchers (one for each year Mandela had spent in prison) to London. The march was to reach London for a rally in Hyde Park on 18 July, Mandela's birthday.

As the demonstration gathered at Glasgow's Kelvingrove Park, near the University of Glasgow (the students had elected Chief Albert Luthuli, ANC President, as Rector in 1962) the platform party, including OR Tambo, were having lunch in the city chambers. OR, who was always reserved and quiet-spoken, and who appeared to be tired, not surprising given his punishing schedule, said a few words of thanks to his hosts. When the march arrived in George Square just outside the city chambers we waved to the marchers from the balcony of the city chambers and then joined the front of the march to Glasgow Green for the rally.

It was a beautiful day with the sun shining from a cloudless sky – not normal Glasgow weather.

The demonstrators were further 'warmed up' by an Angolan band as they waited for the rest of the massive demonstration to arrive and the rally to commence.

Prior to going onto the platform, which was decorated with banners calling for the release of Nelson Mandela and all political prisoners and 'Sanctions Now!', we sat in a caravan behind the stage out of view of the crowd. OR and I chatted. He was very interested in our campaign, asking questions in a friendly way about who was involved, our successes, the difficulties, and how the ANC could help. He also enquired about my family and was pleased when I told him that his son Dali had stayed in my home when he was working with Amandla. He also spent time talking to Allan Boesak about events in the country, the UDF campaign, and he enquired about this and that comrade. After some time we were called to the platform.

When Thozamile Botha (a student in Glasgow at that time, later to be elected as an ANC member of parliament in 1994) introduced me to open and chair the rally there was tremendous applause for the Scottish Committee of the AAM. Among the speakers were Campbell Christie, General Secretary of the Scottish Trade Union Congress; Janey Buchan, member of the European parliament; and Bernie Grant, member of parliament. Although there was a fear among us, as organisers, that we might have booked too many speakers, the crowd was not of that view. Andimba Toivo ja Toivo spoke movingly about the struggle to win independence and freedom for Namibia. Bob Hughes, Chair of the UK AAM, Allan Boesak and Archbishop Trevor Huddleston also spoke and Jim Kerr, of the band Simple Minds, who had flown up from the Wembley concert, sang his song, 'Mandela Day'.

A moving atmosphere was created by the speakers and the by now hugely enthusiastic crowd gave Oliver Tambo a rapturous welcome when he was introduced by me. He thanked the people of Glasgow and Scotland for turning out in such large numbers for the rally, for their boycotting actions and for the many activities in solidarity with the peoples of southern Africa. OR spoke of making South Africa 'unworkable and ungovernable', criticised the British government and Mrs Thatcher's opposition to sanctions and called for increased solidarity in a final push to win freedom for the people of South Africa. He said:

> the issue of the recognition by the nations of the world of the il-
> legitimacy of the apartheid regime is today firmly on the agenda.
> The historic Arusha Conference, which met under the theme
> 'The World United Against Apartheid for a Democratic South Af-
> rica', played an important part in bringing about this result which
> is of central importance in our struggle to liberate ourselves.
>
> Similarly, the hopes of the racists that they could defuse the
> campaign for sanctions have come to nought. Despite the efforts
> of the major Western powers to shield the apartheid regime from
> effective international action, the peoples of the world have taken
> the struggle for the international isolation of apartheid South Af-
> rica yet another step forward. Many areas of the world, including
> the socialist countries and the overwhelming majority of member
> states of the UN, the Non-Aligned movement and the OAU, have
> continued their total isolation of apartheid South Africa. Others,
> such as the Nordic countries, have in the past year adopted import-
> ant measures in this regard. With the sole exception of the United
> Kingdom, the countries of the Commonwealth also resolved in
> favour of further sanctions against racist South Africa, as did the
> group of African, Caribbean and Pacific countries.

As he spoke the crowd grew more and more enthusiastic and this clearly
affected OR deeply. Mainly seen as an intellectual and not renowned as a
powerful orator, OR rose to the occasion and made a wonderfully passionate and moving speech. It was a fantastic performance by a man now in his
seventies. He had spent more than twenty years in exile, campaigning around
the world for international solidarity and for sanctions and at the same time
working tirelessly to maintain unity and give leadership to the national liberation movement.

Afterwards he thanked me for inviting him to Glasgow and said that he
had rarely been so moved by the reaction of an audience. It had lifted his
spirits and given him renewed impetus to continue the struggle. I already
had an understanding of his outstanding political acumen from listening to
and reading his speeches and writings, and through talking with others, but
his humility and modesty made an incredible impression on me.

Inevitably, OR had to fly back to London immediately after the rally to
take up his next duty.

In February 1993 I gave the toast to the Immortal Memory of Robert

Burns[2] at a Burns Supper in London at which Chris Hani, the SACP and ANC leader, gave the main speech. After the Burns Supper I talked with Chris into the 'wee sma' oors' ('wee small hours' – the early hours after midnight) and Chris spoke warmly of OR and his immense contribution over the years.

Six weeks later, on 10 April, Chris was assassinated.

A huge outpouring of grief was unleashed throughout South Africa. The apartheid regime tried to use the situation to its advantage in an attempt to cling to power but it was the ANC which organised and channelled this vast outburst of emotion and anger into pressure to fix an election date of 27 April 1994.

OR, who was in fragile health at the time of Chris Hani's assassination, took Chris's death very sorely and he died two weeks later.

Although OR did not live to see the first democratic election in South Africa nor Nelson Mandela elected as President, there can be no doubt that his leadership and unflinching work in Britain and around the world were of vital importance in the historic victory of the ANC and the South African people.

NOTES

1. Action for Southern Africa (ACTSA) was formed in 1994 as the successor organisation to AAM. John Nelson and I became (and remain) Secretary and Chair respectively.

2. Robert Burns (1759-1796) is Scotland's national poet and Burns Suppers are held annually throughout the world close to the date of his birth on 25 January. In recent years Burns Suppers have been held at the South African High Commission, South Africa House organised by the High Commission in conjunction with ACTSA Scotland.

INDOMITABLE SPIRIT OF OPTIMISM

George Houser

I met Oliver Tambo for the first time in Johannesburg in September 1954. It was my first trip to Africa. The American Committee on Africa, of which I was one of the founders, had been organised the year before this. Our purpose was to support the liberation struggle in Africa. On this first trip I was denied visas to all of British East and Central Africa (from Uganda to Southern Rhodesia). But, by a fluke I was given a transit visa to South Africa from a young consul in then Leopoldville in the Belgian Congo, to travel from Johannesburg to Cape Town to catch a ship. The only person in the world who knew I was travelling to South Africa was Revd Arthur Blaxall, the Secretary of the South African Christian Council. With his help, I went to Pretoria and extended my visa to three weeks. My purpose was to learn all I could about the freedom struggle and meet the leadership of the ANC.

The first person who Blaxall said I should meet was Oliver Tambo, an ANC leader active in the Defiance Campaign of two years earlier, an associate of Father Huddleston and St Peter's College, law partner of Nelson Mandela, and close associate of Walter Sisulu, with whom I had had correspondence. I remember the affection with which Oliver met and embraced me at our first meeting. He offered to drive me around Johannesburg. It was a Sunday, and Oliver asked me if there was anything special I was interested in. A friend in New York, who was particularly knowledgeable in African dance, had urged me to visit Crown Mines on a Sunday afternoon when African dances from various cultures were performed. So we headed off for the Crown Mines' arena. I found out that it was a tourist attraction. As far as I could see, Oliver was the only African in the audience, but there was no racial segregation in the seating and we sat together. After a few minutes, Oliver said to me, 'I almost forgot. This is a gathering and I am under ban. I will meet you outside the arena.' He got up and left. I stayed for only a moment or two before joining him. He explained to me that legally he was allowed to be in the company of only one person at a time. And so I was introduced to 'banning' under apartheid law. We walked a short distance towards his car. I was holding a small briefcase. Oliver reached over to carry it for me and I said, 'I can carry it.' He responded: 'In my country we will do it my way', and he carried my briefcase. This was my introduction to Oliver.

I was not permitted to visit South Africa again for 37 years until 1991 after Nelson Mandela was released from prison. Over the years my contacts with Oliver were by correspondence and meetings in various places while he was in exile. Of course he and the struggle in South Africa were highlighted in the news with the treason arrests in 1956 and the subsequent trial, with Oliver, one of the accused, and the others later acquitted. Even before the Treason Trial ended, the Sharpeville massacre occurred on 21 March 1960. This was a turning point in the struggle. Oliver was chosen by the ANC to escape the country and organise the international work of the ANC. He made his way from Botswana to Ghana, and eventually to London. There, through the Africa Bureau, I reached him by cable and invited him to come to the US: 'Congratulations on escape. Can you come here to help with the campaign against apartheid?' We were elated when we received an immediate reply that he could come for four weeks.

We organised an Emergency Conference on South Africa to be held at the end of May, across the street from the UN, with Jackie Robinson, the famed baseball star, as the Chairperson but headlining Oliver Tambo. Then came a bombshell – the State Department declared Oliver ineligible for a visa. No reason was given, but we had to suspect pressure from the South African government with suspicion of 'terrorism' or 'communist' sympathy as the rationale. This was towards the end of the Eisenhower administration and Christian Herter was the Secretary of State. We mounted protests from labour, church and community groups, and in June the government reversed its decision. It was too late for our conference, but allowed several weeks for a nationwide speaking tour in which Oliver made a great impression with information on the Treason Trial, the Congress of the People, the Freedom Charter and the ongoing struggle against apartheid.

One of my most memorable meetings with OR was in 1967 in Tanzania.

He was in Morogoro, some 190 kilometres west of Dar es Salaam, a centre for ANC education and training. Other major centres for the ANC were in Lusaka (in Zambia) and in Dar es Salaam. Oliver spent much time in Morogoro, not only because of its importance to ANC activity, but because its elevation made it easier to keep his asthma under control. I recall the three-hour drive from Dar es Salaam over the rough road filled with potholes. Oliver had arranged for me to visit him there to discuss ways in which we, the American Committee on Africa, could help with his Welfare Fund, which we had started to provide relief to South African exiles of all political persuasions. At the ANC office I was greeted first by Ruth Mompati, assisting Oliver, and then embraced by Oliver. Our meeting took place, I later learned, only shortly before the doomed joint ANC-ZAPU (Zimbabwe African People's Union) invasion of Wankie.

During my several hours with Oliver, I saw him in operation and caught his sense of mission. The whole strategy of the ANC, he said, was to overthrow the apartheid government of South Africa. He exhibited his usual optimism. 'There is no time factor involved,' he said. 'It will be a long, bitter struggle.' But, he told me, they could win. Looking at my notes of that meeting I wrote: 'He gave me nothing concrete on this, and I didn't ask for anything. But he wasn't just speaking in shibboleths either. I raised the question about the Portuguese territories falling first. He didn't necessarily accept this. He said they would help each other by their separate successes.'

I could see that Oliver was acting with authority. I recalled what Arthur Blaxall had said about his great quality of combining gentleness and sensitivity with conviction. Some critics believed that Oliver was not the real power of the ANC in exile, in spite of his title of Deputy President. What I saw belied this. Stalwart and venerable leaders of the ANC, such as Moses Kotane and JB Marks, were in and out of the office, and they deferred to Oliver. He said to me in the course of our conversations, 'I am not sure when we will be ready. There is so much that has to be done.'

In terms of his Welfare Fund he said he was doing all he could, even helping some PAC members. Then he asked me if I could arrange a new bifocal lens for his glasses, which I subsequently did.

I had great admiration for Oliver's ability to keep perspective when international issues arose. One such issue was the period of so-called détente with South Africa in 1974 when President Kenneth Kaunda of Zambia and Prime Minister BJ Vorster of South Africa exchanged messages. Vorster said that he would not interfere in Mozambique (on the verge of independence) and wanted to normalise relations with independent African states. In response, Kaunda called this 'the voice of reason' and hoped that South

Africa would support 'peaceful change'. This exchange was interpreted by many in the liberation struggle as a Kaunda sell-out. Shortly thereafter I had an hour's discussion with Oliver in Lusaka, mostly on this 'détente'. He had had a long-standing relationship with Kaunda and a major ANC office was in Lusaka. I recall that in our conversation he noted that Kaunda had a 'tarnished image this year'. In my notes I wrote: 'Tambo definitely does not believe Kaunda is a sell-out. For years he has given support to the liberation struggle at great cost to Zambia. This showed courage. Also it shows courage for Kaunda to follow the line he does now. It is not popular with the liberation movements. We will have to wait and see.'

Another issue that tested unity in the liberation struggle came in 1984 with the Nkomati Accord between President PW Botha's South Africa and the independent Mozambique headed by FRELIMO, long a staunch ally of the ANC. The stability of Mozambique was being threatened by a dissident group, the Mozambique National Resistance (MNR), backed by the South African government. Hundreds of schools, health clinics and shops were being destroyed. The oil pipeline and the railroad from Beira to Zimbabwe were blown up. The MNR was the successor to the right-wing resistance to the liberation struggle. This was the background to the Nkomati Accord signed by President PW Botha and President Samora Machel – a non-aggression pact with an agreement to settle differences peacefully, not to allow their territories to be used as a base for an attack on the other. It enraged most of the freedom fighters in South Africa, but FRELIMO looked upon it as necessary for survival.

I recall being in Algiers in November 1984 and meeting with Jorge Rebelo, a FRELIMO leader and the former Minister of Information in the Mozambique government. We discussed the Nkomati Accord, and he said that the ANC was seriously disappointed, but that Oliver Tambo understood the necessity of the agreement. Later, meeting with Alfred Nzo, he echoed the 'keen disappointment' of the ANC. Interpreting Tambo who, he said, maintained a close relationship with President Machel, the ANC 'does not want to make things more complicated for Mozambique'. Nzo was convinced that the Accord couldn't last.

The last time I saw Oliver was at his home in Johannesburg. He had suffered a stroke in exile and was partially paralysed, but he had the same indomitable spirit of optimism and commitment of the young man I had first met almost forty years earlier.

DEDICATION AND
INDEFATIGABLE ENERGY

Bob Hughes

At about 5:00 a.m. on Saturday 24 April 1993, I was awakened by the phone ringing. I had a premonition it would be bad news, and it was; it was a call to say that Oliver Tambo had died.

In a way it was not unexpected, since he had had a massive stroke in 1989 and was no longer in good health. Nevertheless, I was devastated at the passing of such a great ANC leader, someone who was an inspiration to so many people.

I first met Oliver Tambo in 1975 when I was a member of parliament in the UK and I became Vice-Chair of the AAM. The following year I became the Chair of the AAM and from then until Oliver's death I had frequent contact with him.

In order to put the achievements of Oliver Tambo into perspective and understand his contribution to the ANC and to the eventual freedom of the people of South Africa, it is necessary to realise the conditions in which he began his work as the leader of the ANC in exile.

It is difficult to appreciate now that when OR Tambo left South Africa after the Sharpeville massacre in 1960 to found the ANC's External Mission little was known of the ANC outside South Africa.

General observers of events in South Africa were fed the diet that the ANC was not representative of the majority population in the country; that it was a minuscule organisation; and that it was nothing more than a 'front organisation' for the SACP. It was presented as a danger to so-called Western values and as a threat to South African business interests that relied on a high proportion of external capital investment, mainly from the UK and European sources.

Against this background of hostility and with very little in the way of financial resources, OR Tambo had to build an organisation to meet the challenges of making the world aware of the true oppressive nature of the apartheid regime and of the role of the ANC in combating that regime.

Before too long, the ANC had a permanent representative in the capitals of many countries in the world, as well as at the headquarters of the UN in New York.

This was without doubt arduous work and only happened because of OR's dedication and indefatigable energy. Raising the profile of the ANC meant travelling all over the world to engage politicians and governments in argument and discussion.

As someone who saw OR in action, I can testify to his immense patience with those who, either from ignorance or even with malice, denied the true nature of events in South Africa. Many of them would have tried the patience of a saint, but OR understood that only the power of persuasion would make an impact. He knew that bluster and bombast would be counterproductive, although he was assertive in his views and presentations.

At international conferences sometimes organised by the ANC itself, sometimes by the UN, and sometimes by international solidarity organisations, OR was a compelling advocate. He would also spend many hours meeting delegates individually to discuss issues.

At all times, whilst acknowledging the importance of international solidarity work and the need to engage world opinion against the apartheid regime, Oliver made it clear that the people of South Africa themselves would play the decisive role in bringing down the apartheid system.

OR was a man of real compassion and cared very much for individuals. I recall that on 13 March 1983, Joshua Nkomo, Vice-President of Zimbabwe and leader of the Zimbabwe African People's Union (ZAPU), fled the country to the UK, as he feared for his life. This followed the killing of one of his bodyguards at his home in Bulawayo. He claimed that President Mugabe had ordered his (Nkomo's) assassination.

I made contact with Joshua through the offices of Tiny Rowland, co-Chair and Managing Director of Lonhro, the vast African trading conglomerate. We met at a hotel on the perimeter of London's Heathrow airport. We had long discussions and Joshua agreed that he could not simply remain in

London, where his influence on events in Zimbabwe would wither away. He was, however, adamant that he would be killed if he went home and that he needed a guarantee of his safety. He then told me that OR Tambo was the only person who could deliver such a guarantee.

As it happened, the following week I was due to attend an international conference on solidarity with the Front-line States and Lesotho, in Lisbon. I knew that OR would be there and told Joshua this. In order to let OR know that the approach was genuinely from Joshua, I was asked to say to OR that I had a message from 'Someone who claims to be older than him'. This was clearly a piece of private banter between them.

I told OR I needed to speak to him privately and confidentially as I had a message from, 'The one who claimed to be older than him'. He looked a bit startled, but said I should go to my hotel room and remain there until he was available to see me. Very shortly afterwards I met him and explained Joshua's situation. OR agreed that Joshua should return to Zimbabwe and said that he would see what he could do.

Some time later Oliver phoned me from Lusaka to say that he could not manage to travel to London himself, but that Thomas Nkobi, then the ANC Treasurer General would represent him. When I told Joshua this, he was very pleased and said that a meeting with Nkobi was as good as seeing OR himself. Thomas Nkobi came to London and I arranged a private meeting for the two men.

When they emerged, Joshua said simply, 'Thank you, I am going home now.' He returned to Bulawayo on 16 August 1983, with President Mugabe having issued a statement that Joshua Nkomo would not be arrested if he returned home. Whether the guarantee of safe passage was indeed necessary or not, there is absolutely no doubt in my mind that OR *did* provide the re-quired guarantee of safety for Joshua Nkomo for his return.

OR had courage, foresight, and faith in the future. Whatever doubts some people may have had in the dark days when it seemed as though the apart-heid regime was indestructible, he retained an unshakeable belief and de-termination that in the end the ANC and the South African people would triumph.

Life in exile was not easy for OR or his family. He could not have ful-filled his mission without the selfless and dedicated support of his wife Ade-laide and his children.

OR faced great dangers as the regime recognised the calibre of their foe and would gladly have been rid of him. In March 1982 he was due to travel from Lusaka to London to address a UN-sponsored international confer-ence to be followed by a major rally at Trafalgar Square organised by the

AAM. It was common knowledge that OR was an early riser and whenever he was visiting London he would often arrange to meet ANC members at the ANC office in Penton Street. Fortunately, a Front-line States meeting in Maputo meant that he was unable to come to London. On the Sunday morning of the rally, the ANC office was partially destroyed by a bomb planted by agents of the South African regime. I have no doubt that the target was OR and that this was a deliberate assassination attempt.

It was a measure of how far the ANC had travelled and gained in influence that OR was invited to be the guest international speaker at the Labour Party annual conference in Blackpool, on Thursday 3 October 1985.

OR could not be described as a flowery orator, yet he always held the attention of an audience when he spoke. His sincerity and conviction were entirely convincing.

He told the conference of the sacrifices being made by the people of South Africa and that nothing the regime could do would more than postpone the day of freedom when apartheid would be ended. He said:

> But whatever the enemy does, we shall not retreat. [Applause] Rather it is inevitable that we shall win more allies for our cause. Already the much vaunted unity of whites in general and of Afrikaners in particular in the face of the so-called 'black danger' is a thing of the past. We are determined to do everything in our power to draw as many whites to the side of the democratic movement as possible, being certain that the security and happiness of all our people, including that of our white compatriots, lies in the kind of democratic South Africa that is spelt out in our policy document, the Freedom Charter. [Applause]
>
> Yet we have no desire to inherit a country with more graves than it has already. We have no wish to celebrate liberation day surrounded by a desolate landscape of destroyed buildings and by productive machines that have been reduced to scrap metal. Were it in our power, we would have long negotiated a just solution to the South African question on the basis of the democratic principles and practices that govern the political life in this country, but it is clear that the Botha regime is not ready for change. We have no choice but to fight on.

Later, commenting on the inaction of the British government, he said, 'Their recent announced decision to impose limited sanctions is a welcome development. It does not, however, measure up to the demands of the situation in South Africa, Namibia and the rest of southern Africa. That situation cries out for nothing short of immediate and comprehensive sanctions.'

He concluded by saying:

> The phase our struggle has entered demands that we expect of this movement now and when it is in government that it will enter no compromise with apartheid and will not retreat from its commitment to act against that criminal system. Acting in this manner, thus shall we begin to construct relations of friendship between Great Britain and South Africa, relations that are not based on self interest or charity, but on genuine friendship from people to people.

He received a prolonged standing ovation.

Oliver Tambo was known to be a disciplinarian from his early days as a teacher. He always had a steely and unyielding desire for the ANC to succeed, but he was a humane man, and far from being unbending, he was compassionate when dealing with the difficulties faced by exiles and the personal problems that they faced.

Exiles coped or failed to cope with the day to day difficulties in different ways. Most managed very well and were sustained by the belief that one day they would be able to return to a free South Africa. Some found it impossible to cope and were pursued by demons.

During the years of oppression that predated the use of the Internet and satellite communications, the apartheid regime sought to exercise rigid censorship on the press and radio, as well as on such television as existed at the time. It was against the law to quote or make any reference to a banned person or organisation. Some South African journalists, such as Maggie Jackson working in the UK, tried to circumvent this restraint on the freedom of the press by getting British politicians to comment on what was being said by OR Tambo, Thabo Mbeki or others speaking for the ANC. How effective that particular ploy was, I cannot say, but there is no doubt that the message of the ANC did reach inside the country.

One example of this was the international conference on 'Children, Repression and the Law in Apartheid South Africa', held in Harare, Zimbabwe, in September 1987. It was organised by the Bishop Ambrose Reeves Trust (Bart), in conjunction with other organisations. (Bart was an education trust in association with the AAM and was named after Bishop Ambrose Reeves who was the President of AAM before Trevor Huddleston.) We had little idea as to how many delegates, if any, would attend from inside South Africa.

In reality we were overwhelmed with the numbers who arrived in the face of the regime refusing to provide travel documents and defying the threats to imprison anyone who attended the conference.

On the first evening people were sitting around in the hotel entrance lounge talking, discussing, greeting old friends and in the process of making new ones. The ANC delegation arrived and there was a cry, 'There is OR Tambo!'

There was an immediate and spontaneous eruption and hundreds of South Africans who had never seen Oliver stampeded to the entrance hall and engulfed him in joy and exultation.

Censorship cannot prevent the spread of knowledge although it may for a time slow things down. OR Tambo was known and recognised. It was clear that his reputation had reached the people and he was hailed as the leader of the ANC.

OR was always direct in his responses no matter what questions were raised with him. I only saw him angry on one occasion.

In 1987 after some Johannesburg city centre bombings when there had been civilian casualties, there was considerable speculation in the media that the tactics of the ANC and its armed wing MK had changed, and that a decision had been taken to attack 'soft' targets. It had always been the stated intention only to attack military or strategic targets but civilians were never under threat.

Questions were being asked by some of the AAM membership and disquiet was expressed about this possibility. It was agreed that I should meet with OR Tambo, who in addition to being President of the ANC was also Commander in Chief of MK, in order to get the position clear.

I met with OR at the ANC office in Penton Street, London, and explained the position that the AAM was worried at what might appear to be a change of policy. Oliver listened intently and civilly as he always did. He then replied in measured tones, making it clear that he was hurt and angry at the implication that his integrity and that of the ANC was under question. He assured me that what had happened was entirely contrary to the spirit and the letter of ANC policy. He reiterated that the struggle against apartheid was a struggle against the regime and not against people.

There had been no change of policy; civilians would not be targeted. Any action against civilians would not be authorised or tolerated and the ANC would deal with the issue. He was quite specific in stating that, 'The ANC never approved of attacks on civilian targets as it considered them morally wrong, but also strategically senseless.'

I fully accepted the explanation that there had been no alteration of the position of the ANC and was able to report back to assure doubters of this. Oliver's word was good enough and it was immediately accepted by the AAM.

In 1989 OR had a severe stroke and we feared the worst might happen. He survived only because of the excellent medical treatment and care provided by the Swedish health service. However, it did seem that he would never be restored to full fitness.

Shortly before he returned to South Africa after more than thirty years of exile, Archbishop Trevor Huddleston (President of the AAM), Mike Terry, (Executive of the AAM) and I had lunch with OR in North London. He was almost unable to walk and he had great difficulty with his speech, although he was obviously keen and excited about going home. As we were leaving I asked Adelaide if her husband was really fit to undergo such a long and arduous flight. She replied that she understood people's concerns, but said: 'Oliver has to go home; that is what he wants more than anything else.'

Soon afterwards, in July 1991, in Durban at the first congress of the ANC in the country since the banning order was lifted after its imposition in 1960, OR spoke for over two hours accounting for his stewardship of the ANC in exile. It was a wonderful speech and all the more remarkable given the severity of his condition before he had returned home. I commented on this to Adelaide who said, 'From the moment he got on the plane he got stronger and stronger; you could almost see the connections being made in his head. The joy of returning home, the exhilaration of returning home was a magical healing process.' It was truly an example of the power of the body to heal itself, combined with the fierce determination of spirit which was always part of OR's life.

South Africa owes an immense debt of gratitude to the ANC, whose struggle to bring the end to the apartheid regime was simply that, to bring down the apartheid regime. The ANC's credo was based on non-racialism and an end to oppression, which included gender inequality. It was never a black versus white struggle, although obviously black people were the principal victims of the apartheid era. The philosophy can be summed up by OR, who stated: 'It is our responsibility to break down the barriers of division and create a country where there will be neither whites nor blacks, free and united in diversity.'

It is impossible to give proper credit to Oliver Tambo or pay due homage to his achievement as President of the ANC in exile. He was a wonderful man, kind to his fellow human beings, conscientious to a fault. Yet he was steely in his determination to ensure that the ANC would deliver its promise to the people of South Africa that freedom would be theirs.

Oliver always gave credit to those ANC members in exile and at home who carried on the struggle; he certainly never was an egotist. Yet I have no doubt that he was one of the greatest leaders the ANC has had. He was a wise head at the centre of affairs; he was invaluable to the ANC and his influence was beyond estimation.

We remember him with honour and affection as a true patriot.

THE BOROUGH OF HARINGEY

George Meehan

The borough of Haringey in North London is one of the most diverse boroughs in the UK, with some one hundred and sixty different languages spoken. It has a proud record of providing a welcoming haven for exiles and refugees from all over the world, and therefore it was fitting that Oliver and Adelaide Tambo made their home in the borough in the 1960s.

Fifty-one Alexandra Park Road, an unassuming house in suburban Muswell Hill, London N10, was to be a base for the family for some thirty years, as well as a hub for all those fighting in exile for freedom in South Africa, until the family's historic return to South Africa in December 1990.

Shortly before that date, on 22 October 1990, my Labour Party colleagues Councillors Harry Lister and Toby (now Lord) Harris proposed a motion at a full meeting of the Council, as follows:

> This Council, recognising the important contribution that Oliver and Adelaide Tambo have made to the struggle for freedom in South Africa throughout their years of exile and residence in the borough and of the inspiration that this provides for so many local residents, resolves in accordance with Section 249 (5) of the Local Government Act 1972 to confer on them the title of Honorary Freeman of Haringey . . .

Interestingly, even at that time, institutional hostility remained towards the ANC. Conservative Party opposition members on the Council combined to vote against the motion, but it was carried by 36 votes to 17, attaining the necessary two-thirds majority.

A few days before the family's return, at the end of November 1990, fellow Haringey councillors and I welcomed Oliver and Adelaide to the town hall in Tottenham to bestow on them the Freedom of the Borough.

It was a moving ceremony; the presentation to Oliver and Adelaide of their Freedom Scrolls by Councillor Mary Neuner, the Mayor of Haringey, was followed by the ANC anthem played by the local Eclipse Steel band, and sung by the choir of children from the local secondary school, Fortismere.

In her acceptance speech Adelaide paid gracious tribute to the 'peace-loving' people of Haringey. 'The support of the Haringey Anti-Apartheid Group, the support of the successive mayors, councillors and senior officials of the borough, and not least, the support of the masses of the people of Haringey has been immeasurable,' she said.

It was a tribute that meant an enormous amount to my colleagues and I, since the presence of Adelaide and Oliver, and their family, in our borough through the years of struggle against the apartheid regime, had been a significant inspiration for us as local councillors and Labour Party activists.

I think it's true to say that knowing we were hosts to one of the giants of the liberation struggle gave us an added impetus in putting forward arguments for sanctions, locally and nationally, and in taking our own steps in Haringey to ensure that the Council took a lead in bodies such as the UK Local Authorities Against Apartheid grouping.

And, of course, there were other links over the years. Adelaide worked in our local hospital, the Whittington, and as a district nurse, and would have had contact with our social work department.

Adelaide also turned to the Council when the house in Alexandra Park Road had been badly damaged in a fire and she was not able to work. She wrote to the Council 'to tell them that I had had the accident, that I was the bread winner of the family, and that Oliver was in the struggle'. We were happy to help.

We also learnt recently, when Tembi Tambo visited her old home, that Oliver had found time for the occasional game of tennis on our municipal courts at the Albert Road recreation ground a few minutes from Alexandra Park Road.

Those tennis courts are still in operation, and we are now looking into erecting a statue in the recreation ground to commemorate Oliver's stay in our borough.

Today, Haringey Council is keeping the memory and values of Oliver Tambo alive through our Oliver Tambo Science Awards for local children.

Oliver was, of course, originally a science teacher, and he remained committed to education throughout his life. For example, he raised funds internationally for the Solomon Mahlangu Freedom College, enabling children in exile to complete their schooling before joining the struggle.

In Haringey we also see education as key to solving the problems of poverty and unemployment that still affect too many in our community. Through the Oliver Tambo Awards we have been able to link achievement in science to direct help to the developing world. Sponsorship arrangements mean that donations are made to education projects overseas for every child attaining a higher grade.

Two local fourteen year olds, Tsvetelina Hadzheiva and Winfred Adjei, visited South Africa in the autumn of 2006 as the first winners of the award. They were able to meet members of the Tambo family, went to a school in Soweto and took part in the ceremony to rename Johannesburg airport as OR Tambo International Airport, as well as visiting the South African parliament and a safari park.

Separately, seven students from our Alexandra Park School went to South Africa at the same time, to participate in a science project and to attend a ceremony to launch a partnership between Alexandra Park and Ephes Mamkeli Secondary School in Wattville, the township where the Tambo family lived before being forced into exile in 1960, and where Oliver Tambo is buried.

Earlier, we were delighted that our two award-winners were able to be presented with their prizes at the South African High Commission by Tembi Tambo, who said: 'It's not about who gets the best score; it's about who has travelled the furthest. We should celebrate the creativity of Haringey's science project in helping to expand pupil's horizons both here in the UK whilst helping to improve the life chances of children in the developing world.'

For me, it was an occasion that again brought to the fore the vision and values of Oliver Tambo. We hope the awards will inspire successive generations of young people to do their best to make a difference to the lives of others, and act as a fitting commemoration and celebration of Oliver Tambo's life for many years to come.

A CAMPAIGNING POLITICIAN

Kjeld Olesen

On an early morning in 1978 I stood in an airport. I don't remember if it was in Luanda or in Lusaka, but it was one of the Front-line States. Two planes were scheduled to depart and we stood waiting in the hall. My eyes focused on a man standing by himself. Immediately I saw that it was Oliver Tambo and his growing smile told me that he had recognised me too.

I was a member of a mission visiting all the Front-line States on behalf of Socialist International. At that time I was Vice-Chairman of the Social Democratic Party of Denmark and Minister for Transport. The mission was headed by the long-standing Swedish Prime Minister Olof Palme, but at that time he was in opposition to a bourgeois coalition government. South Africa and apartheid were high on the international agenda. For many years the Scandinavian countries in the UN had taken stands against the apartheid regime and had also been main sponsors in channelling money to the various activities of the ANC.

The following ten minutes will be in my memory forever. Oliver took my hand and kept holding it all the time while we stood there talking. His calm voice, sometime interrupted by a little laugh, was exactly as I recalled it from our first meeting back in 1960.

At that time I was Secretary of the Danish Social Democratic Party. I was responsible for the activities in the Copenhagen area and therefore much engaged in the annual rally on 1 May. Our contacts in the British Labour Party informed us that the ANC had decided to urge Oliver Tambo to leave South Africa so that he could contact countries and political parties in Europe and elsewhere and thereby advocate a stronger stand against apartheid. We also learned that he was expected in London at the end of April, and we immediately decided to invite him to address the rally on 1 May in Copenhagen. On 26 April we were informed by the Danish embassy in London that his visa and ticket were ready. Oliver was supposed to arrive from Ghana, but something went wrong.

I had already informed the press about his arrival and a press conference was scheduled for shortly thereafter. Suddenly I had to improvise and alter our plans because he didn't show up in London as expected. An important part of our problem was the fact that the rally was to be broadcast live by television and radio, and they wanted to have a precise timetable.

The first day of May in 1960 was a Sunday filled with sunshine. The day before I was informed by our embassy in London that Oliver would try to reach the rally by flying directly from Dakar to Paris and then to Copenhagen on Air France. Two hours before the rally began I was told that the plane was overdue. When the plane landed I was sitting in a taxi waiting on the apron with the radio on. I could hear the orchestra playing at the rally when the noisy engines were stopped. It had been organised that Oliver Tambo would be the first passenger to disembark, and I recognised him from photos. My welcome was very short as I almost pushed him into the taxi. We drove to the rally at full speed. I had made a plan for communication and I asked the driver to inform his headquarters to transmit to a taxi placed behind the stage that we were on the way. A few seconds later we heard this announced on the radio as the crowd was informed: 'Oliver Tambo has landed and is on his way.'

The daily newspaper *Aktuelt* estimated that the crowd numbered some fifty thousand people. We arrived right after the Prime Minister Viggo Kampmann had delivered his speech. The welcome was warm and enthusiastic. The Chairman of the Workers' Federation of Copenhagen introduced Oliver and he finished by saying: 'What happens in South Africa right now reminds us of the Nazi-occupation of our country. Oliver Tambo has recently left not only his country but also his wife and two children. We are very proud that Denmark is the first country in Europe to be visited by him.'

And then Oliver Tambo stepped forward. The applause lasted for so long that it took several minutes before his first sentence: 'To me it is an exceptional experience to stay here. This is the very first time I address a big white audience.'

After having conveyed greetings from the black workers of South Africa he went on:

In my country the jails are filled up with workers, because they dare to claim equal rights. Think of the wealth of South Africa, and think then of all the black people who suffer from slavery. They are not allowed to organise and they have no influence when they try to sell the only thing possible, their labour. I know that in many countries efforts are made to raise funds to assist us in our struggle for freedom. We are very grateful to the Danish trade union for what you have already done.

We realise that we can only win, if as many countries as possible [exert] even harder pressure on the Verwoerd regime. The best weapon is an effective economic and political boycott. But an economic boycott will also hit the black workers, you could argue. To this I will only say: the black workers cannot become poorer than they already are.

On 1 May 1960 the Danes got acquainted with the ANC and the struggle against apartheid. They could see and hear about it on the television and radio, and the next morning all the newspapers carried a front-page story.

A few hours after the rally Oliver met the Danish press as well as correspondents from various foreign media. For more than an hour he spoke in detail about the unrest in South Africa as Danish television and several newspapers interviewed him. After dinner I accompanied Oliver to his hotel. He was tired, which was understandable, and when we said good night he added, holding my hands: 'To me it has been a very long, but wonderful first day of my life in Europe.'

The following days were very busy. On 3 May the newspapers reported a successful visit to the biggest Danish shipyard Burmeister & Wain with more than three thousand workers. Tambo delivered a short speech in the canteen underlining the necessity of close links between the free labour movement and the suppressed workers of South Africa. Afterwards he saw various activities of the shipyard. All over waving and shouting groups cheered him. As one newspaper stated: 'The visit took place in an atmosphere which Oliver Tambo could feel was genuine and heartfelt.'

From the shipyard we hurried to the Prime Minister's office where Viggo Kampmann hosted a luncheon. Around the table were some other members of the government and certain invited members of the press.

The same evening Tambo met three hundred members of the Social Democratic Party. Almost all of them had heard him at the rally on 1 May, but they wanted to know more about the suppression in South Africa.

During his stay in Denmark Oliver had a very tight programme. He rushed from one appointment to the next like a campaigning politician a few days before election. Of course he was tired at the end of a day, as was I, but it astonished me how he was always in mental balance. He was not the shouting type, more the silent and calm type, and when he spoke people couldn't help but listen to him. And when they listened to him people felt that he had an inner belief, that he was a genuine character without clichés. It was the reason why Oliver Tambo was second to none as a spokesperson for the ANC.

The next time I saw Oliver was during his stay of only a few hours in Copenhagen in 1963. I had been married the year before, and we had dinner in our small flat. The situation in South Africa had deteriorated. In the beginning I asked him a lot of questions. When I told him that my father had been one of the leaders of the resistance movement during the war he began to ask me questions. How was the illegal movement organised? What were the positive or negative experiences?

The suppression in South Africa was harder than ever. An effective international boycott was the best weapon against apartheid, but not the only one. Armed resistance had become a necessity. The next chapter of the long story of a proud black population and its painful way from slavery to freedom was set to begin.

AN EVER-EXPANDING
INTERNATIONAL ROLE

Dorothy Robinson

As an anti-apartheid activist in London in the 1960s I remember how excited we were when Oliver Tambo arrived here. We knew that the opportunity to have such a leading figure from the ANC, the Deputy President, would be an enormous encouragement to the campaign for boycotts and sanctions against the apartheid regime.

Events such as the killing of 69 unarmed protestors at Sharpeville in March 1960 had caused massive protests in London and elsewhere and there was an enormous demand for speakers from South Africa with their own experiences to address meetings all over the UK.

Our speakers' organiser (the late Joan Hyman) arranged most of these meetings. In September 1960 Tambo spoke at the Trades Union Congress's annual conference with Dr Dadoo and Nana Mahomo as the South African United Front (SAUF). I think they would also have spoken at a fringe meeting held at the Labour Party's annual conference but I have not been able to check this. Then they embarked on a two-week speaking tour at centres throughout the UK. This tour finished with a mass rally at Central Hall, Westminster, at the end of September 1960 addressed by the SAUF speakers.

Later that year and in early 1961 AAM concentrated all its efforts around the forthcoming Commonwealth Prime Ministers' Conference due to held at Lancaster House in March.

AAM called for the exclusion of South Africa and after three days of strong opposition to South Africa's continued membership by the newly independent African countries and Canada, Prime Minister Hendrik Verwoerd announced that South Africa would withdraw from membership of the Commonwealth. The BBC interviewed Tambo on 15 March about his reactions to this decision.

This was followed by a visit to the US to lobby the UN as leader of the ANC's External Mission. He also spoke to a very packed and successful South Africa Freedom Day meeting in New York.

But as yet unknown to many of us in London, 1961 was to be the year the ANC turned to armed struggle and MK was formed. Consequently, Tambo's role changed. He began to spend even more time out of the UK on an ever-expanding international role although he still spoke at AAM rallies when he was available.

In 1987 while I was working for IDAF I went to Harare for the International Convention for the Rights of Children and the session addressed by Tambo made a lasting impression on me.

Later on I knew that Tambo's health had been compromised by the severity of the struggle and his dedication to it, but I was truly dismayed and felt a terrible sadness when I heard the news of his sudden death in April 1993.

That he did not live long enough to see the 1994 elections and his people waiting patiently to cast their vote for the first time in their lives to launch their country on the road to democracy was a bitter irony at the end of such a dedicated life.

REFERENCES
British Library Sound Archives.
L. Callinicos, *Oliver Tambo: Beyond the Engeli Mountains* (Cape Town: David Philip, 2004).
A. Lissoni (SOAS), 'Disunited Front?' (26.11.2003).

ONE OF THE GREATEST AFRICAN
NATIONALIST LEADERS

Mike Terry

My first memory of Oliver Tambo is of listening to him address a rally to mark South Africa's Freedom Day in June 1973. Sharing the platform at the Methodist Church's Central Hall in Westminster was Marcelino dos Santos, Vice-President of FRELIMO and one of the key architects of Mozambique's struggle against Portuguese colonial rule.

It was one of those rare events, a political rally which really had an impact on the audience particularly since it was also the central event in the campaign against the British government's celebration of the 600th anniversary of the Anglo-Portuguese Alliance. This Alliance, which dated back to 16 June 1373, was being exploited by the Portuguese to support their colonial policies in Africa.

The hall was full to overflowing and the atmosphere was electric. There was a real sense that at long last the tide was beginning to change for the Unholy Alliance of apartheid South Africa, Ian Smith's illegal regime in Rhodesia, and Portuguese colonialism, which together had been ruthlessly subjugating the entire southern African region.

Marcelino dos Santos was able to bring news of FRELIMO's new front in Tete Province whilst Oliver Tambo spoke with renewed confidence about the struggle within South Africa and of the first tangible signs of resistance to apartheid, especially amongst workers and students, after a decade of the most intense repression following the Rivonia Trial.

Many of those present had already taken part in protests across the country and were to go on to hound the Portuguese Prime Minister Caetano, when he paid an official visit to London a few days later to 'celebrate' the Alliance.

For me personally, the real significance of this rally was the content of the two key addresses. Marcelino dos Santos spoke with genuine confidence of the advances that FRELIMO was making, yet I suspect few, if any, in the audience would have anticipated that Mozambique would be celebrating its independence almost exactly two years later.

However, it was Oliver Tambo's address that had the greatest impact on me. It was a few days before the end of my term as National Secretary of the National Union of Students (NUS). Since 1969 I had become increasing involved in protests against apartheid, initially at Birmingham University where I had been the President of the Guild of Undergraduates and then on the NUS Executive where I had been responsible first for the NUS campaigns on southern Africa and then overall for its international policy. This had drawn me into the work of the AAM at a national level.

I had heard many speeches attacking apartheid. However, as I listened to Oliver Tambo I heard something very different. Certainly he condemned apartheid, but he also spoke of a vision of a new South Africa. It was a message of hope. Above all, Oliver Tambo personified the ANC's determination to make this message of hope a reality and convinced me that the ANC represented the only real hope for the future of South Africa.

Over the next two decades, I was privileged through my involvement in the AAM to work closely with Oliver and to enjoy the friendship of the Tambo family. Throughout this time I became more and more conscious of his exceptional qualities of leadership.

After leaving the NUS, I worked for two years as Deputy Director for Research for IDAF for southern Africa before becoming Executive Secretary of the AAM. Although Oliver and Adelaide had set up home in London in 1960, by the time I started working for AAM, Oliver was mainly based at the ANC headquarters in Lusaka. He was in such demand internationally that his visits to London became fewer and fewer. Indeed, I suspect that I met OR more frequently at conferences and meetings elsewhere in Europe and in Africa than in the UK.

Even when he was able to spend a few days in London he was always torn between the demands of the 'movement' and his desire to be with his family. It could be very disconcerting to be asked to meet OR at their home on Alexandra Park Road in Muswell Hill only to find numerous South Africans waiting to see him to discuss problems, large and small, and to realise that Adelaide and the family had to await their departure before being able to spend any real time with him.

OR participated in many AAM events during my time working there, but the two whose memory I cherish most are the demonstration we organised in November 1985 to protest at the Conservative government's anti-sanctions policy, and the Nelson Mandela 70th Birthday Tribute at Wembley Stadium in June 1988.

The November 1985 demonstration, the largest anti-apartheid protest ever held in Trafalgar Square, represented a total rejection of the attitude Mrs Thatcher had adopted on South Africa at the Commonwealth Conference in the Bahamas the previous month. Britain had blocked the adoption of effective sanctions, but, after extensive negotiations, Commonwealth leaders reached a consensus on a package of partial sanctions, only for Mrs Thatcher to emerge from the meeting to declare that all she had conceded was a 'tiny little bit'.

There was genuine anger in Britain at Mrs Thatcher's indifference to the repression within South Africa – a brutal State of Emergency had been imposed in July 1985 – and in September the AAM National Committee had agreed we needed to organise a major national demonstration to give expression to this anger and to rally support for the AAM's policies. We knew this would require a line up of speakers who would really have an impact and so we sounded out the ANC over the availability of OR. He readily agreed to speak. An approach to Jesse Jackson, then at the height of his popularity in the US, received an equally positive response. The two of them flew into London to join Trevor Huddleston, the veteran anti-apartheid campaigner and President of the AAM. The three together represented the most formidable platform imaginable.

We anticipated a large turnout and so instead of the 'classic' march from Hyde Park to Trafalgar Square, we planned three marches, one from the East End, one from Brixton and one from Hyde Park, which would all meet up in Trafalgar Square for the rally to be addressed by Oliver Tambo, Jesse Jackson and Trevor Huddleston. However, we had completely misjudged the public mood and were overwhelmed by the response. As the main march from Hyde Park arrived in Trafalgar Square with Oliver, Trevor and Jesse at the front, we discovered that the march from Brixton was already in the square and that a group of Rastafarians had 'liberated' the plinth. Photographers captured wonderful images of OR with Jesse and Trevor surrounded by Rastafarian flags. The estimated crowd of 120 000 crammed into Trafalgar Square represented tangible evidence of opposition to the Thatcher government's anti-sanctions policy – indeed, we discovered afterwards that there were still people waiting to leave Hyde Park to join the march even after the rally in Trafalgar Square had ended. As the audience listened to OR's address, there was a sense that the ANC's time had finally come and that the struggle against apartheid was now unstoppable.

However, the rally was not without its problems. A number of anarchists decided to throw their placards at the police line protecting South Africa House. More seriously, we had agreed in advance with the ANC that for security reasons it would not be appropriate for OR to join Jesse Jackson and Trevor Huddleston on the march, but that he would join them at the front as we arrived at Trafalgar Square. Careful plans were made to ensure that this would proceed smoothly. To my eternal shame, however, neither the AAM nor the ANC had anticipated the logistics of leaving the square after the rally. All the roads had been closed off because of the massive turnout and OR and Jesse were both being mobbed by well-wishers. Somehow, if my memory serves me correctly, Frene Ginwala spirited OR away to safety. There were angry words afterwards about how we could have allowed this situation to occur.

Within three years OR was back in London as the guest of honour for an even more impressive event: the Nelson Mandela 70th Birthday Tribute at Wembley Stadium in June 1988. This in turn served as the launch pad for the 'Nelson Mandela Freedom at 70!' campaign, which culminated in activities across the world on Nelson Mandela's 70th birthday on 18 July.

Working with the producer Tony Hollingsworth and Artists against Apartheid, which had been set up by Jerry Dammers of the Specials, whose *Free Nelson Mandela* record had done so much to popularise Nelson Mandela, and OR's son Dali, we had been able to bring together a unique line up of artists for a live performance at Wembley that was broadcast by the BBC to an audience of millions across the world. The event had a profound impact not least because only a few months earlier at the Commonwealth Conference in Vancouver, Mrs Thatcher had described the ANC as 'a typical terrorist organisation'. Yet here was the BBC, the UK's public broadcaster, working, in effect, with the AAM to promote the campaign for the release of Nelson Mandela and the other political prisoners in South Africa.

This required self-restraint on our part. The BBC was neither going to broadcast a propaganda event for the ANC nor one for the sanctions campaign. Inevitably, this meant walking many tightropes and this was where OR's wisdom shone through.

The previous December, when the campaign was simply an idea in our heads, Bob Hughes, the Chair of the AAM and I had attended a major ANC international conference in Arusha. There we were able to sound out the ANC leadership and Thabo Mbeki, in particular, over the idea of marking

Nelson Mandela's 70th birthday. We heard back the following month that the initiative had the ANC's full support. Indeed, when OR delivered the message of the ANC NEC on the 76th Anniversary of the ANC, on 8 January 1988, he said:

> This year our beloved leader, Comrade Nelson Mandela, will be 70 years old. Let us observe his birthday by further intensifying the campaign for the release of this outstanding son of our people and all other leaders and activists imprisoned by the Botha regime.

To appreciate the context of this campaign, we need to go back to a much earlier period. At a South Africa Freedom Day rally organised jointly by the ANC and the AAM on 26 June 1981, OR had pleaded that the campaign for the release of political prisoners:

> *Should not be slackened, let alone abandoned. Our people are trooping into jail. The voice of the rest of mankind will need to be heard more loudly and not merely as a voice. It must be employed to make sure that at least those who have been there for years upon years, like Nelson Mandela and others, are released. That fight should be fought with determination* (emphasis added).

For OR, this appeal reflected much more than simply a statement of the ANC's official policy. He was deeply conscious that his experience of living in exile, while it involved immense sacrifice, bore no comparison to the experience of his closest friends and comrades who had been suffering day in and day out within the dungeons of apartheid for almost two decades. This was brought home to me very sharply during a conversation we once had at his home in Muswell Hill in the early 1980s. He was asking what I felt would be the attitude of public opinion in Britain if the ANC did not respond positively to moves underway at the time for negotiations. I explained that when people involved in the AAM had discussed this, one suggestion had been that we should focus on the campaigns for the release of Nelson Mandela as this would help ensure that no negotiations would be credible without his release. OR's response was immediate. He looked me straight in the eye and simply said, 'No!' He explained that 'this was not why we were campaigning for the release of Nelson and the other Rivonia trialists' or words to that effect. His simple instruction to me, and I could not interpret what he said in any other way than a command, was that everything possible must be done to get them free.

The 'Nelson Mandela Freedom at 70!' campaign represented a determined effort to put OR's vision into effect. It was a campaign with a very specific focus – the release of Nelson Mandela and South Africa's other political prisoners. People felt a real sense of pride when OR joined Trevor Huddleston and other international figures in the Royal Box at Wembley knowing that the consciousness of people across the world was being focused on Nelson Mandela.

I cannot remember ever seeing OR so full of life, other than when with his family, as he was on that weekend. We were able to arrange for him to talk directly on the phone to Winnie Mandela as the sounds from the stage reverberated through the stadium. At a press conference to launch the campaign as a whole, Oliver's enthusiasm boiled over:

> Let the glorious music bursting forth from this world-famous stadium penetrate through the prison walls that the apartheid regime has created for its own defence. Let the sounds of hope that will trill and reverberate from this platform give heart not only to Nelson Mandela and his colleagues imprisoned in Pollsmoor, Pretoria, Robben Island, Diepkloof, Kroonstad and elsewhere, but also to the millions of South Africans who will surely have their opportunity, sooner rather than later, to stage their own concert to salute the peoples of the world who have stood with us in good days and bad, as we struggled to rid the world of the apartheid crime against humanity.
>
> We thank you for your welcome. We extend to you Nelson Mandela's warmest greetings. We shall tell him and his comrades-in-arms what you have done today. The songs you will sing today shall be not only our marching songs but the common music of victory. Let the music of freedom and peace cry out its own message!

Indeed, the music did penetrate prison walls. A few weeks later I received a letter that had been smuggled out of prison from UDF leader, Valli Moosa, who was then in detention, describing how they had watched a video of the concert in prison.

The Wembley tribute was on a Saturday and the Sunday saw OR on the early morning shuttle to Glasgow for the next stage of the campaign – a march from Glasgow to London to arrive on the eve of Mandela's birthday. Despite the previous day's exhausting schedule, he was full of life. It is impossible to describe the atmosphere on the flight. It was like a continuation of the tribute, especially when the air hostesses appeared wearing the campaign badges and it transpired that they had been at Wembley themselves. OR was the centre of attention. With him were Trevor Huddleston and the SWAPO leader, Andimba Toivo ya Toivo, who had spent many years with Nelson Mandela on Robben Island, together with many of us who had been involved with the tribute. Also on the flight were Jim Kerr and the rest of Simple Minds, one of the bands which had played a key role in making the tribute happen, and who had produced a special song, 'Mandela Day', for the event.

We arrived in Glasgow – which had been the first city to award Nelson Mandela the Freedom of the City – on a beautiful summer's day for one of the city's largest ever rallies. OR gave a rousing send-off to the 25 Nelson Mandela marchers, each one representing a year for which Mandela had been imprisoned, as, echoing Mandela's 'Long Walk to Freedom', they started on their long walk to London.

The campaign culminated in a huge rally in Hyde Park on 17 July – the eve of Nelson Mandela's birthday – where Desmond Tutu welcomed the marchers. OR's schedule meant that he was unable to be present for the rally but at the last moment he re-arranged his programme so that he could fly into London to thank the marchers personally at a reception the ANC organised at the Commonwealth Institute on 18 July. He showed his appreciation by presenting each marcher with a maquette of the statute by Ian Walters of Nelson Mandela that OR had unveiled outside the Royal Festival Hall in October 1985.

Over these few days OR and I spent a considerable amount of time together, including a wonderful dinner which the Commonwealth Secretary-General, Sonny Ramphal, organised in OR's honour at Marlborough House on the eve of the Wembley tribute – an initiative which was unlikely to have been appreciated in No. 10 Downing Street. This time together provided me with an insight into the incredible burden that OR bore. Wherever he went, he was in constant demand. South Africans insisted on seeing him even if they only wanted to discuss the most mundane of problems and even when it was evident that he was very tired. In addition, members of the press were relentless in their questioning whenever they had the opportunity. With some notable exceptions they were still almost uniformly hostile to the ANC, but OR showed a capacity to rise to every occasion and handled even the most negative questioning by the media with consummate skill.

When I first started working for the AAM I was very much a 'Young Turk'. I had been schooled in the extra-parliamentary politics of the student movement in the UK and had much to learn from the friendships I developed with South Africans involved in both the AAM and the ANC, many of whom had been instrumental in setting up the AAM in 1959. OR was, however, very much my senior. We were both born in October but 30 years divided us. Initially my relationship with him was as could be expected with an African statesman of his stature. Over time, however, a much more personal dimension developed, largely due to the role of two remarkable Anglican priests, Ambrose Reeves and Trevor Huddleston, both of whom had a very personal relationship with OR and who were successively the Presidents of the AAM whilst I worked for the organisation.

Ambrose Reeves had been Bishop of Johannesburg from 1949 to 1961 and was an outspoken opponent of apartheid who had identified himself with the freedom struggle. During this time he had forged a close political and personal friendship with OR. Indeed, in 1956, just a fortnight before the dawn arrests of the treason trialists, Reeves had accepted OR as a candidate for ordination to the priesthood.

It was Ambrose Reeves who had headed the Treason Trial Fund, or the Bishop's Fund as it was known unofficially, which was the forerunner to the IDAF for southern Africa. On his return to the UK after the Sharpeville massacre in 1960, the Bishop, as he was known affectionately by those of us involved in the AAM, became a key figure in the broad anti-apartheid movement and was elected President of the AAM in 1970.

The special role which the Bishop had played in OR's life soon became apparent to me. Whenever OR and I met he would first enquire about the Bishop's health and that of his wife Margaret. The Bishop had suffered a stroke in 1975 just before I started working full-time for the AAM. Although he continued to be actively involved, he was no longer able to come to London regularly from his home in Shoreham-by-Sea on the south coast. OR encouraged me to keep in regular contact and I used to travel down each month to discuss our work and plans for the future with the Bishop. His health continued to deteriorate but we were able to organise a wonderful celebration at the Co-op Movement's hotel near Euston Station for his 80th birthday on 10 December 1979. OR, who had made special arrangements to be there, hinted during his speech that the ANC intended to honour him for his contribution to the struggle. True to his word, the ANC announced the following June that it had bestowed the Isitwalandwe Award – its highest honour – on the Bishop. This was due to be presented to the Bishop on 16 December 1980, but due to his declining health the ceremony was postponed and he passed away a few days later. OR insisted that the award should still be presented and so at a special ceremony in London on 27 June

1981 the scroll of honour and the medal were given to the Bishop's widow, Margaret, by OR himself.

I was soon to discover that Trevor Huddleston played an even more important role in OR's life. Trevor had been the Superintendent of St Peter's College, the Community of the Resurrection's Secondary School in Rosettenville near Johannesburg where OR taught Physics and Maths in the early 1940s before leaving teaching to set up a legal partnership with Nelson Mandela.

Trevor had arrived in South Africa in 1943 and the friendship which formed between these two young men, one an Anglican priest and the other an African nationalist, was to last five decades. It was an all-embracing friendship which was forged in the struggles of the 1940s and 1950s and renewed and strengthened during the years of exile when OR headed the ANC's External Mission.

It was also a genuinely deep friendship. OR broke down and wept when he heard the news in 1955 that Father Trevor, as he was known universally throughout South Africa, was to be withdrawn from South Africa by his Community. Despite being separated for many years they kept up an extensive correspondence. Just before his death, OR wrote to Trevor, 'I modestly wish to stress that nothing is more precious to me than our unbroken friendship over fifty years.'

Through my own friendship with Trevor, I was able to gain some insight into his friendship with OR. There were many signs of this. In Trevor's little flat at St James's Piccadilly, he gave pride of place to a photograph taken in 1960 of OR seeing him off from Waterloo on the boat-train to Southampton as he took up his new post as Bishop of Masasi in what is now Tanzania.

In the 1980s their paths were to be drawn much closer together. Trevor – now an Archbishop – succeeded Ambrose Reeves as President of the AAM in 1981 and was to become the symbolic head of the worldwide anti-apartheid movement through the following decade and beyond. He was constantly on the move, travelling throughout the UK and across the world preaching against apartheid from pulpit after pulpit and speaking at conferences, rallies and meetings with a single-mindedness which sometimes drove his friends to despair.

Although by this time OR's own health was failing, whenever we met his first concern was for Trevor's well-being. Trevor had been diagnosed with diabetes in the 1950s and his health began to deteriorate during the 1980s. OR would frequently chide me for allowing Trevor to carry out such an exhausting programme. Likewise, Trevor would be extremely critical of the

ANC for allowing OR to bear, as he saw it, almost single-handedly the entire burden of the struggle. The two were able to meet more often during this period and Trevor, I know, drew tremendous strength from their discussions. He felt that his relationship with OR gave him the authority and confidence to speak out so stridently against apartheid.

There was another dimension to their relationship that I only really became aware of in 1990. I had known that OR was an Anglican and that he had once considered becoming a priest, but I had no real appreciation of his deep faith. When OR was recuperating from his stroke at the family home in Muswell Hill, he asked Trevor to visit him so that he could take communion. I used to collect Trevor every Sunday from St James's and drive him to Alexandra Park Road. Together they took communion and I would either wait in another room or leave and return after a while. We would then sit together talking, or sometimes Trevor and I would join the family for lunch. It was very evident to me that there was a deep spiritual dimension to their friendship and that Trevor was still very much Father Trevor, OR's priest, all these many years on. For me, personally, these were very special occasions. These two giants of the struggle were completely relaxed just enjoying each other's company, although the conversation would inevitably turn to the many challenges still facing the struggle.

There is one occasion at the Tambos' home that I remember above all others. This was when Trevor and I, with Bob Hughes, the Chair of the AAM, went to say 'goodbye' to Oliver and Adelaide as they prepared to return to South Africa via Lusaka. Their journey to South Africa represented the end of an era – the era of exile from apartheid.

As we talked together, we shared past memories and thoughts of the future and all its uncertainties. Although we said nothing, all three of us were very conscious that despite OR's good progress in recuperating from his stroke the pressures he would face in South Africa could be life-threatening and that we might not meet again.

In fact, I was only to see OR once more in February 1993. Mendi Msimang, the ANC Chief Representative in the UK had persuaded the ANC to convene an international conference for solidarity movements to discuss their role in the transition from apartheid to the new South Africa and beyond. Fittingly, the ANC had chosen OR to open the conference in Johannesburg. During one of the sessions, Bob Hughes, Abdul Minty and I slipped out to visit the Tambos' new home. It was wonderful to be with OR again. As we sat talking on the veranda, he was so full of life and of confidence for the future. Yet within two months he was dead. I still remember my shock on hearing the news. It was just before a meeting of the AAM National Committee that had been transformed into a protest meeting at the assassination of Chris Hani. Everyone present had his or her own special memories of OR and there was a sense of the most profound grief amongst us all.

OR's death took a terrible toll on Trevor from which he never fully recovered. Indeed, he initially cancelled a series of events that were organised to coincide with his 80th birthday on 13 June that year, and which OR was planning to attend. He asked me to accompany him to South Africa where he had been invited to address the Requiem Mass and officiate at the funeral. I have very few regrets from my twenty years at the AAM, but one of them was to have been persuaded that I should stay behind in London to ensure that the AAM was best placed to respond to the crisis then gripping South Africa. It meant I could not find an opportunity to express my own grief.

It was, in fact, over ten years before the opportunity came for 'closure'. It happened because I now teach Physics at Alexandra Park School, which is a few hundred metres from the Tambos' former home in Muswell Hill. Indeed, I drive past the house on my way to and from work each day. Our school is now linked with the Ephes Mamkeli Secondary School in Wattville, the township where the Tambos lived before coming into exile and where OR is buried. We launched this partnership on the eve of OR's 89th anniversary in October 2006. Before this ceremony I was able to visit Adelaide and the family and to recall my last meeting with OR back in 1993. And on the anniversary itself, I was privileged to be present at the ceremony to rename Johannesburg International Airport as OR Tambo International and to be with the Tambo family at the graveside in Wattville when prayers were said in OR's memory. South Africa is now truly honouring one of the greatest African nationalist leaders of the twentieth century.

BUSINESS LEADERS

DETERMINED TO BUILD BRIDGES

Donald Anderson

In any normal society Oliver Tambo would have probably become a distinguished educationalist. He would likely with great reluctance eventually have been drawn into educational administration after being a well loved and respected headmaster who had inspired generations of students. History thought otherwise and for Oliver this was not to be. The struggle called him to serve his people, but there still remained a slightly scholarly and retiring air about him.

I met Oliver on many occasions during the 1980s, both at his home in Muswell Hill, North London, and in Lusaka, Zambia. I had been appointed Shadow Minister for Africa in Denis Healey's team. It was a fraught time in South Africa: the army was in the townships and the apartheid regime had created the constitutional cul-de-sac of the tri-cameral legislature. The UDF was formed as a response and in fact, though not in name, it became for many South Africans the internal substitute for the exiled ANC. I remember Albertina Sisulu telling me at a UDF rally in Durban that we addressed, that for her, the only real flag was that of the ANC.

Over that period I visited South Africa several times a year, always under respectable auspices, mainly that of the SACC headed by Dr Beyers Naudé and the Revd Frank Chikane. Neil Kinnock, Labour's leader, sent me as his emissary to Durban where the UDF Six led by Archie Gumede, had sought sanctuary in the British Consulate. I was taken around the Vaal townships by Murphy Morobe and met, clandestinely, internal activists such as Popo Molefe and Terror Lekota and, openly, churchmen and ordinary South

Africans. Correspondingly, I had many opportunities to hear the views of representative South Africans on Oliver Tambo. All spoke of him with enormous respect.

Some had known him personally. For example, Fikele Bam, then running a legal resources centre, told me with immense pride that he had been a member of Oliver Tambo's football team. The matron of an old people's home in Soweto showed me a faded *Observer* photograph of Nelson Mandela which she kept hidden on her desk under the blotting pad, and she spoke most warmly of Oliver.

In 1984 I was a co-founder of the Association of West European Parliamentarians for Action against Apartheid (AWEPAA) under the leadership of Dr Jan-Nico Scholten, then a Dutch member of parliament. I became the organisation's Senior Vice-President, which gave me further opportunities to visit the ANC in Lusaka and to explain that Mrs Thatcher did not represent majority opinion on South Africa either in Europe or, indeed, in the UK.

I had the privilege of meeting Oliver in Muswell Hill when he was at home with his family. He was a most genial and generous host. There, and in Lusaka, with the ANC in exile, he made clear to me that he had a fixed determination to return home to South Africa as soon as it became possible. He did in the end, albeit under great physical difficulties because of his stroke. I kept the photograph of our first meeting on my desk in parliament until I retired as a member of parliament in 2005.

I had a small role in one quite significant incident when I was able to introduce Oliver to a Homeland leader. I had known Enos Mabuza of the Swazi-speaking KaNgwane Homeland for several years as a fellow Christian. When I asked him if he would like to meet Oliver Tambo he responded immediately and positively, as did Oliver when I asked him about a possible meeting with Enos. We arranged that Enos and I would be in Lusaka at the same time as the ANC leadership was gathered. We quietly went through the back door of a multi-storey Lusaka hotel and walked to the top floor where we entered the room in which Oliver and senior ANC executive members were waiting to greet Enos. My task completed, I left the room for the South Africans to begin their discussions. I was later told by a UDF/ANC friend, Richard Stevens, that he was surprised when he was in KaNgwane at a subsequent election, to see the youth toyi-toyiing around Enos, a Homeland leader. I, of course, knew the reason.

It was clear to me that Oliver Tambo was determined to build bridges wherever possible. He worked to liberate South Africans of all races from apartheid and thus made his personal contribution to the rainbow nation.

There are two very different styles of political leadership. On the one hand, there are the great inspirational national leaders; on the other, there are those who preside over a committee of strong personalities, reconciling and encouraging. Oliver was firmly in the latter category. He brought together a range of very contrasting personalities, reconciled their different interests and kept the ANC on the road to inclusiveness. He made crystal clear throughout that he had no personal ambitions other than to keep the seat warm for Nelson Mandela; in short, that he was no more than a caretaker leader.

Oliver Tambo, like Moses, had a vision of the Promised Land in which his people would be set free. During those difficult years, wandering in the desert, he kept their eyes fixed on that goal by his example and never showed, at least in public, his frustrations. Tragically, like Moses, Oliver was not to enter the Promised Land, but his leadership role was absolutely vital during that time of travel and should never be forgotten. Few, if any, alternative leaders could have kept the ANC together so effectively and could have kept alive the hope of eventual victory. When I pass through OR Tambo International Airport, I shall bow my head in tribute to a great man. Amandla!

BUILDING A BRIDGE

Michael Young

I first met Oliver Tambo on 24 October 1986 at the London home of Anthony Sampson, a long-time friend of David Astor and Oliver Tambo. The occasion was the first meeting between the ANC in exile and the British business establishment with commercial interests in South Africa.

David Astor and Anthony Sampson had sought to bring the ANC into contact with those whose commercial activities had been seen to place them at polar opposites to the principle opponents of the apartheid administration in South Africa.

It is sometimes difficult, twenty years on, to recall how the world looked in 1986 and how the various guests at Anthony's elegant home in Kensington would have seen each other. To many in the political and business establishment, the ANC was a leftist guerrilla organisation committed to the destruction of the South African state. Furthermore, these businessmen would have not have been accustomed to meeting with those people whom Mrs Thatcher had labelled as terrorists akin to the PLO and IRA.

As the youngest and most junior businessman there I was struck by the thought that, given the august nature of the gathering, my Chief Executive Officer ought to have been present rather than a junior member of the company executive. Nevertheless, I had engineered an invitation from Anthony and was delighted to represent Consolidated Gold Fields since it would not normally have been invited to attend as the company was regarded as right wing and wedded to the status quo in South Africa. Sir Christopher Hogg, Chairman of Courtaulds, attended, as did Sir Alistair Frame of Rio Tinto

Zinc; Gordon Adam of Barclays Bank; Sir James Spooner and David Sainsbury of J. Sainsbury; Patrick Gillan, the Managing Director of British Petro-
leum; and Ray Allen of ICI. All of these senior figures knew that the status
quo could not be maintained indefinitely and some found the apartheid regime distasteful. In addition to these captains of industry, Neil Foster, Chairman of the United Kingdom–South Africa Trade Association attended, and
made his presence felt by his hostile line of questioning.

For my part, I was intrigued by Oliver Tambo and found his economic
thinking interesting and far removed from the command economic model
favoured by many in Africa and elsewhere at the time. I remember thinking
that here was a man with whom to do business. Of the ten men present that
evening, seven, myself included, asked to keep in touch.

On 24 June the following year, Anthony Sampson convened another
gathering of British business leaders at the Connaught Rooms. Under the
auspices of David Astor, twenty-three senior industrialists met to hear Oliver Tambo, this time with a full complement of ANC leadership – Thabo
Mbeki, Mac Maharaj, Aziz Pahad and Jacob Zuma. Tambo wanted to demonstrate that the leadership was more than just himself and Nelson Mandela,
but comprised individuals of calibre and competence. The audience included former Chancellor of the Exchequer Lord Barber, Chairman of Standard
Chartered Bank; Sir Timothy Bevan, Chairman of Barclays Bank; Sir Alistair
Frame, the head of Rio Tinto; Lord Greenhill of SG Warburg and former
head of the British Foreign Office; Sir Martin Jacomb of Barclays de Zoete
Wedd; Evelyn de Rothschild; George Soros of the Soros Fund of New York;
Sir James Spooner of Morgan Crucible; and myself representing Consoli-
dated Gold Fields.

Oliver Tambo spoke about the need for ordered change. Some businessmen doubted that the black population was ready for this, but Tambo remained patient and thoughtful as he developed his analysis of the need for
early change within the political process itself. This was very much in line
with my thinking although some of my colleagues wanted to make gestures
toward black education as a first, but some feared final, step. I found Tambo
thoroughly coherent and plausible, if adventurous. Most importantly, I believed that we should try to promote ordered political change rather than
making token gestures of money designed to create a black educated middle class that might forestall revolutionary sentiment amongst the majority
of the population.

After the meeting ended and my business colleagues left the room, I approached Oliver. Without any corporate remit, I asked him what a company with large interests in South Africa could do to make a difference. My

recollection of this considerable man is interesting. He was short in stature with horn-rimmed spectacles that framed his warm brown eyes. His look was kindly but shrewd and he carried an avuncular air that put one at ease and yet enlisted respect.

I had extended my hand whilst putting my question to him. He took and held it for what seemed an eternity as he looked at me intently and thought about his reply. We remained silent for some time, holding hands, with him looking into the near distance. His eyes returned to mine and he asked if I could help him to build a bridge between the ANC and the Afrikaners close to the then government in Pretoria. My heart sank as he asked this since I knew that my contacts in South Africa were limited and did not extend to the Afrikaans political elite. Gold Fields was an English-speaking mining house and its links with Afrikanerdom were limited. The Boer War was still fresh in the minds of the Broederbond and Cecil Rhodes, the founder of Gold Fields, was hardly a pin-up and role model for the Afrikaans-speaking political class.

Thabo Mbeki was present throughout this exchange and he asked if I could help arrange a meeting between the ANC leaders and the Foreign Office Minister Lynda Chalker, who happened to be a close friend of mine. This was organised following a telephone call I made to Lynda's office and the meeting was held, notwithstanding Mrs Thatcher's edict that Ministers were not to meet the ANC. Lynda felt the chill wind of prime ministerial displeasure as a result of her courage and perspicacity.

With Oliver's request at the forefront of my mind, I needed to develop a plan as to how I might successfully deliver on such an interesting and challenging proposition. I wanted to embrace the idea, but I required at least the acquiescence of my Chairman Rudolph Agnew, who I knew to be amused, sometimes intrigued and usually suspicious of my 'radical thought process' within the conservative mining house. If I could win over Agnew, I stood a chance of delivering on Oliver's request. At the time I was aware of a nervousness within the ANC in exile of just what was happening to and with Nelson Mandela and the South African authorities on Robben Island. I was to learn later that this concern led in part to Oliver's wish to open up some sort of dialogue with the authorities against the fear that P.W. Botha was attempting to divide the ANC by striking a deal with Mandela and marginalising the movement outside the country. Botha believed that the ANC in exile was Marxist in orientation and thus less likely to be cooperative than a man whose long tenure in jail might have made him more amenable. Clearly, at the time, few knew Mandela's condition, what treatment he might have received and thus what his mental state might have been.

I spent two of my regular weekly meetings with Agnew warming him up to the idea by discussing at length the impasse that I saw for South Africa, and indeed for Gold Fields, going forward, unless something of significance was to change in the political equation. Agnew is a bright man and was a brave man in understanding the value of forward thinking and then being prepared to embrace a dangerous opportunity of the sort I presented to him on our third meeting. Put simply, I wanted to tell Oliver Tambo that I would undertake the challenge and that Consolidated Gold Fields would fund the process, which would be conducted in great secrecy. I would be released from many of my daily tasks in economic and political planning within the Company and would devote my time to identifying willing interlocutors and building a secure process between the apartheid administration and the ANC in exile. To his great credit, Agnew agreed, on the condition that if the process was discovered, he would deny any involvement and sack me for inappropriate behaviour.

Three weeks later, Tony Trew of the London ANC office took me to Oliver Tambo's home in North London for my first one-on-one meeting. Here I was able to tell Oliver that I would attempt to build a bridge and that Gold Fields would fund the process. In discussing the operation in detail I spoke of the need for secrecy to protect the process, the individuals involved and the participating institutions. Oliver told me he would ensure that the ANC would be adequately and appropriately represented and that we would liaise through Tony Trew and Aziz Pahad rather than through the London ANC office which was penetrated by the South African Security Service, the Bureau of State Security (BOSS). Additionally, this channel would be important since telephone lines between the UK and South Africa and the UK and Lusaka, the headquarters of the ANC in exile, were tapped by BOSS, which enjoyed a freedom to operate not accorded to others in the same profession. Consequently, these people were free to tap phone lines here, as they did my office and private telephone lines. They also were able to intimidate and threaten those whom the South African state regarded as hostile. Oliver and the ANC leadership were always aware of BOSS's presence and the organisation lost no time in making its presence felt by my family and I. Oliver and I worked out a process which was designed to deliver our goals and frustrate those who would seek to destroy them. We then agreed on a timeframe to bring the two sides together and I discussed with him who I might approach within the Afrikaner community as suitable interlocutors.

My next task was to talk to those in the UK who knew Afrikanerdom better than I did. I was given one name to consider, Professor Sampie Terreblanche, and I set off on my first incognito visit to Stellenbosch, the home of Afrikaner intelligentsia. My task was made more complex by the fact that the closer I got to the centre of nationalist power, the greater the chance of my being betrayed and thus not delivering on my promise to Oliver Tambo.

With fortune smiling on me, and after two abortive meetings with the moderator of the Dutch Reformed Church and the head of the Broederbond, I was able to persuade three key players close to President Botha to attend the first direct meeting between the ANC in exile and the political leadership of the administration in South Africa. Willie Esterhuyse and Sampie Terreblanche were part of the small political cadre close to the apartheid government. Both recognised the need to seek ordered change and Esterhuyse enjoyed great influence with P.W. Botha and Neil Barnard, the head of the South Africa Intelligence Service. Both Esterhuyse and Terreblanche showed great courage in accepting the challenge, not least because P.W. Botha had threatened to withdraw the passports of those who considered talking with the ANC in exile. In addition, not all elements of South Africa's security service recognised, as did Neil Barnard, that the service could secure either the borders of the country or the townships, but not both. Some of the less tutored were prepared to kill those who spoke with the enemy.

Notwithstanding this, Terreblanche and Esterhuyse were prepared to explore the unknown and join the ANC team of Aziz Pahad, Tony Trew and Professor Harold Wolpe in October 1987 at the Compleat Angler in Marlow, England. I had wanted to hold this first meeting at Gold Field's retreat, Mells Park in Somerset, since I knew that my guests would need a quiet location in which to contemplate a conversation with those they regarded with the greatest of suspicion. Rudolph Agnew, however, believed this location would bring things too close to home and I was required to find a different but secure venue for this first make or break meeting. The Compleat Angler was the last place anyone would think of looking for a meeting between these polar opposites. The hotel is a delightful, quaint English rustic retreat that is close enough to Heathrow airport and London to make it practical. Heathrow, because my Afrikaner guests would fly in from South Africa and London because the individuals Oliver Tambo nominated for this first encounter were based in London as well as Lusaka.

I had brokered the initial agenda whilst in Stellenbosch with Esterhuyse and Terreblanche and had taken their wishlist to Oliver so he could understand the white agenda and could add his own items to reflect a joint agenda. I felt that the broad issues at this stage were irrelevant, but would help to set a tone that if useful and conducive, could create the climate necessary for detailed discussion with an enhanced ANC delegation.

The meeting was at first tense and difficult, with my playing a necessary but highly proactive Chairman's role, which encouraged discussion around specific issues.

When the weekend meeting finished I asked both parties to tell me whether or not they each felt that further discussions would be useful. I agreed to speak to Oliver Tambo to establish the ANC interest and Willie Esterhuyse would report back to P.W. Botha via Neil Barnard to establish the government's interest in taking the matter forward.

Oliver was quick to receive me and indicated a willingness to participate further in the dialogue, but with an enhanced level of participation in the shape of Thabo Mbeki, the then International Secretary of the organisation. He would be accompanied by Aziz Pahad and Tony Trew. This speedy response with Thabo heading the ANC team told me all I needed to know about Oliver's interest in taking the dialogue forward.

I had to wait some time for Esterhuyse to get back to me since he needed to speak to Barnard who needed to speak to Botha before any response could be given. The longer I waited, the more concerned I became that Pretoria might decline to take the matter forward. After a week or so Esterhuyse telephoned me. In an eclectic manner he told me that the principals were prepared to engage further, but that secrecy was vital and that a specific set of information requests would need to be tabled as part of the next agenda. I would need to go to South Africa to start the agenda process. Esterhuyse had been warned by Botha that should the dialogue become public then his and Terreblanche's passports would be withdrawn. Such was the interest that Esterhuyse also floated the notion that Neil Barnard might join our discussions at the next meeting.

In the event, Barnard never appeared at any of our discussions and although he became a central conduit, I never met him or talked with him directly. The next meeting was held in Suffolk, again because Rudolph Agnew was nervous about holding the talks at Mells Park, although he was intrigued that both parties felt it worthwhile to take the risk of further and more substantive discussions.

Top of the government's list of requests was the issue of a cessation of violence, since the country was languishing under a State of Emergency in an attempt to quell rising disorder in the townships and an escalation of guerrilla attacks on state installations. The ANC wanted to understand the government's thinking on one man one vote and the unbanning of the ANC. So the talks began in earnest with each side exploring the other's attitude towards violence, the releasing of Nelson Mandela and universal suffrage.

Each of these was understood and debated, including the nature of the post-apartheid economy.

Agreement on each of these issues was achieved over the five-year period of the talks, such that the precise conditions and nature of Mandela's release were brokered in order to ensure that riots and disorder did not follow the event. The explicit nature of the ANC's command and control mechanism for the guerrilla command was explained. The government understood that when civilian targets were inadvertently hit, this was not duplicity on the part of the ANC High Command, but rather a product of the vagaries of the command structure with instructions passing orally rather in written form. Thus as the message was passed from one unit to another the possibilities were there for a distortion of the command. This process of communication on this issue became ever more important as it developed into a cohesive exchange between Oliver Tambo and the ANC leadership, Nelson Mandela and the South African President. The urgency of the talks quickened when F.W. de Klerk became President and his brother Wimpie became a regular participant at the talks. The ANC's link with the President became direct: essentially Oliver Tambo, President of the ANC, was talking directly to F.W. de Klerk, President of the Republic of South Africa, and any attempt by the authorities to divide and rule had long disappeared.

My role during this time had changed from being the proactive Chairman of the talks to facilitator between South Africans, black and white. But I knew that the South Africans were communicating when the two sides embraced on meeting, talked informally in my absence over bottles of Glenfiddich, and viewed me as the stranger and the non-South African. Willie Esterhuyse today describes this type of silent exchange as Glenfiddich diplomacy.

Another change in my role was made when I was asked to present a geopolitical perspective of how South Africa's situation sat in the minds of key world players: Gorbachev, Reagan, Thatcher, Kohl, the EU and the UN. As the momentum of the talks developed and the Soviet Union disintegrated, the whole team asked me to see if Margaret Thatcher might play a role in helping to contain the initiatives that emerged with regularity from these power blocs. Some initiatives were helpful, but most were less so since they were designed to pander to domestic audiences within the various nations. We needed stability and space and my colleagues thought I might persuade Mrs Thatcher to play this important role. I accepted the request and, against my better instincts, went to Downing Street to see the lady who had usurped my former political leader's position, hijacked the Conservative Party, and dragged the nation to the right, thus marginalising Britain in the counsels of the world. As a Liberal Democrat, I had publicly attacked Thatcher during two general elections and one by-election. What right had I to expect her to hear me, let alone receive me? But there was just a chance she might rise to the occasion and be a force for good.

Alas, she would not see me, but her Chief of Staff, Charles Powell, received me at No. 10 Downing Street. He listened attentively to what I had to say and told me he would consult with the British Prime Minister and get back to me. After some two weeks he told me that Mrs Thatcher still regarded the ANC as akin to the PLO and IRA and would not involve herself with these terrorists.

Sadly, I had to report this not only to Oliver Tambo but also to my white South African colleagues who were as keen on this initiative as was the ANC leader. I continued to see if I could unilaterally seek to influence the White House and the State Department in a positive direction.

Gorbachev had told Tambo that Soviet financial support for the ANC was to come to an end and that the ANC would need to seek a negotiated settlement. Thatcher and Reagan were aware of this, but still could not bring themselves to help facilitate this important breakthrough in one of the world's most intractable problems. Such was the limitation of the conservative vision.

Although George Bush Snr was more tutored than his predecessor, he saw South Africa as a low priority for the US. Under-Secretary of State Freeman at the State Department was more interested, but was helpless in the face of White House indifference.

What is clear is that the end of the Cold War and the change in international power politics that followed, embraced South Africa within the mix. Perhaps it could be argued that the resolution of the South African problem helped to break down the old order because it deprived the US and Soviet Union of a major theatre in which power politics could be played. Equally, it might be argued that with the breakdown of the old order, the prospects for a resolution of the South African issue were enhanced since Moscow and Washington pulled away from the African theatre where the East–West conflict was played out in a regional setting.

Either way, at the heart of this global shift was Oliver Tambo – the owlish, brave political leader of the ANC. He was the man who led the struggle overseas and internally and who had to deal with the shifting and swirling problems of global power play. He was the man who needed to fuse the diplomatic with the guerrilla activity of a liberation movement with all the tensions implicit in this pairing. He was the man who was required to keep this disparate movement cohesive in the face of massive challenge by the apartheid government and Western indifference. He was the man who had to network on the grandest yet most complex scale. This was the man who led his countrymen and women through the most difficult and challenging years, and yet did not live to see the full fruits of his endeavours.

Our process of 'silent' discussion and diplomacy came to an end once the ANC had been unbanned and Nelson Mandela had been released – both issues having been resolved through the process which Oliver Tambo had initiated and helped direct. The formal public negotiations then began and Tambo and the leadership in exile were able to return home and take part in the formal process that would bring about the dismantling of apartheid and the creation of democracy in his beloved country.

Oliver attended the ANC Consultation Conference in December 1990 in Johannesburg having already suffered a stroke. He chose to become Chairman of the ANC instead of President, a position that Nelson Mandela assumed. The formal negotiations ran relatively smoothly and swiftly given our detailed talks between 1986 and 1991. Meanwhile, Oliver's health was failing and he died in April 1993.

I attended his funeral in Wattville, Benoni, and remember the warmth and love that surrounded this small but great man. The close harmony of raised African voices in mournful song and the silent tribute of Jesse Jackson and Trevor Huddleston marked the moment when Oliver Tambo was laid to rest in the red earth of the land for which he had struggled for so long. The long silent lines of his fellow South Africans gave ample testament to the love he had carried from his long-suffering people.

A year later, on 9 May 1994, Nelson Mandela was sworn in as South Africa's first black President. The galaxy of the good and great were there to celebrate this wonderful day. As I watched the world pay tribute to this most remarkable achievement in bringing peaceful and ordered change to one of the world's most troubled lands, I couldn't help thinking of the man who had held my hand and asked that a bridge be built. The architect was not there in person, but his spirit was very much alive and present.

CONTRIBUTORS

Lord Donald Anderson of Swansea was born on 17 June 1939. He has worked in the Foreign Service and as a lecturer; and has played an active role as a member of parliament for Monmouth and later Swansea East. In 2005, he moved to the House of Lords as Lord Anderson of Swansea. Lord Anderson is currently a member of the EU sub-committee on Foreign Affairs, Defence and International Development. He has been a member of the Executive of the Inter-Parliamentary Union and Commonwealth Parliamentary Association since 1983, and was Chairman of the UK branch of the Commonwealth Parliamentary Association from 1997 until 2001. During this time, Lord Anderson also served as leader of the North Atlantic Assembly UK Delegation and of the Socialist Group. In 1984 he helped form the Association of West European Parliamentarians for Action against Apartheid (AWEPAA, now AWEPA) and was subsequently appointed as its Senior Vice-President. He is married to Dorothy Anderson, and has three sons.

HE Chief Emeka Anyaoku was a member of the diplomatic service of Nigeria and the Commonwealth Secretariat for 34 years. He served as Foreign Minister of Nigeria in 1983 and as Commonwealth Secretary-General from 1990–2000. He is currently, among other things, Chairman of the Presidential Advisory Council on Foreign Affairs in Nigeria, International President of the World Wildlife Fund (WWF); a member of the governing board of the Geneva-based South Centre and a trustee of the British Museum.

Professor Kader Asmal was born in Stanger in KwaZulu-Natal. He studied at the University of South Africa (UNISA), and later in London and Dublin. Professor Asmal was a founder member of the British AAM in 1960, founder and chairperson of the Irish AAM from 1964–1990, rapporteur of UN international conferences on apartheid in Havana (1976), Lagos (1977) and Paris (1986). He was an ANC delegate to the

443

Convention for a Democratic South Africa (CODESA) in 1992, a member of the ANC's negotiating team at the Multi-Party Negotiating Forum in 1993 and a founder member of the ANC's Constitutional Committee in 1986. He has been a member of the NEC of the ANC since 1991 and a member of parliament in the National Assembly since 1994. He is a former Minister of Education (1999–2004), Minister of Water Affairs (1994–99), Chairperson of the Cabinet's National Conventional Arms Control Committee (1995–2004) and Chair of the Portfolio Committee on Defence in the National Assembly (2004–05). Asmal was also Chairman of the Intergovernmental Committee of experts at UNESCO, negotiating the draft Convention on Cultural Diversity during 2004–05; and has been presented with several awards, including the Prix UNESCO for human rights in 1983. Asmal was awarded the Order of the Légion D' Honneur in 2006 – the premier order of France.

Dr Sandi Gladstone Baai was born on 21 December 1942. He is currently Director of Research based at the head office of the Public Service Commission in Pretoria and is a homeboy of Comrade Oliver Reginald Tambo. He is a former Rhodes university lecturer and the recipient of the Dr Beyers Naudé Christian Fellowship Trust scholarship and the Overseas Research Student Award (ORS) from the Committee of Principals and Vice-Chancellors of the universities of the UK. In 1988 he gained a Ph.D. from the University of Durham in the UK. He is a theologian and author of the book *O.R. Tambo: Teacher, Lawyer and Freedom Fighter* (2006).

Sir Geoffrey Bindman qualified as a solicitor in 1959 and has practised in London since 1960, specialising in civil liberty and human rights issues. From 1966–76 he was legal adviser to the Race Relations Board and thereafter, until 1983, to the Commission for Racial Equality. He edited the report of the International Commission of Jurists' 1987 mission to South Africa, *South Africa: Human Rights and the Rule of Law* (1988, 1989). He has won awards for a lifetime's achievement in human rights from Liberty (December 1999) and has represented the International Commission of Jurists, the International Bar Association, Amnesty International, and other bodies in human rights missions in various countries, including the former Soviet Union, Germany, South Africa, Chile, Uganda, Namibia, Malaysia, Israel and the Occupied Territories, and Northern Ireland. In 1994, Bindman was a UN observer at the first democratic elections in South Africa. He was knighted in the New Year's Honours List in 2007.

George Bizos was born in 1928 in Kirani, Greece. He and his father arrived in South Africa in 1941 as Second World War refugees. In 1950 he completed his law degree at the University of the Witwatersrand. During apartheid, Bizos committed himself to fighting for basic human rights and represented many political activists (such as Walter Sisulu and Nelson Mandela) in high-profile cases. He involved himself in the Truth and Reconciliation Commission, representing families of those who died during the struggle against apartheid; and also provided representation to the families of Chris Hani, Steve Biko and the Craddock Four. In 2004, Bizos represented Morgan Tsvangirai, the leader of

Zimbabwe's main opposition party (the Movement for Democratic Change), on a charge of high treason brought by the Zimbabwean government. In the same year, he received the International Bar Association's (IBA) prestigious Bernard Simons Memorial Award at Auckland, and the annual Sydney and Felicia Kentridge Award from the General Council of the Bar.

Paul Boateng is the British High Commissioner to South Africa and the British High Commissioner to the Kingdoms of Lesotho and Swaziland. He was born on 14 June 1951 and was educated at the Ghana International School, Accra Academy and in the UK at Apsley Grammar School and Bristol University (LLB Hons). He is a qualified Solicitor and practised as Barrister at the Eight Kings Bench Walk Chambers. He has had a distinguished career in politics, including being appointed as Financial Secretary to the Treasury (2001–02) and as Chief Secretary to the Treasury (2002–05) before his current appointment.

Victoria Brittain has worked as a journalist for many years. She was employed by *The Guardian* for twenty years, where she became Associate Foreign Editor. She worked as Research Associate at the London School of Economics and was also on the editorial board of *Race and Class*, as well as the National Executive Council of the Respect Coalition. She compiled the play *Guantánamo* with Gillian Slovo and has written several books.

Revd Brian Brown, a minister of the Methodist Church, was Administrative Director of the Christian Institute of Southern Africa when served with a banning order in 1977. During the 1980s he was Secretary of the South African Coalition which coordinated anti-apartheid activities in Britain.

Baroness Lynda Chalker is founder and chairperson of Africa Matters Limited, which provides advice to business, international bodies and governments on activities in sub-Saharan Africa. Baroness Chalker has been a member of the Lower and Upper Houses of the UK parliament for over thirty years. For twelve years she was Minister of State at the Foreign and Commonwealth Office, holding responsibility for Africa and the Commonwealth and for Overseas Development. She was made a Life Peer in 1992. Baroness Chalker is a non-executive director for a number of major companies, and Chairperson of the Board of Medicines for Malaria Venture. She is also Coordinator of the Nigerian Honorary International Investor Council, a member of both the Tanzanian and Ugandan Investment Round Tables, and of the Kenyan Economic and Social Council. She is a founder Executive Trustee of the Global Leadership Foundation, and of the Nelson Mandela Legacy Trust.

Sir Evelyn Robert Adrian de Rothschild was born on 29 August 1931. He began his career in the family business, NM Rothschild & Sons banking house, at the age of 26. In addition, Evelyn de Rothschild has been involved in numerous other organisations and has held prestigious business positions, such as Chairman for *The Economist*, and Director of Lord Black's *Daily Telegraph*. In 1989, he was knighted by HRH Queen Elizabeth II. Sir Evelyn has given much support to the arts, as well as numerous charities.

Ambassador Ismail Coovadia was born in Johannesburg on 9 September 1939. He joined the anti-apartheid movement during his student days. He was treasurer of the South African Students Association (UK) in the 1960s. He participated in organising anti-apartheid meetings and conferences. He was the Secretary of the ANC Logistics Committee (UK). He was one of the two persons responsible for the purchase and renovation of the ANC premises in Angel, London. His responsibilities included working closely with the ANC National Treasury and the Treasurer-General, Cd. Thomas Titus Nkobi. He was responsible for Cd. Oliver Tambo's travel during his visits to London. He accompanied the representatives of the Mass Democratic Movement to Brussels during their meetings with the European Commission. He represented the ANC as its Chief of Foreign Affairs and he served briefly as the Deputy Director General (Corporate Services). He was South Africa's first High Commissioner to Pakistan and is currently Ambassador to Norway and Ireland.

Dr Nkosazana Clarice Dlamini Zuma was born on 27 January 1949. She matriculated at Amanzimtoti Training College (1967), and went on to study at the University of Zululand where she was awarded a B.Sc. in Zoology and Botany. During this time she became an active underground member of the ANC, and was elected Vice-President of SASO (1976). She then went into exile, where she furthered her studies, and was awarded an MBChB from the University of Bristol (1978). Dlamini Zuma then worked at hospitals in KwaZulu-Natal, England, Swaziland and Zambia, and then at the Medical Research Council in Durban. She returned to the UK in 1985 to complete a Diploma in Tropical Child Health from the School of Tropical Medicine, University of Liverpool (1986). She then joined the ANC Regional Health Committee, followed by a job as director of the Health and Refugee Trust, a British NGO. During the CODESA negotiations, she was a member of the Gender Advisory Committee. She was awarded an Honorary Doctorate from both the University of Natal (1995) and the University of Bristol (1996). Dlamini Zuma was appointed as Minister of Health in 1994, and then as Minister of Foreign Affairs in 1999 – a position she still holds.

Jerry Dunfey is the co-founder of Omni Dunfey Hotels, Dunfey Group, and Global Citizens Circle whose mission is to 'foster constructive change in our global community by assembling diverse groups of concerned individuals – from world leaders to local activists – for challenging discussions, which will stimulate meaningful and enduring resolution of our world's pressing concerns'. Many of the Circles have featured South Africans including Oliver and Adelaide Tambo, Walter and Albertina Sisulu, Nelson Mandela and Graça Machel, Desmond and Leah Tutu, Beyers Naudé, Johnny Makathini, and Donald and Wendy Woods. Dunfey has been in South Africa on numerous occasions, including as a member of Senator Kennedy's 1985 fact-finding mission and as a guest of state at President Mandela's 1994 inauguration.

Brian Filling has been a campaigner against apartheid since the 1960s. He became Chair of the Scottish Committee of the AAM on its foundation in 1976, remaining in this position until its dissolution in 1994 with the end of apartheid. He was the Chair of ACTSA Scotland (Action for Southern Africa), the successor organisation to the AAM, from its inception in 1994 until the present. He chaired the AAM meeting on the day that Nelson Mandela was awarded the Freedom of the City of Glasgow in 1981. He also chaired the huge rally in Glasgow in 1988, addressed by OR Tambo, which launched the march from Glasgow to London calling for the release of Nelson Mandela. He was the joint editor of *The End of a Regime? An Anthology of Scottish-South African Writing Against Apartheid* (1991), and was the lead organiser of the visit of Nelson Mandela to Glasgow in 1993 to receive the Freedom of nine UK cities. He is the author of *From Colonialism and Apartheid to Ten Years of the New South Africa* (2005), and is the Chair of Community HEART, which has sent over two million books to South Africa since the end of apartheid.

Dr Frene Ginwala is a member of the NEC of the ANC and is the Chancellor of the University of KwaZulu-Natal. She is the Special Adviser to The Minister on Anti-Corruption and a member of Ministerial Review Commission on the Intelligence Services. She became the first Speaker of the National Assembly and served for two terms (1994–2004) as well as becoming a member of the Pan African Parliament. She left South Africa immediately after the Sharpeville massacre to arrange for Oliver Tambo to travel illegally to Tanganyika; and helped to establish the External Mission of the ANC. Later she assisted Nelson Mandela and other ANC leaders to exit and return to South Africa covertly. She was the spokesperson of the ANC in London and head of the political research unit in President Tambo's office. On her return from exile she joined Nelson Mandela's Secretariat, was appointed head of the ANC Research Department and a member of the ANC negotiation team. Ginwala has served as the Presiding Chair of the Global Coalition for Africa and Chairperson of the AU Steering Committee on the Pan African Parliament. She was a member of the Commission on Human Security. She has been presented with several awards including the Order of Luthuli and the North South Prize of the Council of Europe.

Jonas Moses Gwangwa has played a significant role in the development of South African jazz music. Gwangwa was a member of the Jazz Epistles until 1959. Thereafter, he continued to involve himself in music, both in South Africa and overseas, becoming popular in America during the 1960s. Gwangwa was not embraced by the apartheid government and, after it was made illegal for black people to congregate, Gwangwa entered into exile in the early 1970s. He was musical director for the ANC's cultural ensemble tour Amandla for a decade and, in the late 1980s, teamed up with George Fenton to compose the score for Richard Attenborough's film, *Cry Freedom*. In 1988, he performed at Wembley Stadium at the Nelson Mandela 70th Birthday Tribute. Gwangwa returned to South Africa in 1991.

447

Nadine Hack is the President of beCause, a global firm with the tagline 'bringing causes to life' that conceives, develops and executes cause-related strategies and initiatives for corporate and non-profit clients in order to build awareness of and support for humanitarian efforts. She served as NYC Commissioner for the UN, Consular Corps and International Business, the city's senior liaison with the diplomatic and business communities. She is Adjunct Professor in the International Program at the Wagner Graduate School of Public Service at New York University.

Peter Hain MP spent his childhood in South Africa until his parents – Walter and Adelaine – who had become leading anti-apartheid activists in Pretoria, were successively imprisoned, banned and forced into exile in Britain in 1966. Peter Hain later led the British campaign which forced an end to all-white South African sports tours by disrupting them. Elected Labour member of parliament for Neath in 1991, he has been a government minister since 1997, including Minister for Africa, joined the Cabinet in 2002 as Secretary of State for Wales, and has since served both as Leader of the Commons and Secretary of State for Northern Ireland and since June 2007 as Secretary of State for Work and Pensions.

Michael Holman was brought up in Gwelo, Rhodesia (now Gweru, Zimbabwe). His opposition to minority rule led to his arrest in 1967 and a one-year restriction order. Holman left Rhodesia on an exit permit in 1968 to complete an M.Sc. in Politics at Edinburgh University. He returned in 1971 and then left illegally in 1976 to avoid military service. From 1977–84, Holman was based in Lusaka, Zambia, where the ANC had its headquarters. Thereafter, Holman served as editor for the *Financial Times* in London, reporting on the African continent. More recently, Holman has written and published *Last Orders at Harrods* (2005) and its sequel. *Fatboy and the Dancing Ladies* (2007)

George Houser, a Methodist clergyman, was born in 1916 and devoted much of his life to the advancement of racial equality. In 1942, he helped establish the Congress of Racial Equality (CORE), with James Farmer and Bernice Fisher, and served ten years as CORE's Executive Secretary. With Bayard Rustin, he co-led the Journey of Reconciliation in 1947 through the South. For their efforts, Houser and Rustin were presented with the Thomas Jefferson Award for the Advancement of Democracy. In the 1950s, Houser began to focus on African liberation heading the American Committee on Africa (for 26 years) and supporting decolonisation. He has written *No One Can Stop The Rain; Glimpses of Africa's Liberation Struggle* (1989) and *I Will Go Singing*, with Herbert Shore, memoirs of Walter Sisulu (2000).

The Rt. Hon. The Lord Geoffrey Howe of Aberavon, CH, QC, was born in December 1926 in Wales. He served for two years with African troops as a lieutenant in East Africa, and went on to study law at Cambridge. Called to the Bar in 1952, he was appointed QC in 1965 and served (with Geoffrey Bindman) as one of the three members of the Street Committee, whose report helped to shape Britain's 1968 Race Relations

Act. He joined Edward Heath's government as Solicitor General in 1970 and became Trade Minister in 1972. He served in Margaret Thatcher's Cabinet for all but the last three weeks of her government, as Chancellor of the Exchequer (1979-83), Foreign and Commonwealth Secretary (1983-89), and Deputy Prime Minister (1989-90). Geoffrey Howe paid his first of several visits to Soweto in 1975. During 1986, as Foreign Secretary and President of the EU Foreign Affairs Council, he conducted two missions throughout southern Africa. He resigned from the Thatcher Cabinet in November 1990, and next came to South Africa as one of the Commonwealth observers of CODESA. He has been an active member of the House of Lords since his appointment there in 1992.

Archbishop Trevor Huddleston was born in 1913. While at Oxford in the 1930s, he committed himself to being ordained into the ministry of the church. After taking his vows, Huddleston was sent to South Africa at the age of thirty. Here his enduring dedication to the anti-apartheid struggle began. He was invited to attend ANC meetings, and participated in protest meetings during the 1950s while this was still possible. Huddleston met Oliver Tambo at St Peter's College where Tambo was employed as a schoolmaster. Huddleston was President of the AAM and was instrumental in encouraging a cultural boycott of South Africa as well as economic sanctions.

Lord Hughes of Woodside (Bob Hughes) was the Labour member of parliament for Aberdeen North constituency from 1970 until 1997 when he retired and became a working peer in the House of Lords. He became Vice-Chairman of the British AAM in 1975, became Chairman in 1976, and remained in this position until elected as Chair of Action for Southern Africa (the successor body to the AAM). He is currently Honorary President of ACTSA. From 1996–2006 he served as a trustee of the Canon Collins Educational Trust for Southern Africa. He is the holder of the South African Order, Grand Companion of the Order of OR Tambo (conferred April 2004) by President Mbeki in Pretoria.

Helen Jackson is a British politician, born on 19 May 1939. She received a History degree from Oxford. After teaching children with special needs, Jackson entered into politics and was elected to the Sheffield City Council. From 1992, she served as member of parliament for Sheffield Hillsborough before retiring in 2005.

Zweledinga Pallo Jordan was born in 1942 in B Location, Kroonstad, in the Orange Free State. He joined the ANC in 1960 and left South Africa in 1962 to study in the US at the University of Wisconsin. Jordan holds a number of degrees, including a postgraduate degree from the London School of Economics. In 1975 he worked full-time in the ANC's London office as part of the research unit of its Department of Information and Publicity. In 1977 he moved to Luanda, Angola, to head up Radio Freedom, and also became involved in MK's training programmes for new recruits. In 1979, on Oliver Tambo's recommendation, Jordan was appointed Director of the ANC's first internal mass propaganda campaign, *The Year of the Spear*, which marked the centenary of the

Battle of Isandlwana of 1879. In 1980 he became head of the ANC's research unit of the Department of Information and Publicity, based in Lusaka, Zambia. At the ANC's Kabwe Conference of 1985 Jordan was elected to the NEC and served as Administrative Secretary of the NEC Secretariat from 1985–88. From 1985–89 he served on the NEC's Strategy and Tactics Committee as convener. In 1989 he became the ANC's Director of Information and Publicity. Jordan returned to South Africa in June 1990 after the unbanning of the ANC and other political organisations. He was the ANC's main media spokesperson before and during the 1994 elections. In April 1994, Jordan was sworn in as a member of parliament and the Minister for Posts, Telecommunications and Broadcasting. In May 1996, he was appointed the Minister for Environmental Affairs and Tourism, a position he held until June 1999. Jordan is currently the Minister of Arts and Culture.

Minister Ronnie Kasrils is currently Minister for Intelligence Services in the South African government. He was formerly Minister of Water Affairs and Forestry and before that Deputy Minister of Defence. Born in Johannesburg in 1938 he joined the liberation movement in 1960, was a member of the ANC's military wing MK from its inception, became Chief of military intelligence and served under Oliver Tambo in various capacities in exile from 1965–90.

Sir Sydney Kentridge was born in Johannesburg in 1922. He studied at the University of the Witwatersrand, and served with South African forces in the Second World War from 1942. After the war, Kentridge took first-class honours in jurisprudence at Exeter College, Oxford. In 1949, he was admitted to the Johannesburg Bar where he would appear for the defence in cases such as the Treason Trial (1958–61), the Prisons Trial (1968–69), and the Steve Biko inquest (1977). He was later admitted to the Bar in England, and worked as Judge of Appeal in Botswana, Jersey and Guernsey.

Horst Kleinschmidt was twice elected as the Vice-President of the National Union of South African Students in the 1960s. Thereafter he joined the staff of the South African Christian Institute which he served until its banning in 1977 in terms of the Suppression of Communism Act. During this time Kleinschmidt was prosecuted for leading students who called for the release of detainees without charge or trial. He was also charged for being found in possession of banned literature and for refusing to testify before a secret Security Police Commission of investigation. In 1975 he was detained in solitary confinement for 73 days under the Terrorism Act, without being charged or tried. He fled South Africa in 1976. From 1979–92 he worked for IDAF in London; from 1983 as its Director. Upon being able to return to South Africa Horst worked for the Kagiso Trust. From 2000 until 2005 he worked as head of Marine and Coastal Management, the government department concerned with fisheries. He now runs his own consultancy on environmental matters from Cape Town. He was awarded the Bruno Kreisky prize for Human Rights in 1990 and was knighted by the King of Sweden in 1998.

Thandi Lujabe-Rankoe was born in 1936 in the Eastern Cape, South Africa. She has held numerous positions in the ANC, most notably, Chief Representative for Norway, and ANC Women's Section Chairperson in Botswana and Zimbabwe. She has diplomas in Public Administration and Diplomacy. Lujabe-Rankoe is currently the South African High Commissioner in Mozambique for the Department of Foreign Affairs South Africa, as well as the Head of the South African Government Mission.

HE Dr Lindiwe Mabuza was born in Newcastle, KwaZulu-Natal. She started her working career as a teacher in Swaziland and then as an academic in the US. From 1977–79 Mabuza worked as a radio journalist with the ANC's Radio Freedom – broadcasting into South Africa from Lusaka, Zambia – and as the Editor of *Voice of Women*, a journal by ANC women. She was also the Chairperson of the ANC's Cultural Committee in Lusaka. This was followed by positions as the ANC's Chief Representative to Scandinavia (1979–87), where she opened the organisation's offices in Denmark (1985), Norway (1986) and Finland (1987), and then as the ANC's Chief Representative to the US (1989–94), where she also opened the ANC office. In 1995 Mabuza was appointed as the first South African Ambassador to the Federal Republic of Germany. From 1999–2001 she was the High Commissioner of the Republic of South Africa to Malaysia, the High Commissioner of the Republic of South Africa to Brunei Darussalam (non-resident), and the South African Ambassador to the Republic of the Philippines (non-resident). In 2001 Mabuza was appointed as the South African High Commissioner to the UK, a position that she still holds. Over the years she has been involved in numerous publications, including of her own poetry, has received two Masters degrees, and has been the recipient of various awards and honorary doctorates.

Nomzamo Nobandla Winnifred Madikizela-Mandela was born on 26 September 1936 in Bizana, Transkei. She received a Social Work diploma from Jan Hofmeyr School in Johannesburg, followed by a B.A. degree from the University of the Witwatersrand. Winnie Madikizela-Mandela actively involved herself in the struggle against apartheid, and endured several prison sentences as a result. She was on the last National Executive Committee of the original ANC Women's League before it was banned, after which she worked with other women leaders through the Federation of South African Women. In May 1977, she was banished to Brandfort.

Nelson Rolihlahla Mandela was born on 18 July 1918. He was expelled in 1940 from Fort Hare with Oliver Tambo after participating in a student strike. Mandela completed his degree by correspondence, and later registered at the University of the Witwatersrand. He was one of the founding members of the ANC Youth League, and was instrumental in organising the Programme of Action which was accepted by the ANC in 1949. Mandela and Tambo worked together as lawyers, opening up the first black legal firm in South Africa. He was one of the accused in the Treason Trial, and was detained after the Sharpeville massacre in 1960, at the same time that the government banned the ANC. Mandela later became known as the Black Pimpernel because he successfully evaded the police. Under Mandela's leadership, MK was formed as the military wing of the ANC, and executed acts of sabotage against government and economic installations. After illegally exiting South Africa to arrange training for MK members, Nelson Mandela was arrested and charged upon his return. While serving this sentence, he was charged with sabotage in the Rivonia Trial and sentenced to life imprisonment. He was released on Sunday 11 February 1990. In 1993, he accepted the Nobel Peace Prize for all South Africans involved in the struggle against apartheid. Nelson Mandela became the first democratically elected State President of South Africa in 1994. After holding various positions within the ANC, including ANCYL President, ANC Transvaal President, Deputy National President and ANC President, Nelson Mandela retired in June 1999.

Gail Marcus is a South African artist currently living and working in London. Marcus was born in Johannesburg, in 1950, to a family that was heavily involved in the struggle against apartheid. She left South Africa in 1963 with her family, on her parents' exit visas. Her teenage years were spent in Israel. She came to England in 1967 to complete her education, and has lived most of her adult life in the UK. She has been an active member of the AAM and the ANC.

Dr Joe Matthews was born on 17 June 1929. He matriculated at St Peter's Secondary School, Rosetterville, Johannesburg (1947). He was awarded a B.A. with English and History from the University of Fort Hare (1951), followed by an LLB from the University of London (1956), and a Master's Degree in History from the University of London (1968). He became a member of the ANC Youth League in 1944, and was involved in the Defiance Campaign (1952). He was one of the accused in the Treason Trial of 1956. Dr Matthews was admitted as an attorney of the Supreme Court of South Africa in 1958, and went on to practise in Durban, Lesotho and Botswana. He returned to South Africa in 1991, and went on to be appointed the Deputy Minister for Safety and Security under Mandela's government – a position he retained until 2004.

President Thabo Mvuyelwa Mbeki was born on 18 June 1942 in Idutywa, Transkei. He joined the Youth League at age fourteen and quickly became active in student politics. While studying for his British A-levels he was elected secretary of the African Students' Association (ASA). He went on to study Economics as a correspondence student with London University. Mbeki left South Africa in 1962 under orders from the ANC. From Tanzania he moved to Britain where he completed a Masters Degree in Economics at Sussex University in 1966. He remained active in student politics and played a prominent role in building the youth and student sections of the ANC in exile. Following his studies he worked at the London office with the late Oliver Tambo and Yusuf Dadoo before being sent to the Soviet Union in 1970 for military training. Later that year he arrived in Lusaka where he was soon appointed Assistant Secretary of the Revolutionary Council. In 1973–74 he was in Botswana holding discussions with the Botswana government about opening an ANC office there. In 1975 he was acting ANC representative in Swaziland. He was appointed to the NEC in 1975, and served as ANC representative to Nigeria until 1978. On his return to Lusaka he became Political Secretary in the office of Oliver Tambo, and then

CONTRIBUTORS

Director of Information. From 1989 Mbeki headed the ANC Department of International Affairs, and was a key figure in the ANC's negotiations with the former government. After the April 1994 general election he was elected one of two Deputy Presidents of the new Government of National Unity. After the National Party withdrew from the Government of National Unity in June 1996, Thabo Mbeki became the sole Deputy President. In December 1997, Thabo Mbeki became the new President of the ANC. He was elected President of the Republic of South Africa in June 1999, and then re-elected in April 2004.

Zanele Mbeki is currently the Chairperson of the WDB Trust, a fund created for South African women's economic empowerment. The Trust owns a Women's Investment Company (WDB-IH) whose role is to promote women business leaders and to create revenue streams in support of the Fund. The Fund supports principally credit for poor rural women (WDB-Microfinance) as well as business and literacy training, gender research and documentation. Mbeki is a Trustee/Director of several national and international boards which promote social and economic development in poor communities (Schwab Foundation for Social Entrepreneurs [Geneva]; El Taller for Human Rights [Tunis]; and SAWID [South Africa]). She studied Social Work in South Africa (at Wits University) and completed postgraduate studies in the UK (at the London School of Economics and Institute for Social Work Training) and the US (at Brandeis University). She has social-work-related experience in Africa, the UK and US and with the UN High Commissioner for Refugees (Africa and Asia).

Baleka Mbete was born on 24 September 1949. She received her teacher's certificate from Lovedale Teachers' College, and later went into exile. In May 1976, Mbete joined the ANC. She worked for the party in numerous positions throughout Africa before serving as Secretary-General of the ANC Women's League from 1991–93, Deputy Speaker of the National Assembly of South Africa from 1996–2004, and Speaker of the National Assembly since 2004. Mbete has been a member of the Presidential Panel on the Truth and Reconciliation Commission since 1995 and of the ANC NEC since 1994.

George Meehan came to London from County Donegal in Ireland in 1963, and has lived in the borough of Haringey with his wife and family ever since. He was first elected to the Haringey Council as a Labour councillor in 1971, and has now served for more than thirty years. He served as Leader of the Council from 1983–85 and from 1999–2004, and was re-elected Leader in May 2005. He has a strong commitment to improving educational opportunities for all, and has served for many years both as school governor in a number of Haringey schools and as the Council's Executive Member for Children and Young People.

Rita Mfenyana, born in Russia, married South African student **Sindiso Mfenyana**, who was sent by the ANC to study in the then USSR in the early 1960s. After Sindiso had completed his studies the family moved around on various ANC assignments given to him until the end of 1974 when they arrived in Zambia where the ANC had its headquarters. An engineer by profession, Rita was able to find employment in Zambia, and participated in the activities of the ANC Women's Section. Her main preoccupation in the ANC was the formation of the South African Children's Club in Lusaka for which she became known as 'Auntie Rita'. The Club was later transformed into the ANC Pioneer/Masupatsela organisation. Rita Mfenyana later became a full-time cadre of the ANC, specialising in projects for women and children, at first in the ANC settlements in southern Africa, and later in South Africa after the peaceful transition. The family moved to Tanzania in 2004 where Sindiso Mfenyana serves as the South African High Commissioner.

Ambassador LMS Mngʼikana is presently serving as the South African Ambassador to the Republic of Turkey and non-residentially accredited to Azerbaijan, Uzbekistan, Turkmenistan Kyrgyz Republic and Tajikistan. He served as the Deputy Representative of the ANC in London (1969–73) responsible for the UK and Western Europe and as Chief Representative of the ANC in Stockholm (1974–79), responsible for Nordic countries. Ambassador Mngʼikana played rugby for the Border African Rugby Football Union XV uninterruptedly from 1956 until his enforced exile from South Africa in 1965. He is also an accomplished musician, and played trumpet and saxophone in various bands in East London and at Fort Hare University College, and was music director and leader of the ANC Youth and Students' Choir in London. He is known as the 'singing ambassador' in the diplomatic circles in Ankara.

Mayor Ruth Segomotso Mompati was born on 14 September 1925 in Ganyesa Village in the district of Vryburg. She started her career as a teacher at the Dithakwaneng Primary School near Vryburg. In 1953 she studied typing and shorthand and immediately thereafter was employed by Mandela and Tambo Attorneys as a typist, where she remained until 1961. It was at this stage that she officially joined the ANC, and became a member of the NEC of the Orlando branch. In 1953 she became a member of the NEC of the ANC Women's League and was a founder member of the Federation of South African Women. Mompati was an organiser and leader of the 1956 Women's March. Shortly afterwards she went into exile, and between 1962–64 she underwent military training as a combatant of MK. She then served as the head of Administration in the ANC President's office from 1964–1970. In 1965 she became Head of the Women's Section, and in 1966 was elected to the NEC. In 1970 she became a member of the Internal Reconstruction Committee, and in 1976 she was appointed to the Secretariat of the Women's International Democratic Federation as a representative of the Federation of South African Women. In 1981 the ANC sent her to the UK as their Chief Representative, and then in 1984 she was sent back to Lusaka to work on the Coordinating Committee of the NEC of the ANC. She was once again elected to the NEC in 1985. In 1990 she was chosen to be part of the ANC delegation that negotiated the peaceful transition with the government at Groote Schuur. In 1994 she was elected to the National Assembly of the Republic of South Africa. In 1996 she was awarded an Honorary Masters Degree in Education by the University of the North West and an Honorary Doctorate in Education from UNISA. In 2000 Mompati became the Mayor of the Naledi Municipality, a position that she still holds.

CONTRIBUTORS

Mosie Moolla was born in 1934. He was expelled from high school for participating in the Defiance Campaign and, at 22, was the youngest person to be arrested during the Treason Trial. He worked as Joint Secretary of the Transvaal Indian Youth Congress during the 1950s. During the May 1961 stay-at-home, he was arrested and tried for incitement, and two years later was detained under the 90-day law. He later served as the Asian representative of the ANC in New Delhi and Cairo. Moolla is the former Ambassador and High Commissioner to Tehran and Islamabad respectively.

Tony Msimanga was born and grew up in Mamelodi, near Tshwane (Pretoria). He was highly active in student politics under the banner of the Congress of South African Students (COSAS). In 1979 Msimanga left South Africa for exile through Swaziland then Mozambique and finally Angola. He joined MK in 1983 and received military training in Angola. Thereafter he became part of the security and intelligence structures of the ANC in Angola and Zambia, and was based at the ANC headquarters in Lusaka for a further ten years. In 1993 Msimanga joined the ANC Foreign Affairs Unit and worked as a public servant until 2001. He was appointed as the South African Ambassador to Angola in 2001 and, in 2005, as the South African High Commissioner to Kenya, a position that he still holds.

Minister Sankie Mthembi-Mahanyele was born in March 1951. After graduating from the University of the North (Turfloop) with a B.A. and a teacher's diploma, she went into exile. Here she worked for the ANC as editor of their Women's Section journal *Voice of Women* (VOW). She began working as ANC Chief Representative for Germany and Austria in 1989. On her return to South Africa in October 1993 she was appointed Deputy Head of the ANC's Department of International Affairs before assuming the position of Deputy Minister of Welfare in May 1994. Mthembi-Mahanyele was later promoted to Minister of Housing, and is now the ANC Deputy Secretary General.

General Godfrey Nhlanhla Ngwenya was born in Johannesburg in 1950. After witnessing the violence of the student uprisings in 1976, as a senior clerk at Baragwanath Hospital, he joined the ANC and MK. He received military training in exile: in Angola he held the positions of Military Instructor, Camp Chief of Staff and Company Commander. Before the democratic elections of 1994, he served as the MK's Chief of Personnel and Training. He was presented with the Merit Medal in Silver (MMS) and is currently the Chief of the South African National Defence Force.

Thembi Nobadula grew up in the Ekuthuleni area (east of Johannesburg). She was heavily involved in politics, and took part in the 1956 Women's Anti-Pass March to the Union Buildings. In 1962 she went into exile in the UK, where she still lives.

Thami Ntenteni was born in Johannesburg in 1953 and matriculated at Morris Isaacson High School in 1971. He became a political activist while studying at the University of Zululand. At that time he was involved in the BCM and the South African

Students' Organisation (SASO). Ntenteni was expelled from the University of Zululand in 1974 and became a teacher at Morris Isaacson High School. In 1975 he joined the underground structures of the ANC. He went into exile in February 1976 where he was trained as a member of MK in the then USSR. In 1977 he started to work for Radio Freedom and in 1983 was appointed as its Director. In 1992 he returned to South Africa after the unbanning of the ANC and other political parties. He holds a B.A. degree majoring in communication from University of South Africa and is currently the head of Public Broadcasting Services Radio at the South African Broadcasting Corporation.

HE Dr Sam Nujoma, Founding President of the Republic of Namibia, was born on 12 May 1929. In 1959, he was elected Leader of the Owambo People's Organisation (OPO), the forerunner of the South West African People's Organisation (SWAPO), which was formed on 19 April 1960. He spearheaded the national liberation struggle until Namibia's independence on 21 March 1990. In 1971, he was the first leader of an African nationalist movement to address the UN Security Council in New York leading to the UN General Assembly passing a Resolution declaring SWAPO as the sole and authentic representative of the Namibian people. Nujoma was elected by the Constituent Assembly and was sworn in as the first Namibian Head of State on 21 March 1990. He was popularly re-elected for two more terms of office in 1994 and 1999, respectively. Through his leadership, SWAPO adopted the Policy of National Reconciliation under the motto: ONE NAMIBIA, ONE NATION. In recognition of his dedication to his selfless sacrifices to the national liberation struggle and nation building, the parliament of the Republic of Namibia enacted legislation in April 2005, declaring him Father of the Namibian nation. He stepped down on 21 March 2005, handing over the reins of power to his successor His Excellency President Hifikepunye Pohamba.

Revd Canon Dr Paul Oestreicher was founder, with Revd Brian Brown, of the Christian Institute of Southern Africa Trust. A former Chairman of Amnesty International UK, he was, until 1998, Director of the Centre for International Reconciliation at Coventry Cathedral. In retirement he is honorary Quaker Chaplain to the University of Sussex and lives in Brighton.

Kjeld Olesen was born in 1932 in Copenhagen. From 1958–66, he was Secretary of the Social Democratic Party. Thereafter, he became a member of parliament until 1987, and served as Minister of Defence (1971–73), Minister of Transport (1977–78), and Minister of Foreign Affairs (1979–82). After his departure from politics, he took up his original profession and sailed until 2002 as a mate in the merchant marine.

Enuga S. Reddy was the Assistant Secretary-General and Director of the Centre against Apartheid of the United Nations. He is the editor of *Oliver Tambo and the Struggle against Apartheid* (1987) and *Oliver Tambo: Apartheid and the International Community* (1991). He compiled and edited Oliver Tambo's speeches and articles from between 1960 and 1993. The collection is available on the ANC website.

Dorothy Robinson was Administrative Secretary of the AAM from 1960–66 and also worked at IDAF mainly on political prisoners' issues, from 1983–90.

Justice Albie Sachs worked as an advocate at the Cape Bar, defending people charged under racist statutes and repressive security laws, and went into exile in 1966. During the 1980s, working closely with Oliver Tambo, he helped draft the organisation's Code of Conduct, as well as its statutes. In 1990 he returned home, and after the first democratic election in 1994 he was appointed by President Nelson Mandela to serve on the newly established Constitutional Court.

Sally Sampson was married to the late writer Anthony Sampson, who was a close friend of Oliver Tambo and his family. He edited *Drum* magazine in the 1950s, and wrote the authorised biography of Nelson Mandela as well as many other books about Africa. Anthony Sampson was awarded a posthumous Order of the Grand Companions of OR Tambo Silver in 2006. Sally knew Oliver and Adelaide Tambo when they lived in North London, and she has close contact with post-apartheid South Africa where an Anthony Sampson Foundation has been set up. She works as a family court magistrate in London.

Ambassador Bengt Säve-Söderbergh was born in 1940. He visited South Africa for the first time in 1960 as a young mate on a merchant ship. From 1978–85 he headed the International Centre of the Swedish Labour Movement (later renamed the Olof Palme Centre), and from 1985–91 he was Deputy Minister for International Development Cooperation at the Swedish Ministry for Foreign Affairs. Säve-Söderbergh is the founder of the International Institute for Democracy and Electoral Assistance (IDEA), of which South Africa is a member, and was its first Secretary-General (1995–2002). Lately he has been working with South Africa in the Four Nations Initiative to reform the UN. In October 2007 Säve-Söderbergh will retire from the Swedish Ministry for Foreign Affairs after having served in many different capacities since 1967. He holds an MBA from the Stockholm School of Economics and in his spare time is President of the Swedish Jazz Federation, in which capacity he initiated an exchange programme for musicians between South Africa and Sweden.

Stan Sangweni and **Angela Sangweni** (née Dladla) were born (in 1933 and 1936) in KwaZulu-Natal, in Newcastle and Port Shepstone respectively. They both completed high school and trained as teachers at St Francis College, Marianhill, outside Pinetown. In the mid-1950s, Angela taught at high schools in South Africa and Swaziland from 1958–74, and at a secretarial school in Nairobi, Kenya, from 1984–92. Stan completed his university education in Lesotho, Canada and the US between 1958 and 1964 and subsequently became a lecturer at the University of Swaziland (1964–74) and a professor at the University of Natal (1992–94). He also worked with the UN from 1974–92 in the fields of regional economic cooperation and environmental management. He joined the government's Public Service Commission in 1994 where he is currently Chairperson of the Commission. Angela and Stan have been active within the ANC since 1974 in Lusaka, Nairobi and South Africa where they have been involved in the education, environment and branch structures of the ANC.

Pierre Schori is a Swedish diplomat with vast experience in foreign affairs, development cooperation and peacekeeping operations. As part of his long career at the Swedish Ministry for Foreign Affairs, Schori was the Minister for International Development Cooperation, Migration and Asylum Policy, and the Deputy Foreign Minister (1994–99). In 2000, he was appointed as the Swedish Ambassador to the UN, a position he held until 2004. From 2005–07 he served as the Special Representative of the Secretary-General and Head of Mission in Côte d'Ivoire, responsible for the 10 000 civil and military personnel that integrate the complex peacekeeping mission. Schori has also served as a member of the Swedish parliament, and the European parliament for the Swedish Social Democratic Group. He is currently the Director-General of FRIDE, a think tank based in Madrid that aims to provide the best and most innovative thinking on Europe's role in the international arena.

Judith Scott first visited South Africa in 1953. She later met South African exiles, including Adelaide and Oliver Tambo, and, after marrying in 1959, she moved from London to Cardiff. Scott offered hospitality to numerous South African exiles, including Edward Matethe, who became the first African nuclear physicist to qualify at Oxford University. When Revd Simeon Nkoane became Bishop he invited Scott to South Africa to help with some of the township projects for youth. In the 1980s, Scott was instrumental in getting student leaders to the UK to continue their disrupted education. After Nkoane became seriously ill and died in 1989, Scott and her family formed a trust in his memory. In 1989, 'The Bishop Simeon Trust' came into being. Scott retired from the trust in July 2006, and was appointed by the trustees as its President.

Tony Seedat (Mahomed Moosa Seedat) was born on 6 June 1936. Seedat was one of the first Indians to have matriculated from Newcastle. He later left for Durban in the mid-1950s, where his political orientation began. He went into exile in London in 1958. The early 1960s and late 1970s were spent as a scholar in Germany (studying for his Masters in Economics), the former Soviet Union as well as Africa, studying and training. During the 1980s he was posted as the ANC Chief Representative in Bonn, Germany, after which he returned to the ANC head office in London where he was active in the ANC structures. In 1993 he returned to South Africa where he was active in the projects office in Luthuli House. During the amalgamation process he was instrumental in the setting up of the South African Intelligence Services, and worked in the South African Secret Service up until his retirement in 2000.

Ronald Segal was born in Cape Town in 1932, and banned from 1959–92. He published and edited *Africa South*, an anti-racist international quarterly from 1956–61, the last few issues as *Africa South in Exile*. In 1964, he convened the International Conference on

Economic Sanctions against South Africa in London; and in 1966 the International Conference on South West Africa in Oxford. He is the author of well over a dozen books.

Michael Seifert has practised as a solicitor in London for 40 years. His clients have included the ANC, the AAM, the National Liberation Front of South Vietnam and the Socialist Republic of Vietnam, the Cuba Solidarity Campaign, the Palestinian Liberation Organisation, the National Union of Mine Workers, the Morning Star, Friends of the Earth, Greenpeace and many other socialist, anti-racist, human-rights, environmentalist and international solidarity organisations. He is a Vice-President of the Haldane Society of Socialist Lawyers.

Reginald September was born in 1923. In 1938, he joined the National Liberation League and, by the 1940s, he was committed to trade unionism. He was active in organising the Franchise Action Council when disenfranchisement became a concern for coloured people. September was a founding member of the SACPO (known as the South African Coloured People's Congress after December 1959), and worked as the organisation's General Secretary until the apartheid government ordered him to resign in 1961. He was a defendant in the Treason Trial from 1956, although charges against him were later dropped. During the 1960 State of Emergency, he was detained without trial for five months, and again in 1961 after playing a role in the May stay-at-home. He went into exile in 1963. He is currently the ANC's Chief Representative for Western Europe.

Mongane Wally Serote was born in Sophiatown in 1944. Influenced by the BCM, the subject matter of his poems was often closely tied to political struggle and black identity. In June 1969, Serote was arrested under the Terrorism Act. He was released without being charged after nine months in solitary confinement. After winning the Ingrid Jonker poetry prize, he was awarded a Fulbright scholarship. This allowed him to complete a Fine Arts Degree at Columbia University in New York. He later chose a life of exile, living in Botswana and London. He returned to South Africa in 1990, and in 1993, won the Noma Award for Publishing in Africa. After the ANC won the democratic elections in 1994, he became a member of parliament and was selected as Chairman of the ANC's portfolio committee for Arts, Culture, Language, Science and Technology. In 2004, the Chilean government presented Serote with the Pablo Neruda award. Serote has written poetry, novels, short stories and essays, and is currently the Chief Executive Officer of Freedom Park – a national heritage site that is due to open in 2009.

Gertrude Shope was born in Johannesburg. After joining the ANC at the age of 29, she left her teaching career in protest against Bantu Education. From 1958, Shope served as Chairperson of the Central Western Jabavu branch of the Federation of South African Women, until she was promoted to Provincial Secretary in the late 1960s. Shope later joined her husband, Mark Shope, in exile, where they represented the ANC in several countries. Shope also served as Secretary to the head of the ANC Women's Section. Florence

Mophosho, during this time. In 1981, Shope was promoted to head of the Women's Section and, in 1985, became a member of the ANC's NEC. Shope served as President of the ANC's Women's League from 1991–93 and, in 1994, became a member of parliament in the Government of National Unity.

HE Mrs Nomasonto Maria Sibanda-Thusi was born in Johannesburg. She served in the ANC from 1978–2000 in various capacities, in Angola, Tanzania, Sweden, Finland and South Africa. From 1994–98, she served as National Administrator in the Office of the Secretary-General of the ANC, and from 1998–2000, she was the Personal Assistant to the Head of International Affairs in the office of the President of the ANC. She completed her college studies at Nora Real in Sweden in 1990, after which she enrolled for a degree in Social Anthropology, Demographic Studies and Development Studies at the University of Stockholm. Sibanda-Thusi joined the Department of Foreign Affairs in 2000 and served as Minister/Deputy Head of Mission at the South African Embassy in Berlin from November 2000 to August 2004. This includes a period of almost a year as Chargé d'Affaires at the South African Embassy in Berlin. She was appointed as Ambassador to France at the beginning of September 2004. On 28 September 2004, she was also accredited as South Africa's Permanent Representative to UNESCO.

Gillian Slovo was born in 1952 to South African political activists Joe Slovo, leader of the SACP, and Ruth First, a journalist. She has lived in England since 1964, working as a writer. One particular novel, *Red Dust*, published in 2000 and made into a film in 2004, deals with contemporary South African issues. Set in the courtroom, the story examines the effects of the Truth and Reconciliation Commission. Her memoir, *Every Secret Thing: My Family, My Country* (1997), is a recounting of her childhood in apartheid South Africa. The book explores what it meant to be the daughter of two major figures in the struggle against apartheid: from exile to armed resistance to her mother's murder in 1982.

Lord David Steel, a British and Scottish politician and a Liberal Democrat in the UK House of Lords, was born in March 1938. He spent his childhood in Scotland and Kenya, and studied at the University of Edinburgh where he involved himself in Liberal politics. By 1965, he had been elected to the House of Commons. In 1997, he retired and was made a life peer as Baron Steel of Aikwood. He was elected as a Liberal Democrat member of the Scottish parliament in 1999 and, in 2004, the Queen made Lord Steel of Aikwood a Knight of the Order of the Thistle, which is the highest honour in Scotland.

Dr Adelaide Frances Tambo (née Tshukudu) was born on 18 July 1929 in Vereeniging, South Africa. As a high school pupil, she began working as a courier for the ANC. At the age of eighteen she joined the ANC Youth League, where she was soon elected as Chairperson of the George Goch branch. She met Oliver Reginald Tambo at a meeting of the Eastern township branch of the ANC. The couple married in December 1956 and had three children, Tembi, Dali and Tselane. After going into exile with her husband in 1960, she continued her struggle against apartheid in London: she was a founder member of the Afro-Asian Solidarity Movement and the Pan-African Women's Organisation (PAWO), and worked with the IDAF to assist a number of families whose children left South Africa after 1976. She returned to South Africa in 1990 and, in 1993, was elected Treasurer-General of the ANC Women's League. She became an ANC member of parliament in 1994. Adelaide Tambo passed away on 31 January 2007.

Michael Terry teaches Physics at Alexandra Park School in the London borough of Haringey where he is an Assistant Head Teacher. His school is situated a few hundred metres from the Tambo family's home during their time in exile from apartheid South Africa and it is now the partner school of Ephes Mamkeli Secondary School in Watville where the Tambo family lived before going into exile. For twenty years from October 1975, Terry was the Executive Secretary of the AAM. During this period he worked closely with the ANC and its President, Oliver Tambo, and became a close friend of the Tambo family. In 1994 he was awarded the UN Medal for his contribution to the international campaign against apartheid and in 2001 was awarded an OBE for his services to human rights. He is currently the Secretary of the Anti-Apartheid Movement Archives Committee and was Secretary of the South Africa 2004 Advisory Committee, consisting of prominent individuals in the UK, that was initiated by the South African High Commissioner to promote activities to mark South Africa's first Decade of Freedom.

Prof Ben Turok was born in Latvia in 1927 and arrived in South Africa with his family in 1934. He graduated from the University of Cape Town in 1950. In 1953, he joined the South African Congress of Democrats (COD) and, by 1955, was working as the COD's Secretary for the Western Cape. In 1955, he was served with a banning order and was arrested the following year for treason. The charges against him were dropped in 1958. He was appointed National Secretary of the COD in 1958 and Secretary of the National Secretariat of the Congress Alliance. Turok was active underground in re-establishing Congress organisation during the 1960 State of Emergency and, in 1962, was arrested under the Explosives Act. He spent three years in prison. Although placed under house arrest after being discharged, Turok fled to Botswana. He later lived in Tanzania and Britain.

Archbishop Desmond Mpilo Tutu was born in Klerksdorp, South Africa, on 7 October 1931. In 1978, in the wake of the 1976 Soweto uprising, Bishop Tutu was persuaded to take up the post of General Secretary of the SACC, which challenged white society and the government, and afforded assistance to the victims of apartheid. For several years Tutu was denied a passport to travel abroad as he became a prominent leader in the crusade for justice and racial conciliation in South Africa. In 1984 he received a Nobel Peace Prize in recognition of his extraordinary contributions to that cause. In 1985 he was elected Bishop of Johannesburg and, a year later, was elevated to Archbishop of Cape Town. In this capacity he did much to bridge the chasm between black and white Anglicans in South Africa. As Archbishop, Tutu became a principal mediator and conciliator in the transition to democracy in South Africa. In 1995 President Nelson Mandela appointed him Chairperson of the Truth and Reconciliation Commission. Tutu has been granted the honorary title of Archbishop Emeritus and has received numerous prizes in addition to the Nobel Peace Prize, most notably the Order for Meritorious Service Award (Gold) presented by President Mandela, the Martin Luther King Jr Non-Violent Peace Prize, and the Sydney Peace Prize.

Ian Walters was born in 1930. He worked as a sculptor, producing numerous busts and statues of significant political figures, most notably Nelson Mandela and Oliver Tambo. For his depiction of Fenner Brockway, Walters won the Jean Masson Davidson Medal awarded by the Society of Portrait Sculptors. He died in 2006 before his three-metre-tall clay sculpture of Nelson Mandela was cast in bronze.

Per Wästberg was born in 1933 in Stockholm. He spent 1959 in Rhodesia and South Africa. There he met Oliver Tambo and wrote two books on his experiences: *Forbidden Territory* and *On the Black List*. He received his Ph.D. from Uppsala University in 1962. Wästberg founded the Swedish Anti-Apartheid Committee and was co-founder of Swedish Amnesty in 1963, and was President of International PEN from 1979–87. He is a member of the Swedish Academy and President of its Nobel Committee for Literature. He has published over fifty volumes of novels, essays, poetry, and travel, and has written six books on modern African politics and culture.

Pauline Webb was a former Vice-Moderator of the WCC and a founder member of the Commission of the WCC's Programme to Combat Racism which gave strong support to liberation movements in southern Africa. In Britain she chaired End Loans to South Africa and was an active participant in the AAM. In Muswell Hill, North London, where the Tambo family were living in exile, Webb became a close neighbour and friend of Adelaide Tambo. Later, as Organiser of Religious Broadcasting for the BBC World Service, she maintained a well-informed and constant interest in events as they developed in southern Africa.

Cora Weiss, President of the Hague Appeal for Peace, was the Director of The Riverside Church Disarmament Program from 1978–88, during the ministry of Revd William Sloane Coffin. During the early 1960s she helped to organise the annual Africa Freedom Day events at Carnegie Hall and was the Executive Director of the African–American Students Foundation (1959–63) which brought students from East Africa to schools and colleges in the US. During apartheid, Weiss persuaded the Trustees of Hampshire College to accept the student initiative to divest from companies doing business in South Africa.

Peter Weiss is an international lawyer and currently Vice-President of the Centre for Constitutional Rights and the Paris-based International Federation of Human Rights (FIDH). He was a co-founder and long time Board member of the American Committee on Africa including twelve years as its President.

Michael Young, a specialist in conflict resolution and strategic evaluation, is the mediator who initiated and chaired secret talks that led to the dismantling of apartheid in South Africa and subsequent free elections. Between 1986 and 1990 Young facilitated covert negotiations between the ANC in exile and the ruling Afrikaner elite. These talks helped to pave the way for a more formal and public negotiating process that later resulted in democratic government in South Africa. Young is Chairman of Michael Young Associates Ltd.

PHOTOGRAPHIC CREDITS

Photo of OR and Samora Machel © UWC-Robben Island Museum Mayibuye Archives

Photo of OR with Julius Nyerere and Sam Nujoma © UWC-Robben Island Museum Mayibuye Archives

Photo of OR and Nelson Mandela © UWC-Robben Island Museum Mayibuye Archives

Photo of OR meeting Fidel Castro in Cuba © UWC-Robben Island Museum Mayibuye Archives

Photo of OR with Yusuf Dadoo © Wits Historical Archives, used with the permission of the Tambo family

Photo of OR at the People's Parliament Against Apartheid in Stockholm © Mats Åsman

Photo of OR with Trevor Huddleston © Alan Wylie

Photo of Brian Filling addressing the Glasgow Rally © Alan Wylie

Photo of OR, Alfred Nzo and Joe Slovo in conversation © UWC-Robben Island Museum Mayibuye Archives

Photo of OR, Johnny Makhathini and Pearl Robinson © Nadine Hack

Photo of OR, Thabo Mbeki, Zodwa Sisulu, Themba Vilakazi, Aggrey Mbere and Zwelakhe Sisulu © Nadine Hack

Photo of OR with Edward Kennedy © UWC-Robben Island Museum Mayibuye Archives

Photo of OR dancing © Wits Historical Archives, used with the permission of the Tambo family

Photo of Adelaide Tambo with Tselane on her hip and Dali looking on © Wits Historical Archives, used with the permission of the Tambo family

Photo of OR and Johnny Makhathini in China © UWC-Robben Island Museum Mayibuye Archives

Photo of OR with Indira Ghandi and Morarji Desai © UWC-Robben Island Museum Mayibuye Archives

Photo of OR at the unveiling of the statue of Nelson Mandela courtesy of Paul Boateng

Front cover
© Reuters/Corbis

Back cover
Photo of Oliver and Adelaide Tambo crossing the street courtesy of Dali Tambo

Photo of Oliver and Adelaide Tambo with Bantu Holomisa courtesy of Dali Tambo

Photo of OR with Yusuf Dadoo © Wits Historical Archives, used with the permission of the Tambo family

Photo of OR dancing © Wits Historical Archives, used with the permission of the Tambo family